"This rich collection will be widely welcc
in opening up and developing mainstrea
gender, sex, and sexuality, after the British Psychoanalytic Council's
'moving on' statement of 2011. The critical deconstruction of heteronormativity is achieved without discarding all that is essential and valuable
about psychoanalytic theorising and method. The commitment to a more
open-minded and self-reflective approach shines through the diverse and
highly nuanced clinical accounts. This book will be an essential part of
psychoanalytic education and invaluable to the many clinicians who want
to think differently about their practice."

—**Joanna Ryan, Ph.D.,**
Site for Contemporary Psychoanalysis; co-author (with
Noreen O'Connor) of *Wild Desires and Mistaken Identities:
Lesbianism and Psychoanalysis* (Routledge, 2003)

"The fields of psychoanalysis and psychotherapy, like societies at large
around the world, recognise that it is difficult to integrate rapidly developing ideas of identity, especially gender identities and sexualities, without falling back on normative models. This challenge is daunting, and
has been side-stepped for too long. It has the potential to be genuinely
creative for our field and for those we try to help. The editors of this
book are both experienced therapists with the essential qualities of lively
engagement, compassion and wisdom, together with the openness to
bring together a diverse set of contributors. They include a long contribution from a brave patient, who brings alive for us the experience of
recognizing and crystallizing a transgender identity. The wide range of
perspectives will give all readers further understanding, and – as with
all good books – still more to understand."

—**Professor Mary Target (now Hepworth),**
Psychoanalysis Unit, Research Department of Clinical,
Educational and Health Psychology, University College London;
Fellow, British Psychoanalytical Society

"In this innovative book, Hertzmann and Newbigin bring together a
diverse group of authors who show us how far we have come and how
much more we have yet to do in the reappraisal of psychoanalytic theories of gender and sexuality. They address theoretical and clinical issues
of desire and gender in the consulting room, in the children's clinic, in
supervision, and in the emotional life of clinicians as well as patients,
helping us to recognize complexities of desire and gender previously
obscured. Most usefully, the authors do not simply provide new rules
and categories to render gender and sexuality coherent, or to regulate or

liberate desires and identities. Instead, they point the way for clinicians and patients to explore the complexities of conscious and unconscious meaning in personal experiences of gender and sexuality. Readers will expand their vocabularies and find helpful suggestions for working with patients whose subjectivities may at first feel unfamiliar. For example, cis therapists new to working with trans patients will find help in getting oriented. They will also be helped to challenge their own limitations of theoretical understanding and categorization, to expand and deepen their range of meaning-making, and to appreciate the advantages of uncertainty—for the benefit of clinical explorations with their own patients."

—**Paul E. Lynch, M.D.,**
Psychoanalyst, Boston, MA, USA; Faculty, Boston
Psychoanalytic Society and Institute, Massachusetts
Institute for Psychoanalysis, and China America Psychoanalytic
Alliance; co-editor, with Alessandra Lemma, of *Sexualities:
Contemporary Psychoanalytic Perspectives* (Routledge, 2015)

SEXUALITY AND GENDER NOW

Sexuality and Gender Now uses a psychoanalytic approach to arrive at a more informed view of the experience and relationships of those whose sexuality and gender may not align with the heterosexual "norm". This book confronts the heteronormative bias dominant in psychoanalysis, using a combination of theoretical and clinical material, offering an important training tool as well as being relevant for practicing clinicians.

The contributors address the shift clinicians must make not only to support their patients in a more informed and non-prejudicial way, but also to recognise their own need for support in developing their clinical thinking. They challenge assumptions, deconstruct theoretical ideas, extend psychoanalytic concepts, and, importantly, show how clinicians can attend to their pre-conscious assumptions. They also explore the issue of erotic transference and countertransference, which, if unaddressed, can limit the possibilities for supporting patients more fully to explore their sexuality and gender. Theories of psychosexuality have tended to become split off from the main field of psychoanalytic thought and practice or read from an assumed moral high ground of heteronormativity. The book specifically addresses this bias and introduces new ways of using psychoanalytic ideas. The contributors advocate a wider and more flexible attitude to sexuality in general, which can illuminate an understanding of all sexualities, including heterosexuality.

Sexuality and Gender Now will be essential reading for professionals and students of psychoanalysis who want to broaden their understanding of sexuality and gender in their clinical practice beyond heteronormative assumptions.

Leezah Hertzmann is a senior couple and individual psychoanalytic psychotherapist at the Tavistock and Portman NHS Foundation Trust and in private practice. She has a career long interest in psychoanalytic theory and technique with LGBTQI populations and is a member of the British Psychoanalytic Council special advisory group on sexual diversity. In 2015, Leezah was the recipient of the British Psychoanalytic Council Award for Innovation. She teaches and publishes widely.

Juliet Newbigin is a psychoanalytic psychotherapist with a long-standing interest in the impact of the wider social context on the development of individual identity within the family. She has been particularly concerned about the troubled history of the heteronormative understanding of sexual orientation in both psychoanalysis and Jungian analysis, and their failure to recognise the experience of the LGBTQI community. She currently chairs the British Psychoanalytic Council's Advisory Group on Sexual and Gender Diversity.

Tavistock Clinic Series

Margot Waddell, Jocelyn Catty, & Kate Stratton (Series Editors)

Recent titles in the Tavistock Clinic Series

Doing Things Differently: The Influence of Donald Meltzer on Psychoanalytic Theory and Practice, edited by Margaret Cohen & Alberto Hahn

Inside Lives: Psychoanalysis and the Growth of the Personality, by Margot Waddell

Internal Landscapes and Foreign Bodies: Eating Disorders and Other Pathologies, by Gianna Williams

Living on the Border: Psychotic Processes in the Individual, the Couple, and the Group, edited by David Bell & Aleksandra Novakovic

Making Room for Madness in Mental Health: The Psychoanalytic Understanding of Psychotic Communication, by Marcus Evans

Melanie Klein Revisited: Pioneer and Revolutionary in the Psychoanalysis of Young Children, by Susan Sherwin-White

New Discoveries in Child Psychotherapy: Findings from Qualitative Research, edited by Margaret Rustin & Michael Rustin

Oedipus and the Couple, edited by Francis Grier

On Adolescence: Inside Stories, by Margot Waddell

Organization in the Mind: Psychoanalysis, Group Relations, and Organizational Consultancy, by David Armstrong, edited by Robert French

Psychoanalysis and Culture: A Kleinian Perspective, edited by David Bell

Researching the Unconscious: Principles of Psychoanalytic Method, by Michael Rustin

Reason and Passion: A Celebration of the Work of Hanna Segal, edited by David Bell

Short-Term Psychoanalytic Psychotherapy for Adolescents with Depression: A Treatment Manual, edited by Jocelyn Catty

Sibling Matters: A Psychoanalytic, Developmental, and Systemic Approach, edited by Debbie Hindle & Susan Sherwin-White

Social Defences against Anxiety: Explorations in a Paradigm, edited by David Armstrong & Michael Rustin

Surviving Space: Papers on Infant Observation, edited by Andrew Briggs

Talking Cure: Mind and Method of the Tavistock Clinic, edited by David Taylor

The Anorexic Mind, by Marilyn Lawrence

The Groups Book. Psychoanalytic Group Therapy: Principles and Practice, edited by Caroline Garland

Therapeutic Care for Refugees: No Place Like Home, edited by Renos Papadopoulos

Therapeutic Approaches with Babies and Young Children in Care: Observation and Attention, by Jenifer Wakelyn

Thinking Space: Promoting Thinking about Race, Culture, and Diversity in Psychotherapy and Beyond, edited by Frank Lowe

Towards Belonging: Negotiating New Relationships for Adopted Children and Those in Care, edited by Andrew Briggs

Turning the Tide: A Psychoanalytic Approach to Mental Illness. The Work of the Fitzjohn's Unit, edited by Rael Meyerowitz & David Bell

Understanding Trauma: A Psychoanalytic Approach, edited by Caroline Garland

Waiting to Be Found: Papers on Children in Care, edited by Andrew Briggs

"What Can the Matter Be?": Therapeutic Interventions with Parents, Infants, and Young Children, edited by Louise Emanuel & Elizabeth Bradley

Young Child Observation: A Development in the Theory and Method of Infant Observation, edited by Simonetta M. G. Adamo & Margaret Rustin

SEXUALITY AND GENDER NOW

Moving Beyond Heteronormativity

Edited by
Leezah Hertzmann &
Juliet Newbigin

Routledge
Taylor & Francis Group

LONDON AND NEW YORK

First published 2020
by Routledge
2 Park Square, Milton Park, Abingdon, Oxon OX14 4RN

and by Routledge
52 Vanderbilt Avenue, New York, NY 10017

Routledge is an imprint of the Taylor & Francis Group, an informa business

British Library Cataloguing-in-Publication Data
A catalogue record for this book is available from the British Library

Library of Congress Cataloging-in-Publication Data
Names: Hertzmann, Leezah, 1963- editor. | Newbigin, Juliet, 1948- editor.
Title: Sexuality and gender now : moving beyond heteronormativity / edited by Leezah Hertzmann and Juliet Newbigin.
Description: Milton Park, Abingdon, Oxon ; New York, NY : Routledge, 2019. | Series: Tavistock clinic series | Includes bibliographical references.
Identifiers: LCCN 2019011792 (print) | LCCN 2019012930 (ebook) |
ISBN 9780429287633 (Master) | ISBN 9781000022643 (Adobe) | ISBN 9781000022797 (Mobipocket) | ISBN 9781000022940 (ePub) | ISBN 9780367254100 (hardback : alk. paper) | ISBN 9781782205296 (pbk. : alk. paper)
Subjects: LCSH: Sexual minorities—Mental health. |
Sexual minorities—Counseling of. | Sexual orientation—Psychological aspects. | Sex role—Psychological aspects. | Cultural psychiatry. | Psychotherapy.
Classification: LCC RC451.4.G39 (ebook) | LCC RC451.4.G39 S47 2019 (print) | DDC 616.890086/6—dc23
LC record available at https://lccn.loc.gov/2019011792

ISBN: 978-0-367-25410-0 (hbk)
ISBN: 978-1-78220-529-6 (pbk)
ISBN: 978-0-429-28763-3 (ebk)

Typeset in Palatino
by Swales & Willis, Exeter, Devon, UK

Note about the cover image: "The Moon and Sleep" by Simeon Solomon (1840–1905)

Solomon was a British painter, associated with the Pre-Raphaelite Movement. He was initially successful, but his career never recovered from two prosecutions and brief periods of imprisonment in 1873 and 1874, for having sex with men. This painting dates from 1894, oil on canvas, 514 x 762 mm. It was presented to the TATE collection by Miss Margery Abrahams in memory of Dr Bertram L. Abrahams and Jane Abrahams in 1973.

CONTENTS

II
Desire

III
Perspectives on gender

SERIES EDITORS' PREFACE

Margot Waddell, Jocelyn Catty, & Kate Stratton

Since it was founded in 1920, the Tavistock Clinic—now the Tavistock and Portman NHS Foundation Trust—has developed a wide range of developmental approaches to mental health which have been strongly influenced by the ideas of psychoanalysis. It has also adopted systemic family therapy as a theoretical model and a clinical approach to family problems. The Tavistock is now one of the largest mental health training institutions in Britain. It teaches up to 600 students a year on postgraduate, doctoral, and qualifying courses in social work, systemic psychotherapy, psychology, psychiatry, nursing, and child, adolescent, and adult psychotherapy, along with 2,000 multi-disciplinary clinicians, social workers, and teachers attending Continuing Professional Development courses and conferences on psychoanalytic observation, psychoanalytic thinking, and management and leadership in a range of clinical and community settings.

The Tavistock's philosophy aims at promoting therapeutic methods in mental health. Its work is based on the clinical expertise that is also the basis of its consultancy and research activities. The aim of this Series is to make available to the reading public the clinical, theoretical, and research work that is most influential at the Tavistock. The Series sets out new approaches in the understanding and treatment of psychological disturbance in children, adolescents, and adults, both as individuals and in families.

Sexuality and Gender Now: Looking Beyond Heteronormativity is the first volume in the Series on this subject and one that is long overdue. Editors Leezah Hertzmann and Juliet Newbigin remind us that while we live, increasingly, within political and social cultures whose official language opposes discrimination and celebrates difference, the effects of prejudice continue to be felt in subtle and more explicit ways by those whose sexuality and gender do not fit within heterosexual norms. Despite significant developments in approaches to sexual and gender variance, these remain complex and contested categories within psychoanalytic communities. This ambitious and necessary book invites the reader to consider the extent to which psychoanalytic theory continues to be indebted to "heteronormative" assumptions and urges us, in the words of the editors, to think about the "undercurrents of homophobia and casual cruelty", the "misunderstandings" and "unconsidered judgements", that creep into the consulting room when we leave these unquestioned.

The chapters assembled here set out to challenge these normative assumptions, and to examine the binds and blind spots of our theory and clinical practice. Collectively, they take an enquiring approach to the narratives that have historically linked identity, desire, gender, and sexual behaviour in psychoanalytic theory, and propose new frameworks for thinking about the dilemmas arising from the clinical encounter. Their aim is to encourage a more nuanced attitude, a fluidity in our thinking, a space in which ideas can be explored and developed rather than shut down, cut off, or hidden away.

As the editors point out in their lucid introduction, Freud's definitive statement in the *Three Essays on the Theory of Sexuality* (1905d) makes it clear that he viewed human sexuality as infinitely variable. Yet he famously concluded that "the final sexual organisation" is a heterosexual one. The longstanding tensions between the emancipatory and the conservative impulses within psychoanalysis are picked up by many of the contributors to this volume. Several of the chapters attend to the legacy of the pathological interpretation of homosexuality that was dominant for so long in psychoanalysis and include explicit recognition of the suffering that this caused. All the contributions push against too-facile approaches, encouraging the reader to struggle with complexities, while looking afresh at received psychoanalytic ideas; all are informed by clinical experience and include examples, often described in moving detail, of work taking place in different settings.

The authors represented here are diverse in their beliefs and approaches. In the three parts of this volume—"Sex and the Consulting

Room", "Desire", and "Perspectives on Gender"—they make use of a broad range of theoretical models, drawing on Kleinian and Freudian ideas, French psychoanalysis, post-Jungian analysis, and queer theory. They do not seek consensus but aim for thoughtful elaboration, bringing different ideas to bear on one another to raise important questions. How, for example, are clinicians to gain greater awareness of their own internal systems of what constitutes "naturally" acceptable and unacceptable gender and sexual expression? As Hertzmann and Newbigin explain in their Introduction: "The authors here take a critical approach to conventional theory, deconstructing and extending psychoanalytic concepts. But we believe that what is most important for the clinician is a process of reflective self-awareness, including both unconscious and embodied responses, which attends closely to the transference and countertransference and does not shy away from uncomfortable reactions that may appear prejudicial or pathologizing."

In its determination not to shy away from the difficult and uncomfortable, this is a volume that makes room for the professional and the personal, the supportive, the sceptical, and the unsure. It will be an invaluable training text for teachers and students as well as a vital resource for all practising clinicians who are seeking to broaden their thinking and to develop enlightened and hopeful ways of engaging with an area that is so important for us all.

ACKNOWLEDGEMENTS

Every effort has been made to contact the copyright holders for their permission to reprint selections of this book. The publishers would be grateful to hear from any copyright holder who is not here acknowledged, and we will undertake to rectify any errors or omissions in future editions of this book.

Chapter 4: first published as L. Hertzmann, "Losing the Internal Oedipal Mother and Loss of Sexual Desire", *British Journal of Psychotherapy*, 34 (2018, 1): 25–45. Reprinted by permission of John Wiley & Sons, Inc.

Chapter 5: originally adapted from Dianne Elise, "Woman and Desire: Why Women May Not Want to Want", *Studies in Gender and Sexuality, Vol. 1* (2000, No. 2): 125–145. By permission of The Analytic Press, Hillsdale, NJ. Copyright © 2000 by The Analytic Press. It appeared adapted as "The Primary Maternal Oedipal Situation and Female Homoerotic Desire", *Psychoanalytic Inquiry*, 22 (2002, No. 2): 209–228. Reprinted by permission of Taylor & Francis, LLC.

Chapter 7: first published as J. Drescher, "From Bisexuality to Intersexuality", *Contemporary Psychoanalysis*, 43 (2007, No. 2): 204–228. Reprinted by permission of William Alanson White Institute of Psychiatry, Psychoanalysis & Psychology and the William Alanson White Psychoanalytic Society.

Chapter 9: first published as M. Suchet, "Crossing Over", *Psychoanalytic Dialogues*, *21* (2011): 172–191. Reprinted by permission of Taylor & Francis Group, LLC.

Chapter 10: first published as K. Corbett, "Gender Now", *Psychoanalytic Dialogues*, *18* (2008): 838–856. Reprinted by permission of Taylor & Francis, LLC.

ABOUT THE CONTRIBUTORS

Ken Corbett, PhD, is Assistant Professor, New York University Post-doctoral Program in Psychoanalysis and Psychotherapy. He is the author of *A Murder Over a Girl: Justice, Gender, Junior High* and *Boyhoods: Rethinking Masculinities*.

Jack Drescher, MD, is a psychiatrist and psychoanalyst in private practice in New York City. He is Clinical Professor of Psychiatry, Columbia University; Faculty Member, Columbia's Division of Gender, Sexuality, and Health; Adjunct Professor, New York University; and Training and Supervising Analyst, William Alanson White Institute. He has served on work groups revising sexual and gender diagnoses of *DSM–5, ICD–11*, and *PDM–2*. He is the author of *Psychoanalytic Therapy and the Gay Man*, Emeritus Editor of the *Journal of Gay and Lesbian Mental Health*, and the editor of more than 20 books dealing with health and mental health issues in LGBT community. He is a Distinguished Life Fellow of the American Psychiatric Association, and Past President, Group for the Advancement of Psychiatry.

Dianne Elise, PhD, is a Personal and Supervising Analyst and Faculty member of the Psychoanalytic Institute of Northern California and a Training Analyst member of the International Psychoanalytical Association; she has served on the Editorial Boards of the *Journal of the*

American Psychoanalytic Association and *Studies in Gender and Sexuality*. Her over 30 publications include wide-ranging papers on the subjects of gender, sexuality, and erotic transference, appearing in the *Psychoanalytic Study of the Child*, *The Psychoanalytic Quarterly*, *Journal of the American Psychoanalytic Association*, *Psychoanalytic Dialogues*, *Studies in Gender & Sexuality*, and *Psychoanalytic Inquiry*. She has recently developed the concept of *analytic eroticism* to portray the role of libidinal vitality in treatment. Elise's book, *Creativity and the Erotic Dimensions of the Analytic Field* (Routledge, 2019) expands her work in innovative ways and presents her contemporary thinking on erotic life in psychoanalysis. She is in private practice in Oakland, California.

Giorgio Giaccardi is a Jungian Analyst and supervisor in private practice in London. He is Training Analyst of the British Jungian Analytic Association and Member Analyst of the Associazione per la Ricerca in Psicologia Analitica (Milan). He has published, taught, and presented, both in the United Kingdom and abroad, on the process of symbolization. He is a contributor of book reviews to various psychoanalytic journals. With Routledge, he has previously published a chapter on "Apolline and Dyonisian pathways to the Numinous" (in *The Idea of the Numinous*, 2006), and in 2019 he will contribute a chapter on archetypal processes involved in same-sex desire as part of a volume edited by Pilar Amezaga and Elizabeth Brodersen, *Jungian Perspectives on Indeterminate States: Betwixt and between Borders*. His paper "Unconscious Processes, Instrumental Music and the Experience of the Sublime" was commended in the 2014 Rozsika Parker Prize and was published in the *British Journal of Psychotherapy*.

Leezah Hertzmann is a couple and individual psychoanalytic psychotherapist at the Tavistock and Portman NHS Foundation Trust (London) and in private practice. Leezah has previously led the development of several mentalization-based interventions based on psychoanalytic concepts and practice for couples and parents whose relationships become dysregulated and violent. One of these interventions was successfully evaluated in a recently published research trial, of which she was co-principal investigator. In 2015, she was the recipient of the British Psychoanalytic Council Award for Innovation. Leezah has a particular interest in psychoanalytic theory and technique with LGBT individuals and couples. She teaches and publishes widely and is a member of the British Psychoanalytic Council Advisory Group on Sexual and Gender Diversity.

Juliet Newbigin is a psychoanalytic psychotherapist with a long-standing interest in the impact of the wider social context on the development of individual identity within the family. She has been particularly concerned about the troubled history of the heteronormative understanding of sexual orientation in both psychoanalysis and Jungian analysis and their failure to recognize the experience of the LGBTQ+ community. She currently chairs the British Psychoanalytic Council's Advisory Group on Sexual and Gender Diversity.

David Richards is a psychodynamic psychotherapist and supervisor in private practice, working both with individuals and in organizational settings. He has been a senior tutor on the MSc in Psychodynamic Counselling and Psychotherapy at Birkbeck College, University of London. Over the last three decades he has worked extensively in the public and private sectors, initially in the HIV field and later managing a community counselling service for older adults. He has particular experience of working with the LGBTQ+ communities, and within his wide theoretical interests has a particular focus on issues of sexuality and identity. He has served on the Board of the British Psychoanalytic Council, holding a portfolio of diversity, and is also a member of the BPC Advisory Group for Sexual and Gender Diversity.

Poul Rohleder is a clinical psychologist and psychoanalytic psychotherapist, and member of the British Psychotherapy Foundation. Alongside having a private practice in central London, he is an academic and researcher and is on the editorial board of the *British Journal of Psychotherapy*. He is a senior lecturer at the Department of Psychosocial and Psychoanalytic Studies at the University of Essex, where he is involved in the training of psychodynamic counsellors. His research interests are in sexuality and marginalized identities, and he has published a number of academic papers in these areas. He is a member of the British Psychoanalytic Council task group on sexual and gender diversity within psychoanalysis.

Melanie Suchet is clinical Associate Professor, NYU Postdoctoral Program in Psychotherapy and Psychoanalysis, and Faculty member at the Stephen A. Mitchell Center for Relational Studies. She is an associate editor of *Psychoanalytic Dialogues* and a contributing editor of *Studies in Gender and Sexuality*. She is the recipient of Division 39's 2014 SGI award and of Division 39's 2016 Scholarship award. Her private practice is in Manhattan. She is the originator and co-editor of *Relational Psychoanalysis: Volume 3*, dedicated to bringing to the fore newer ideas, especially political and social issues. She is co-editor of the Routledge book series *Psyche and Soul*. She works on the edges of psychoanalysis, attempting to bring into the centre what has been excluded and dissociated. Her interests also lie in the analyst's subjectivity and, specifically, in the subject positions the analyst holds with respect to race, class, gender, and sexuality.

Bernadette Wren trained as a Clinical Psychologist and Systemic Psychotherapist and was, until recently, trust-wide Head of Psychology at the Tavistock and Portman NHS Trust. She has degrees in philosophy and psychology and a continuing interest in the relevance of each discipline to the other. She works clinically with transgendered young people and their families in the Trust's Gender identity Development Service. For many years she taught clinical research methods across several Tavistock courses, has been a Teaching Fellow in the Department of Health and Human Sciences, Essex University, and an Honorary Senior Research Associate in the Department of Clinical, Educational and Health Psychology at UCL.

Introduction

Leezah Hertzmann & Juliet Newbigin

There is currently much debate about the varied forms that gender and sexual expression can take. Are we in the grip of a media-induced hysteria that encourages perverse behaviour? Or are we finally facing a reality that has been hidden or ignored for years—that both gender and sexuality are far more fluid than we have cared to admit? Psychoanalysis is one of the sites where this debate is taking place—unsurprisingly, in view of the fact that Freud was one of the first to ignite it at the turn of the nineteenth and twentieth centuries. The book intends to make a contribution in this important area.

It would not have been possible without the British Psychoanalytic Council's initiative to break decisively with the troubled history of psychoanalysis' pathological reading of non-heterosexual behaviour. For many years, this had led not only to the psychoanalytic treatment of homosexuality as an illness, but also to the exclusion of anyone who had "crossed the line sexually" from the opportunity to train with one of the institutes that offered courses in psychoanalysis or intensive psychoanalytic psychotherapy. In 2011 a Position Statement was issued that read: "The BPC does not accept that a homosexual orientation is evidence of disturbance of the mind or in development." Following this, the BPC set up an Advisory Group to explore ways of making the profession more welcoming to LGB people, and the group went on to extend its brief to include gender, as well as sexual, diversity. This collection has emerged from this process of opening our thinking.

Looking beyond heteronormativity

Freud's *Three Essays on the Theory of Sexuality*, first published in 1905 and revised several times between then and 1920, show him as simultaneously both radical and conservative in his attitude to sexuality. In the *Three Essays*, he declares that human sexual behaviour can and does take many forms, that homosexuality is found "in people whose efficiency is unimpaired, and who are indeed distinguished by specially high intellectual development and ethical culture" (1905d, p. 139). Yet he concludes that "the final sexual organisation" is a heterosexual one (1905d, footnote p. 207fn). So, although Freud states in the first essay on the sexual aberrations that "the exclusive sexual interest felt by men for women is . . . a problem that needs elucidating and is not a self-evident fact . . . " (1905d, p. 146fn), in the third essay, "On Puberty", he states that the libido, in its mature, procreative state, leads to a search for a partner of the opposite sex. Dana Birksted-Breen has stated that Freud chose to maintain conflicting ideas on sexuality and saw masculinity and femininity as "a conundrum" (Birksted-Breen, 1993a). In this book, we are focusing on contemporary ways of reading this "conundrum", taking as our starting point the radical Freud of "The Sexual Aberrations". Our title, "Looking Beyond Heteronormativity", follows on from Freud's stated intention in the opening paragraphs of this first Essay, to "look more closely" into the "errors, inaccuracies and hasty conclusions" (1905d, p. 135) that creep in if we leave unquestioned the conventional assumption of heterosexuality as the "natural" biologically determined expression of sexuality.

As Foucault has described, Freud was one of the pioneering nineteenth-century psychiatrists who developed a new way of observing and classifying human sexual behaviour:

> This was an important time. It is easy to make light of these nineteenth century psychiatrists, who made a point of apologising for the horrors they were about to let speak, evoking "immoral behaviour" or "aberrations of the genetic senses", but I am more inclined to applaud their seriousness: they had a feeling for momentous events. It was a time when the most singular pleasures were called upon to pronounce a discourse of truth concerning themselves, a discourse which had to model itself after that which spoke, not of sin and salvation, but of bodies and life processes—the discourse of science. [Foucault, 1976, p. 64]

Freud's *Three Essays* contain some good examples of what Foucault is describing here. In the opening pages of this work he does indeed call upon the most singular pleasures to pronounce their own discourse of scientific truth. Freud was criticized in his own time, for example, by Jung, for having reduced the fundamental life drive—the *libido*—to a matter of sexuality. From the start of his career as a psychiatrist, Freud studied this aspect of human life and behaviour, which was considered shameful and lived out in silence, in spite of being a familiar part of everyone's experience in a society where privacy was usually more limited than we would expect today.

Freud came from a respectable Jewish family, but, as Rosemary Balsam (2017) reminds us, he grew up in a small, crowded apartment, in which he would have been in intimate contact with other members of the family and no stranger to the facts of life, including pregnancy. He writes to Fliess of his earliest sexualized memory of his mother with striking delicacy:

> [l]ater (between the ages of two and two-and-a-half) my libido was stirred up towards *matrem*, namely on the occasion of a journey with her from Leipzig to Vienna, during which we must have spent the night together and I must have had the opportunity of seeing her *nudam*. [1950 [1892–1899], pp. 261–262]

In spite of his fastidious language here, Freud went on to become the doctor who spoke fearlessly to his patients, including young women, about their sexual life and fantasies. When we read case histories such as that of Dora (Freud, 1905e), we can feel shocked at Freud's boldness in unhesitatingly speaking to this adolescent girl about what he imagines to be her private and inarticulate thoughts. However, Dora's complex family situation suggests how irregular sexual practices in the bourgeois family could be, and it must have been a dramatic experience for a young woman to come across a doctor who could name sexual matters clearly, even if, in the process, he revealed his own limitations in understanding and empathy.

In this book we have collected papers that demonstrate, we hope, an open-minded, enquiring approach to matters of gender and sexuality, one that allows these matters to evoke questions, and to speak for themselves. The term "heteronormativity" may sound like clumsy jargon to some, but it is simply a way of naming the position from which sexuality is conventionally understood. Freud was right in saying that "errors, inaccuracies and hasty conclusions" can obscure the view when we assume an expertise that ceases to question our own assumptions, and it has been amply demonstrated that this began to happen in the field of psychoanalysis in the years after Freud.

Heterosexuality is encoded in the social, cultural, religious, and economic institutions of our society. And although a more tolerant attitude is developing in our own and other Western countries, those whose gender identity and sexual orientation do not conform to heterosexual norms still experience discrimination and bias. The changes brought in by the 2010 Equality Act that promote equal rights for LGBT+ people may appear to have provided protection against prejudice, but a backlash against "political correctness" continues to produce undercurrents of homophobia and casual cruelty towards those whose gender and sexuality do not "fit" with the heteronormativity that some regard as "natural". We would add here that these normative assumptions are still producing misunderstandings, often simply the result of ignorance of other people's lives, that find their way into psychoanalytic theory and clinical practice.

The philosopher Thomas Nagel (1986) has argued that the scientific attitude falls prey to a belief that its knowledge is "a view from nowhere", leading its champions to claim that the insights of scientific rationality are the final word on a given area, and he warns us that we forget at our peril that every view is a view from "somewhere". Because the "Darwinian" Freud, who equated heterosexuality with full maturity, has assumed a dominant position in the psychoanalytic field of enquiry, we intend here to present essays on sexuality and gender that name this psychoanalytic "heteronormative" tendency and look beyond it.

This is the first book in the Tavistock Clinic Book Series on this theme, and, like others in the series, most of the chapters here are by authors working in or influenced by the object relations tradition of psychoanalysis. The book intends to question our psychoanalytic assumptions and unreflective judgements, but we certainly do not claim to provide final answers. The chapters in the section dealing with gender will inevitably be the area where this is most obviously true, as this is an emerging field that poses the starkest challenges for the contemporary psychoanalytic clinician. It is appropriate to think of these papers as celebrating the pioneering work begun by Domenico Di Ceglie and colleagues in the Gender Identity Development Service (GIDS) at the Tavistock Centre. We hope to show clinicians and their patients facing together the challenges in understanding that emerge in the course of psychotherapy. As the French analyst Collette Chiland said of this area of work: "The analyst needs to work on himself or herself as much as on the patient" (2000, p. 33).

This collection aims to serve as a training text for students as well as a resource for practising clinicians. The authors here take a critical approach to conventional theory, deconstructing and extending psychoanalytic concepts. But we believe that what is most important for the clinician is a process of reflective self-awareness, including both unconscious and embodied responses, which attends closely to the transference and countertransference and does not shy away from uncomfortable reactions that may appear prejudicial or pathologizing. This often proves crucial in understanding where significant difficulties lie for both partners in the therapeutic couple, and exploring them may feel risky but will better enable the clinician to survive the dilemmas with which s/he is presented in treatment. The authors here address these issues, including work with erotic feelings in both transference and countertransference—something clinicians can feel reluctant to acknowledge, but which, if left unaddressed, can limit the possibilities for supporting patients to explore their sexuality and gender more fully.

The Oedipus complex

When we speak of "deconstructing" psychoanalytic concepts, we certainly do not mean that they should be abandoned. The Oedipus complex has occupied a central place in psychoanalytic theory, bringing together three aspects of human experience relevant to our topic—namely, desire, gender identity, and sexuality—across the generations. The earliest evidence in Freud's writing that he was formulating what he later defined as the Oedipus complex occurs in notes that he sent to Fliess on 31 May 1897, in which he refers to having identified "hostile impulses against the parents (a wish that they should die)" (1950 [1892–1899], p. 264) At that time he was engrossed in his self-analysis and had uncovered these wishes in himself, finding in them the origins of his own "hysteria". This exploration of his dreams and fantasy life eventually led Freud to abandon his earlier theory that neurosis was the result of an actual seduction in childhood by a parental figure or older sibling. By October of that year, he had found, in the classical story of Oedipus Rex, a mythological representation of the experience of desire for his mother and jealous rivalry with his father that he had recognized in himself. The discovery that this "complex" of feeling—the child's intense emotional response to the discovery of his parents' sexual relationship—was reflected in a well-known myth from ancient times indicated to him the universality of this experience: "we can understand the riveting power of Oedipus Rex, in spite of all the objections raised by reason against its presupposition of destiny" (1950 [1892–1899], p. 265).

By 1910, in the fourth of his five lectures on psychoanalysis, he was speaking confidently of the Oedipus complex as an inevitable challenge of individual maturation, and one that "constitutes the *nuclear complex* of every neurosis" (1910a, p. 47). In the *Three Essays on the Theory of Sexuality* (1905d) Freud had outlined his ideas about infantile sexuality. He broadened the meaning of "sexuality" to encompass all forms of preverbal bodily pleasure of an auto-erotic kind, culminating in the genital desire for the parent that resulted in the oedipal crisis. Subsequently, during latency, these desires became repressed, until adolescence reawakened eroticism in a more mature and related form. In *Totem and Taboo*, he claimed that the origins of the Oedipus complex lay in an inherited memory of mankind's prehistoric trauma. He theorized an early society in which there had been a "primal horde"—the sons who had been driven out by the "violent and jealous father who keeps all the females for himself" (Freud, 1912–13], p. 141)—who came together and killed and devoured their father. "United, they had the courage to do and succeeded in doing what would have been impossible for them individually" (p. 141)

An echo of this murderous impulse, passed down through the generations, Freud argued, was the "phylogenetic" origin of oedipal guilt and the intense anxiety about the possibility of castration. Here, he was intending to build firm foundations for psychoanalysis by rooting them in the emerging scientific disciplines of archaeology and anthropology. However, we no longer accept his idea of "phylogenetic" memory, and we have come to see his picture of the "primal horde" as belonging alongside Frazer's *Golden Bough* (1894) as something taken seriously at the time but now regarded largely as a work of Eurocentric fantasy about "primitive" people.

Freud's view of the Oedipus complex as based on a scientific view of human infantile development and linked with the evolutionary history of the species, has aroused controversy, and as a theory is obviously complicated and contestable. Indeed, it can be argued that it is the nature of Freud's theory, situated as it is on the border between scientific evidence and Freud's unflinchingly honest but subjective examination of his internal life, inevitably inflected with his own unexamined cultural assumptions, that lends it a particular complexity, creating rich possibilities for development in different directions. The various paths these developments have taken have given rise to different schools of psychoanalysis.

Freud was initially influenced by Wilhelm Fliess' biologically based ideas about human bisexuality. Fliess, an ear, nose and throat specialist, hypothesized a link between the nose and the genitals and argued for a male equivalent of the female menstrual cycle, lasting 23 days, as opposed to the woman's 28 (in Gherovici, 2010, pp. 65–68)). Freud adopted Fliess' idea of "an innate bisexual disposition" (Freud, 1908a, p. 166) but transformed it into a theory of psychological masculinity and femininity. He developed an account of the Oedipus complex that was firmly rooted in the boy's experience of his anatomy, assuming that the significance accorded to the penis reflected the "natural" cultural superiority accorded to masculinity: "active", "dominant", over femininity: "passive", "receptive". For the boy, and particularly for Freud, the oldest son of a mother who adored him, this account appeared objectively coherent; his anatomy destined him to move from his earliest intense love affair with his mother, through castration anxiety and painful submission to his father's authority, to arrive at identification with him, accepting his father's superior status but comforted by the prospect that in the future he would possess a woman of his own. But Freud also suggested that the boy, before settling on this "positive" oedipal outcome, could also experience the complex in a "negative" form—a homosexual desire to be sexually dominated by his father, in which he was the passive partner, subjectively identified with his mother. This picture, while involving the boy's fantasy about the function of his penis, is further complicated by Freud's assertion that the boy assumes his mother to possess a penis like himself. It is the discovery that this is not so that provokes the oedipal crisis, initiating castration anxiety and facing him with his guilty recognition of his sexual wishes towards his mother.

Freud later developed his ideas about the oedipal situation of women (1931b, 1933a) to correct his earlier mistaken assumption that the girl's development was simply the mirror image of the boy's. The work of other colleagues, particularly women analysts, had led him to recognize that both girl and boy shared the mother as their earliest love object. It is here that Freud moves further from observed anatomy, into the territory of subjective meaning, when he asserts that the girl does not recognize her vagina, but only her clitoris, which she assumes to be a penis. In fact, she sees herself as "a little man" and assumes that her mother is similarly equipped. Like the boy, it is the discovery of this mistake that ushers in her oedipal crisis, leading her to reject her mother in disgust and resolving her envy of the penis she lacks by turning to her father who will give her a baby—preferably a male child—in compensation.

As previously noted, in spite of his belief in this phallocentric fantasy of narcissistic completeness, and the polymorphously perverse sensual pleasures that prevail in early infancy, Freud required the genital stage of development, which initiates the complex, to come to a heterosexual resolution, the "positive" outcome. Underlying this assumption was his Darwinian view that the dominant function of sexuality was to ensure the survival of the species. At this point, the contra-sexual or "negative" aspect of the complex became repressed and consigned to the unconscious, in service of the requirement that each individual prepare him or herself to play the part assigned by their biological sex. Successfully negotiated oedipal development allowed the complex to "dissolve". Failure to complete the process led to neurosis.

There is a great deal of literature in psychoanalysis drawing out different aspects implicit in Freud's picture, giving rise to specific schools of psychoanalysis. There are those that have pursued Freud's view of his discipline as a science. Much work has been done on child development, to find supporting evidence based on observation that elaborates Freud's theories. Anna Freud herself, Melanie Klein, Donald Winnicott, and Margaret Mahler all worked with children and extended Freud's ideas very creatively. Currently the work of the Boston Change Process Study Group, arising from the work of the neo-natal psychologist, Daniel Stern, is observing minutely the way infant and care-giver develop emotionally entrained pre-verbal communication. Most psychoanalytic trainings in the United Kingdom require the candidate to undertake an infant observation, in order to develop attunement to children during their earliest stages of development, on the understanding that such close attention informs the therapist's sensitivity to the patient's infantile and pre-verbal experience.

There have also been, from the outset, colleagues of Freud's who contested his assumption of the primacy of the phallus and his argument that the pre-oedipal girl has no knowledge of her vagina and its function. Beginning with Karen Horney and Helene Deutsch, there were analysts, mainly women, who argued that "anatomy is destiny" but assumed women's innate knowledge of their biological capacity. Women may lack a penis, but they can bear children. They claimed that it was possible to define essential differences between male and female psychology based on observable physical differences, but without the phallocentrism assumed by Freud. Melanie Klein, who situated oedipal development at a much earlier stage and took for granted the infant's innate awareness of his or her anatomy, has contributed to these ideas. These participants in the psychoanalytic discussion of gender and sexuality have offered creative insight into how women's experience is informed by their bodily reality, notably of menstruation and childbirth, and the intimate links between mothers and daughters. It is a line of thinking that further develops Freud's ideas about psychic bisexuality and is being currently explored fruitfully by the Committee on Women and Psychoanalysis (COWAP) of the International Psychoanalytical Association.

In the United Kingdom, Kleinian psychoanalysts have developed a line of psychoanalytic thinking that has foregrounded the oedipal stage as the development of an acceptance of reality, leaving its implications for bodily awareness somewhat obscured. This approach, which draws particularly on the ideas of Melanie Klein, Hanna Segal, and Wilfred Bion, focuses on the capacity for tolerance of the so-called third position, an Oedipus complex of the mind that recognizes the separation from a primal unity of mother and infant and introduces the capacity for reality testing and reflection. These developments have been central to the Tavistock tradition. Money-Kyrle (1971) described how the Oedipus complex establishes three crucial "facts of life": the fact of gender difference, the fact of generational difference, and the required deferment of gratification. This creative line of thought has been taken further by subsequent thinkers, including Herbert Rosenfeld, Betty Joseph, Ron Britton, and John Steiner. It has travelled abroad and has impacted on Roy Schafer and Thomas Ogden in the United States. In the United Kingdom it is perhaps one of the reasons why interest in the implications of Freud's ideas about sexual development as such has waned, and there has been an increased focus on the here and now exchange in the analytic encounter.

Alongside those schools that maintain the "scientific" inheritance of Freud's work, there has been ongoing interest in developing his subjectivist viewpoint, which is particularly engaged with his thinking about sexual identity. This perspective recognizes the body's existence as a fantasy construction that can include the assumptions that the mother shares a penis and that the little girl is a "little man": ideas that may seem true to a child but come from somewhere other than physical reality.

This reading of Freud has been given traction by the work of Lacan, which has been influential in academia. Lacan's Freud is understood from a phenomenological perspective, which recognizes the crucial contribution of the social context in which we develop our sense of identity. Although Freud did not recognize it himself, the Oedipus complex in his own account can be read as a description of the child's earliest introduction to the world interpreted through the cultural construction of sexual difference, the dominance of "masculine" values and "the repudiation of femininity" (1937c), which the child takes in as he or she attempts to decode the social meaning of bodily treatment and family dynamics. Other French analysts are significant here, such as Jean Laplanche (1997), who stresses the asymmetrical nature of the child–parent relationship, and Janine Chasseguet-Smirgel (1985b) and Bella Grunberger (1989), who argued, like Money-Kyrle, that the Oedipus complex introduced the child to the fact of generational, as well as sexual, difference.

All these schools aim, in different ways, to develop Freud's ideas about what are essential aspects of human behaviour and experience, which Freud described as scientific truths that were being uncovered by psychoanalysis. Perhaps for this reason, the language in which these developing theories were expressed has tended to lead to their being construed as "facts", which have been at times misused to claim the "moral high ground" in debates about the correct view (Milton, 2000) in relation to gender and sexuality. "Deconstruction", as we use it here, refers to the attempt to develop an understanding of the evolving history of psychoanalytic ideas and the truth claims that they make.

The book

These multiple ways of developing the theory of Freud's Oedipus complex demonstrate how it can be read as the crucible of our unstable sense of our identity. In placing sex at the heart of psychic development, Freud highlighted its capacity to destabilize the psyche, requiring each individual to develop her/his defences to deal with the power of this drive. His work maintained in sharp focus a connection between psychoanalysis and the physical body, in both its material and its fantasy form, a conundrum that it is difficult to keep in view. As Nancy Chodorow (1992) has pointed out, the developmental history of everyone's sexuality, whatever their orientation, should be understood as "a compromise formation".

We advocate here a position that recognizes the contradictions we inevitably face in trying to theorize our own internal world. For us, the "scientific" achievement of psychoanalysis is the development of a particular kind of attention and reflection in a special setting. Although we need theory to think within, it can foreclose further questioning if we allow it to take primacy in dictating our understanding of what we see. We hope that the reader will be able to find congruence with the not-knowing, open stance we have tried to convey here—"without memory or desire . . ." (Bion, 1967). This frequently quoted line advocates an attitude that is, of course, impossible to achieve but indicates an approach where theories and assumptions are not adhered to rigidly, allowing the clinician to engage more directly with the patients' dilemmas and conflicts. We believe that this psychoanalytic stance can enable an openness to the atypical developmental trajectory of relationships for those whose sexuality and gender may be fluid, and to think about the place of them in the mind. Developing a wider and more flexible attitude to sexuality in general could illuminate our understanding of all sexualities, including heterosexuality, in addressing the internal experience of individuals who are forming their own identities in our rapidly changing world.

The book is written both for clinicians involved in training and supervising students in psychoanalytic settings, as well as for students themselves. We are aware that practising clinicians may not have had the opportunity to explore sexuality and gender more widely in their original trainings, and may want to develop a greater depth of understanding. We hope it will be of interest to clinicians, supervisors, teachers, academics, and students in the fields of psychoanalysis, psychoanalytic psychotherapy, psychodynamic counselling and therapy, couple and family psychoanalysis, and child psychotherapy and analysis.

The chapters and authors

These collected chapters that comprise the book contain a selection of new essays, alongside several by authors who have already had a significant impact on the development of psychoanalytic theory and practice. All the authors in this book have endeavoured to develop new ways of extending psychoanalytic theories, always informed by the clinical experience, with patients at the centre. They include clinicians working with a wide range of populations, in settings in both the medical and the voluntary sector, but also educators in psychoanalysis, committed to teaching, supervising, and training coming generations of psychotherapists. The authors of these collected essays on issues of gender and sexuality represent a range of theoretical standpoints, which include object relations, Kleinian and Freudian, those of French psychoanalysis, post-Jungian, and queer theory.

Part I: Sex and the consulting room

Juliet Newbigin explores how the development of psychoanalysis in the English-speaking world has foregrounded infant–care-giver relationships and relegated erotic experience to a less prominent position than Freud proposed. She explores the work of Laplanche and of others influenced by his thinking who emphasize the unmirrored and enigmatic nature of sexual excitement. She suggests that the unexplored heteronormative bias of psychoanalytic clinicians has led to a neglect of the therapist's own psychosexuality, leading to an unconsidered judgemental stance on non-normative sexual behaviour. Her chapter emphasizes the need for a greater openness to our patients' sexuality from a perspective that is informed by the clinician's own experience of erotic desire.

Poul Rohleder draws on psychosocial research outside the psychoanalytic field that demonstrates the shame-inducing impact of homophobia on the development of a boy who grows up with an awareness of a gay identity. He explores the psychoanalytic literature on shame and, drawing on clinical and cultural examples, demonstrates the defensive behaviour that underlying shame can produce, which can include a paradoxical hyper-masculinity. He suggests that it is the aspects of a gay man's identity that are associated with vulnerability and weakness that are particularly shame-inducing, as they evoke a misogynistic fear of becoming like a woman. These feelings and their link with internalized homophobia can be difficult to address in therapy but should not be avoided, as they have inevitable consequences for the patient's self-esteem.

David Richards' chapter is a significant contribution to a discussion that barely exists as yet, about the impact on the supervisory relationship of an awareness of diverse sexuality. Richards considers the impact on the supervisee, gay or straight, of the supervisor's sexuality, if it is known or intuited from the context in which the work takes place. Because of the silence about sexual orientation that psychoanalysis has required of its practitioners, Richards suggests that sexuality, as an aspect of the clinician's lived experience, has come to be ignored; he describes the effect that it can have when it becomes available for lively consideration in the supervisory context. He considers the various settings in which clinical work takes place and the particular impact that these settings may have on the supervisory dynamic.

Part II: Desire

These chapters address the use and relevance of the Oedipus concept in its classical depiction of desire and challenge the traditional heteronormative use of the concept. The authors address, in different ways, how desires develop across time and how the trajectory of early infantile sexuality can persist in the mind and the body in adult relational life.

Leezah Hertzmann explores how the loss of the unconscious oedipal mother can be manifested as a loss of sexual desire in a couple's relationship. Her paper is focused on women's desire for women, but she also considers the relevance of these ideas for other gender relationship pairings and how crucial it can be for couples to understand and acknowledge a wide range of identifications with, and desire for, both genders. The move from a fantasy state of merger and a wish to possess the oedipal mother to a more reality-based relationship can induce feelings of abandonment and loss, particularly of sexual desire. She suggests that to transcend sexual and gender binaries, gender and sexual fluidity should be acknowledged in therapy and can contribute to enhanced awareness of the desires of all our patients, regardless of their sexual orientation or gender identity.

Dianne Elise is a senior and influential figure in psychoanalysis the United States. She has written extensively on gender, sexual orientation, sexuality-inhibited desire, and infidelity, as well as on other issues such as creativity and ageing. In this chapter, she also examines the classical version of the female oedipal complex in order to elucidate aspects of same-sex object choice. Elise explores whether a mother can see her daughter as a sexual subject and whether mother–daughter homoerotic desire can be experienced and validated by the mother. She suggests that the fate of eroticism in the early mother–daughter relationship can obscure female desire, and she proposes the relabelling of the "negative oedipal complex" in girls as the "primary maternal oedipal situation". She emphasizes that female desire, what she wants and *that* she wants, is rendered invisible by heterosexual structures that psychoanalytic theories have, until more recently, all too readily accepted without question. She makes clear that she is referring to qualities in the mind, not proposing that, in actuality, people need to live bisexual lives, and in this sense she remains close to Freud's ideas on psychic bisexuality.

Giorgio Giaccardi writes about the effect on gay men of the lack, or inadequacy, of symbolic representations for their desire. Drawing on a rich range of sources, which include psychoanalysis and post-Jungian and queer theory, he describes how gay men have had to create forms of relationship in which they can find themselves and their desire reflected. His account promotes a sympathetic understanding of the need that drives this search, which arises from an internal deficit that can permanently undermine a sense of wholeness for the individual. He argues, nevertheless, that the creative work of improvisation can be reparative and has a considerable contribution to make to the wider culture.

Part III: Perspectives on gender

In this part the chapters consider gender and gender identity; they will inevitably present a challenge to historical psychoanalytic ways of theorizing this area. These authors write from clinical experience and demonstrate their own struggles to question their own assumptions.

Jack Drescher is a senior figure in psychiatry and psychoanalysis in the United States. He has made significant contributions to ways of thinking more open-mindedly about gender and has been actively engaged in the negotiations to arrive at the psychiatric classification of gender dysphoria. Here he begins by describing his own early encounter with an intersex patient, to demonstrate how the biological evidence of gender nonconformity that such patients exhibited was routinely eliminated through surgery to enable them to occupy a place in the "natural" gender binary. His chapter takes the reader systematically through the terms involved in the classification of gender and sexuality, explaining, as he goes, their history and the development of the ongoing debate about gender and sexual variance, including the narrative provided by psychoanalysis. He suggests that everyone, including therapists, has his/her own internal system of what constitutes "naturally" acceptable and unacceptable sexual and gender expression, arranged hierarchically, and he points out how important it is for clinicians to be aware of their own. "What analysts hear through their own filters may inevitably affect the kind of interventions they do and do not make with patients."

Bernadette Wren describes the work of The Gender Identity Development Service (GIDS), which is the one NHS highly specialist service in England and Wales for children and adolescents. She addresses the quandaries around gender diversity urgently facing children, parents, carers, GIDS clinicians, and NHS commissioners, and how pressing questions arise for clinicians attempting to find their feet with these young people and their families. She describes how difficult it can be to make sense of their unhappiness, and how challenging it can be to address their struggles imaginatively, compassionately, and safely. There are, as yet, few published papers that illuminate how a service operates at the centre of this whirlwind in a highly contested area. While politicization of gender identity in children proceeds unabated, and arguments about professional practice are regular news events, the voices of the clinicians rarely heard. This chapter is not a personal record of this anxious, watchful clinical work but, rather, one in which Wren outlines how these responsibilities are thought about and managed, as well as describing some of the impacts of the disputatious context on the work. She illustrates the way that GIDS sits at the heart of a set of contested issues of our time.

Melanie Suchet has been the recipient of two significant awards for her work in psychoanalysis by the American Psychological Association, and she is also on the editorial board of several journals. This seminal chapter describes her work with a patient who, through a long process of analytic exploration, came to choose to transition from female to male. The chapter attempts to replicate Suchet's experience of the work: the sense of uncertainty, of not knowing, and having to "stay in the dark and let things emerge organically" (Suchet, personal communication, August 2018). It also resonates with the patient's experience of living with and through the uncertainty of gender and sexuality to reach a place of greater understanding and acceptance. Suchet describes undergoing her own process of change, re-evaluating her relationship to psychoanalytic theories and concepts and issues of technique. She comes to a different understanding of the body and the central issues of how to own and inhabit and body that have not been sufficiently theorized in the psychoanalytic literature.

A person beyond gender

This chapter is an account by a patient. We felt it important to be reminded how these issues of gender, so delicate and often so anxiety-provoking for the professional, can seem to the person who is undergoing them. We are grateful to the author for letting us use his account of his experience as a trans man who spent many years depressed and confused by a baffling sense of wrongness and difference from those around him. He makes no claim to have found a magic solution, but his moving story conveys vividly the reality of one person's honest attempt, with the help of a therapist, to confront the issues. It is longer than the other chapters, but we felt it justifies its length.

Ken Corbett is an influential figure in psychoanalysis the United States, drawing on his wide experience of working with gender-variant children to question the impact that normative developmental expectations have had on nonconforming boys in particular. Here, he argues for a model of development that does not adhere rigidly to the picture that is reflected in the Oedipus complex, but one that makes room for expressions of gender that are individual and unexpectable. He describes gender and bodily coherence as an "intricate lattice work", "too complex for . . . simplistic causality". He invites us to question our tendency to equate gender variance with pathology, in order to maintain an open mind and a therapeutic capacity to listen to the other's experience. He says: "we struggle still to find a way to speak about non-normative genders outside a split that moves between phobia and advocacy". "We have been too quick to categorize, too quick to diagnose, and insufficiently attentive to the complex and perplexed relations established between individuals and cultural mandates."

A note about patient confidentiality

The chapters in this book contain a variety of clinical examples that have been approached in different ways. Some are fictional, some are composite case examples, and some are from patients or supervisees whose consent has been given to include their material. Above all, the authors of these chapters have considered the issue of confidentiality with the utmost care and thought.

Readers of this book may like to be aware that Melanie Suchet's chapter was written with her patient's consent and involvement. She said about this process: "As an analyst one has to be very careful about the timing of when to write a piece. It feels to me, that only when coming to an end, does it feel less of an interference and less likely to feel exploitative."

She explained that she was greatly encouraged by "Raphael", who has told her how helpful the paper has been for him. He said that he has read it many times, as a way to remember who he was and as a way to remember his struggles. He moved to a different city, and, when comfortable with his new therapist, he allowed her to read the paper and get a sense of all the work he has done.

PART I

SEX AND THE CONSULTING ROOM

CHAPTER ONE

Sex and the consulting room

Juliet Newbigin

I n this collection, psychoanalytic clinicians are reviewing theoretical ways of thinking about the sexual behaviour and gender presentation of individuals they meet in their consulting rooms today. And here, my subject is sex itself: sexual excitement, its nature, and its impact on other aspects of our lives. These things have, of course, always been the focus of psychoanalytic study. Freud is often caricatured as the Viennese doctor who saw sex everywhere. But, since the first decades of its development as a discipline, psychoanalysis in the English-speaking world has shifted its perspective in a somewhat different direction. Indeed, ironically, psychoanalysts have been accused of tending towards an attitude to sex—particularly sex in its experimental and non-heterosexual forms—that is even conservative and disapproving. The British Object Relations School has developed Freud's original ideas in a highly creative direction, but one that has moved away from Freud's nineteenth-century drive-based model. Susan Budd, in a paper called "No Sex Please—We're British" (2001) argued that the school's inter- and intra-personal model of relating made the focus of its concern, not bodily adult sexuality, but the emotional quality of attachment, seen through the lens of infant/parent dynamics. Because in the United Kingdom there has been from the beginning a tradition of accepting lay (i.e. non-medical) analysts, many of these were women involved in education and child-development, like Anna Freud and Melanie Klein. Significant male figures, such as Bowlby and Winnicott, were paediatricians. Presenting psychoanalysis as a way of thinking about the nature of the bond between mothers and children proved a valuable route towards the acceptance of psychoanalytic ideas, and these ideas have played a significant part in the culture of post-war Britain (2001, p. 62).

The timing and nature of the Oedipus complex was an important area of disagreement in the Controversial Discussions (King & Steiner, 1991) that led to the setting up of the different groups in the Institute of Psychoanalysis, and a tendency to avoid reopening these differences may also have inhibited exploration of bodily sexuality, according to Marilyn Lawrence (2012). But the subtle shift of psychoanalytic interest in the direction of pregenital experience has had a significant impact on the way in which relationships are described. Peter Fonagy (2008) reports on the results of a survey that he conducted with Mary Target into the incidence of language related to sexual behaviour in psycho-analytic journals. He says:

> Some still consider the hallmark of psychoanalysis to be its concern with sexuality (Green, 1995, 1999; Spruiell, 1997). Yet it is an open secret that this cannot be the case. The major theories of psycho-analysis today place the crux of their clinical accounts elsewhere— principally in the domain of emotional relationships. A frightening survey of the use of sexual and relational language in the electron-ically searchable journals of psychoanalysis showed a dramatic decline in words in psychoanalytic articles directly concerning sexuality. Contrasting this decline with relational theoretical words indicates that the decline is not in jargon words per se but in con-cepts specific to sexual theoretical language. . . . Even contrasting general relational words (such as love, affection, intimacy) with general sexual words (referring to body parts, sexual orientation, and sexual acts) shows the divergence of slope between the two domains. [Fonagy, 2008, p. 11]

He agrees with Budd that object-relations theorists have produced a highly nuanced understanding of interpersonal dynamics in the con-sulting room, but one that tends to steer away from details of bodily sexual experience. He says:

> Psychosexuality . must be rooted in sensorimotor embodied experience. An explanation that fundamentally sees the psychosexual as a symptom of object relations misses an essential aspect. Erotic experience is

unarguably intensely physical, and the failure to incorporate this aspect, or the reduction of physical arousal to a social construction, appears to us to create a distorted and shadowy representation of human sexuality that cuts it off from its roots in bodily experience. [Fonagy, 2008, p. 17]

Dagmar Herzog describes similar developments in the United States in the recent collection edited by Alessandra Lemma and Paul Lynch, *Sexualities: Contemporary Psychoanalytic Perspectives* (2015). In Lemma's chapter, entitled "What happened to psychoanalysis in the wake of the sexual revolution?" she describes psychoanalysts' resistance to the Kinsey reports published in 1948 and 1953 (Kinsey, Pomeroy, & Martin, 1948; Kinsey, Pomeroy, Martin, & Gebhard, 1953) and, later, to Masters and Johnson's book, *Human Sexual Response* (1966). In both cases, the profession came out strongly against the broad and varied picture of sexual behaviour that emerged from this research, which included a much higher incidence of homosexuality than had been previously thought. Instead, at the time, psychoanalysts placed an emphasis on the need for stable heterosexual relationships for sexual health and stressed the importance of love and kindness in the sexual encounter. Promiscuity and thrill-seeking sex were roundly condemned, and homosexuality, which became stereotypically associated in many clinicians' minds with the practice of meeting up with partners for casual sex, was firmly pathologized, as detailed in Kenneth Lewes' well-known book, *Psychoanalysis and Male Homosexuality* (1995). Speaking of the attitudes prevalent among US psychoanalysts in the years after World War Two, Herzog says:

> . . . I want to propose that the animus against homosexuality could also be seen as part of a much deeper-seated ambivalence within the psychoanalytic community about the centrality of sex of *any* kind to the psychoanalytic project. For sex was both the topic analysts thought they were experts on *and* they were deeply anxious about being too strongly associated with. This uncertainty and discomfort had as much to do not least with the aggressive Nazi, as well as the conservative Christian, attacks of the 1930's on psychoanalysis as not only an overly "Jewish" enterprise but also an overly sex-obsessed and therefore "dirty" one. [Herzog, 2015, p. 23; italics in original]

Freud, recognizing the unruly, excessive aspect of the libido, saw its inhibition or attempted suppression as the foundational cause of neurotic symptomatology. However, he also argued for the value of sublimation, and he believed that sexuality should be expressed in an appropriately managed way. In the *Three Essays on the Theory of Sexuality*, he suggested that lingering too long on foreplay led to perversion (1905d, p. 211) and that, although we were all familiar with the polymorphous pleasures of early childhood, these should be sidelined in adolescence, when genital sexuality became "subordinated to the reproductive function" (p. 207). Any other outcome led to psychological problems. Peter Fonagy (2008) argues that in spite of Freud's bold free-thinking, his eventual developmental model was shaped by evolutionary theory. Although his embodied picture of sexual excitement captured its compulsive and often ruthless quality, Freud's concept of libido was finally described in Darwinian terms as a manifestation of biological necessity. Fonagy points out that the impulse behind the development of object relations theory was need to correct the "scientism" of this picture, and, in spite of its tendency to foreground infantile experience and parent–child dynamics, it adds the emotionally engaged dimension that is downplayed in Freud's earlier drive-based account of psychosexuality.

In this chapter, I introduce a discussion of psychosexuality that is relational, but also more reflective of the world we currently inhabit. I am intending here to reevaluate the excessively judgemental stance of psychoanalysis in relation to "perversion". I see this as an aspect of the austere view that tended to be taken towards the sexual freedom that emerged after contraception released women from the threat of unwanted pregnancy and allowed people to pursue sex for pleasure and excitement, both in and outside the context of committed relationships. In addition, the demographics of the psychoanalytic profession— a preponderance of older, white middle-class people—also threatens to leave the attitudes of clinicians out of touch with the modern world.

Contemporary theoretical approaches

I have been quoting the work of Mary Target and Peter Fonagy, UK clinicians who have drawn attention to the recent lack of focus on psychosexuality. They have explored the ideas of the French analyst, Jean Laplanche and the US analyst Ruth Stein. Fonagy and Target have produced an influential body of work, which convincingly links the capacity in childhood to develop affect regulation to the experience of secure attachment to caregivers. They suggest that it is the caregiver's appropriate "marking" of the child's emotional communication that allows the child to recognize its own mind in the mirroring capacity of the other. Recognizing that a child's active sexual behaviour, such as masturbation, tends to meet with negative responses from adults and that incest fears cause adults to shield children from adult sexuality, both Fonagy and Target suggest (Fonagy, 2008; Fonagy & Allison, 2015; Target, 2015) that negative or inscrutable mirroring leads the child to internalize an ego-alien sense of its own sexual pleasure, which contributes an air of mystery to sexual experience when the adolescent comes to approach it for him or herself. They both reference the thinking of Jean Laplanche and Jean-Bertrand Pontalis (Laplanche, 1995; Laplanche & Pontalis, 1968).

The particular character of the French context gives Laplanche's theory an emphasis that is different from that of Anglophone psychoanalysis. He was a psychoanalyst and a translator of Freud's writing into French, and although Lacan was his teacher, his own position is distinct. But he was also a philosopher, within a tradition of Continental philosophy that has been particularly concerned with phenomenology. This approach differs from that of the British and American schools, rooted in a position born of logical positivism and analytic philosophy, which takes for granted an objective world. Instead, since Husserl and Heidegger, Continental philosophy has viewed the individual as entering a world that is met through pre-existing interpretation. Laplanche's theoretical approach to Freud is concerned to go beyond what he thought of as the limitations in Freud's revolutionary ideas. Freud was unable, thought Laplanche, to maintain what he describes as Freud's "Copernican" insights into the intersubjective origins of the mind and strayed back into the "Ptolemaic" world of scientism and evolutionary biology (Laplanche, 1997). He adhered to Freud's early seduction theory and argued against its abandonment. But Laplanche's interpretation of the adult's "seduction" of the infant is different, seeing it as the necessary means by which the infant's own internal world comes into existence. Laplanche claimed that, as well as the basic relationship between mother and child based on the day-to-day business of survival, the mother inevitably unconsciously transmits traces of her own sexuality to the child in the process of handling and feeding, sending the child "enigmatic" messages that the child responds to with excitement (2002). This excitement is, however, beyond the child's capacity to understand, and, as it is also mysterious and unrecognized by the mother, the child is left to struggle with this arousal alone. Nevertheless, it is in the struggle to grasp the communications from this lost object of excitement that the child's internal world comes into being. Laplanche argues that Freud was wrong in describing this early stage of infant development as "auto-erotic", as it arises from an experience that is profoundly related, but in a way that endows it with a mysterious and tantalizing quality, where something enormously desirable is sought but never completely grasped. Only afterwards, in a hopeless attempt to process the experience, does the infant find a means to prolong the pleasure in an auto-erotic form, thus giving rise to the infant's earliest experience of sexual fantasy. Laplanche's picture emphasizes the relationship between infant and mother as an asymmetrical encounter with a much larger, mysterious other, who evokes a powerful mixture of feelings that are always beyond reach (2005).

It is his practice to describe this area as *"le sexuel"*, in order to distinguish it from the term "sexual", which exists in English but not in French. When Laplanche uses the term "sexual", he means it to designate the objectifying, Darwinian attitude that he thinks Freud slips in and out of while describing this crucial aspect of development in the *Three Essays*—reverting to the Ptolemaic language and losing sight of his revolutionary insight. Laplanche argues that this enigmatic and frustrating search for a lost object of desire will come to underlie all later sexuality, which will never quite match the promise of fantasy. The view of Fonagy and Target where the adult's disapproval of the child's excitement or the failure of attunement on the part of the mother makes sexual excitement feel as if it is alien to the self, is understood in Laplanche's terms as an inevitable aspect of human existence, but one that is also creative and accounts for what is excessive and momentous in sexual experience.

Target's version of Laplanche's view is expressed within the language of British Object Relations, which stresses the reciprocity of mother–infant relationships as opposed to the asymmetry that is more familiar in the context of French philosophical thinking. For her the difficulty of sexuality arises from moments of maternal failure, or moments when the baby's demands are unbearable for the mother, making the difficulty between the mother and baby a mutual one:

> One may imagine a number of linked reasons for this sort of misattunement. The mother may unconsciously associate frustration and insistent drive pressure from another person with a sexual relationship: the baby implores and bullies the mother in a way she may unconsciously associate with a partner in a state of sexual desire . . . .
>
> In both of these situations of repeated inadequate mirroring, desexualisation and sexualisation of the baby's drive pressures, he may internalise a representation of his state coloured by his mother's mind especially her unconscious associations. [2015, p. 51]

In spite of these differences, the important issue that I wish to take up here is that these authors' ways of thinking give us an account of sexual excitement as something unmirrored and enigmatic, which takes place outside the bounds of socially sanctioned ways of relating. Fonagy has described it as "borderline", in that sexual behaviour assumes a freedom to violate body boundaries that would, in other circumstances, be outlawed (2008). I have been arguing that psychoanalysis has developed a tendency, for understandable reasons perhaps, to downplay what is unruly, excessive, and aggressive in sexual experience, in pursuit of a more domesticated fantasy of a "healthy" sexuality that is "non-perverse", loving and properly practised in the context of stable relationships. I think that, if we are prepared to open this up to include what I would suggest is a more truthful picture of actual sexual behaviour, we will be able to recognize with more acceptance the highly unstable mixture of feelings associated with sexual response, which can ignore body boundaries and include cruelty, disgust, and shame, all of which, as Freud himself pointed out, contribute to excitement in the process of overriding them (1905d, p. 152).

The writings of Ruth Stein are very helpful in finding this more complex, darker emotional register. Like Fonagy and Target, she uses the theories of Laplanche to develop the psychoanalytic theorizing of sexuality beyond drive theory and object relations, to take account of its particular quality.

> She says: in my recent work (Stein, 1998a, 1998b, 2006) I have suggested that we are in need of a phenomenological, experience-near probing into actual sexual experience, sustaining a stance that differs from our habit of reducing the meaning of sexuality to the workings of the impersonal drive of drive theory, or to a sexualized derivative of, or defence against, early object relations. Both drive theory and object relations theory have been used to encase too narrowly the complexity of human sexual experience, and their reductionist use in totally explaining sexual experience may have been an important factor in the insidious marginalization of sexual experience and the forgetting of its otherness. The theoretical reduction of sexuality within psychoanalysis has enabled many of us to hurry over experiential aspects of sexuality our patients describe (or defend against describing) to us. Patients tell us of encounters or practices that are sometimes strange, excessive, "perverse", and irrational, and we at such moments hastily reach for explanations that help us normalize such experiences. [Fonagy, 2008, pp. 44–45]

She suggests that we need to find a language that recognizes better its enigmatic quality. She says:

> I have proposed that we look at sexual experience as comprising three strands. Psychosexuality is characteristically woven with specific,

uniquely poignant body sensations; it is excessive of normal functioning, of work rationality and purposefulness, and even of containment; and, finally, it is enigmatic, being based on the mystery of the desired other's unconscious intentions and the mystified longings they call forth in our embodied mind. [2008, p. 46]

Stein's approach lays a stress on the excessive quality of sexual arousal that involves overriding the strictures of self-control imposed by the superego, which is the legacy of early social relationships. In sex, we claim for ourselves the right to a pleasure that, in childhood, under normal circumstances, seemed mysterious and unmirrored by parent figures. Robert Stoller, coming from the direction of US Ego Psychology, nevertheless was aware that one of the main components of sexual excitement was the transgressive feeling of overcoming internal inhibitions. He said: "To judge by the evidence thus far available regarding erotic excitement (versus dull rubbing), tension is either necessary for or improves excitement. Excitement is tension is psychic friction is anxiety-to-be-surmounted is anticipation of danger (pseudo-danger) is elements of hostility" (1991, p. 1095).

Sexuality today

Like Ruth Stein and Robert Stoller, I think the truth is that sexual excitement is sought precisely for its excessive quality of self-abandonment. The Elizabethan and Jacobean poets likened the moment of orgasm to death:

Since thou and I sigh one another's breath,
Whoe'er sighs most, is cruellest, and hastes the other's death.
[John Donne, 2005, p. 66]

While sexual intimacy involves identifying with the other's pleasure, it also, simultaneously, involves a release of the requirement to keep the other in mind, in favour of a letting go in pursuit of one's own climax. It offers the unusual opportunity—which, in Fonagy's terms, would be "borderline" in other circumstances—of an intense interaction in which both parties freely use each other's bodies for mutual enjoyment.

The precariousness of this experience makes us feel vulnerable, and it can be difficult to speak about it with our partners, not to mention with our therapists. It feels in conflict with other aspects of the self, because it is "in excess of normal functioning" and involves behaviour that has not been recognized and endorsed by internal parent figures.

Resistance may, therefore, build up in an ongoing relationship, until access to passionate sexual feelings is lost:

> A young woman in her twenties had enjoyed a close relationship with her mother, who had impressed upon her the message that men will take advantage of a woman who is too sexually willing. This had not prevented her from leaving home and establishing sexually active relationships. But now that she had moved in with her boyfriend, she recognized that, although she was very attached to him, she had to overcome an unwillingness to agree to sex. Particularly at times when she had been involved in domestic activities, such as tidying their flat, she found herself dreading the prospect of his physical presence and wanted nothing to do with him sexually. In her mind, sex had become associated with mess and confusion.

Back in 1912, Freud argued in "On the Universal Tendency to Debasement in the Sphere of Love" (1912d) that it was frequently difficult for men to bring together the "sensual and affectionate current" (1905d, p. 207) in their sexual life, feeling that the former was driven by primitive, instinctual needs, which felt shaming in the presence of a well-brought-up female partner. This split could lead a man to conduct his sexual relationship in secret with a prostitute or mistress, who filled the role of the "debased sexual object, a woman who is ethically inferior, to whom he need attribute no aesthetic scruples, who does not know him in his other social relations and cannot judge him in them" (1912d, p. 185). In the case described above, the young woman was in danger of seeing herself through her mother's eyes as just such a "debased sexual object" that her mother had warned her she would become. Now that she was "the well-brought-up female partner", keeping their home tidy, she needed to distance herself from sexual involvement and was inclined to reject her boyfriend when she imagined him wanting to use her in that way. Stephen Frommer, speaking of gay as well as straight relationships, describes the conflict involved in combining love and lust in our interactions with one person:

> Lust and love live psychically in various relational configurations, both more and less easily. The ability to lust where one loves depends on psychic multiplicity. This involves the capacity to bring the otherness of self forward in the context of attachment, to transit between states of mind that can feel radically different in their experience of self, other, and the form(s) of relatedness that are desired between the two. Because lustful states of mind are fashioned from fractures within the self, the product of actual and/ or feared shame and

humiliation during early identity development, it follows that the conscious and unconscious experience of lust contains the affectively charged psychic residue of these assaults and can threaten what we think of as both the more familiar and acceptable senses of ourselves. [2006, p. 663]

Although we live in a society that appears to be very open about sex, these traditional attitudes described by Freud persist alongside a pervasive atmosphere of sexual knowingness. A research project published in 2004, by a group of women exploring how heterosexual young people were able to deal with the challenges of safeguarding their sexual health in an age of HIV and sexually transmitted diseases, discovered that these young men and women arrived at sex with private expectations of a surprisingly traditional heteronormative kind, organized around an idea the researchers called *The Male in the Head* (Holland, Ramazanoglu, Sharpe, & Thomson, 2004). Both sexes embarked on their first sexual experience assuming that the man should be confident and assertive and that the woman should be hesitant but eventually available. Challenging the distraction caused by these noisy cultural messages required self-confidence and trust on both sides that the partner would respond sympathetically. It can be difficult, even for sexually experienced women and gay men who are signed up to dating websites to meet a potential partner, to insist on using a condom when first having sex. The quality of sexual experience, which is distanced from the everyday self and foregrounds impulsiveness in preference to negotiation, can make it impossible to intrude on the intimate encounter by bringing in the important relational issue of mutual physical safety. In the absence of a relaxed sense of shared intimacy, the individual's private need for security can be difficult to mention, for fear that it will produce a collapse of the fantasy that sustains sexual excitement.

A recent piece by Zoe Heller in the *New York Review of Books* described two books based on research into straight female sexual behaviour in the age of the Internet which gloomily concluded that young women were increasingly prepared to participate in sexual acts such as anal intercourse, because they believed it was expected of a sexually confident young woman, even though it made them anxious and they did not necessarily enjoy it (Heller, 2016). It is significant that, in so much of the above evidence, including the short case study, the woman conceives of herself, while engaging in sex, through the eyes of her male partner. She is thus predisposed to be alienated from her own psychosexual experience. It must surely be the case that, in order to move from this position, she must not only feel confident with her partner, but also understand her own bodily responses sufficiently to know what gives her sexual satisfaction. As detailed recognition of the nature of the female orgasm is a relatively recent thing; women may only now be beginning to become assertive about their own sexual pleasure.

However, anyone currently working with young people will tell us that the role that social media play in their lives cannot be overestimated: it saturates them with messages that they take to represent social expectations. They have access from an early age to pornography that informs them about sexual behaviour and to online role models who demonstrate the aura of self-confidence that one is required to display. All this complicates the prospect of embarking on a sexually active life oneself with one's own imperfect and mysterious body. The activity of sharing intimate pictures of body parts in text messages between members of a couple, known as "sexting", can be used cruelly when those images are passed on to others or put up on the Internet. This form of bullying derides the vulnerability and trust involved in sexual behaviour, thereby increasing the danger of openness.

Everyone is familiar with the binary distinctions that define gender differences in the popular mind: "men are from Mars; women are from Venus"; femininity is associated with receptivity and openness, while masculinity is outgoing and assertive. In "Analysis Terminable and Interminable" Freud described the "repudiation of femininity" as a fundamental human trait.

> In males the striving to be masculine is completely ego-syntonic from the first; the passive attitude, since it presupposes an acceptance of castration, is energetically repressed, and often its presence is only indicated by excessive over-compensations. In females, too, the striving to be masculine is ego-syntonic at a certain period—namely in the phallic phase, before the development to femininity has set in. [1937c, pp. 250–251]

In spite of his earlier questioning of this equation, which "does not tell us enough" about sexual difference (1920a, p. 171), Freud here assumes a correlation between activity and masculinity, and femininity with passivity. In his theorizing of the individual's developing awareness of her or his sexual identity, gender definition is centrally mapped onto binary characteristics of assertiveness and vulnerability, insistence and receptivity, wholeness and lack. The boy must inevitably face the threat of losing his penis, a castration that, he fears, will "feminize" him. The girl must give up the belief that her clitoris qualifies her as "a little man" and adapt herself to her "feminine" recessive role. A turn to Freud's theory of "psychic bisexuality" does not resolve the issue, because the bisexual "masculine" and "feminine" characteristics of an individual's internal world are conceived along these pairs of opposites. It remains very difficult to describe the physical nature of sexual activity, or to think psychoanalytically about gender identification as the complex process it actually is, without becoming entangled in the reductionism of this binary way of understanding sexual difference. In a sexual encounter, whether between members of the opposite sex or members of the same sex, it is not correct to describe either partner, in whatever position, as passive, but Freud's theorizing of "femininity" has perpetuated its association with vulnerability or openness: the more precarious and apparently "weaker" state. We might think of the "femininity" that he describes as "repudiated" as simply equating with an attitude of trusting dependency. Although occupying this position can feel like a risk, if it can be sustained by both members of the couple, it becomes a significant ingredient in a satisfying sexual relationship.

However, these characteristics of gender essentialism that Freud made central to his theory have great power in our internal fantasy life. Robert Stoller suggested that the sado-masochistic component of sexual excitement arose from our capacity to convert our experience of childhood vulnerability into active erotic stimulation. He described what was usually classified as perverse behaviour as "the erotic form of hatred" (Stoller, 1975), arguing that transgressive sexual behaviour was a way of transforming early narcissistic injuries and traumatic experience into excitement: "An essential quality in pornography (and perversion) is sadism—revenge for a passively experienced trauma" (p. 79). The hatred that Stoller describes is the child's hatred of the powerful parent, who uses and humiliates the child, possibly without acknowledging it. Sexualizing that earlier state of helplessness allows it to be reexperienced in a controlled way. In the cross-dressing fantasies Stoller describes, there are dominant women who force the man to wear women's clothes, but he is intensely excited by these fantasies, no longer the helpless boy who suffered castrating treatment at the hands of his mother or female relatives. However, it would be a mistake to dwell too much on the "hatred" aroused by the original trauma, because, in consensual sadomasochistic sexual games, it often seems that what allows the scenario to become sexually exciting is the care taken by the dominant partner towards the submissive. While such an encounter may take place outside the boundaries of a committed relationship, careful attention to the submissive partner's responses nevertheless appears to be the compelling ingredient that provides erotic stimulation and combines aggression with a form of tenderness. The dominant and submissive partners are bound together in a mutually trusting relationship that, paradoxically, suggests a form of security. It has been suggested that this is a practice that can potentially be reparative, when it takes place within the context of a stable relationship involving mutual trust (Weille, 2002). The popularity of *Fifty Shades of Grey* (James, 2012) and its sequels demonstrates the popularity of this idea, even if it exists, for many people, at the level of a masturbatory fantasy.

In sexual experience there is excitement in overriding shame barriers and giving oneself up to pleasure that can incorporate oral or anal sadism and masochism; but there is also risk. The Latin root of the word "passion" is *"patere"*: to open. The adjective "passive" comes from the same derivation. The surrender to sexual excitement in itself involves letting go of normal inhibitions and allowing oneself to be taken by the experience. However, this surrender, which heightens the excitement, involves risking being open to an impulsive and unboundaried way of being with another, makes us vulnerable, and, crucially, exposes us to shame if we are not met receptively. Even in the context of a community of shared rules of social engagement, alcohol and/or drugs are often used in pursuit of disinhibited sexual experience, perhaps because it helps to "forget" vulnerability, and this can sometimes be used in a compulsive way to escape from unhappiness in everyday life. Tim Dean has written about the "barebacking" culture that exists in some communities of gay men, where sexual receptivity is converted into a form of heroic endurance, rather than vulnerability (2008). Giaccardi explores this in his chapter here.

A young gay man, who worked in a responsible job involving adolescents, began twice-weekly therapy with a female therapist, intending to explore the possibility of training as a psychodynamic psychotherapist himself. He had been in a relationship for some years, and, although he openly discussed his difficulties with his partner, whom he felt to be dominating, the relationship seemed stable, and he used the therapy to become more assertive in order to improve communication between them. However, after a while, a pattern began to develop where he would miss the Monday session without notice being given, and would even, at times, disappear for a week or more. When he returned, he would be full of remorse, saying that he had simply found himself unable to face coming to therapy. Eventually, what emerged was that he and his partner often spent weekends partying with other men, taking drugs and having sex with a number of different people. But, after a weekend spent in this way, he felt unable to come to therapy because of the imagined criticism he expected to face from his therapist. He was also afraid that, if this hidden aspect of his life were to be found out, he would be jeopardizing his career. Although the therapist attempted to explore this behaviour, which she saw as arising from his own internalized homophobia, it felt as if this approach did not reach the patient but, rather, accentuated the painful gulf that separated them. It was very difficult for the young man to move beyond the cycle of wild uninhibited weekends, followed by terrible shame and self-loathing. The absences continued, and eventually the man left therapy and did not return.

The therapist was saddened and frustrated by this outcome and was inclined to think of this man's behaviour as perverse. It occurred in a state of mind that was split off from his highly responsible professional identity and seemed driven by self-destructive excitement that horrified and worried him on Monday morning, when he returned to his work-day self. He had a tendency to blame his partner for getting him involved, but, when he was able to think about it, he recognized that he could not disavow his own responsibility. Indeed, it was clear that this man expected his therapist to share his judgement of his own behaviour, and it served to increase his sense of his own shame. This proved intolerable in the end and led to his sacrifice of the therapy, while the self-obliterating sexual episodes continued.

At the European ChemSex Forum that took place in London in April 2016, participants emphasized how important it was for their clients—some women, but predominantly men—who used the specialist sexual health services catering for people who were habitually involved in sexual activity while taking drugs, to feel that they were meeting medical and therapeutic staff who were familiar with the phenomenon of chemsex, were able to speak in an informed way about the risks, and had some sympathetic insight into the compulsion that was driving it. The report from the Forum linked high-risk sexual practices with multiple partners to low self-esteem and a history of shame, rejection, and trauma. The report quoted a survey conducted by Stonewall in 2013 which found that half of gay and bisexual men felt their lives were not worth living (compared to 17% in men in general). In 2012, 3% attempted suicide (rising to 5% in black and ethnic minorities) compared with 0.4% of men in the general population.[1] Contributors to this Forum stress that this vulnerable group will resist seeking help, including the counselling they badly need, unless it is available in an environment where they anticipate that they may meet a non-judgemental response. Rohleder and Richards explore this area further in their chapters.

With the availability of effective medication, the risks of contracting HIV through sex have fallen substantially since the early days of the AIDS epidemic. Taking retroviral drugs consistently after diagnosis can reduce infectivity level to practically zero, and the existence of the prophylactic drug, PrEP, can protect against becoming infected. However, the impact of the early days of AIDS continues to be felt. Gay men are still stereotypically regarded as promiscuous and disease-ridden. The queer theorist David Halperin explored why gay men participate in sexual practices like chemsex, which are sought out by some in spite of the risk that still exists (2009). He rejects the shame-based explanation of internalized homophobia, refusing to subscribe to a view that, he believes, contributes to the pathologizing of gay men by portraying them as self-destructive victims. Instead, he cites Genet, who, in spite of an early life spent in poverty and deprivation, nevertheless triumphantly asserted his capacity to survive humiliation and social rejection and fashioned creative work out of that experience. Halperin describes Genet as defiantly asserting his "abjection"—the term Kristeva uses to define that which we cannot bear, that which fills us with horror (1982). And he argues that the gay man who courts sexual risk is, like Genet, defying society's expectation that he will live quietly and responsibly, practising safe sex at all times.

Halperin says:

> Modern post-industrial societies produce social conditions that seem to foster in their citizens a yearning for escape, exemption, "small vacations from the will itself", self-loss, transcendence. Abjection offers one such opportunity; the voluntary pursuit of risk offers another; pleasure (whether it involves sex, eating or shopping) holds out a third. It is because risky sex manages to conjoin and condense all three modes of wished-for transcendence—abjection, risk and pleasure—that it remains so seductive and so unmanageable. [2009, p. 97]

Queer theory emerges from a place of resistance to stigmatizing attitudes that have placed LGBTQ people at the margins of society and pathologized their behaviour while maintaining a hostile ignorance about the reality of their experience. Queer perspectives developed particularly during the initial period of HIV/AIDS, which fuelled a moral panic that targeted LGBT people. This atmosphere of panic was particularly strongly expressed by Conservative religious groups in the United States. The Conservative American Family Association circulated this funding letter to its members:

Dear Family Member,

Since AIDS is transmitted primarily by perverse homosexuals, your name on my national petition to quarantine all homosexual establishments is crucial to your family's health and security(.)These disease carrying deviants wander the street unconcerned, possibly making you their next victim. What else can you expect from sex-crazed degenerates except selfishness? [quoted in Bronski, 2011, p. 227]

In the face of the demonization of the "perverse homosexual" as the "sex-crazed" carrier of disease, oppositional writing developed from queer thinkers, who developed a critique of heteronormativity designed to shed light on how it felt to be inhabitants of a world "under the overarching, relatively unchallenged aegis of a culture's desire that gay people *not be*" (Sedgwick, 1993a, p. 164; italics in original). This literature included a close examination of psychiatry and psychoanalysis, concluding that these disciplines bore considerable responsibility for constructing medicalized ways of reinforcing the stigmatization of LGBTQ people. Halperin's rejection of the concept of internalized homophobia arises from that position. His account of the excitement at playing the part of the "abjected object" reminds us of Stoller's description of the masochistic thrill of triumphing over the mockery of the dominant female figure from childhood, although, in this case, the triumph can be seen as a current act of social defiance.

Halperin suggests that we can

think of abjection not as the symptom of an unconscious drive to self-annihilation but as *a strategic response to a specific social predicament*—as a socially constituted affect that can intensify the determination to survive . . . and can lead to the creation of various devices for extracting heightened pleasure, and even love, from experiences of pain, fear rejection, humiliation, contempt, shame, brutality, disgust or condemnation. [Halperin, 2009, p. 94]

Cast in this light, it can be seen as a form of resistance.

I would question the optimism of Halperin's view that states of abjection, sought through unprotected sex, can be seen as "a strategic response" that can "intensify the determination to survive", but he is describing a complex mixture of feelings that it is important to consider. I think it is possible to understand why risky sex provides an escape from feelings of individual vulnerability for a while, even though, on Monday morning, the man in the case vignette previously quoted found himself in another state of mind. Similarly, a woman's capacity to enact a rape scenario during uninhibited consensual sex could feel exciting at the time but lead her to feel guilty and ashamed of herself later, because she does not understand where those desires came from. Sex between two partners, whether of the same or opposite sex, which uninhibitedly enacts masochistic fantasies can provoke a shameful backlash, making the event unavailable for reflection and thus further understanding. In acute cases, where erotic fantasy relies on cruel, abusive imagery, orgasm is only possible through masturbation, as such fantasies produce such guilt and shame subsequently that they cannot be introduced into sex involving a partner who is seen as a caring figure.

Clinical considerations

Psychoanalysis has had a tendency to focus on Stoller's use of the word "hatred" in describing perversion and forgets his caveat that we are all familiar with the excitement that arises from the aggressive/masochistic element in sex. This has led to psychoanalytic perspectives that place a stress on the "destructiveness" of perverse behaviour, which, in some cases, includes any sexuality that is not heterosexual. Chasseguet-Smirgel argues that sexuality that deviates from genital heterosexuality is "an imitation or parody of the genital universe of the father" (1985a, p. 11): it denies the difference between the sexes and between the generations, the fundamental value of heterosexual love, and cannot be creative. "It is an attempt to substitute a world of sham and pretence for reality" (p. 12).

This use of the term "perversion", which resoundingly describes it as a "turning away" from the right path, has been revisited by authors, such as Benjamin (1995), Dimen (2001), Saketopoulou (2014b), and Lemma (2015a), who search for an attitude that encourages an openness to the various forms embodied sexuality can take. This can include a choice of open relationships rather than settled ones, sadomasochistic enactments, body modification, and the assumption of transgender and transsexual identities—phenomena that, in the past, psychoanalysts have usually regarded as indicative of pathology, or even of psychosis. As previously argued here, sexual excitement takes us outside the boundaries of our everyday selves and can involve behaviour that makes us vulnerable to shame. If we are met by a therapist who confirms the "badness" of our desires, we may be angry but all too ready to accept what was already expected. So it is refreshing to find clinicians who can take a more open-minded view, which encourages reflection. Saketopoulou (2014b, 2015) has suggested that transgressive sexual enactments that provoke an ecstatic masochistic response can be creative, allowing the emergence into awareness of unrepresented psychic longings. She references Laplanche and the literary critic, Leo Bersani, who has described such sexual experience in positive terms as "shattering" the ego's "illusory power", the antidote to the dangerous fantasy of mastery of a life lived with a narcissistic denial of difference. He speaks of masochistic surrender as positive thing—"an evolutionary conquest". With the ideas of Laplanche in mind, he says that it originates in early life: "it allows the infant to survive the gap between a period of shattering stimuli and the development of resistant, defensive ego-structures" (Bersani & Phillips, 2008, p. 121).

The authors above all suggest that therapists' readiness to forget their own experience of sexual arousal, when hearing about a patient's unconventional sexual interests or sexual encounters that are pursued for ecstatic self-abandonment, allows them to objectify the patient and veer away from what they themselves might find uncomfortable. Ruth Stein suggests that there may be something about the practice of analysis itself that provides the therapist with a relief from vulnerable aspects of her/himself:

> May it not also be that the attracting power of this therapeutic activity for analysts lies in the fact that by following, by "shadowing", the patient with sensitive dedication, we in a sense fulfill a longing to shed our occasionally burdensome selves and identities. . . . May we not be nourishing the fantasy that, by being empathically immersed in the patient's experiential world, we can spare ourselves our own exposure, our coming forth and showing ourselves in our naked individuality? [1997]

Talking openly about sex in the consulting room increases the risk of taking both patient and analyst into uncomfortable areas.

Although most analysts no longer present themselves to their patient as a "blank screen", Stein suggests that the therapist's own spontaneity and excitement in responding to the patient are felt to be non-analytic, associated as they are with impulsivity and non-reflective states of mind. This may make it seem dangerous even to allow these feelings into awareness, with the result that both parties may collude in avoiding them.

A touchingly honest account of this is described by Fonagy in his paper about sexual excitement, in which he describes how his own emotional difficulty in hearing his young patient, Dan, short-circuited the immediacy of their work together for some time. Fonagy noticed vaguely that their work had moved away from a focus on Dan's relationships.

> But it was Dan who drew my attention to it when one day he referred back to a session some weeks earlier when he asked me about a fantasy he had had during intercourse of being a medieval knight in a complete suit of armor. He said, "You did not really know what I was talking about then, did you? You were talking about me wanting to protect myself from women who I feel might attack me. It is nothing to do with that. It is to do with being hard and rigid" [and he held up his right arm clenching his fist.]
>
> Going back to my notes, [says Fonagy] I found that I had not recorded the fantasy; the session (as I saw it) had been about his unconscious wish to be able to retain his father's interest in him outside and my interest in him in the transference. I did not know if I had got it wrong, but obviously from Dan's point of view I had been way off beam. But as I tried to get into the image he was now suggesting, I sensed myself running into a countertransference block. I did not really want to put my mind into the gear where Dan's wish to have a sense of steely stiffness in his penis made emotional sense. It made me feel quite uncomfortable; obviously it touched on sexual anxieties never properly dealt with in my own analysis. The image I was aware of was being a woman whose body is asked to contain Dan's metallic, cutting, painful excitement. The sadism was clear; I could have said something about it, but this felt intellectual and mechanistic. In retrospect I can see that while in the past I had found it easy to identify with Dan's anxieties, his current triumphant feelings of sexual conquest led me to identify instead with the subjugated woman. [2008, p. 30]

This vignette is a tribute to Fonagy's capacity to create a relationship with his young patient that is frank and open enough to allow Dan to tell him he had not felt heard. Far more frequently, I think, we are likely not to receive this kind of feedback, and authors have commented on the paucity of literature on the subject of the therapist's countertransference experience in relation to sexually arousing material, particularly in relation to the even more sensitive area of gay and lesbian patients (Frommer, 1995; O'Connor & Ryan, 1993; Ryan, 1998).

If we are seeking to create a level of trust between our patients and ourselves similar to that which Fonagy describes here, we are required to be more open to the nature of sexual excitement and its often disturbing qualities, without seeking to label it perverse or sadistic. Psychoanalysis has been written from a heteronormative perspective that assumed that children are born in a family with heterosexual parents, where boys and girls would grow up to follow the path that their parents had taken. Today's young people in urban environments are growing up in a very diverse world, where they are faced with a smorgasbord of identities—gay, lesbian, bisexual, queer, bi-curious, and so on—in which they are encouraged to appear knowing and confident. Indeed, the trying on of different sexual and gender identities may sometimes be a means of finding an enclave to retreat into from the apparently hypersexualized world that we now inhabit.

The legacy of the pathological interpretation of homosexuality that was dominant in psychoanalysis until relatively recently can still be seen in the tendency to link gay men with promiscuous sexual behaviour. However, there appears to be a general movement in psychoanalysis and psychotherapy to move towards a style of work that attempts to combine spontaneity and reflectiveness—something that is so difficult—what Schafer describes as the capacity for the analyst to be "better prepared to be unprepared" than the patient (Schafer, 1997, p. 188).

Conclusion

I have argued here that we, as clinicians, should develop a greater openness to our patients' sexuality from a perspective that is informed by our own sexual experience. It is interesting to note that it is in our dealings with LGBTQ patients, that we have been alerted to our profession's neglect of psychosexuality—as if, in a heterosexual life, it has become something that can almost be taken for granted. It is only those people who have been seen as problematic through a heteronormative lens who have focused our attention on their sexual activity. As Foucault has pointed out, nineteenth-century sexology created the "homosexual" as "a personage, a past, a case history, and a childhood, in addition to being a type of life, a life form and a morphology, with an indiscreet anatomy and possibly a mysterious physiology" (1976, p. 43). While we are trying to move on from this position, it still persists in the requirement to enquire into the aetiology of a person's homosexuality, while seeing no need to question another person's heterosexuality in the same way. We still tend to assume heterosexuality as "natural" and unquestioned unless something happens to throw it off course. To counteract this tendency, Nancy Chodorow (1992) has proposed that all sexuality, in whatever form, should be viewed as a "compromise formation". This would help us to regard each individual as unique and to call into question our reliance on causal explanations based on psychoanalytic theories of developmental lines. In reality, we know that human development is far too complex for reductive views to be convincing. We may speak of influences but, I would argue, remain agnostic about causes. Adrienne Harris, in her well-known paper, *Gender as Soft Assembly*, describes herself as:

> drawing on dynamic systems theory, the forms of chaos theory particularly developed by Thelen and Smith (1991), to imagine these multiplicities of developmental outcomes. Their general-systems approach would see phenomena like gender or sexual desire not as structure but, rather, as "softly assembled" sets of behavioral attractors whose form and stability would be quite variable, depending on the task at hand, the context, and the individual's life history and experiences. With this approach variability of pathway and of experience are privileged. [Harris, 2000, p. 231]

Ruth Stein and Laplanche remind us that sexual experience is by nature enigmatic and occupies a state of mind that evades reflection and makes for vulnerability. Although, as Dagmar Herzog (2015) remarks, we have been encouraged to think of our psychoanalytic inheritance as having provided us with "expertise" in sexual fantasy and orientation, I am arguing here that this has allowed us to remove ourselves from the immediate impact of the patient's sexuality, particularly in its bodily aspects. We examine our patient's disclosures in order to decode hidden oedipal accommodations or pre-oedipal anxieties, but this has distracted us from staying more closely in touch with the immediacy of what we are told and its impact on our countertransference.

In overcoming this disengagement, we may feel more vulnerable but, in the longer term, may be helped to remain open rather than reaching for theory prematurely, and, where the other's sexuality differs from our own, come to see it not as the defining aspect of that individual, but discover its appropriate place in their unique picture.

Note

1. European ChemSex Report, 2016: www.gmfa.org.uk/Blog/european-chemsex-forum-report

CHAPTER TWO

Homophobia, heteronormativity, and shame

Poul Rohleder

> Homosexuality is assuredly no advantage, but it is nothing to be ashamed of.
>
> [Freud, 1935/1951, p. 786]

Although homosexuality remains illegal in some parts of the world, and gay men and lesbian women are actively persecuted, other countries have come a long way in recognizing the human rights of people who identify as gay, lesbian, or bisexual. In the United Kingdom, we have gay men and lesbian women enjoying the right to have their relationships recognized, to be married, to have children, to be parents. There are some prominent individuals in business, politics, science, and many other fields who are openly gay, lesbian, or bisexual. At the time of writing this chapter, the Taoiseach (prime minister) of the Republic of Ireland, a country that historically has had a predominantly conservative Catholic population, is an openly gay man. Nigel Owens, an internationally lauded professional rugby referee from Wales, is openly gay, as are some celebrated Olympic athletes.

Nevertheless, while the headlines of same-sex marriage and equality suggest that everything is fine, there remains a persistent and insidious homophobia and heterosexism, and a social environment where many gay, lesbian, and bisexual individuals grow up with a sense of there being something "wrong" with them, something to be ashamed about. As readers will know, homophobia is a term used to refer to the hostile attitudes towards gay, lesbian, and bisexual people. The term refers broadly to a fear (phobia) of the homosexual. However, the diagnostic term *phobia*, suggesting an irrational fear, a "mental illness", has been critiqued (e.g. Wickberg, 2000) on the grounds that it actually refers to a pervasive prejudiced attitude, a hatred. Nevertheless, it remains a usefully familiar term, encompassing the name-calling at school and in other social arenas: "faggot" (for gay boys and men), "dyke" (for lesbian girls and women), "sissy", "queen", "pansy", "fairy". It describes anti-homosexuality attitudes that can be so deeply entrenched that, in some cases, people have gone as far as to describe extreme weather as divine retribution for society's permissiveness towards gay marriage (BBC News, 2014). We hear about people who equate homosexuality with paedophilia, and with bestiality ("if we allow men to marry each other, what next, men can marry animals?"). We know about violence and abuse—even murder—inflicted on gay men and lesbian women. However, homophobia is not just about these prominent examples; it is also the everyday, small disapproving gestures and looks, throw-away remarks ("that is so gay!"), and homosexuality as the target of giggles and ridicule. The reality is that the many celebrated gains made for equality (like same-sex marriage) did not come without some rather rabid debates about what is moral and natural vs immoral and unnatural.

As Freud mentioned in his letter to a concerned mother of a gay son, homosexuality is "nothing to be ashamed of", and, at a superficial level, one would be assured to think that in societies like the United Kingdom, this is indeed so. However, for many people who identify as gay, lesbian, or bisexual, feelings of shame may be a significant, persistent difficulty. This is reflected in research that has shown poorer rates of psychological health among gay, lesbian, and bisexual people, as compared to the general population (King, 2011). A recent published meta-analysis of 12 UK population health surveys found that adults who identify as gay, lesbian, or bisexual were almost twice as likely to report symptoms of depression, anxiety, and suicidality than adults identifying as heterosexual (Semlyen, King, Varney, & Hagger-Johnson, 2016) gay men and older gay, lesbian, and bisexual adults being particularly vulnerable. King (2011) argues that these higher rates of psychological distress can mainly be attributed to stress arising from discrimination and a hostile social environment.

In this chapter I explore shame in relation to homophobia and a current of misogyny that underlies homophobia. I draw on some clinical material and other illustrative examples. I explore this in relation to the psychoanalytic literature on shame and also how psychoanalysis has contributed to the "shaming" of homosexual individuals. Finally, I also consider how shame around sexuality and gender plays out among the gay "community" and the challenges of naming and talking about shame when working with gay men. I focus on gay men, because this is what I am most familiar with from scholarship, research, and clinical work, and because most of the psychoanalytic writing on homosexuality has focused on the gay male. However, I acknowledge that this continues to contribute to the relative silence in the psychoanalytic literature about female homosexuality. One of the criticisms levelled against psychoanalytic writing on homosexuality is its blindness to non-psychoanalytic research and evidence (Lewes, 2009), so I also draw on non-psychoanalytic research to deepen understanding of what happens socially (and not just psychically). The psychoanalytic literature typically uses the term "homosexual", but the terms "gay men" or "lesbian women" or "lesbian, gay, and bisexual" are also often used, more frequently so in the non-psychoanalytic literature. I use these terms interchangeably, although I acknowledge that many readers will have specific preferences.

Understanding shame

Shame is regularly defined as a deeply painful experience of self-consciousness in the presence of others, where the individual feels exposed as having a real or imagined deficiency in their identity or self (e.g. Kaufman, 1989). This sense of exposure may leave the person feeling small, undesirable, worthless, fearing rejection, and wanting to hide from others. In comparison with other affective states, shame has been less written about in the psychoanalytic literature.

Freud (1905d) linked shame to the Oedipus complex and emerging superego demands to repress forbidden sexual impulses. He saw shame as representing the tension between the ego and the ego ideal, which refers to ideal self-representations and introjects of parental ideals. Here shame (along with guilt) was linked to narcissism and castration anxiety. Piers and Singer (1953) and, later, Levin (1967) differentiated between guilt, which they saw as linked to transgressions against the superego and consequent castration anxiety, and shame, which they understood as linked to the ego ideal, involving fear of rejection and abandonment (rather than punishment), although the two affective states may be linked.

This early conceptualization of shame views it in terms of internal drive dynamics. Later psychoanalytic theorists placed more emphasis on the interpersonal dynamics of shame. Amsterdam and Levitt (1980) argue that shame has its source when the young child, capable of self-awareness, encounters parental disapproval at their sexual exhibitionism. In such moments, excitement and joy is suddenly disrupted, resulting in shame. This is supported by observations from infant development research (Schore, 1991). Broucek (1982) argues that at such a moment of contact, the parent becomes a stranger to the child, and shame may develop as a result of the child feeling like an object of (negative) observation. Thus, shame has been understood as a social emotion and linked with a sense of self and identity (Pines, 1995). Pines describes the experience of shame in these terms:

> shame is the affect of un-desire, one that comes through the painful realisation that I, and you, feel rejected, unwanted, repulsive, ugly, deformed, shrivelled—the vocabulary is extensive. In shame we are no longer the object of desire, either of our *own* or that of others. The experience of shame is the inner language of failure, demoralisation and of painful comparisons. It is a perverse viewing of the self by a detached condemning observer under whose scrutiny the defect in the self, however small it may be, remains magnified. We are microbes under the microscope. The observer, the observing part of the self, is the perverse viewer who objectivises the person being looked at. [1995, pp. 251–352]

The psychoanalytic writing on shame dates the first onset of shame feelings to an early, pre-oedipal age. Read uncritically, locating an understanding of shame almost entirely within this timeframe is to suggest that shame, and its link to narcissism, is a response to a sort of trauma moment, in which the subject retreats into himself. States of shame and narcissistic rage were understood by some psychoanalytic writers as intrinsic to the pre-oedipal character of "the homosexual" (e.g. authors such as Bergler and Socarides, reviewed in Lewes, 2009). While the patients written about by these authors may indeed have struggled with feelings of narcissistic shame and rage, there was no consideration on the authors' part that the rage might be due to the trauma and damage caused by persistent social hostility and oppression, nor the shame to repeated parental, familial, and social rejection. Some gay men may have long-standing struggles with shame that have their roots in early parental rejection, while others, having had a nurturing early relationship with parental figures, may later develop shame as a result of subsequent rejections.

It is important to note that shame in itself is not a measure of pathology. Indeed, shame is experienced by individuals who have had a healthy development (Morrison, 1983). Broucek (1982) asserts that some experience of shame is necessary to help the child to learn to differentiate self from other and become aware of his/her "separateness from the important other" (p. 371). Broucek (1982) goes on to state that regulated (as opposed to unregulated) experiences of shame act as a socializing agent, as the child learns the socially acceptable limitations to his behaviour. Schafer (2002) argues that superego values about gender and sexuality are transmitted by introjection and projection through the medium of language, which we come to take for granted as objectively reflecting reality. However, as social constructionists point out, language always implies a particular perspective and is, in many cases, socially "structured to serve sexual and gender biases" (p. 25). Schafer suggests that language has a coercive power that regulates our moral and social behaviour. Currently there are plenty of anxieties being expressed in the social discourse about "trans" identities, with appeals made to the need for "boys to be boys and girls to be girls", as if the word "boy" or "girl" reflects a set of truths. What does it mean to be "boy"?

Heteronormativity and homophobia and growing up gay

As we have learnt above, shame is related to attachment and misattunement, and to rejection from important others. This relates to Winnicott's (1967) conception of the parent as the mirroring object, in relation to which the child develops a sense of self. For the boy who is growing up to be the adult gay man—what Corbett has referred to as the "proto-gay" boy (1996)—such misattunement can be repeated and gradual. This sort of misattunement to his emerging sexuality occurs as his sexuality expresses itself.

Target (2007) notes that there is often some degree of misattunement by the parent who turns away from the child's sexuality, suggesting that shame is a part of all our sexual lives, regardless of sexual orientation. Newbigin provides (in chapter 1) a detailed overview of the work by Target and others on sexuality. As Newbigin argues, psychoanalytic writing (particularly British writing) has tended to pursue a rather domesticated, heteronormative fantasy of sex and sexuality as healthy, non-perverse, and loving; the more complex. "darker" emotional aspects of sex, such as shame, or aggression, have tended to be ignored. When it comes to sex and sexuality, everyone has some feelings of shame. However, where sexuality is unsanctioned, feelings of shame may be more dominant. Parents may have more anxiety and worry and may respond with fear to sexuality and behaviour that they may interpret as non-normative. Solomon (2014) provides a common example of such disapproval in his recollections as a proto-gay boy:

> I was popular at home, but I was subject to corrections. My mother, my brother and I were at Indian Walk Shoes when I was seven, and as we were leaving, the salesman asked what colour balloons we'd like. My brother wanted a red balloon. I wanted a pink one. My mother countered that I didn't want a pink balloon and reminded me that my favourite colour was blue. I said I really wanted the pink, but under her glare, I took the blue one. [p. 7]

In psychoanalytic theory we are predominantly focused on the early parent–infant relationship and its mirroring function, but these are not the only important mirroring objects: there are siblings, peers, and society more broadly. As Akhtar (2014) states, a minority is defined as such by the distorted gaze of the majority. For some proto-gay boys, the misattunement can be insidious. As the proto-gay child is developing a self and expressing his or her sexuality, he or she comes gradually to learn through the affective, verbal, and behavioural response of others (family, teachers, peers, and society at large) that there is something wrong, something to be ashamed of. Indeed, some of the more vociferous psychoanalytic writers on homosexuality, like Socarides (quoted in Doty, 1963), argued in the *New York Times* that social acceptance of homosexuality should be discouraged, as it would reduce in "the homosexual" patient the feeling of his being ill, and thus he would not seek treatment for his homosexuality.

Herek and McLemore (2013) have reviewed the empirical research on homophobia, which has consistently found that heterosexual men express more negative and hostile attitudes towards gay men and lesbian women than do heterosexual women. Furthermore, heterosexual men tend to express more hostile attitudes towards gay men than towards lesbian women. Lesbian women, notably feminine lesbian women (or what some might refer to as "lipstick lesbians"), might even be a source of excitement in the erotic imagination of some heterosexual men. There is therefore something gendered about homophobia. Herek and McLemore (2013) explain these findings in terms of socio-cultural constructions of masculinity and femininity, and, in particular where masculinity—more so than femininity—is seen as something that is to be achieved, performed, and proved. Plummer (2014) argues that it is gender transgression, rather than the (homo)sexual practice per se, which seems to be a necessary pre-requisite for homophobia. Homophobia is a "hot-button issue" for men in particular, because homosexuality transgresses masculine ideals and male social power. In this way, Plummer (2014) sees homophobia as a form of policing of masculinity and manhood. Thus, underlying homophobia may be misogyny: the hatred against gay men who have betrayed masculinity because they are "like women". It is hatred of effeminacy, the feminine. Moss (2002) argues that while homophobia is most relevant for gay men, internalized homophobia (discussed further below) is also something to be considered for heterosexual men, who may deny themselves certain experiences or pursuits because they may be considered by others (and themselves) as "feminine" or "gay".

Taywaditep (2002) cites research that indicates that while there may be some element of "truth" in gay men showing characteristics of effeminacy, many have no effeminate characteristics. In fact, studies suggest that it may be more accurate to say that a majority of gay men have more androgynous (both masculine and feminine) gender characteristics than heterosexual men who are more simply masculine. Gay men are reported to have shown more consistent gender nonconforming behaviours and interests in childhood than heterosexual men. Research has shown that many of these proto-gay effeminate boys gradually become "defeminized" during adolescence and young adulthood. It is suggested that this is due to the pressure to conform to gendered behaviour—faced with peer rejection, bullying, name-calling, and public shaming, masculinity gets enforced.

Heteronormativity and psychoanalytic theorizing on homosexuality

Psychoanalytic theory has, for the most part, tended to focus on homosexuality in terms of how it has *developed*. Although Freud could be considered to have held a liberal understanding of homosexuality, he also saw it as something of a "mystery" (Freud, 1920a), because of its otherness to "normal", heterosexual development, thus describing it in some of his writing as an "arrest" in normal development. Psychoanalytic writing on homosexuality, mental health of gay men, relationship dynamics, shame, and other aspects typically focuses on the impact and effects of early childhood experiences. While these are important, less attention is given to the later social influences. Psychoanalysis, too, has played a significant role in maintaining—even shaping—some of the homophobic views people have, most notably seeing homosexuality as a mental illness and as perverse. For a fuller review of psychoanalytic theorizing of male homosexuality readers can refer to Lewes' (2009) important analysis, and other authors in this book will make some reference to this body of work. But the points I wish to make link to the above discussion on heteronormativity and homophobia.

Although in psychoanalysis we are concerned with the complexity of individual psychic experiences, with individual nuances and the vicissitudes of psychic phenomena, psychoanalytic language is saturated with binary language that describes gender and sexuality—masculine/feminine; homosexual/heterosexual; passive/active; maternal/paternal—which are, in fact, what Schafer (2002) refers to as "organising concepts" (p. 26) rather than facts or truths. Furthermore, these constructs are arranged in terms of a hierarchy of value with the *masculine-active-heterosexual* being seen as the norm against which the "opposite" sex is constructed and non-normative men seen as deviant.

Barden (2011) argues that psychoanalysis set out to disrupt norms and the idea of normality. Yet, for the most part, psychoanalysis has rigidly adhered to a heterosexual norm. Sexual orientation—either heterosexual or homosexual—develops as a solution to the Oedipus complex. Psychoanalytic theorizing of the Oedipus complex has taken a heteronormative perspective, and, indeed, for the male, the complex starts from a heterosexual position: the boy desires his mother (opposite sex) first. Freud (1937c) considered the repudiation of femininity as bedrock in psychoanalysis—the girl, lacking the penis, has a wish for one, and the boy fears femininity and the loss of the penis (castration). When psychoanalysis approached homosexuality as something to be treated, successful treatment of gay men was understood in terms of their becoming more masculine and less feminine, more active and less passive, more heterosexual and less homosexual (Schafer, 2002).

Thus, in psychoanalytic theory, homosexuality has, for the most part, been perceived "as threatening a known certainty—the binary (masculine–feminine) heterosexual gender arrangement" (Corbett, 1993, p. 345). Barden points out how during Freud's time homosexuality was at first construed as a gender identity issue, where the gay man was generally seen as having "a female mind in a male body" (2011,

p. 326). Jung and his concept of Anima and Animus allowed for a more fluid understanding of gender, yet, as Barden (2011) argues, this theory rested on the notion of balance between the two, and a "healthy" balance still tended to include conservative ideals of what was conventional for men and for women: men could thus be "too soft" and women could be "too masculine". Corbett (1993) writes that psychoanalytic theorizing has often equated male homosexuality with femininity and passivity, viewing gay men as "counterfeit women" (p. 346). He advocates seeing male homosexuality within a spectrum of masculinities, rather than aligning it with femininity. Some gay men may be more passive and may be more effeminate than other men, but much of the psychoanalytic literature tends to stereotype gay men in this way and does not consider the ways in which gay men can be active and passive, masculine and feminine. Indeed, as Newbigin and Giaccardi suggest in their chapters in this book, in a sexual act it seems somewhat absurd to describe either partner—regardless of sex—as passive, when they are both actively, mutually involved.

Barden (2011) argues that heteronormativity "is bad for theory, gendered as well as sexualized identities" (pp. 324–325). The barring of homosexual men and women from psychoanalytic training, and the general dismissal by early psychoanalytic theorists of non-psychoanalytic literature (Lewes, 2009), has meant that alternative theories, research evidence, and perspectives have received little attention. In recent years, other, non-pathologizing theories of the development of sexuality of homosexual men have been formulated, based on a broader research base than the few clinical cases that were typical of earlier writers.

For example, Isay (1986, 2010) has drawn on considerable clinical experience and a number of cases to observe an oedipal complex of gay men formulated around the desire for the father as primary sexual object, rather than the mother. Many gay men describe feeling "different" from an early age (from age 4)—more sensitive, less aggressive, not liking "rough-and-tumble" play, enjoying aesthetic pursuits more than other boys. Likewise, many proto-lesbian girls who grow up to become lesbian adult women recall a "tomboy" childhood, more than do than heterosexual women (Jalas, 2003). The website www.rucomingout.com, is a support organization offering readers inspirational and personal stories by gay men and lesbian women about their coming-out experiences. Many of the gay men and lesbian women posting their stories make mention of always having felt "different" in the ways described above. Isay (1986) argues that part of the experience of feeling different includes the "perception of same-sex fantasies and early homoerotic arousal patterns" (p. 471). Drawing on his clinical work with over 40 cases, he goes on to argue that homoerotic fantasies are often present in proto-gay boys at the ages of 3–5 years, with the fathers being the primary erotic attachment object. Building on this work, Scott Harms Rose (2007b) presented research with in-depth case studies of 5 gay men and observed evidence of oedipal rejection from the fathers at an early age. Isay and Rose challenge the accepted view that distant fathers contributed to the development of homosexuality in males, arguing instead that fathers may become distant *because* of their fear and discomfort of their son's same-sex desires.

The proto-gay boy's homoerotic fantasies underlie the experience of being different, provoking feelings of guilt and shame, and may contribute to the experience of low self-esteem among many adult gay men. As Lynch (2015) argues, the proto-gay boy learns from an early age that his sexual desires are "unsanctioned by others" (p. 140), experiencing his sexuality as "an outlaw" (p. 151), resulting in feelings of shame. Isay's (1986, 2010) and Rose's (2007b) patients describe prolonged attempts to deny and repress same-sex desires, fearing that they would be incapable of falling in love and having (hetero) sexual feelings. Coming out represents the breaking down of this denial and repression and the start of recognition, acceptance, and integration. However, if the boy does not meet this acceptance, it will have far-reaching consequences for his self-esteem. Early oedipal paternal rejection can lead many gay men to have difficulties with developing sustained intimacy in their relationships (Rose, 2007a, 2007b), an issue also understood with reference to internalized homophobia.

Internalized homophobia and shame

As noted earlier, Broucek (1982) makes a distinction between regulated shame, which can healthily allow the child to experience himself as separate from his object(s) but acceptable to them, in contrast to unregulated shame, where the child is left to make sense of the painful emotion on his own. Blum and Pfetzing (1997) point out that children of other oppressed groups, for example Jewish or black individuals in countries where they are in the minority, may also be recipients of hostile and rejecting attitudes, which produce feelings of shame and guilt. However, such children typically have parents who are also Jewish or black, who can respond to their child's conflict and distress in a containing and affirming manner that helps to instil a counter-narrative. The gay child is typically alone, with straight parents, and few people, or no one, to turn to for help in understanding what being "gay" is. For some, the most damaging hostility comes from the parents themselves. Blum and Pfetzing thus equate the proto-gay boys' experience to that of ongoing trauma.

Internalized homophobia refers to feelings of self-hatred and shame among some gay men and lesbian women arising from the introjection of negative and hostile responses from significant and important others—including social messages. As discussed above, much of this homophobia experienced by gay men contains an underlying misogyny. Moss (2002), therefore argues that "internalized misogyny" exists in parallel to internalized homophobia (p. 26), or fear and rejection of the "feminine". From a self-psychology perspective, internalized homophobia is understood as causing a disturbance in the sense of a coherent self (e.g. Shelby, 1994).

Before continuing, I offer an example of the sort of internalized homophobia I have been describing. I use the core storyline in the award-winning 2016 film, *Moonlight* (spoiler alert for those readers who still want to see the movie!). The story follows the coming-of-age story of an African–American boy called Chiron through three chapters—childhood, adolescence, and young adulthood. First, we follow Chiron as a child and his painful experience of living with a drug-abusing, volatile mother and an absent, unknown father, and with constant bullying from peers who ridicule his softness. He goes by the name of "Little". One afternoon, while hiding from a bunch of bullies from school, he is found by an African–American man, Juan, who takes Chiron under his wing and treats him in a paternal, empathic manner. During one poignant scene, where Chiron starts to open up to Juan about his hidden shame, he asks Juan, "what does faggot mean?" Juan responds by saying, "it is a word people use to make gay people feel bad". In adolescence (Chapter 2 of the movie), the bullying continues. Juan has since died, but at school one young man, Kevin, shows kindness to Chiron, and they strike up a friendship. In the film we get a sense of the emerging desire that Chiron feels towards Kevin, as one night he has a wet dream of Kevin having sex with his girlfriend. Later, on a beach at night, after smoking a joint, the two boys kiss, and Kevin masturbates Chiron. The next morning, back at school, the bullying gang coerces Kevin into punching Chiron repeatedly as part of a hazing ritual. The following day Chiron attacks the main bully, witnessed by teachers, and he is then escorted out of the school for being violent, which brings to an end his developing friendship with Kevin. In the third part, the audience is taken aback by the striking, slightly shocking image of Chiron as an adult: a big, muscular, tattooed man going by the name of "Black". He is now a tough, detached gangster dealing in drugs: the little "faggot" boy has grown into the hypermasculine man. Towards the end of the movie, he receives a call from Kevin, who is now living in another city, and Chiron goes to meet him. At this reunion with Kevin we learn that Chiron, who is gay, has not been intimate with anyone else since that time on the beach, and we get a sense of how split-off his sexuality has become.

The film powerfully portrays themes of masculinity and, in particular, gay African–American masculinity. In movies, African–American masculinity is often associated with stereotypes of the gangster, the thug, or the rap artist, with a strong anti-gay attitude. In Chiron, we have an example of how, in this social context, internalized homophobia and shame produces a homosexuality that has to be outlawed and denied.

In their psychometric study of 90 gay men, Allen and Oleson (1999) found that shame was significantly related to internalized homophobia. Participants scoring higher on measures of internalized homophobia scored higher on measures of shame. Furthermore, they found that some of the characteristics of shame rated as significant by participants included those related to notions of "failed" masculinity: "effeminate", "weak" "passive". The researchers also found that the stereotypical gay man whom participants most associated with a sense of shame was one who was "lacking masculinity". In *Moonlight*, Chiron adopts a hypermasculine self as a defence against his shame and his homosexuality. He has a tough, un-feeling exterior, to conceal his secret shame. We witness how denied his sexuality has become as we learn only when he reunites with Kevin that he has lived without intimacy since the time on the beach. Some gay men, struggling with internalized homophobia, split off and compartmentalize their sexuality (Blum, Danson, & Schneider, 1997); they can only live openly in a more accepting environment, such as a big metropolitan city. In *Moonlight*, this is what Kevin has done. His sexuality is not explicitly stated, but his affection for Chiron is clear. In the closing scenes we see the two men sitting together, facing each other, opening up and sharing— Kevin seemingly more comfortable facing Chiron, who is somewhat withdrawn, in his bulky body.

Homophobia and accompanying shame have serious consequences for mental health (McDermott, Roen, & Scourfield, 2008). Rates of poor mental health (such as suicidality) are higher for gay, lesbian, bisexual, and transgender people. Shame is associated with higher rates of "self-destructive" behaviours, such as drug and alcohol abuse. In McDermott and colleagues' study, they found that this self-destructive behaviour is mostly linked to shame as a result of homophobia and homophobic abuse. This can be illustrated with clinical material from my work with Mr B, whom I saw for once-weekly psychotherapy.

Clinical material: Mr B

Mr B was a gay man in his late-20s and living with HIV. He was referred to therapy via an HIV support worker, because Mr B was struggling with loneliness and "rejection issues" related to his HIV status. He also had a history of self-destructive behaviour (binge drinking, previous drug use, and frequent casual sex). In my first session with him, he said that previous bouts of "binge sex" were prompted by feelings of loneliness and frustration. Since his HIV diagnosis (less than a year previously), he was trying to live a healthy life and had controlled his drinking, stopped taking drugs, and stopped "binge sex". It became apparent that his HIV diagnosis weighed heavily on Mr B and that he thought of it as a "punishment", which "a part of me feels like I deserve".

Mr B described being close to his mother. However, she seemed to have had emotional difficulties as a result of traumatic life events of her own and was not always emotionally available to him. He was not close to his father or his younger brother. He described his father as "emotionally cold" and verbally aggressive. He said he had nothing in common with him and had grown up feeling different. Although the eldest, he said that "I was never the prized son that my brother was." In contrast he felt that he was "pushed away" by his father. He described his childhood and adolescence as difficult, growing up in a small town; he was mocked, teased, and bullied by his peers for being effeminate. His first gay sexual relationship was with a man some years older. They lived together for four years, but Mr B had difficulties with intimacy and was always jealous and insecure with his boyfriend. There was some indication that he was in fact having other sexual encounters. At around the time of starting therapy, he had met and begun a relationship with a new man, and the relationship, as with the previous one, soon ran into difficulties. Mr B was insecure and easily became angry, leading to frequent arguments.

Initially my work with Mr B was set up as time-limited supportive therapy in the context of his HIV diagnosis. Recognizing some of his long-standing difficulties, we soon discussed the possibility of ongoing work. However, almost from the start, Mr B felt insecure with me. He found the space beneficial, and he recognized his need to work through things, but he feared my rejection and so was ambivalent about whether he should come for more or not. He started to miss sessions, questioning, with some anger, whether he needed therapy. The sessions started to feel a little chaotic, with Mr B denigrating therapy but at the same time seeming to need it. I was left feeling unsure whether he would stay or go. In one session he talked about his frustration at work (in a hotel), complaining that the managers were "cold" towards the kitchen and cleaning staff whom Mr B saw as "desperate", poor, and in need of help. It was not a stretch to suggest to him that he was talking about his own desperate need for help but also his fear that I would find him unacceptable and reject and humiliate him. Eventually, Mr B agreed to come for ongoing therapy but warned me of his "badness" to come. I interpreted that he longed for a relationship but was aware of the anger that disguised a damaged, ashamed part of himself, which he did not want others to see.

During one session, after some months, he was talking about his struggles with HIV, his fear, and his loneliness. He was very tearful in the session, saying, "this is not how I imagined my life would turn out to be". When I announced the end of the session, he became angry that we could not continue, asking whether I had another patient after him. Two days later he called me to say that he had paid his outstanding bill into my bank account and confirmed his appointment for the following week. On his return we spoke of how angry he had felt when I turned him away at the end of the previous session. He said how he had wondered whether he should "fire his therapist". I acknowledged his anger and sense of rejection and interpreted his phone call as his checking to see if I was still OK; that his rage had not damaged me. He then proceeded to talk about his adolescence and the build-up to his coming out at age 17. Struggling to talk through tears, he spoke about how he was "treated like a disease", how he was beaten up at school by the other boys, how his parents took him to a "Christian conversion therapy camp", and how he felt total rejection from his angry father.

In this brief synopsis of my work with Mr B, there are issues of narcissism and early trauma at play, and we can understand Mr B's difficulties as a result of the oedipal rejection he felt from the father and the added pain of his father's favouring his younger but more masculine brother. The themes of not been acceptably masculine (like his brother), the rejection from his father, the bullying by his peers, his expected, perceived, and actual rejection by other men, including me, a male therapist, were live throughout our work. His momentary wish to "fire" me was due in part to his own feeling of being rejected in favour of another patient who was taking his place—a more favoured sibling. His past binge drinking and binge sex were used as a means of defending against the feelings of shame—feeling good, if only momentarily. His fears of rejection were projected onto others, whom he then mistrusted and with whom he felt insecure. In the therapy, Mr B projected his feelings of rejection and guilt into me. In the countertransference, I felt repeatedly that my offer of help was being rejected, leaving me feeling not good enough. I had a sense of warmth and nurturance towards Mr B, but at times felt frustrated and even irritated with him for missing or cancelling sessions. In the session where I called time, I was moved by his feelings of loneliness, and I was left with a sense of guilt for having ended the session, as if it was cruel to do so. I felt as if he was testing me to find out whether I liked him/accepted him enough. It was important for me to remain consistent and reliable, so that trust could develop and I could become an object that he could start to use (Winnicott, 1969) in a helpful way.

Hertzmann (2011) observes how internalized homophobia acts as a punitive agent, provoking hostile attitudes towards one's own homosexuality and that of others, and in couples, this may result in difficulties with intimacy, where sexual desire towards the partner is met with shame, hatred even, from one partner in the couple or both. This was observed in the case studies by Rose (2007b), who noted that some gay men may defend against shame, anger and fears of rejection by looking for relationships with others who are likely to reject them. This is also evident in the shaming that may occur among the gay "community",[1] which I discuss in the next section, where shame is split off and located in others. For Mr B his deep sense of shame and isolation about his sexuality was further deepened by contracting HIV—an actual disease which brought to the surface the shame of his perceived disease of homosexuality (I've discussed elsewhere shame in relation to gay men living with HIV in Rohleder, 2016).

Gay pride vs shame

McDermott, Roen, and Scourfield (2008) argue that lesbian, gay and bisexual identity for the most part is formed along the binary of shame–pride, where pride dominates shame, and shame is left hidden. For some in the gay "community", to talk publicly about gay men and shame is seen as a return to pathologizing gay identity and as an attack on pride identities. Matthew Todd (2016)—a gay activist and editor of one of the prominent UK gay publications—in his book *Straight-Jacket*, a semi-autobiographical account of his experience of growing up with his own feelings of shame at being gay, describes the reluctance of many gay men to admit to shame, which is associated with the pejorative description of the "self-loathing gay". It is humiliating to be consistently and repeatedly made to feel that there is something unacceptable about you. Gay pride, then, stands as a repudiation of this oppression. Probyn (2000) suggests "pride operates as a necessity, an ontology of gay life that cannot admit its other" (p. 19). Shame gets silenced.

Shame and internalized homophobia and misogyny may then get projected and located in certain individuals, who are, in turn, shamed. Anti-effeminacy is not limited to homophobic heterosexual men and women: research has shown that anti-effeminacy attitudes are also pervasive among gay men. Blum, Danson, and Schneider (1997) noted that the trauma of homophobia and internalized homophobia is defended against through splitting and dissociation. Shame becomes located in more effeminate gay men. Taywaditep (2002) looks to history to illustrate how in the 1910s and 1920s some gay men, wanting to dis-identify themselves from effeminacy, took on the identity of "queer", against which effeminate men were labelled "faggot" or "fairies" or "queens" and were viewed with resentment and scorn. During a strengthening gay liberation movement, two stereotypical "pride" identities began to emerge: that of camp and drag, which appreciated gender-nonconformity and strengthened a sense of cohesive identity, and the macho, hyper-masculine look among many gay men—a shift to "butch" gay men, with "femme" men increasingly marginalized. Many gay men viewed camp and drag as politically incorrect, as they were seen as reinforcing heterosexuals' conceptions of the gay male stereotype. This marginalization of effeminate gay men is continued among contemporary gay men, where "straight acting" is seen as a badge of honour. Heteronormative binaries seep into gay relationships where people are defined in terms of "femme" or "butch"; "sissy" or "straight-acting"; "queen" or "manly". Thorne and Coupland (1998), for example, conducted a text survey of dating advertisements for 100 gay men and 100 lesbian women in prominent UK gay publications. They found that ads by gay men accentuated traits of masculinity. Lesbian women similarly referred to definitions of personality ranging from "butch" to "femme" or "lipstick" lesbian. In the contemporary equivalent of personal ads, the online ads for communities of men who have sex with men promote masculinity as the ideal and marginalize effeminacy (Miller, 2015).

Talking about shame can be difficult when many gay men are trying to reach a sense of self-acceptance and pride, which may require a life-long struggle. Some gay men may already be, understandably, cautious about the assumptions and attitudes of psychotherapists. A fairly recent UK survey by King and colleagues (cited in King, 2011) found that a large percentage of psychotherapists reported having treated at least one patient with a view to changing or reducing their homosexuality. Gay-affirmative psychotherapy emerged to facilitate a sense of pride and security among gay patients, through the support of psychotherapists who were often themselves gay, and could provide appropriate role models that gay young people so often lacked. However, as King (2011) points out, having a gay psychotherapist is not a necessity for psychotherapy to be affirming. A psychotherapy becomes gay-affirming where homosexuality is recognized as a normal variant of sexuality, that it is in itself not the cause of gay men's—and lesbian women's—psychological difficulties, and where a therapist has an understanding of the contextual and social realities of gay patients (King, 2011). Facilitating a sense of acceptance and pride for someone struggling with shame is important work. But important, too, is the analysis of the impact that trauma and internalized homophobia have had on internalized object relationships and character development. Much can be fruitfully explored in the transference between heterosexual therapists and their gay patients about difference and acceptance. This work requires the heterosexual therapists to consider their own countertransference, blind spots, and possible anti-homosexual biases. To ignore the impact of the broader social environment on the development of gay men is potentially harmful and re-enacts the shame.

Note

1. I use community in scare quotes to identify this as a figure of speech, rather than a reality. There is no such thing as a gay *community*, as we are talking about a heterogeneity of individuals, interests, hobbies, means of socializing, professions, and so on.

CHAPTER THREE

Working with sameness and difference: reflections on supervision with diverse sexualities

David Richards

I n this chapter I explore themes that emerge from my experience of supervising counselling and psychotherapy with patients identifying as gay and lesbian, as well as the experience of supervising practitioners identifying themselves as lesbian and gay. The interpersonal triangle of supervisor, supervisee, and patient both represents and embodies a complex and powerful set of dynamics and emotional states and implicitly involves the sexual identity of each of the three parties present in the supervisory consulting room and the various meanings this has for each of them personally and historically.

The psychoanalytic supervisory tradition has not tended to allow for, let alone encourage, the active use of the supervisee's sexual identity within discussion of clinical work; even less encouraged is any acknowledgment that the supervisor also has a sexual identity, and that both these identities will play their part, implicitly or explicitly, in the exploration of the clinical work being supervised. I propose that it is vital for both supervisor and supervisee to be able to acknowledge, at least in their own minds, their own personally identified sexuality, and, equally, to hold an awareness of the complex web of associations that constitute their lived experience as a gay man, lesbian woman, heterosexual or bisexual individual. For therapists identifying as gay or lesbian themselves who work with patients of a similar identity, it can be seen as essential for the supervisor to be able to assist in articulating areas of self or experience active in the clinical process that might otherwise remain hidden or repressed, just as they have so often been in external reality and the social world until relatively recent times.

The psychoanalytic community as a whole may still remain ambivalent or unclear about whether and to what degree there is anything intrinsically different about analytic work with lesbian, gay, and bisexual people; and equally in focusing on the supervision of such work we may raise the same question in relation to gay, lesbian, and bisexual practitioners. It seems to me important for us to recognize that while lesbian and gay individuals are, of course, identical in so many fundamental human respects with heterosexual individuals, there are equally significant ways in which the formation of their identities and their lived experience is different, not least as a result of growing up and living in societies that may deny, degrade, or abuse their sexual identity and preferences.

In this chapter I reflect on my supervisory work with both individuals and groups, where clinical work with gay men and lesbian women is presented. I reflect on supervisory work with gay, lesbian, and heterosexual therapists, working with lesbian and gay patients; and I also reference my own identity as a supervisor in these contexts who is himself a gay man—a fact that may or may not be explicitly known by the supervisee, but which element of identity can potentially be utilized by me within the work. This capacity for supervisors to make reflective use of their own identity and experience within the work of supervision is a central point of my argument here. I concentrate on what is particular to the work of supervision and the relationships within the supervisory space.

In supervision, as in therapy, we always encounter sameness and difference and are presented with an opportunity to question and reflect on ourselves and what in our own identity and experience may be brought into awareness by the prompt of the patient's or the supervisee's material. More specifically, in supervision we encounter a triangular relational situation: the therapist/supervisee, the patient under discussion, and ourselves as the supervisor. In much of traditional psychoanalytic thinking and the literature on supervision the person of the supervisor is neglected at the expense of the other two. This is, of course, in many ways for good reasons, as the patient's experience and identity are, rightly, at the heart of the supervisory enterprise, alongside the therapist's, and equally their joint relational contact and experience. However, I wish to avoid the temptation—and perhaps equally the reassurance—of concentrating only on the patient's or supervisee's identity, psychopathology, and sexuality by reflecting on the supervisor's own presence and sexual identity in the room and the effect this may have on what material emerges and how it is discussed. Such a position encourages the principle that the supervisor's identity should not be split off but should, rather, be included in the reflection of supervision and, hence, be available to be utilized for the benefit of the supervisee's work with his or her patient. This can include in particular the scope to make active use of one's countertransference to develop understanding of the clinical material, an idea promoted by certain writers referenced below; however, this can only be done effectively if the supervisor is able, at least internally, to reflect on his or her sexual self and gender identity within supervision.

The supervisor's use of self

The supervisor's use of self is an idea explored by two writers, in particular, in ways that I find extremely valuable. First, there is Ogden's paper "On Psychoanalytic Supervision" (2005), which presents the idea of "dreaming up the patient" in supervisory discussion. This can be described as an opportunity for the person of the patient, who has been mentally taken in by the therapist/supervisee, to be, as it were, recreated during the supervisory session; it is a kind of "fiction", as Ogden describes it, "bring[ing] to life in the supervision what is true to the analyst's experience of what is occurring at a conscious, preconscious and unconscious level in the analytic relationship" (p. 1268). This implies a degree of fluidity that involves the therapist internalizing the patient and then reproducing him or her in discussion with the supervisor, rising above what we could see as restricted or over-concrete notions of identity such as gender or sexual orientation, at least in the way these terms tend to be used in everyday life. The patient is, in a sense, transformed, and his or her presence, or aspects of it, are heightened through this experience, but in a way that can serve to help therapist and supervisor develop their understanding of the therapist's knowledge and lived experience with the patient. It is a way of acknowledging and also appreciating the subjectivity of the process, and encouraging the potential for supervisory discussion to benefit from such subjectivity, rather than maintaining any pretence that the patient and the way they are presented are totally objective. It is important to acknowledge that aspects of the therapist's own identity will inevitably influence how the patient is experienced and mentally taken in in the course of the work; and, equally, that aspects of both therapist's and supervisor's identity will influence how the patient and the therapeutic relationship are then reproduced and explored in supervision. We should also keep in mind that the route of the patient from therapy to supervision is only through the person of the therapist, and that the supervisor's primary task—certainly to my mind—is to concentrate on helping the therapist (rather than directly aiming to help the patient); and thus, again, the identities of both therapist and supervisor are important and benefit from active and thoughtful attention.

The subjective co-creation involved in "dreaming up the patient" referred to above can also be helpful in reflecting on our relation to identities that may present as more fluid and less binary: for example, an individual identifying as bisexual or transgender. A person who positions themselves beyond the binary norms can produce significant and complex responses in others, including therapists and supervisors. The desire to step out of the binaries of heterosexual and homosexual, or male and female, and to identify as bisexual or pansexual, and "third" or non-binary, in terms of gender identity can present a significant challenge to traditional psychoanalytic thinking and prac- tice. Thus, in therapeutic work, and in the discussion of this work in supervision, there may be assumptions and reassuring certainties in the practitioners' minds that will be unsettled by patients who describe— and perhaps embody—a different way of being that moves beyond the binary; and who, equally, will be, implicitly or explicitly, expecting or indeed demanding a therapeutic response that recognizes rather than refuses their chosen identity.

Schaverien's paper, "Supervising the Erotic Transference and Coun- tertransference" (2003), presents valuable observations about the three identities and, equally, the three bodies engaged in supervision. She emphasizes the idea of the "analyst-as-person", which can come into play at times of significant erotic material, leading to a challenge to the therapist's self-concept and professional identity. She argues that the gender and sexual orientation of each figure in supervision (patient, therapist, supervisor) has a significant impact on the experiencing and exploration of so-called "erotic" or eroticized material. She suggests, further, that the supervisor's countertransference can be particularly helpful in trying to unpack what is going on in the therapeutic rela- tionship. "The erotic reveals much about the patient's way of being in the world" (p. 167)—and hence it will also reveal much about the ther- apist's and the supervisor's ways of being in the world. Thus opportunities arise in supervision for examining important relational dynamics, such as parallel processes. One theme that these thoughts prompt is the extent to which a group that is defined by its sexuality may tend to be thought of only in terms of sexual or sexualized features—an idea I return to. While this is, of course, to be avoided, at the same time the particular feelings and associations that may be stimulated by material related to sexual identity in the consulting room (whether same or different) must be thought about in the context of supervision, and I find Schaverien's ideas of great help here.

Alongside these internal and interpersonal dynamics we are, I believe, also required to keep in mind the external reality and history that will be part of an individual's life and development; and for lesbian, gay, and bisexual people there will inevitably be an experience of growing up within a society that does not in any straightforward way validate their identity and, indeed, may actively work to dismiss or deny it. There may be experience of discrimination or abuse that will have affected the psychic and psychological development of the individual, effects that will continue to reside in some form in the unconscious, however resolved they may appear to be on the surface.

As mentioned by many authors referenced in this book, discrimination and pathologizing of sexual minorities became incorporated into the tradition of psychoanalysis after Freud. This history is part of the personal and professional development of those who train as analysts or therapists (regardless of sexual orientation). It is understood that this has made it extremely difficult, if not indeed impossible, until relatively recently, for applicants to analytic training to disclose a homosexual orientation, and, equally, that this may have led to difficult and painful personal narratives for those who were thus obliged to hide their true natures throughout long training analyses and subsequent professional work. While times can be seen to have changed in many ways, we might consider an article in a recent issue of *New Associations*, the newsletter of the British Psychoanalytic Council (Anonymous, 2015), in which a gay man reflects both on his experience of being interviewed for a psychoanalytic training and also on the literature referenced within the institution's teaching on sexuality. His comments serve to remind us that there is still work to be done to ensure that different sexual identities are considered as equal and of equal value. It is also to be noted that the author felt it advisable for him to remain anonymous, for reasons related to fears he powerfully identifies and which are not difficult to understand.

Both the internal and more fluid personal identity and the externally recognized and socially located identity, including the erotically embodied, are vitally important for us all; and in therapy, and in certain ways more explicitly in supervision, they are vividly present and are, indeed, what much of the clinical work is about.

The "known" and the "unknown"

The notion of sitting with the unknown is a familiar and important principle for analytic practitioners, who think of Bion's use of the poet Keats' original concept of "negative capability" (Keats, 1899) in encouraging the therapist to approach each session "without memory or desire" (Bion, 1967). Alongside this is the idea of maintaining neutrality, emerging from Freud's early advocacy of "evenly-suspended attention" (1913c) and the aim to establish and hold a space for the development of the patient's transference towards the therapy and the therapist. This presupposes that the therapist does not gratify the patient's curiosity by making him or herself "known" to the patient, in order to facilitate working with phantasies, projections, and symbolic meanings. At the same time, however, we, as therapists, may feel it is necessary, or at least beneficial, to consider the meaning for the patient of aspects of his or her identity that have led to neglect, discrimination, or abuse, as discussed above. It is in this context that issues of trust are significant, and where the knowledge of a therapist's also being part of the same cultural group may be vital for developing the potential security of therapeutic (or, equally, supervisory) work. Such reflections should encourage us to maintain a complex sense of the meaning of the terms "known" and "unknown", keeping in mind how subtle are the workings of the unconscious and how sensitive the intuition we may have towards those we might identify as the same as or different from ourselves.

We might also reflect on what may be publicly known about a practitioner and how this knowledge may be understood and perhaps made valuable use of by a patient or supervisee. To date, we have no tradition in the UK psychoanalytic community of "openly gay analysts"—that is, analysts or therapists who openly identify themselves as gay or lesbian—such as certain American analysts (for example, Blechner, Drescher, Isay), who, through writing, public speaking, and clinical practice, include their self-identification as gay men in their engagement with the world of patients, trainees, and supervisees, as well as the analytic community of colleagues, local, national, and international. This greater openness in the US psychoanalytic community has developed since the decision by the American Psychiatric Association in 1973 to remove homosexuality as a pathological category from the *DSM* (*DSM–III*), and the American Psychoanalytic Association Position Statement admitting lesbians and gay men to psychoanalytic training which was issued in 1991. In the United Kingdom it was only in 2011 that the British Psychoanalytic Council agreed a similar position statement, and the British analytic community is still involved in ongoing discussions about theoretical concepts and views about symptomology and pathology relating to sexuality and sexual object choice.

While there has been a gradual increase in the UK literature on therapy with gay and lesbian people, little has been published on the supervision of work with sexual minorities—unlike in the United States, where various papers have appeared over the last 20 years or more. Pett's 2000 paper comes from a humanistic/existential perspective and applies principles of a gay affirmative approach from therapy to supervision; this reflects the humanistic tradition's generally more open and accepting history with regard to sexual minorities. There is otherwise no further text until a short but very stimulating paper by Bruce Kinsey in 2011. This presents valuable personal reflections and clinical vignettes and also references the idea, familiar from the American analysts, of being sought out for supervision as a practitioner known to be gay. It thus confirms the value for other gay and lesbian therapists of making oneself known and thus available to be used in important ways that benefit supervisees and their patients—a position I can identify with myself from my own supervisory experience, which is explored further on in the chapter.

A central dilemma of "gay affirmative" therapy or supervision is that, while it is essential to have a positive and supportive stance on the part of the therapist in relation to being gay (i.e. non-pathologizing, at the very least), there is equally the need to be able to identify and explore any internal conflicts the patient (or supervisee) may need or wish to explore in order to grow. However, this may be easier—or, even, only possible—within the kind of "safe" setting referred to above. Reflecting on his own experience as a gay supervisor, Kinsey writes:

> It is true that my work with gay men has had a particular liveliness that comes from a sort of tribal affiliation. There is much shared and much different, but the community of experience in the gay world brings a deep understanding that can't just be learned: it has to be lived. [Kinsey, 2011, p. 11]

I can identify with this very much from my own experience. Kinsey goes on to say:

> It also feels rather strange to be writing an article about "gay supervision" as if there was such a thing, and that my voice could represent it. I am not a spokesman for such a thing, nor is this the only perspective there might be. It feels odd to identify with the part of me that makes me different from, rather than all that is ordinary or the same as everyone else. [pp. 11–12]

This neatly sums up the duality I touched on earlier—namely, that we are all the same, except for the significant elements about us that are different. Kinsey's thoughts also address the dilemma for lesbian and gay practitioners, one aspect of which is well articulated by Blechner (2009), who identifies as fundamental the integration of one's personal and professional identity—a conflict or challenge that simply does not exist in the same terms for heterosexual practitioners. Blechner eloquently writes:

> Not being in the closet has had a very healthful effect on all my clinical work. I don't bring up my sexual orientation . . . needlessly with patients. If [they] ask, I may tell them, after suitable exploration of their own fantasies and motives. But even if the subject never comes up, the fact that I am not afraid if it does is certainly freeing. . . . To bring my true private self into alignment with my public self has given me much more freedom to work as an analyst on any issue with any patient. [2009, p. 29]

One could say there still remains a dearth of role models for gay and lesbian therapists in training, just as is still significantly the case for lesbian and gay people growing up. While they are more visible in public roles than in the past, it must, inevitably, remain the case that those in a minority will always be less fully reflected in the world around them than the majority can take for granted. There is a lack of automatic validation that the heterosexual therapist/trainee might quite naturally expect and that is confirmed by our hetero-normative society. Neutrality is important yet also arguably impossible to attain, and sometimes the disclosure or knowledge of a therapist's or supervisor's identity may be experienced as more important than remaining apparently neutral. There are, of course, pitfalls, conflicts, and tensions to be mindful of, but also great potential benefits and, indeed, one could say, important achievements. Glazer (1998) in her paper "Homosexuality and the Analytic Stance: Implications for Treatment and Supervision" helps us to recognize an essential component of the complexities when trying to address neutrality:

... it is important to address issues of sexual orientation in supervision. Supervisors and supervisees often politely collude in not discussing the effects of the therapist's sexual orientation on the treatment. This can result in inhibitions in listening for both heterosexual and homosexual therapists dealing with both heterosexual and homosexual patients. [1998, p. 410]

We know from collective history as much as from individual experience that that which remains unknown—whether unseen or ignored—can become something hidden, which can, in turn, lead to fears of exposure and shame, and so often to painful and even violent enactments. Indeed, the Oedipus myth so central to Freud's thinking about early development embodies this truth most powerfully; and is effectively explored in Steiner's appositely entitled "Turning a Blind Eye" (1985). That which remains unspoken can so easily become that which is unspeakable. The phrase powerfully adopted within the early AIDS campaign can also be evoked here: "Silence equals death" (Act Up, 1987). It is a significant and fascinating conundrum that the psychoanalytic enterprise, founded to address that which is hidden to the point of being unconscious, has stood for so long against the "knowing" that is represented by sexual orientation and identity.

Safety and separateness: the container and the ghetto

Reflecting on themes of silence and safety, it is helpful to turn to a text that addresses the minority experience more broadly. Akhtar's "The Mental Pain of Minorities" (2014) addresses primarily ethnic and cultural minorities, but what he says is relevant to any minority group. He proposes that for any minority group, the power imbalance and the resulting invisibility is as important as the numerical size of a community; and he points out that the group can become an object of—often malign—projections from the majority, an idea that has implications for the psychoanalytic world, both practitioners and patients. Akhtar references Sandler (1960) in saying "that a sense of safety is the most basic requirement for normal psychic functioning" (Akhtar, 2014, p. 147). This safety is mostly likely and most naturally to be looked for in a context of "sameness" for any minority group and is, for example, fundamental to agencies set up to provide services for any specific minority group, such as LGBTQ+ (Lesbian, Gay, Bisexual, Transgender, and Queer) where everyone within the agency, service providers as well as service users, identifies as belonging to that group.

However, such a setting also prompts an implicit tension. It can provide a container (which creates an opportunity where something of value can potentially be found that could not be found outside, and establishes it safely within a boundaried space); but this is inevitably in tension with the possibility of becoming a ghetto (where the community is safely contained but isolated from the rest of the world, which can serve to restrict potential and where that which is other/different can be avoided and vital experience and learning thus lost). This confronts us with significant contraries and, especially, the need to find and work with the differences within a context of apparent sameness, which may raise difficult and painful confrontations and may, indeed, feel as if it puts the safety that is so important at risk.

Clinical material and reflections

The dynamics of the supervisory couple, and the potential avoidance or collusion that may play out within supervision, are clearly identified in Russell and Greenhouse's paper "Homophobia in the Supervisory Relationship: An Invisible Intruder" (1997). The authors are a supervisory couple (a heterosexual supervisor and a lesbian supervisee) and the paper presents several vignettes from their work together, one of which addresses internalized homophobia very directly. A lesbian patient requests confirmation that her therapist is also a lesbian, as she has heard rumours about this; the therapist, feeling cornered and uncomfortable, seeks to unpick the meaning in the transference but does not validate the rumour; the supervisor supports this position, and they agree that the therapist's countertransference of discomfort is an understandable reaction. The authors explore this and conclude that there is an avoidance of personal challenge in the therapy and a collusion within supervision, when the shared identity in the consulting room and its meaning for both parties is directly encountered, one issue identified being that of the integration of personal and professional identity, as referenced by Blechner above. The suggestion is that the therapist's avoidance of disclosure is, in this instance, an expression of internalized homophobia, which leads her to engage defensively with the patient's pathology at the expense of the interpersonal significance of sexual orientation in the consulting room. Here we have an example that illustrates how something that is not spoken may come to equal something that is unspeakable.

What began as an avoidance of sexual orientation in the supervision has now compromised the therapy itself. The patient has rightly felt misunderstood. Three overlapping dimensions contributed to her asking the therapist about her sexual orientation. The first is the meaning of the patient's membership in the lesbian subculture. The second has to do with the relational implications of two members of the same stigmatised subculture who encounter each other in a therapy relationship. The third includes the real and transferential aspects of this particular patient's relationship with any therapist. [Russell & Greenhouse, 1997, p. 36]

The authors make it clear that they do not automatically encourage personal disclosure in such a situation, and one could argue that the scenario is too simplistic in presentation, but I feel that it does prompt important reflection about how we experience and work with this kind of intervention from a patient, including in supervisory discussion.

I now reflect on some of my own experiences in supervision that speak to the theme of what is known/disclosed and how this affects the unfolding supervisory process. Some of these experiences take place within the setting of an agency providing counselling for people identifying as LGBTQ+ and thus can be seen as sidestepping the issue of direct disclosure in that my sexual orientation is known as a matter of course: everyone in this agency, service users and service providers, is required to identify as LGBTQ+. As touched on above, this serves to embody a particular situation that can potentially lead to avoidance and collusion in a different way from the example discussed above. Equally, a supervisory situation where my sexual orientation may be known but is not explicitly disclosed can prompt other dynamics that affect the process, as described in the first examples below.

The following clinical and supervisory scenarios are either simplified or adapted in order to preserve confidentiality and are used with permission.

Mixed sexualities: disclosed or undisclosed

First, I present a scenario from my work in a university counselling service, where I provide individual supervision for the members of the counselling team. In this example I am supervising the case of a young gay man who is presenting with relational difficulties. The therapist is a young man who has identified as heterosexual insofar as he has referred to a female partner; he may be aware that I am gay, but I have not explicitly identified this. He describes, from the first session with this patient, a reference to "different sexual interests" between the patient and his partner. I ask whether he enquired further about this and hence whether he has any more particular knowledge of their different sexual interests, as it seems likely that these may play a part in the relational tensions. He says he didn't ask but agrees that this would have been helpful. This is a straightforward clinical discussion, and the therapist seems, as he usually does, grateful for guidance and for my prompt to pursue an area that he acknowledges he finds quite delicate. I am aware, when later reflecting on this scenario, that a similar situation within the LGBTQ+ agency would be likely to feel different to me; a therapist there might also feel wary of approaching potentially delicate sexual material within a same-sex scenario, but the area seems somehow more accessible than in this generic setting—or is it just somehow more "normal" in the specialist setting that is in a way defined by its relation to sexuality? A further thought is that the idea of "different sexual interests" is, of course, present in the room as represented by the supervisee and myself; and it strikes me that, had I pursued this sense of parallel process in our discussion, it might have served to activate our shared thinking more vividly.

A more overt example from work with the same therapist is another gay patient, in this case a young Muslim man whose family is extremely hostile towards his sexuality, which they have discovered inadvertently and responded to very punitively, restricting his movements and, indeed, behaving in a manner both disturbing and potentially even illegal (in terms of human rights). I find myself feeling a sense of outrage and speaking very intensely about the situation, expressing strong feelings about the family's behaviour and the legal implications, and am suddenly aware of feeling rather exposed, as if the sexual orientation I share with the patient might have become visible. I have no reason to believe that the therapist would have any kind of antipathy to my sexual orientation, even if he had identified it; he was himself expressing equally strong and disturbed feelings about the patient's situation, and we were able to think constructively about it together, so there is no logical reason for me to feel self-conscious. However, this reaction, which I would understand as an expression of my own internalized homophobia, is powerfully evoked and leaves me feeling deflated.

The concept of internalized homophobia has become a familiar cultural construct in Western society, alongside other examples of similar processes related to histories of difference, discrimination, and oppression, such as internalized racism. We could thus understand that in this instance I was reacting to experiences from elsewhere in my life and history and re-enacting a protective response that in the (relatively distant) past has prompted me to be wary of revealing my sexual orientation in a setting that may not feel safe. I do not believe that the university itself or any of the counselling staff are homophobic, nor that there would be a hostile reaction to the knowledge that I was gay; however, I think the replication of a social situation that has affected me in younger days may be inevitable, even if at a pre-conscious level, perhaps exacerbated in a generic setting dealing with young people and their troubles. In addition, and more significantly, I may unconsciously expect or fear an identification to be made by the therapist between me and the gay patient, thus placing me in a psychologically vulnerable position, in which I stand to lose my supervisory authority. Although logically my mature self can recognize that these dynamics are neither accurate nor helpful, the powerfully internalized message from years ago proves hard to resist in the moment. Both these university scenarios evoke a sense of something sexually "different" or even potentially transgressive, producing tension in me that originates from what may remain unspoken/unspeakable: that is, my own sexual identity and its place in the world.

It is equally important to reflect on this in a specialist same-sex setting, where I think different and subtler dynamics and tensions can play out. Here the minority sexual identity is shared and explicit, and therapists do not need to leave at the door whatever aspects of their external experience feel transgressive. Nevertheless these reactions, arising from internalized homophobia or previous experiences of discrimination, may be repressed or otherwise avoided and hence become enacted within the clinical work or in supervision. This may, of course, originate with me as supervisor just as much as with the therapists. These two settings, one generic and one specialist, can serve to represent the outside world and its oppositions and oppressions very powerfully and effectively.

Identification and desire

Focusing on the LGBTQ+ agency setting prompts awareness of various individual and interpersonal elements that require attention. These include identification, desire, and the erotic. In a setting characterized by a shared sense of sexual identity and, beyond that, the implication of shared sexual interests and activity, it is vital to find a way of reflecting on this in supervision that aims to be open and honest while also abiding by important boundaries of care and respect. In a group setting in particular, where the supervisor is one of several gay or lesbian people in the room, he or she is available to be thought about, fantasied about, identified or misidentified with, projected into, and so forth; and the same is true of the patients and supervisees. The role of the supervisor's authority is also at play, with other aspects of the relational dynamics, explored below in several vignettes.

An agency setting that is formed and characterized by a particular sexual identity will naturally and also importantly include various aspects of the group's experience and behaviour in the world outside. For patients identifying as LGBTQ+, there may be sexual dynamics that play a significant part in their external social and interpersonal life, and that may well be part of the difficulties that have brought them to therapy; this is the case regardless of whether or not the patient is sexually active and, if active, whether s/he is sexually satisfied. There may be various kinds of understandings or assumptions, on the part of both patient and therapist, about relational contact between two LGBTQ+ people in an intimate setting that are powerfully evoked by the therapeutic encounter. Such expectations can be brought into active play in the consulting room and may well include important unresolved and challenging interpersonal dynamics of a sexual nature that will explicitly or implicitly affect the developing process of the therapy. Naturally, this material will also affect the supervisory experience, which has a central role to play in helping recognition, understanding, and possibly resolution of these dynamics. As the supervisor in this setting also brings his/her own active and potentially unresolved internal and external sexual experience, this is valuably kept in the supervisor's awareness and attention paid as to where and how it can be utilized in the interests of the clinical discussion and, equally, what is its potential for disrupting the discussion.

A particular example of this can be seen in the shape of the phone app Grindr, a facility for gay men to locate each other geographically and hence to meet up if interested, primarily for sexual contact. This has featured in various scenarios in group supervision within the agency, including a pertinent exchange where a female therapist is presenting a new male patient who talks about Grindr, which she says she is not familiar with. She seems to indicate by a particular look at her male colleague in the group that she expects him to be more familiar with it, to which he responds with apparent discomfort that he is not. One aspect here is that the male therapist is known to be in an established relationship, so that it might be imagined that his discomfort touches delicately on a familiar expectation/assumption about gay men's sexual behaviour: that is, that all gay men have multiple sexual partners, regardless of whether they are in a relationship. The group chooses to find his denial of knowledge of Grindr amusing, and a smile is shared, including by me. But I feel that there is, equally, a judgemental undertone, the recognition that he may not care to be publicly associated with the familiar idea of open relationships or, indeed, with what might, in other circles, be referred to as sexual promiscuity. I am also mindful that neither of them (therapists under 40) is suggesting that I (a supervisor in his 50s) might be familiar with this app. I relate this both to my role and authority as the supervisor but also to my age: perhaps in their minds, consciously or otherwise, I am too old to be sexual, or perhaps they prefer not to imagine that if I am sexually active, I would be likely to use a facility like Grindr.

This raises a theme with which I am familiar from previous experience, as supervisor in an older adults agency, where the idea or evocation of the erotic and, especially, the fantasy of intergenerational couplings (in the transference and countertransference of older patients and younger therapists) tended to cause disturbance in supervisory discussion. Age and sexuality can combine to be an agitating force in the clinical setting; and within the LGBTQ+ agency I found myself equally spot-lit in other scenarios involving older gay patients, where as supervisor I was aware of a tendency to feel identified (generally by younger supervisees, but also within my own mind) with an older patient who might be expected to be non-sexual. I am mindful that I did not feel able to voice this degree of self-consciousness at the time and thus not only sat with the projection/identification but also left the group without the opportunity to explore this aspect of the work.

Another scenario featuring Grindr is in the case of a young male patient whose phone blinks repeatedly throughout his sessions with his male therapist. The therapist imagines that the blinking may be caused by messages on Grindr, which he knows the patient is preoccupied with, and that the patient does not want to lose any time in receiving these. This patient is rather desperately trying, through various behaviours, to ward off anxieties about himself and his future. In supervision we think about the phone, which he clearly does not want to turn off, and its blinking as an important "third" in the room: a transitional object, or perhaps more the symbol of a fantasized other who is out there waiting for him if only he can get the message quickly enough. This imaginary other thus serves to keep at bay the therapist as an important other who is actually available to him. While the therapist expresses frustration with his patient and with himself for not handling the situation robustly enough (for example, by making the right interpretation, or by asking the patient to turn his phone off), in supervision we also reflect on the subtle threads of intimate contact and ambivalent desire that seem to echo in the work and affect the possible interventions.

There may be a degree of envy at play between patient and therapist, and again a shadowy transgressive fantasy evoked: the patient is unable to relinquish an attachment to what his blinking phone seems to represent, and the man sitting with him may seem too threatening in his very degree of availability. The therapist may likewise be almost too careful in aiming not to disrupt the sexual/relational fantasy so seductive for the patient, partly because he is in touch with the patient's vulnerability and his tendency to feel attacked or undermined, as he has previously demonstrated in the transference. As the therapist and I reflect together, we recognize the importance of such care to be taken, while at the same time the need for a gradual challenge to the patient's defensive structure, which holds him back from developing more genuinely intimate relationships. Thus in the supervisory couple there is some capacity to sit more thoughtfully with the complexity of this case and what it evokes for us both personally.

Projections into the "other"

The broader theme here, which I have reflected on through my experience in this agency, is a sense of a split into "good" and "bad" elements of gay sexuality, certainly for men: the sense of a choice being made by therapists who come to work in this setting with their own kind, and the resulting opportunity to see themselves as "good" (for example, secure partnerships, sometimes children, "responsible citizens"), as well as the meaning of inhabiting the professional role of therapist, especially the fantasy of being psychologically healthy—all difficulties resolved through personal therapy. This is, then, in opposition to the shadow of something "bad" that can, in turn, be located in the patients (for example, casual or anonymous sex, apparent lack or avoidance of responsibilities, frequently linked with use of recreational drugs and alcohol). If this idea bears some examination, then I, too, as the supervisor am implicated in it. The work in this setting represents not only the interest and pleasure of working with my own cultural group, but also offers an ideal opportunity for splitting off and projecting complex unresolved aspects of my psychosexual self into the "other" of the patients. The "other" is then inevitably identified with what could even be thought of as "sick"—a symptom or a psychological difficulty that calls to mind the old and hateful idea of the "sickness" of homosexuality as an identity. Here is the presence of potentially shameful aspects of self, desire, and behaviour that can be reflected on by therapists (and, crucially, be available for discussion in supervision), which the nature of a specialist LGBTQ+ setting might serve to hide or keep at a distance. This projective potential could be thought of as the shadow side of the "liveliness" referred to by Kinsey in the quote above, in terms of the pleasure and complex engagement for the gay therapist or supervisor in working with his or her own community.

To return to identification and desire: it is required, arguably, that in this setting therapists both explore the identity they share with the patients as well as reflect on the meaning of the many differences between them and, in doing this, become aware of and reflect on the desire that has brought them there. This is evoked in various ways in the consulting room and in supervision, where I, too, as the supervisor, have to identify my own desire and how it plays out. It is likely that the average patient turns to this specialist agency in order not only to gain the support and understanding of a therapist who is seen (and promoted) as the same as themselves, but also to work with a therapist who can be identified as someone who has resolved similar kinds of personal/sexual difficulties. This tension may be unconsciously welcomed by therapist (and supervisor), as it can act as confirmation of the "healthier" kind of gay man evoked in my reflections above. We might wonder how this particular tension would be expressed in lesbian therapeutic couples: the scenario below describes a powerful encounter that evokes related and significantly erotic dynamics.

Eroticized encounters

Desire, in my experience, can usually be thought about constructively in an abstract or conceptual way within supervision; it is usually much harder to address if a more powerful attraction or even physical arousal is involved in the clinical work. It is important for a therapist to be able to bring an experience of attraction or arousal with a patient for exploration in supervision without undue shame or embarrassment, which will be easier if a working relationship of stability and trust has been established. Again, the supervisor's shared identity within the specialist LGBTQ+ setting will play its part and may feel sufficiently supportive and encouraging for the therapist to be able to address this area. More generally, eroticized transferential and countertransferential dynamics are always troubling to encounter and can, within a setting characterized by same-sex desire, set up dynamics variously arousing, stimulating, and/or disturbing. An example of the latter arose in the work of a female therapist with an older woman who exhibited extremely powerful erotic feelings towards the therapist, which the therapist found almost unbearable. This patient was extricating herself from a painful relationship, which had included violent enactments, and she seemed to turn to the therapist as an available erotic object. This made it difficult for both of them to think about in symbolic terms, as the patient would make very intrusive comments about the therapist's body and what they might do together, and the therapist would feel paralysed in response, unable to comment or interpret in the way she usually would. In supervision she actually had to break down on one occasion: she became unable to speak and started to cry, before she could stabilize herself and make some sense of what was happening.

As the group discussed the work, we felt that the patient had required the therapist to be available for an aggressive kind of erotic enactment, partly in order to punish the ex-partner for hurting her (literally and metaphorically) and, more importantly, to try to push out old internalized messages from the patient's mother that her sexuality was unhealthy and unwanted. Within the intense intrusive transference, the therapist had lost her capacity to reflect and respond; the violent, intrusive transference made her unable to access her countertransference in a productive way, and only in supervision could she start to make contact with it and make use of it. I was aware of my own concerns about a situation that threatened to become unmanageable. My immediate consideration prompted me to question whether the work could continue, mirroring the therapist's desire to stop; but my countertransference (which felt parental towards the therapeutic couple) told me that the real meaning of this behaviour was historical. The therapist responded with relief as she recognized that her real role with this patient was maternal, and that, if she could resist the erotized attack on her creativity and separateness, the work could continue. It later became clear that interpretations recalling the patient's relationship with her mother did serve to move the work forward. My role could be seen as that of a protective father/partner, intervening in the mother's relationship with her child in order to facilitate containment, as Winnicott describes (1965). But equally, the presence of a male and another female supervisee also in the group serves to illustrate, in the context of same-sex couplings, a different family grouping, an alternative and effective working group that provided a sensitive holding (a kind of loving attention, one could say) for this deeply bruised woman.

The powerful erotic dynamic described above could equally develop in the context of a male therapeutic couple, or, indeed, in a "heterosexual" or male/female couple. However, it may be the case that the agency's specialist identity makes it possible to explore same-sex couple relations with a particular intensity. The setting creates the potential freedom to bring sexuality more openly into therapy and may come to be seen as permitting or even encouraging a sexualized kind of engagement. Thus the "gay" setting can sometimes seem tantalizing as well as relieving for the anxious but also desiring patient; and the therapist and supervisor also have to allow themselves to be open to such projections and phantasies. These processes have to be managed, not least through the work and relationship with the supervisor but, as the previous vignette shows, can be meaningfully thought about only if they have first been experienced and allowed into the therapist's mind.

Any gay, lesbian, or LGBTQ+ community setting—whether a gay bar, a social or support group, an agency, or a counselling/therapy service—will provoke customary tensions that are part of the group's identity and particular complexes, in which a central question in a mixed gender setting is how "other" the other may seem. It is an interesting fact that the LGBTQ+ agency described above saw more gay male patients than lesbian ones. This may be because women would often prefer to go to an all-female environment, so that gender is prioritized over sexuality; or, perhaps, as a female supervisee in the agency suggested to me, that the customary societal identification of women with greater emotional openness and/or vulnerability than men might be reversed or at least challenged among the gay community. Interestingly, however, there were roughly equal numbers of male and female therapists in the agency, indicating that all members of the professional group shared an interest in the setting and its potential.

A "sexual" setting and its opportunities

A parallel setting from another part of my supervisory experience provides some final clinical reflections. This is a sexual health clinic and a generic service that, as is often the case in this area of work, actually contains a significant number of gay men in both patient and staff groups. Thus the organization, with its explicit emphasis on sexual life and sexual relating both within and beyond the gay male community, raises many of the themes touched on above in terms of an LGBTQ+ specialist service, but here with a more specific focus arising from the sexual nature of the clinic's work. Many gay male patients are likely to come to the clinic expecting that gay men will be significantly represented on the staff team. It is worthy of note that many gay male staff members, who may be qualified nurses and counsellors as well as sexual health advisors, are attracted to work in this area, where an intimate encounter is provided in ways that parallel the LGBTQ+ therapy agency setting previously described. The clinic provides counselling alongside sexual health consultations, and I describe a supervisory vignette to illustrate this particular setting and its dynamics.

In this case, I am supervising another middle-aged gay male therapist, and the patient in question is a younger gay man presenting with what we identify as an extremely powerful experience of internalized homophobia that has a significant developmental history. He has presented in the clinic with high anxiety about sexual infection but with apparent low risk, based on his stated sexual activity; and it seems as if his internal response to the fear of infection is related to a fear that it is his gay body itself that puts him at risk. The sense of interwoven shame and envy is powerfully evoked in the various scenarios he describes, resulting in a kind of manic defence, which is made visible in his highly muscled body, built up, as it were, to protect him from what threatens him from both within and without.

In our discussion the therapist and I acknowledge the power of the patient's presentation, which is moving but also disturbing to us both; we are able to identify the degree of discomfort we each feel as fellow gay men sitting with such a painful experience of self-hatred, but we are equally able to think about this and what it means. I feel in such an example that the shared identity of all three parties creates an opportunity in supervision that may be challenging but is also highly productive. I am not aware in any detail of the therapist's personal history, but we are able in the context of our clinical and theoretical discussion to share an understanding of how such a homophobic attitude can be taken in and identified with by another gay man. I imagine that for the therapist, as for me, this is reflective of our own developmental experiences, which we can put at the service of the patient and the work. In addition, I feel we may embody a parental gay male couple symbolically holding this vulnerable and distressed young man in our minds, in our joint reflections and shared thinking.

I am not suggesting that a heterosexual or sexually mixed couple in supervision would be unable to share similar themes and reflections, nor to develop a similar understanding; however, the gay supervisory couple can, I believe, provide a further degree of recognition, which potentially deepens and enhances the therapeutic process. My understanding is that this recognition arises from the significant contribution made by the gay individual's personal experience and sense of shared identity, however different specific histories may be. This is a particular dimension of understanding that is forged in the context of growing up within a society marked by the hetero-normative and often homophobic attitudes referred to earlier in the chapter.

It is pertinent to reflect on my own personal and professional development as a further parallel here. The first decade of my therapeutic career took place in the HIV field at a time—the 1990s—when the majority of my patients were gay men, and the setting I worked in (a voluntary organization) also attracted many gay men as staff and volunteers. I can therefore identify with the attraction that gay practitioners may feel towards the setting of the sexual health clinic and the opportunities it offers to work with our own community. Such a setting can provide valuable opportunities for practitioners as well as for patients; and while identification must be recognized and carefully reflected on and its complexities worked through, it does not follow that we should avoid such a setting in order to protect ourselves (or our patients) from degrees of identification. Rather, as I hope to have shown, there are important, creative, and personally meaningful components in such a setting and such an encounter that are potentially extremely valuable.

Conclusion

A central argument of this chapter is that as practitioners we should be "out" to ourselves in terms of our sexual and gender identity, regardless of whether and where we might choose, as therapist or supervisor, to express this openly. As supervisors, it is especially important to make space for reflection in a more active way on the personal identities of both supervisee and supervisor, including the dynamics that our respective identities provoke in the supervisory relationship. With or without disclosure as therapists, I suggest that as supervisors there can be significant value in using ourselves in clinical reflection and discussion. I see this as a way of furthering those principles enacted by equality legislation, which could also be termed good professional practice. I believe this is what the BPC's position statement on homosexuality was intended to promote. I believe we are required to be willing to reflect on who we are and how we relate to different "others", although this may remain in some tension with traditional notions of analytic neutrality and absence of personal disclosure. I suggest that this process vitally includes but also goes beyond the fundamental idea of making use of our countertransference in clinical reflection. Blechner prompts us to reflect on the integration of our personal and professional identity as one way of expressing this; and as supervisors we can have an important role in encouraging and assisting this process of integration in our supervisees.

Note

I would like to acknowledge the work of my supervisees and to thank them for their permission to use their experience in this chapter. My supervisory work is an important part of my clinical caseload, which I both value and enjoy.

PART **II**

DESIRE

CHAPTER FOUR

Losing the internal oedipal mother and loss of sexual desire

Leezah Hertzmann

Adult couple relationships offer the chance for powerful early infantile sexual experiences to be reawakened and thereby provide a unique bonding experience sexually. However, a common problem for couples and individuals coming for therapy is loss of sexual desire. The problems that may be specific to same-gender couple relationships particularly in the area of sexual desire, have generally not been so widely explored in psychoanalysis compared to those of opposite-gender couples. Furthermore, there are noticeable gaps in the literature on the issue of same-gender desire in the transference and countertransference with therapist of either gender (Burch, 1996; Frommer, 1995; Ryan, 1998). Building on earlier ideas about same-gender desire and couple relationships (Hertzmann, 2011, 2015), this chapter aims to examine how it might be possible to use psychoanalytic concepts, specifically the loss of the unconscious oedipal mother, to explore a deeper understanding of the difficulties with conscious and unconscious same-gender sexual desires in psychoanalytic psychotherapy.

Using a composite case example[1] at various points throughout the chapter, I describe the loss of sexual desire in a lesbian couple's relationship, including how an erotic transference developed to the therapist and the challenges this can present. I consider some of the possible unconscious reasons for the loss of desire and its relationship to the move from what I refer to as the longed-for state of being in "perfect" harmony with the maternal object, and the accompanying belief that this has been finally found, to a more realistic state of imperfect harmony. I suggest how the longed-for state of merger can, for some, bring about the *recovery of an unconscious belief* that you can possess the oedipal mother, and that this belief can play a part in the loss or lessening of sexual desire. I suggest that this may be driven by a reluctance to both relinquish this belief, as well as give way to feelings of grief. The importance of aspects of technique, as well as the need for non-pathologizing concepts to support the clinician's formulations and therapeutic interventions when dealing with erotic transference and countertransference, are discussed.

The particularity of a sexual encounter with another woman both brings alive and echoes early unconscious interactions with primary caretakers.

The bodily sexual experience affecting the mind deeply pulls it back into a much more regressed state. I discuss how the necessary temporary collapse of boundaries of the self so central to sexual relating allows access to unconscious experiences from early infancy.[2] These boundaries may not be so immediately restored in some patients, and this can contribute to further difficulties in relationships. Although this chapter focuses on women's desires for women—specifically, women whose lesbian identity is felt by them to be stable and a given—the relevance of the ideas presented here for other gender pairings are also explored.

Conscious and unconscious desires: the longed-for state of perfect harmony

Maintaining and sustaining an adult couple relationship is not easy. Relating and, particularly, sexual relating involves encountering difference while making a deep emotional connection. To be truly intimate with another human being, to understand someone else's experiences in depth, involves sustaining difference between partners, not doing away with it. It would be tempting to assume that lesbian relationships are often unhelpfully lacking in separateness, something several authors have described as a state of fusion or enmeshment (Burch, 1985; Igartua, 1998). Ossana (2000) defines this as "a relational process in which the boundaries between the individual partners are blurred and a premium is placed on togetherness and emotional closeness" (p.

281). However, in my experience. lack of separateness is not necessarily always problematic for lesbian couples. Indeed, Burch (1997, pp. 93–94) found relationship longevity and satisfaction for lesbian couples was highly correlated with close involvement alongside relatively few experiences of feeling distinctly separated.

A central developmental feature of all adult relationships is the inevitable transition from the heightened sense of intense merger with excitement and apprehension of initial sexual exploration, to a less pressing and, for many, a more profound encounter with one's partner. Indeed, every long-term relationship needs to find a way to manage this evolution from first sexual encounters and longing to something more mature, yet still retaining some capacity for excitement and creativity. It is not always possible to maintain this objective consistently, and most couples will need to find a way to manage the inevitable ups and downs of life.

There are obvious conscious reasons for changes in sexual desires in all adult couple relationships, such as pressures of work responsibilities, parenting, the process of ageing, physical problems, the unavoidable tensions or difficulties in the relationship itself, as well as simply knowing one's partner better. Difficulties with sexual desire are often consciously understood as being caused solely by these kinds of demands and can be a common problem for couples of all gender pairings and sexual orientations. However, in my experience, loss of desire tends to come to light in the course of assessment rather than as the presenting problem, and for each couple it will have a unique trajectory and meaning. Clinically it would seem that for some lesbian couples, particularly those for whom there has been an initial wonderfully heightened state of merger with intense desire, the process of separation and the transition to linked separateness can be intensely painful—something I discuss in more detail below.

The internal parental couple and loss of the unconscious oedipal mother

Psychoanalysis views our encounter with the internal parental couple relationship as a fundamental psychic event in the course of our development (Ruszczynski, 1993). Whether the treatment is with a couple or an individual, the psychotherapist's task will involve exploring our encounter with the internal parental couple in earlier development. However, it is important to note that traditionally this concept of the internal parental couple has been heteronormatively constructed.

I have described elsewhere (Hertzmann, 2015, pp. 162–164) how, for some lesbian and gay couples, both partners desire to be in a couple relationship, but not like the heterosexual parental relationship they had grown up with. As well as dealing with their own internalized homophobia (Hertzmann, 2011), which can prevent partners inhabiting their sexual orientation fully, unconsciously some couples may in fact *"object"* to the intrapsychic presence of the internal heterosexual parent couple as a dynamic object residing within their shared unconscious world (Bannister & Pincus, 1965). I have named this predicament "objecting to the object" (for a more detailed description see Hertzmann, 2015, p. 157).

Extending these ideas further, I discuss the implications of what may be an important developmental moment prior to the internalization of the heterosexual parental couple—that is, the experience of losing the unconscious primary maternal oedipal object. This is a fine-grained moment in development and one that may, I think, be of crucial importance to couples generally, but especially to lesbian couples. Specifically, the oedipal mother is such an exciting object of passionate exclusive attachment, but, of course, this is necessarily lost in the process of development.[3] The shift a child has to make when she or he encounters the reality of the presence of the adult couple relationship involves dealing with a rival for the mother in the form of the father, partner (whether or not it is actually a male figure), or other important person in the mother's life, and ultimately, the realization that it is impossible to remain in this exclusive state.

In this chapter, I want to examine how this necessary developmental moment of transition which in the course of development is revisited, can unconsciously shape interactions for lesbian couples. In particular, it may be one of the drivers for the loss of sexual desire, also described by some as "lesbian bed death" (for a full description of this idea including the pejorative tone associated with it, see Iasenza, 2002). However, firstly I want to elaborate on a number of psychoanalytic ideas about early psychosexual development which have influenced the development of the ideas in this chapter.

Psychosexual development and contemporary psychoanalytic ideas

Psychoanalysis brings to the fore and elaborates an understanding of the powerful human drive to pair, begun in infancy, continued in development, and, for many, culminating in the formation of adult couple relationships. This drive and the complexity of that which is deeply desired, including sexual desire, emphasizes the connection between adulthood and infancy, conscious and unconscious, between past and present. Psychoanalytic theories speak to the interactions of children with parents of both genders in early infancy and childhood and how these experiences set the stage for psychosexual development. It is understood that the physical handling of the child's body contributes to the emergence and development of the infant's psychosexuality, in part through the attention to and tending of bodily functions. As Freud wrote in 1912, sexual instincts and "components of erotic interest" (1912d, p. 180) are discernible and correspond to the child's primary objects:

> . . . sexual instincts find their first objects by attaching themselves to the valuations made by the ego-instincts, precisely in the way in which the first sexual satisfactions are experienced in attachment to the bodily functions necessary for the preservation of life. [1912d, pp. 180–181]

Freud's papers that describe childhood sexuality (1905d) identified powerful, passionate, sexual feelings accompanied by intense and sometimes frightening fantasies. He recognized a period of psychosexual development preceding the formation of the Oedipus complex where the attachment to mother predominates in both sexes. Concerning female sexuality specifically, Freud emphasized the centrality, complexity, density and duration, of the primary relationship between the little girl and her mother (1931b).

Contemporaneously, Zepf, Zepf, Ullrich, and Seel (2016) discuss how Freud's original seduction theory is seen as neglecting the critical role of the parental unconscious, and they question the idea that children compete with mother or father for the love of the "rival" parent. They suggest that the child's oedipal experience should, rather, be considered as staged by the parents' unconscious oedipal strivings. These parental strivings are seen as unconsciously projected into the child and then processed by the child through identification. They go on to suggest that in this sense the father and mother could be seen as competing with the child for the love of the other parent, an idea that puts a different perspective on oedipal strivings in the triadic scenario and rearranges the direction of unconscious desires between parents and child.

Intimate adult sexual relationships recall early unconscious aspects of genital sexuality and fantasy, as well as experiences with parents during infancy and childhood. Such powerful feelings and fantasies from infancy are brought unconsciously to adult couple relationships by both partners, echoing early interactions with parents, a link that Target (2015, p. 44) describes as: "So obvious as to be easily missed. Adult sexual relating and foreplay suggests their roots in parent–infant interaction (kissing, hugging, tickling, nuzzling, stroking, baby words, names and voices), but the direction of this relationship may not be so obvious." The reawakening of infantile bodily feelings, the echoes of early interactions with parents of both genders, and the felt desires in adult sexual relating can collectively contribute to satisfying sexual desire.

Building on aspects of classical Freudian, object relations, and attachment theories, Target (2007, 2015) and Fonagy (2008) have constructed a clinically relevant model of adult psychosexuality incorporating the work of Laplanche (1976, 1987b, 1995; Laplanche & Pontalis, 1968), and Stein (1998a, 1998b, 2008). Their extension of these ideas and development of new concepts has provided clinically useful theories that elucidate the mystery (Stoller, 1985b) and the unfathomably profound quality that imbues erotic experience. Both Laplanche and Stein explain the influence on the child of the adult's unconscious sexual mind. They describe how the adult transmits an unconscious enigmatic message—enigmatic because of the repressed dimension of the nurturing adult's behaviours and speech towards the child, transmitted via gestures of ordinary care and handling of the infant. In the process of these interactions with the child, the mother touches and arouses the child's body parts, which, through her unconscious sexual mind, become eroticized. Thereby, the infant's mind is aroused to respond to the mother's sexuality that is always present and somehow expressed without her being conscious of it. Laplanche and Stein also speak of such a seduction establishing a child's sexuality and functioning as an enhancing, developmentally normative influence on a child's psychosexual development. Stein particularly describes the enigmatic and excessive (1998b, 2008) nature of the mother's sexuality—enigmatic owing to the non-transparency of her message even to herself. This may include a whole spectrum of unconscious sexual fantasies, such as same-gender sexual desires or sexual fantasies about a parental couple, being seduced or the seducer, sadomasochistic fantasies, and fantasies and experiences from the current adult sexual relationship. The mother's sexuality may also have been shaped by her experiences of the oedipal father, and these, too, may be present in her interactions with her infant, though not necessarily in her conscious awareness.

Stein (1998a) describes how the early confrontation of the infant with the adult world includes something intangible and nonverbal, exuding from the other in nonverbal powerful ways, and asks:

. . . —Can we retrieve this sense of enigmatic sexual experience, this stimulation of imagination experienced while the body is being stimulated, pleasured, tantalized and overwhelmed by an other? [Stein, 1998a, p. 620]

I would suggest that adult couple relationships offer the chance for such powerful early sexual experiences to be rekindled, reawakened, and thereby provide a unique bonding experience sexually. The enigmatic quality that is contained in the infant's experience of the excitement provides intensity of both bodily and psychic sensations and becomes a central and insistent driving force in adult sexuality, with the potential to shape the shared unconscious world of the couple's relationship. This may, in turn, bring alive the desire for and inevitable loss of the unconscious oedipal mother.

At this point I would like to introduce the reader to the composite case example to which I return in the course of the chapter to illustrate various points. To begin, I outline the individual histories of Anja and Christie, a lesbian couple whose unconscious couple fit was driven by early childhood oedipal issues that came to be understood as very problematic for their relationship.

Anja and Christie

Anja and Christie had been together for five years. They described their initial meeting as feeling that they had each found the soulmate they had long been seeking. For both, this was evident in the ways that they understood aspects of each other very deeply, including difficult experiences from their childhoods and their subsequent responses to these events.

Anja's parents were unhappily married and split up when Anja was 7. Her mother was a rather fragile self-interested woman, and her father was a charismatic though avoidant man. In childhood Anja had been her mother's confidante for the unhappy relationship with Anja's father. Anja's mother was frequently annoyed by the moments where Anja and her father would spend time together, for instance playing in the garden, and she objected to being left out of these fun times. She complained bitterly about all the tasks she felt she was left to do in the home, finding it unbearable to be excluded. This situation was the cause of frequent arguments between Anja's mother and father, as if they were in a competition for Anja's love and to be the preferred parent. However, something of an oedipal triumph occurred when Anja's father absented himself from the family home. Although these times of being her mother's confidante in part felt close and warm, her father's departure left Anja in utter disbelief, always hoping that he would return to release her from the burden of having to cope with her mother alone. Furthermore, in adolescence her mother viewed her early romantic partners and peer group friendships as rivalrous to their relationship, which became a source of many disputes.

For Christie, her parents had also been unhappily married. Her mother had been depressed and preoccupied for many years after several miscarriages and the death of a baby girl born after Christie. At these times, Christie felt her mother to be very distant from her, and this was exacerbated by her father's more tender involvement with her mother. Although this occurred rarely, it was difficult for Christie to witness. Not only was there an inevitable rival in the form of Christies' father, but, in addition, her mother's preoccupation and depression in response to both the baby death as well as her miscarriages became like another rival to Christie. When her mother was in less of a retreat, she sought out Christie, and these were times of closeness where Christie felt as if she was the most important person in the world to her mother and where her father would become sidelined. However, these occasions of closeness were often interrupted by her mother's depression and retreat, leaving Christie feeling very abandoned. From early on, she came to expect these abandonments as inevitable.

Re-finding the lost internal oedipal mother

Freud's idea, emphasized several times in his work, that the first seducer of the infant is the mother (Freud, 1905d), makes it possible to understand how in forming an adult couple relationship, each partner, regardless of sexual orientation, is unconsciously searching for that early oedipal experience with mother. Although this exclusive connection and attunement is ordinarily lost in development by the inevitable awareness of the adult sexual parental couple, it is possible to rekindle something of this early intense connection in the sexual life a couple creates together.

However, the feeling that the mother is ever fully possessed totally is an illusion. Laplanche (1976, pp. 19–20) posited that in the process of handling and feeding the mother unconsciously transmits traces of her own sexuality—"enigmatic messages"—to the child, that the child responds to with excitement. Newbigin (in chapter 1, this volume) explains clearly how: this excitement, however, is beyond the small infant's capacity to understand and process, and, as it is also mysterious and unrecognized by the mother, the child is left to struggle with her/his arousal alone. According to Laplanche, when such an instinct as hunger, feeding, changing and so on, having created excitation in the instinct, loses its natural object—the mother in this case—the ego is turned in on itself and left in an aroused state, what he termed "autoerotism" (1976, p. 19). He emphasizes that it is not an objectless state, rather:

> . . . the object to be rediscovered is not the lost object, but its substitute by displacement; the lost object is the object of self-preservation, of hunger, and the object one seeks to refind in sexuality is an object displaced in relation to that first object. From this, of course, arises the impossibility of ultimately ever rediscovering the object, since the object which has been lost is not the same as that which is to be rediscovered. [1976, p. 20]

Laplanche emphasizes that what is desired is not the object itself but, rather, the idea or feeling of the internal mother as object, elaborated in fantasy by the infant.

I am suggesting that, for some lesbian couples, the reawakening of early unconscious experiences with mother can have meaning in ways that are different from those experienced with someone of the opposite gender. (For a further detailed discussion of maternal erotic desire, transference, and countertransference see Wrye & Wells, 1994, pp. 33–87.) As far as the unconscious is concerned, a sexual relationship between two women may well constitute a real hope of finding the lost experience with mother again, or even induce a feeling that it has been found. The difficulty is that such an unconscious hope can then make psychic separation between the partners more difficult. Early oedipal experiences of merger and simultaneous loss, which are very challenging for an infant to manage, are reawakened and now have to be managed in adulthood, but this time with all the "un-done" boundaries, conscious and unconscious vulnerabilities, and investment that adult sexual relating involves.

Coming home

For many women, the choice of a female partner will likely include masculine fantasies and projections formed in development not just from encountering a male carer (where and if that has been the case), but also from the unconscious and conscious fantasies about male figures including those that the mother herself may carry and convey in her enigmatic messages to the infant. However, being with another woman in a lesbian couple can very directly tug at earlier infantile sexual experiences with the enigmatic sexual mother (although sexual fantasies may well include those of both genders as well as fantasies which are non-gender-specific). It is in this very moment that the early sexual experience lost to consciousness can be so powerfully rekindled in a relationship between two women. The sense of harmonious merger with another woman's body, the passion for someone of the same gender, unconsciously bring both partners up against the inevitable fact: the loss of the internal oedipal mother. I am proposing that the harmonious merger and longed-for state of being in perfect harmony brings about a *recovery of the unconscious belief* that you have, or can indeed possess, the oedipal mother. However, this presents something of a paradox, because as much as this early experience of both bodily and enigmatic aspects from early infancy may feel *as if* it has been re-found, simultaneously this is accompanied unconsciously by the knowledge of the inevitable and certain loss of the internal oedipal mother.

The particularity of a sustained sexual relationship with another woman brings alive and echoes early unconscious bodily interactions with mother, as well as, in its wake, the repetition of loss. I have often heard lesbian patients describing their sexual experiences with another woman as a feeling of *"coming home"*, and how in these moments there is a deeply profound and word-defying enigmatic quality. It is as if an early regressed and embodied state with the internal oedipal mother is made contact with again and finally symbolized. The experience for one woman of being with another is that the woman's body provides no concrete confirmation to the unconscious of the contrary. It is as if the unconscious is saying: "I know what another woman's body feels like, how it feels to be in this aroused state in the presence of someone of the same gender." In the context of a couple relationship this can have a unique meaning for each partner and influence the unconscious beliefs (Morgan, 2010) about the relationship, as well as driving interactions between them, including sexually.

I have found that it is not uncommon for couples presenting for therapy to describe quite lucidly their observation of a move from being in something like perfect harmony, a perfect partnership, to something much more disappointing. The ordinariness of life together feels as if it has destroyed, or at least severely impacted on, their unique earlier expectant union. A wonderfully intense initial encounter as a couple, perhaps even lasting for some time, comes to an end, the relationship takes on a different character, and sexual desire becomes problematic for one or both partners. Part of the work of therapy is to enable the unconscious conflicts and phantasies to become consciously known, so that the couple can accommodate to the lived reality of imperfect harmony, a more flawed partnership.

The initial state of being in perfect harmony can in itself bring about in the unconscious the *recovery of the belief* that you can indeed possess the internal oedipal mother. Of course, this process of adjustment—from the loss of the fantasy partner to a more true-to-life appraisal of the reality-based partner—is common to all relationships where development takes place. For most couples this is a significant shift to make and one which frequently causes difficulties for the relationship. I am proposing that the difference for lesbian relationships is that the deep connection brought about through sexual relating, these very moments of intense merger, not only allow but can facilitate the hope or belief that it is possible to possess the longed for internal oedipal mother. However, the difficulty is that in fact there are two losses being negotiated. There is not only a developmental pull necessary to make the adjustment from the fantasy to reality-based adult partner, but the loss of the unconscious oedipal mother is being simultaneously negotiated. The transition from fantasy to reality at two very distinct and important levels of encounter is not to be underestimated. Even where the loss of the internal oedipal object of desire in the mother may have been managed more or less well in development, it is in adult couple relationships that earlier aspects of unresolved oedipal losses and experiences can re-emerge, causing difficulties for the couple.

Desire and loss

It is understood that the revival of the original fantasy of possession, bringing with it the unconscious repetition of loss can ordinarily lead to an intensification and further elaboration of desire. However, I am suggesting that for some couples, it can instead lead to an intensification of loss rather than desire and that this occurs because of the couple's shared projective system. Specifically, within a couple relationship both partners' valency to receive the other's projections and to conform to that same projection shapes their shared unconscious world. Their experiences of loss in relation to early infantile experiences with mother, reawakened in their adult sexual encounter, are mutually projected into the other. That same projection, landing and taking root in fertile territory, matches the structure of the partner's internal world, thus exacerbating the already existing experience of loss. I am suggesting that the reciprocal projective encounter can then result in an intensification of the loss as opposed to an increase in desire.

The mutuality of these projections as well as the experience of another's body the same gender as one's own, could for some lead to particular kinds of unconscious beliefs driven by loss (Morgan, 2010) which then shape the relationship, along the lines of: "we can have this state of wonderful merger even though we know it was lost in the past". However, shared unconscious beliefs bring with them a shared unconscious accompanying defence which may be something like—"In order not to experience this loss of the primary maternal oedipal object, we need to remain in this unseparated merger to prevent this loss from occurring—again." Given the loss of both the oedipal object of desire and the loss of the fantasy partner to a more reality-based partner, it is perhaps not surprising that there might be a pull to try to avert these losses from occurring, as the demand on the psychic economy of the couple to make such a shift is considerable. I return to Anja and Christie here to illustrate some of these points.

> The presenting problem for this couple was that, over the past two years, Anja had had several sexual encounters with other women, the nature and duration of which she refused to talk about. These encounters had been preceded by a mutual loss of sexual desire in the relationship on both their parts, which was particularly upsetting to them as their initial coming together had been intense and powerful, unlike anything either of them had experienced before. Previously, the expression of their sexual desires for each other had just "happened with ease", and they described being able to read the other with such accuracy that it felt as if they were quite literally residing in each other's minds. As this initial excitement and intensity gave way to something less urgent between them, they found that sexual relating became more problematic. The adjustment to this now developmentally different phase of their relationship, which required them to talk about their sexual desires and fantasies, proved difficult and upsetting. Anja said that she felt her sexual desires had become dulled, and Christie reported that she was upset by the loss of passion, replaced, instead, by a palpable feeling of sadness. Anja responded to this loss of desire between her and Christie by seeking out other sexual experiences in order to reignite her sexual feelings, but this had not provided the hoped-for solution. Christie was extremely hurt and felt very betrayed. Anja was full of guilt and remorse, and Christie was the injured party, justified in her anger.

In the initial stage of the work it felt as if they were dealing with a profound loss, which seemed to have the gravity of something akin to a death. In terms of their couple projective system, the feelings of grief seemed to be particularly located in Christie—perhaps understandably, given her position as the injured party. However, it became clear that for Anja, her efforts to recover her sexual desire through her encounters with other women were in fact an attempt to re-find the lost sense of passion with Christie as well as the fantasy partner she had wished her to be. They were trying to deal with the grief surrounding the loss of feeling completely at one, which had been so profound and intense. However, although it was still unclear what might be behind their loss of sexual desire, it seemed more important at this stage of the work to try to get hold of their mutual projections in order that these could become more conscious.

The collapse and restoration of boundaries within the unconscious

Projections play a crucial role in so many aspects of a couple's relationship. The fit between a couple, their valency both to receive the other's projections and to conform to that same projection, contribute to the construction of the couple's shared unconscious world. Early experiences with primary caregivers, so powerfully reawakened in adult couple relationships, call for a deeper understanding of sexual desire for couples. Target (2015, pp. 51–52) describes how one's own pleasure is attained through taking control in fantasy of the thoughts and feelings of the other, occupying them in this moment of sexual intimacy as if to make their experience one's own, and then finally returning these thoughts and feelings to the other. Target states that it is not that experiencing oneself as the other inevitably brings pleasure and satisfaction; rather, she elucidates the way in which one's own pleasure can only be experienced when it has been inserted—or projected—into the other, in fantasy. These ideas make it possible to see how an integral part of sexual relating is the way in which one's own desires are lived out through being projected into the other, seen and experienced physically in the body, and thereby transformed and incorporated psychically as part of the self.

The capacity for mutual projections and fantasies, so necessary in sexual relating, crucially involves the temporary collapse of boundaries within the self at the intersections between the unconscious, the conscious, and the body, which, subsequent to sexual fulfilment and orgasm, can usually be restored to a pre-fantasy state. However, such a temporary collapse of boundaries within both body and mind can allow access to unconscious experiences from early infancy to be sharply rekindled. These experiences are then brought into the landscape of the couple's shared unconscious world, sometimes finding their expression not only in the sexual relationship, but in ordinary day-to-day encounters, ways of being together, perhaps playfulness, or in tensions and arguments—in essence, a whole range of behaviours and interactions.

Sexual relating requires that we abandon our internal stability, allow ourselves to come undone, step beyond normal body boundaries, behave in ways which might be described as unruly, excessive, insistent and eventually, these permeable boundaries can be flexibly restored. This moment of the collapse of boundaries, physically and in the mind, can be such a pleasurable moment of merger. However, in my clinical work with couples and individuals I have found that for some, the recovery of the boundaries within the self may not be so immediately possible. Where this is the case, the continuation of this vulnerable, opened-up state can lead to the exploration of sexuality becoming inhibited or defended against. In terms of projections, Morgan's idea of the "projective gridlock" (1995, pp. 3–48), while not referring specifically to sexual relating, speaks of a particular kind of experience in a couple, where projective identification is used by both partners to create a projective gridlock. This means that the couple have a problem feeling psychically separate and different from each other. Projections cannot be taken back in and re-introjected, so that each partner can find a way back to their own separate self. I am suggesting that the need to sustain mutual projections—and not to recover oneself—in sexual relating may be more pressing if the fantasy of possessing the unconscious oedipal mother is an ingredient. Then, projections may be less amenable to re-introjection. For the enigmatic nature of psychosexuality to find expression, some aspects of the fantasy partner will also have to remain in the partner's mind. The partner cannot become "too real", because in sexual relating there has to be space for fantasies and projections. However, this can collide with the psychic work required to address the boundary between the fantasy and reality partner, which developmentally, is the task the couple are trying to navigate. To illustrate this further, I return to the case example and, in particular, to the couple's sexual life together.

Anja and Christie described their previous ways of relating sexually together as highly mutually satisfying. They felt transported by each other to places of word-defying intensity, accompanied by vulnerability. These were feelings that were at times difficult to recover from in the immediate aftermath of sex, by which they meant it took a long time before they could "restore themselves from this opened-up state". They explained that what had been problematic and something of a downer was that, after making love, one or both would feel overwhelmed and tearful without quite knowing why. As they carried on with their day, these vulnerable feelings did not easily recede. While they had attributed this to their intense and fulfilling sexual relating, they had become aware of what they referred to as "an air of sadness" after sex. Over time, these sadder feelings intensified and became something both Anja and Christie wished to dodge; consequently, they found they were avoiding sex as a way of side-stepping these feelings. This was puzzling and upsetting, especially as previously their desires had been expressed with such apparent ease and intensity. They reflected that it was at around this time that each experienced a loss of sexual desire for the other, and they described how bitterly disappointing this was. Anja said, "We just can't find our way back to each other." Initially they tried to address their difficulties by talking about their feelings, exploring whether they could provide some comfort to each other, as well as the hope that by sharing their sexual fantasies, things might improve. However, none of these attempted solutions helped, and not only were they both distressed, their significant resentments towards each other quietly festered as a backdrop to their shared sadness and disappointment.

A while later, Anja and Christie came to a session having had a difficult argument. They had been talking about their lack of sexual desire, and Christie was demanding to know whether Anja had sexual feelings towards anyone at all, or whether her lack of desire was specific to her. In this difficult discussion, Anja had told Christie that she had had several erotic dreams over the past months involving me as the therapist and her together, but that she regarded these as irrelevant and unimportant because the therapy relationship was professional and not a real relationship anyway. In the session, Anja said her feelings were confusing because she wanted to feel desire for Christie again and, after all, that was why they were coming to therapy. My attempts to help them think about what Anja's sexual feelings towards me meant symbolically in terms of their relationship had little traction, and Christie was unable to shift her position from that of humiliated, aggrieved partner. Instead, she took what had happened as meaning that Anja, having had her desires brought alive in the therapy, would inevitably leave her for another—it was simply a matter of time. However, in my countertransference I had the feeling of having been involved in a highly illicit encounter, and this felt as if I had somehow been party to a betrayal. It was particularly perplexing because they had come to therapy for help with their sexual desires, and now one of the couple, Anja, had developed sexual feelings for another—me. I felt as if I was now the interloper, the rival coming between them, which I put to them. Christie's responded very concretely, congratulating me on the accuracy of my understanding. She said, "Yes, this is exactly how it is, you ARE the hated one coming between us."

Their polarized positions as guilty betrayer and injured betrayed partner, with me as hated other, remained fixed, and they began discussing the possibility of splitting up. Anja tried to reassure Christie she would not leave or betray her again, and yet Christie could not move from her position that something illicit had already taken place here in the therapy. Her struggle at the cusp of unconscious belief, fantasy, and reality was expressed most fully when she said, "I know it was a dream, but I can't get away from the fact that Anja has desires for you and not for me." The very thing Christie feared in her mind had happened. At this stage I was worried Christie would decide to leave the therapy, the relationship, or both.

An obvious triangular crisis had unfolded, and it was striking how different aspects of the oedipal scenario were distributed, alternating between the three of us. To each of them I became either the hated rival, or, at other times, I found myself in an overly cosy dyad being part of an interaction that excluded the other. I was not quite able to establish how exactly this had happened (couple psychotherapists working psychoanalytically would be acutely aware of this kind of scenario and watchful for its occurrence). Not only was there a lack of desire sexually between them, there was a striking lack of desire for an intercourse in the mind about what was happening in the therapy. This seemed to have got split off and projected into me. Through their polarized positions, they could avoid being put in mind of their own unresolved and painful oedipal dilemmas in each of their histories—namely, the loss of the desired object, witnessing and being observer of a couple, the inevitable experience of exclusion, and the burden of oedipal triumph. At around this time they told me that together they had considered that perhaps Anja should carry on in the therapy with me on her own, and that Christie should try to solve her problems elsewhere. Christie's belief that Anja would leave and, in effect, had already done so seemed irrefutable.

Issues of technique in the therapy when working with a couple where one partner has an erotic transference are demanding. In terms of Anja's erotic feelings emerging in the transference to me, I found that it was almost automatic to interpret these erotic feelings, and something that at the time felt important to do. Their sexual feelings as a couple, which had appeared to evaporate, were now located between Anja and me. Interventions designed to explore feelings and thoughts and which, by their very nature, introduced curiosity, doubt, or uncertainty were treated by Christie as a threat to be extinguished, because they hit up against the certainty of her belief that Anja would leave. Her conviction that she could control events as well as me in the therapy was striking. She thought that by holding on to this belief, she could not only correct past losses, but, if she lived as if these events had already occurred and related to them accordingly, she would be protected from further abandonments. Any different view, ambivalence, or doubt was experienced by Christie as betrayal. There was simply no reality other than that which she held. For Christie, Anja's erotic preoccupation with me replayed her own mother's preoccupations and abandonment of her. Although their turmoil and anger was striking during this part of the work—particularly Christie's towards me—what was also noticeable was the atmosphere of sadness in the room, which it seemed important to explore further in due course.

The enactment of abandonment and loss

A phenomenon that I have encountered in my clinical work is where there is simultaneously a loss of sexual desire and a sense of abandonment, expressed by either member of the couple thinking their partner has already abandoned or is about to abandon them. This then organizes the relationship in such a way that the couple behaves as if the other—this time their partner—has already been lost. A feared or anticipated abandonment is related to as if it has already happened or is about to happen again. The unconscious knowledge that the oedipal mother has been lost before and symbolically will be again is then related to as if it is happening in the here and now. The paradox is, of course, that unconsciously the loss of the oedipal mother has already happened, but the difficulty is this: the hope that as a couple they could possess the oedipal mother again has been rekindled and reawakened in the unconscious, and therefore the feelings of loss, including loss of sexual desire and abandonment, are felt even more acutely. Returning to the clinical example of Anja and Christie, this was an issue that became very problematic in the therapeutic work.

At this time, my interventions highlighted how, in the transference, I was alternately either a hated rival or in a cosy dyadic encounter that left the other excluded and betrayed. For Anja and Christie to be a couple in the room and in the presence of an observer—whether I or their own capacity to stand aside from their interactions and note what was happening in their relationship—was challenging. Even to allow some curiosity about what was occurring in the therapy felt as if it was a betrayal against Christie's certain belief that Anja would leave. Furthermore, in Christie's mind Anja had already done so through channelling her feelings towards me and not her, and she related to Anja as if this had already occurred.

It would have been tempting to try to counter this belief, which Christie so firmly held about Anja, to attempt to loosen its grip. However, I was also aware that if I took up the material in this way, then the erotic transference would risk not being attended to. The exploration of Anja's erotic transference and sexual feelings towards me made for some difficult sessions, where Christie felt again betrayed and humiliated. For me to be in the presence of these erotic feelings as well as Christie's hatred, and not to rush to interpret or skip over them, was taxing. In my countertransference, I felt under intense pressure to demonstrate to Christie that I was not a threat, but I also felt that something primal and erotic was alive between Anja and me.

In terms of the erotic transference, I regarded Anja's sexual feelings not only as belonging to her, but as a communication on behalf of them both about their sexual life together as a couple. The nature and content of Anja's erotic fantasies and dreams bore similarities to what she and Christie described having lost. It felt important to stay with Anja's exploration of sexual desires without either rejection or enactment and to try to work with these desires in the transference, with the eventual aim that sexual feelings could be reintrojected between them in their couple relationship. This was especially difficult for Christie, as it involved the elaboration of Anja's desires in her presence. Furthermore, Christie's feelings of anger and betrayal towards me in the transference needed frequent exploration.

Gradually, through linking their experiences of me as both rival and desired object to their respective experiences in childhood, unconscious oedipal desires could become more conscious, accompanied by the pain at the recognition of what had been lost. Anja's erotic feelings became less foregrounded and she faced the reality of the nature of the therapy relationship—that she could never possess me, the desired object in the ways she had fantasized. As Anja became more in touch with the sadness of the loss of me as a potential sexual partner, she was able to feel the pain of the loss of the exclusive merger she and Christie had experienced together. Christie's experience of witnessing an exclusive coupling had been unbearable, both in the therapy and in childhood. However, her expectation of being abandoned became less certain, and she was now able to notice that she had not been deserted by Anja, nor by me as the therapist. She came to understand how important this belief had been, serving the function of protecting her. With this firm belief "in her armour", as she put it, she could exert control over painful events, predict being abandoned, and always be prepared for this certain eventuality. In addition, she was able to begin to think about how her certainty of the future shaped the present, how she then related to Anja in ways that could push her to enact the very thing she feared.

By attempting to stay with and interpret these uncomfortable feelings in the transference, informed by my countertransference experience, it became possible for this couple to begin to grieve the oedipal losses that had played a part in their loss of sexual desire. To understand that neither could totally possess the other was an important unconscious belief they had held, which informed the way their relationship developed. Many of their oedipal dilemmas and losses had not only been played out in their couple relationship, but had come alive in the therapy.

Discussion

Anja and Christie's relationship difficulties brought to light the need to deal with some important oedipal losses. The temporary collapse of boundaries within the self, as previously outlined, allowed access to unconscious experiences from early infancy to be sharply rekindled. Crucially, their experience of sadness post love-making was an important indicator of the pre-existing knowledge of the inevitable loss of the oedipal mother who can never be fully possessed. The loss of the sexual desire stood as the symbolic manifestation of the loss of possessing the oedipal mother and was expressed in their sadness. This sadness thwarted the developmental task of both dealing with the loss of the fantasy partner and, simultaneously, accommodating to the more real-life partner in an adult couple relationship.

In terms of the couple's projective system, it was striking how some distinct aspects of loss and grief had been split between Anja and Christie. The recognition that the lost object cannot be replaced was located in Christie, whose valency for this was shaped by her firm belief that she would eventually be abandoned. However, Christie's belief of certain abandonment was projected into Anja, who became the abandoning, betraying partner. Anja's internal landscape fitted the shape for this projection, and her response to the disbelief she felt in relation to this loss, accompanied by an intense need to actively recover the lost object, led to her seeking out encounters with other women. Anja described the loss of her and Christie's intense and profound sense of merger as akin to what happens following a death: "It's like expecting the person will walk through the door again . . . and I suppose that in the same way I keep expecting that we will get this passion and connection back, just like before." Holding the reality of what had been lost for them as a couple seemed to be Christie's role, while Anja actively tried to restore the previous state they had inhabited together.

I came to understand Anja's erotic transference to me in the therapy as the rerouting of their sexual desires as a couple, and although this was intensely painful for them, I regarded it as a developmental step. Their sexual desire had not been lost entirely but, rather, came to be known about in the therapy, so that oedipal losses from the past could be worked through in the transference. The aspects of felt betrayal, attendant with the Oedipus situation, had important meanings for Christie and Anja. Anja's sense of betrayal by her father for leaving her with her mother, which she found a tremendous burden, and Christie's sense of betrayal by her mother's psychic retreat were part of their unconscious couple fit.

Their powerful and intense pull at the start of their relationship promised the hope of being able to recover and maintain an exclusive connection they had lost without either the abandonment or rivalry by a third. This wonderful sense of merger was cruelly interrupted by a bewildering loss of desire, which caused them much distress. In the transference, I came to represent the betrayal they had both experienced. It emerged that the exclusive connection they had both longed for and thought they had found had, in the past, also been very burdensome to them. Contained within their intense connection there was, simultaneously, an unconscious need to get away from this merged state in order to find their true and separate selves.

Working with erotic feelings in the transference and countertransference is technically challenging but perhaps especially so when working with couples. Oedipal issues are already foregrounded by the configuration of three people in the therapy setting, which primes the shared unconscious world of the couple, bringing to awareness early childhood experiences of inclusion and exclusion. Target (2015, p. 61) writes of an intensive therapeutic relationship offering a way forward because, like a sexual relationship, it can provide recognition of sexual feelings without the weight of rejection that can be felt in a relationship in the outside world. However, like a parental relationship, it helps the patient to develop, regulate, and represent feelings without fulfilling the need to enact them.

Working with couples who are already struggling with oedipal losses to explore the erotic transference located in one partner while the other tolerates the inevitable exclusion this involves requires the therapist to not be pushed off balance, either by the anger in one partner or the wish for exclusive connection in the other. As Stein (2008), writes so clearly, to not

> hurry over experiential aspects of sexuality our patients describe (or defend against describing) to us. Patients tell us of encounters or practices that are sometimes strange, excessive, "perverse", and irrational, and we at such moments hastily reach for explanations that help us normalize such experiences. [p. 56]

Appropriately interpreting the unconscious while simultaneously enabling patients to stay with and experience a wide variety and range of sexual desires and fantasies can be technically demanding for therapist and patient, but perhaps particularly so when working with couples.

Concluding thoughts

This chapter has described how, for some lesbian couples, the longed-for state of being in perfect harmony and the temporary collapse of frontiers within the unconscious may allow more direct access to aspects of early infantile sexual experiences with the unconscious experience of the oedipal mother. This can bring about repeated moments of recovery of an unconscious belief that you can, indeed, possess the internal oedipal mother. However, the transition from intense merger with a partner to developmental separation necessitates facing the loss of that state of pleasure of being in perfect harmony and unconsciously once again relinquish possession of the internal oedipal mother. This can be symbolically expressed as a loss of sexual desire and can often be accompanied by a sense or fear of abandonment. The unconscious knowledge that the internal oedipal mother has been lost before and symbolically will be again can then organize the relationship in such a way that the couple behaves as if the other—this time their partner—has already been lost.

For some couples and individuals, this can present as a loss of sexual desire, as one or both partners struggle to flexibly inhabit a relationship where they can adjust to a more reality-based relationship, while still retaining the capacity for fantasies and projections that can enrich their experiences together. The paradox is that, of course, the loss of the oedipal mother has already happened. Therefore, the feelings of loss and abandonment can be felt even more acutely and may risk being dealt with in an unreconstructed state of grief.

While this chapter has focused on women's desire for women, I want to briefly consider the relevance of these ideas for other gender relationship pairings. I have described elsewhere (Hertzmann, 2015, pp. 158–159) how crucial it can be for couples to understand and acknowledge a wide range of identifications with, and desire for, both genders. I described how, for a gay male couple (Hertzmann, 2015, pp. 164–168), their struggle with being able to flexibly inhabit these identifications and desires led to considerable difficulties with desires in their relationship. In my clinical experience I have also encountered heterosexual couples whose loss of sexual desire seemed best understood as having its roots in an unconscious prohibition in both partners to identify with and feel sexual desire for the same gender, as well as an embargo on erotic same-gender fantasies and the wish for enactment. These were felt to be a threat to the very survival of the relationship. To acknowledge that a range of gender-fluid fantasies and desires could be part of a heterosexual relationship can enable some couples to find new ways to explore their sexual desires, which may have previously been blocked by an unconscious ban. Whatever the gender pairings in a relationship, the need to flexibly inhabit, identify, enact, and explore gender fantasies, identifications, and roles is central to understanding what happens to sexual desire in relationships. To transcend sexual and gender binaries, for gender and sexual fluidity to be more foregrounded in the therapy and in psychoanalysis could provide possibilities to deepen our understanding of the conscious and unconscious nature of desire in our patients, regardless of their sexual orientation or gender identity.

Therapeutic relationships and couple relationships both provide the arena for intimacy to be achieved on an adult level, coloured and enhanced by the richness of childhood oedipal wishes. Elise (2015, p. 284) describes the working through of unrequited oedipal longing within the therapeutic relationship as "one of the most profound gifts of an analysis. The child's confrontation with thwarted desire (generationally) for either parent is central to the development of the mind, the personality, and one's erotic life." There are, of course, inevitable differences between how this might be managed in work with a couple or when working with an individual patient. However, I think it is not only possible but crucial to also work with couple issues very directly with individual patients, because when an individual seeks help, for whatever reason, they are in fact treated by a couple relationship: the intimate relationship of patient and therapist (Ruszczynski, 1993, p. 9).

Enabling patients to explore sexual and erotic feelings, to lift prohibitions and encounter a range of desires in the transference and countertransference, can be challenging for therapists, but particularly when working with both partners of a couple together. Yet, if approached with sufficient flexibility and close attention to the unconscious, it can potentially support patients to develop and come to know about aspects of their own psychosexuality in treatment, which may help their capacity to make and sustain adult couple relationships.

Notes

1. I have chosen to include a composite case example to protect patient confidentiality. This example is based on several cases seen in treatment, both in clinic and private practice settings, dating from 2006–12. Characteristics of different cases have been combined to illustrate overarching themes. The balance of potential problems of privacy with scientific reporting in this chapter has therefore been considered in significant detail. I am grateful to the editor and reviewer of earlier drafts of this essay for help with this matter.

2. Regarding the idea of unconscious experience, this is an area of much philosophical debate within psychoanalysis. It includes the idea that to speak in terms of one's capacity to "experience" the unconscious if the very concept of the unconscious refers to that which is beyond one's experience, does not make sense. Indeed, the idea of suffering "unconscious experiences" may be seen as highly contradictory if one is not consciously aware of the experiences that are presumed to be suffered by the patient. In this chapter, the approach regarding unconscious experience is that "experiences" that have been repressed reside "in" the unconscious, engendering psychic conflicts. The manifestation of these account for psychopathology and can be brought to consciousness in the transference and countertransference in the therapy relationship, as well as in the couple's relationship. However, the question of "experience"—and the many different philosophical positions within this debate—is beyond the scope of the chapter.

3. In this chapter, I am focusing on the oedipal mother rather than the pre-oedipal mother, which can be regarded as a separate topic. In terms of oedipal mother, I am particularly thinking of the difficulty for the child in recognizing the parental relationship and the ways in which they may wish to link with each parent separately, having an exclusive union with one and therefore excluding the other parent.

CHAPTER FIVE

The primary maternal oedipal situation and female homoerotic desire

Dianne Elise

About ten years ago, I was asked to teach a psychoanalytically based course on lesbian object choice. I was at a loss regarding what literature to assign; there seemed to be very little analytic literature that addressed female same-sex object choice without being a priori pathologizing. I finally realized that the classic papers that I taught on female psychosexual development needed only to be examined for their implicit content regarding female homoeroticism. I assigned these papers, and we read them through a lens that focused on lesbian rather than heterosexual developmental paths. I found it quite ironic that at that time the literature trying to explain the "circuitous route" (Freud, 1931b) to female heterosexuality was actually the best place in the analytic literature to get a fair accounting of female homosexuality. One does not have to read far to see that psychoanalysis has not found female heterosexuality to be very "straightforward". By implication, lesbianism can be seen as a quite understandable developmental outcome. In this chapter, I intend to examine closely classical theory on the female oedipal complex in order to shed light on same-sex object choice.

In spite of what I have just described regarding the analytic literature, for many years it became customary within psychoanalysis—mirroring the homophobia of the culture at large—to feel that it is homosexuality that needs explaining: how is it that a woman comes to have a female object choice when heterosexuality would be the normal and expected path? In her 1992 paper, "Heterosexuality as a Compromise Formation", Chodorow challenged this thinking by emphasizing that it is just as important to explore the development of a heterosexual outcome to the oedipal complex. Freud and other early analytic theorists most definitely felt that female heterosexual object choice needed explaining: how is it that a girl would come to choose her father as her erotic object when her mother was already in that place (as she was for the boy). Unless one invokes innate heterosexuality (as Horney and Klein were to do) and denies the erotic nature of the early mother–daughter relationship, exclusive female heterosexuality is a puzzle.

In our efforts to understand female development, psychoanalysis has frequently slipped into a quicksand of assumptions. It is important to be able to think conceptually about girls' development without automatically making assumptions about the body, gender identifications, and sexual orientation. Tyson (1982) has taken pains to distinguish and separately define core gender identity, gender identity, gender role identity, and sexual orientation, but often in theory elaboration these concepts collapse into one another. Horney (1924), Jones (1927), and Klein (1932b), in refuting Freud, argued that a girl does not begin life as "a little man"; instead, they leapt to a conclusion that has her start out as a little woman: innately feminine and inherently heterosexual.

In order to understand that lesbianism is just as "natural" as female heterosexuality, one need only consider the concept of bisexuality. I believe bisexuality to be a very rich and useful concept that has been underutilized. Stoller (1972) emphasized the centrality of this concept for Freud as an essential building block in theory from Freud's first writings to his last. Freud (1905d) himself stated: "Without taking bisexuality into account, I think it would scarcely be possible to arrive at an understanding of the sexual manifestations that are actually to be observed in men and women" (p. 220). Freud believed that an inherent, constitutional mix of male and female traits influenced both object choice and the degree of a person's masculinity and femininity. Unfortunately, Freud's theory of bisexuality—itself not internally consistent—included the proposal that the girl's earliest sense of herself was not truly bisexual, but male and masculine.

Stoller (1972, 1974) critiqued Freud's effort to ground bisexuality in a constitutional basis and stressed, instead, the psychological basis of bisexuality. Stoller (1974) maintained that "bisexuality should still serve as a central theme in understanding human psychology" (p. 392). Object choice and overt sexual orientation, along with gendered sense of self, are encompassed within this concept. I agree that we can utilize, as did Stoller, the concept of psychic bisexuality without putting the girl in a male or androgynous body. As Tyson (1982) clarified, core gender identity, gender identity, and sexual orientation are distinct. Thus, one can have a self-concept as female and be bisexual or lesbian in object choice. Much work has been done emphasizing that the mother is the first love object for the girl as well as for the boy. The girl's object relational constellation centrally involves the experience of homoeroticism as well as heteroeroticism.

As mentioned above, however, psychoanalytic theory has tended towards accepting heterosexual outcomes as "natural" and not in need of examination or explanation (Chodorow, 1992; Schafer, 1974). In contrast, anything other than heterosexual object choice appears as deviation from the "norm", pathological, and, thus, in need of explanation. This attitude prevails despite Freud's (1905d) statement that psychoanalysis "has found that all human beings are capable of making a homosexual object choice and have in fact made one in their unconscious" (p. 145). Schafer notes that, as early as 1905, Freud "had come to realize that genital heterosexuality is a difficult, imperfect, more or less precarious achievement" (Schafer, 1974, p. 469), and Schafer concludes: "It is one great consequence of Freud's discoveries that our psychoanalytic explanations may no longer presuppose any natural or pre-established culmination of human psychosexual development" (p. 471). While Horney challenged Freud's formulation, she invoked innate heterosexuality and the naturalness of motherly feeling—a step in a much more conservative direction than that of Freud. I believe we must incorporate the concept of psychic bisexuality in order to follow, with an open mind, *various* developmental paths regarding object choice in females.

Freud (1931b, 1933a), in particular, devoted much attention to the "riddle of femininity". In taking bisexuality quite seriously, Freud could see that a girl's early erotic relationship to her mother was no less significant than it was for the boy. Why would the girl let go of this first object of desire and reroute to the father—a relative stranger to her erotic life? Although Freud developed the very convoluted explanation that the turn to the father could be understood in terms of penis envy (versus an object-related erotic desire that could be easily encompassed within the theory of bisexuality[1]), Freud seemed to be puzzled by female psychosexuality to the end of his career.

Possibly the most central and perplexing question in the history of psychoanalysis has been, "What does a woman want?"—almost a lament as initially posed by Freud (1925j), who seemed frustrated enough with this dilemma to hand it over to female colleagues and future generations of theorists. This has led to numerous responses and further questions, with a recent and most cogent answer by Benjamin (1988) that women *want to want*, to have a sense of agency and desire: sexual subjectivity. I propose that the obscuring of female desire has centrally to do with the fate of eroticism in the early mother–daughter relationship.

A woman wants her mother

Freud admitted to being at a loss regarding female desire and deferred to female analysts, who, he felt, might be better equipped than he to probe the early relationship with the mother for potential answers. I believe, however, that Freud (1931b) had nine tenths of the answer to his query but could not quite bring himself to believe it (Young-Bruehl, 1990), and many theorists since have been similarly perplexed. Zak de Goldstein (1984) points out that some of Freud's own metaphors, like the "dark continent", worked to obscure further the subject of female sexuality, "thus *a priori* making the key question 'what does a woman desire?' difficult or even impossible to answer" (p. 180) (see also Olivier, 1989). I suggest that Freud was actually closer to the heart of the matter than has been much of the subsequent literature.

Freud became clear that the first thing a girl wants is her mother. That desire is most often denied (Butler, 1990, 1995; De Lauretis, 1994; Laufer, 1986; Lax, 1994, 1997; Rubin, 1975). However, unlike the boy's situation, where this desire is *acknowledged* and then forbidden, a girl's desire for her mother is typically erased, negated, made invisible, non-existent. That a girl wants her mother is generally not seen or registered by the mother; it remains an *unrecognized* desire. Benjamin (1988) writes of the importance of mutual recognition and of the need to see the mother as a sexual subject. Both are essential to a girl's sexuality: but can the mother *see the daughter* as a sexual subject? Can mother–daughter homoerotic desire be experienced and validated *by the mother*? The heterosexual gaze sees the boy's desire for the mother and, eventually, the girl's desire for the father but is blind to the girl's directing of these impulses and wishes to the mother (Burch, 1997; Butler, 1990, 1995; De Lauretis, 1994; Kernberg, 1991; O'Connor & Ryan, 1993; Zak de Goldstein, 1984).

Zak de Goldstein (1984) writes that the infant receives precise instructions through the mother's gaze:

> The mother neither looks at nor manipulates the girl in the same way as the boy. Her gaze summarizes expectations and wishes that order and define the sexual profile of each . . . She receives from a distance her father's sexual instructions as well. [pp. 182, 183]

Kernberg (1991) considers the impact on the girl of the "mother's subtle and unconscious rejection of the sexual excitement which she would freely experience in relation to the boy": the girl would "gradually become less aware of her own genital impulses" (p. 356).

Although mothers might be anxious about erotic feeling in relation to sons (and thus, not consciously experience such desire "freely"), the anxiety itself indicates the registering of heteroerotic desire (Chodorow, 1978). Olivier (1989) describes the contrasting situation, where the girl is a nonoedipal object for the mother and as a result of her mother's nondesire comes to feel that she is "unsatisfactory, incapable of satisfying" and later is "never satisfied with what she has or what she is" (p. 44).[2] (see also Bergmann, 1995; Halberstadt-Freud, 1998). In Butler's (1995) terms, the daughter's desire for the mother is foreclosed in a never-never land of the "sexually unperformable" (p. 178)—a possibility that can no longer be conceived of and, thus, cannot be grieved.

For every child, object loss and hunger occur first in relation to the mother and are focalized in the experience of "weaning". Girls, however, are not just weaned from the breast as a source of milk and comfort. If their future is to be heterosexual, they are not going to get the breast back as a source of sexual gratification. Klein (1932b) believed that in response to oral frustration in relation to her mother, a girl turns to the father and takes his penis as her object of satisfaction. However, this explanation fails to account for why the same sequence would not occur for a boy. It seems unlikely that he would experience less oral frustration than the girl. Unlike a boy, who, of course, is also weaned, a girl loses the nipple, and her mother as sexual object, forever.

Data indicates that suckling is sexually stimulating to infants of both sexes; in the case of girls, vaginal stimulation and lubrication result (Kestenberg, 1956, 1982; Kleeman, 1976). Analytic writers beginning with Freud (1905d) have acknowledged the sexuality in the mother–infant relation: "The sexual instinct has a sexual object outside the infant's own body in the shape of his mother's breast" (p. 222). This bodily component adds to the intensity of the experience with the mother as first love object for both boy and girl. What has been less acknowledged is the nature and degree of the impact for a girl in giving up her mother as her first sexual object as she moves from pre-oedipal development through the various oedipal stages.

It is evident that preoedipal and oedipal development does not involve distinct phases in strict linear sequence, nor does a girl abruptly turn from her mother to her father (Laufer, 1986). Much over-lap occurs in relating to mother and father, both preoedipally and oedi-pally. However, in heterosexual development, a girl *resolves* the oedipal complex with her father as sexualized love object. Freud's (1931b) insight must be kept in mind that many women never completely relin-quish their original libidinal attachment to their mother, and some women insistently retain it, never achieving "a true change-over towards men" (p. 226).

Freud (1931b) stated that with the girl's turn to the father and cir-cuitous winding into femininity, she relinquishes (not without a struggle) her sexuality, her desire, and her activity, as well as her mother as love object. She stops masturbating, he thought. Her sexu-ality is permanently injured (see also Lampl-de Groot, 1927). How much more explicit could these statements be? Freud notices that in female sexuality something that was previously in motion comes to a halt. This halt is coexistent with the turn from mother to father as primary sexual love object, and Freud notes that this shift is unlikely to occur completely or without conflict; the oedipal relation to the father inherits qualities of the original relationship with the mother, and women are often looking to refind their mothers in their hus-bands. A girl's desire seems to lose something after the "negative" oedipal, and this may be where a certain sexual "diffusivity" sets in.[3]

Freud (1924d, 1925j), writing on the dissolution of the Oedipus com-plex, emphasized that things go very differently for the two sexes. Yet, boys and girls are *not* so different in their oedipal experience if the focus is kept on the first love object. This perspective leads to another way of understanding the girl's longer "preoedipal" period as actually encompassing her initial oedipal situation. It is the desire for the mother that is "smashed" (Freud, 1925j) for both sexes—even more totally for a girl. It is what each sex does next in relation to the father that greatly differs, and it is here that lesbian object choice may diverge as well.

Certain commonalities in oedipal experience for the two sexes become much more apparent if one thinks of oedipal situations (Klein,

1928, 1945) in terms of a *primary-maternal*—first temporally and in archaic intensity—and then a *secondary-paternal*, rather than a positive and negative Oedipus complex. This latter conceptualization is a view through a heterosexual lens that obfuscates important realities. Thinking in terms of primary and secondary oedipal experience follows more closely the developmental reality for most children of early female caretaking (Chodorow, 1978) and stays with Freud's emphasis on the centrality of bisexuality.[4]

The primary oedipal situation—each child with the mother under predominant child-rearing arrangements—is quite similar for each sex, which is why Freud thought of the girl as a little man; he could not quite get his theory of bisexuality fully into his own language possibilities. Schafer (1974) notes that

> it is not inaccurate to attribute to Freud a relative neglect of bisexuality . . . for his theory of development the important thing was to get the girl to become *feminine* and ready to receive love and babies *passively* from an active man . . . he needed a sustained phallic perspective. But that perspective is not inclusive enough for his own psychoanalytic discoveries. [p. 477]

It is the secondary oedipal situation—the relationship each sex has in desiring the father—that truly brings up sharp gender differences. This is the phase where heterosexual complementarity gets established (Benjamin, 1988, 1995), leading to a repression for theorists frequently, as well as for children, about what went before. As Freud emphasized, this repression regarding the relationship of desire for the mother is especially strong for girls. However, I would add that not *all* girls repress this desire.

Speaking of the girl, Enid Balint (1973) stated: "I assume that if she was satisfied by her mother's body she rightly felt that her own body satisfied her mother" (p. 200). I do not believe we can necessarily make this assumption: something potentially traumatic does seem to be evidenced in girls' sexual development. The existence of girls' "castration depression" (Brakel, 1986; Mayer, 1995)—or, in separation–individuation terms, the "depressed mood" of rapprochement girls (Mahler, Pine, & Bergman, 1975)—argues against any attribution of confidence to a girl regarding her body's ability to satisfy either her mother or, subsequently, herself. I find taking a close look at Lampl-de Groot's early work quite intriguing.

Lampl-de Groot (1927), like Freud, refers to the greater degree in females than in males of libidinal repression—a "sacrifice" of her active strivings towards the mother in order for passive feminine love of the father to be "victorious" (p. 340). Lampl-de Groot emphasizes "how extraordinarily difficult it is for a child to give up the possession of the mother, who has been his love object since he was capable of object-love at all" (p. 333). Lampl-de Groot intends this previous statement to include the girl:

> To the boy castration was only a threat, which can be escaped by suit-able modification of behaviour. To the girl it is an accomplished fact, which is irrevocable, but the recognition of which compels her finally to renounce her first love-object and to taste to the full the bitterness of its loss. [p. 337]

This, I believe, is the depression and trauma of "castration" for a girl; it concerns object relational loss (Elise, 1998a). This point raises interest-ing issues regarding lesbian development: does a girl who retains a homoerotic focus feel less castrated, less injured in her sexuality? Or, if she too is feeling erotically devalued but keeps the mother as object choice, what might this tell us about her particular experience of the oedipal phase? I am not envisioning a single experiential path, but I am emphasizing the relevance of these issues in varying ways for les-bians as well as for heterosexual women.

Lampl-de Groot (1927) underscores that the castration complex in girls is *preceded* by the negative oedipal complex. Castration ends this mother love in that a girl is typically pressed to abandon completely her negative oedipal stance and instead to present herself passively to the father: "Thus, in female children the castration-complex deals a deathblow to the negative Oedipus attitude and ushers in the posi-tive Oedipus complex . . . *a secondary formation*" (p. 340; italics added). This statement is in accord with my thinking in proposing to relabel the negative oedipal complex in girls as the primary maternal oedipal situation.

Lampl-de Groot's position is that a girl's castration reaction has to have a prehistory. It is only due to its precursor—the negative oedipal love—that the castration complex in girls assumes its great significance. Freud (1926d, p. 139) was aware that for a boy the narcissistic value of the penis is its guarantee of eventual (re)union with the mother. It was difficult for both Freud and Lampl-de Groot to see that the penis has this same "narcissistic" value for a girl, even though Lampl-de Groot (1927) does emphasize that a girl "can never succeed in securing her first love-object, while the man, when he grows up, has the possibility of doing so" (p. 339).

Freud was in somewhat of "a pickle" with regard to his developing theory of female sexuality. He also had an interesting and confused relationship to Lampl-de Groot and her theory (which is widely taken to be merely a restatement of Freud's ideas). Both Freud and Lampl-de Groot understood the intensity of a girl's desire for her mother and Freud (1933a) states his complete agreement with Lampl-de Groot's (1927b) paper. However, Freud's thinking slips in logic when he moved to the idea that a girl experiences the lack of a penis as a purely narcissistic wound separate from her oedipal desire for the mother. *Penis envy needs to be understood as reflecting a negative oedipal, object relational injury.* Freud (1923b) neglects his own theory regarding the negative oedipal:

> The simple Oedipus complex is by no means its commonest form, but rather represents a simplification or schematization. . . . Close study usually discloses the more complete Oedipus complex, which is two-fold, positive and negative [or, in the girl's case, negative and positive] and is due to the bisexuality originally present in children. [p. 33]

Freud continually had trouble holding onto his own contribution regarding "this complicating element introduced by bisexuality" (p. 33), and this is most apparent when he ends up with a penis envy dislocated from a girl's desire for her mother.

Most subsequent theorists have picked up on Freud's use of "pre-Oedipus" to then focus on an early, *nonsexual* mother–infant relation. Oedipal then becomes synonymous with the girl's turn to the father, and the negative oedipal slips out of view in most later theoretical formulations. From this theorizing lesbians are often pathologized as pre-oedipally fixated in an infantile merger with the mother. Freud (1931b) acknowledged the difficulty he had previously encountered in crediting "the very surprising sexual activity of little girls in relation to their mother . . . even in phallic trends directed towards her" (p. 237). We see once again confusion in his statement of agreement with Lampl-de Groot (1927) regarding "the complete identity of the *pre-Oedipus* phase in boys and girls" (Freud, 1931b, p. 241; italics added) when she is describing the complete identity of the girl's negative oedipal with the boy's positive oedipal.

It is necessary to refer clearly to a girl's negative oedipal as paralleling a boy's positive oedipal in order to understand fully the role of the castration complex as the foreclosure of desire. Freud's statement that the castration complex ends the boy's oedipal and begins the girl's fails to take account of her negative oedipal relation; this is ironic, given that Freud himself introduces the concept and reality of the girl's negative oedipal. For both sexes, castration is about the oedipal relation to the mother.

At the very end of his 1925 paper, Freud states:

> In girls the motive for the demolition of the Oedipus complex is lacking. Castration has already had its effect, which was to force the child into the situation of the Oedipus complex. Thus the Oedipus complex escapes the fate which it meets with in boys. [1925j, p. 257]

Freud can only be understood here as referring to the girl's *positive* oedipal; a girl is castrated/desexed, and *then* she turns to the father oedipally. What, then, is the nature of her sexuality in the positive oedipal and after? And what of girls who do not turn to the father? Or of those who do, but who then return to the mother?

Freud (1933a) addressed his readers:

> I have no doubt you are ready to suspect that this portrayal of the abundance and strength of a little girl's sexual relations with her mother is very much overdrawn. After all, one has the opportunity of seeing little girls and notices nothing of the sort. [p. 121]

However, Freud went on to say that enough can be seen if one knows how to look and also emphasized "how little of its sexual wishes a child can bring to preconscious expression or communicate at all" (p. 121). We need to consider the ramifications of the fact that mothers frequently do not see their daughters' desire for them. Nonrecognition of a little girl's "sexual relations" with her mother will lead to vicissitudes in lesbian as well as heterosexual female development. In exploring further girls' confrontation with their mother's heterosexuality, I now shift focus from early classical theory on the female oedipal complex to literature from more recent decades.

A mother wants her man

Several authors (Barnett, 1966; Bergmann, 1995; Halberstadt-Freud, 1998; Kestenberg, 1982; Laufer, 1986; Lax, 1994; Montgrain, 1983; Rubin, 1975; Schalin, 1989; Torok, 1970) have described girls' erotically desirous relations to their mothers as well as the resulting wish for a penis when a girl discovers that her genital is "the wrong one". Laufer (1986) sees a girl's desire to have a baby with her mother as her primary libidinal aim. However, "at some point in her development she must give up the fantasy of being able to keep her mother's love to herself" (p. 265), because, unlike the boy, who possesses "at least the potential of a potent penis" (p. 266), the girl must recognize that the father can gratify the mother in a way that she can "never hope to replace" (p. 265).

Lax (1994), referring to the negative oedipal phase, states that masturbation fantasies in 2- to 3-year-old girls focus on the mother as the erotic object (p. 286). At some point the girl realizes, however, "that the boy has the potential she lacks for the type of relationship with mother she would like to have" (p. 287). Depression over perceived maternal object loss is "evoked when the erotic longings and fantasies which the little girl has directed toward her mother are confronted by the reality of the mother's unattainability as an erotic object" (p. 291).

I emphasize that Laufer and Lax are referring to unattainability of the mother due not to generational and incestuous boundaries, but to confrontation with the mother's heterosexuality, which favours the penis—the father and the boy (at least in fantasy)—and eliminates the girl's possibilities with the mother even on the level of fantasy: "someday, later, when I grow up. . . . " A girl suffers a serious defeat in her first, most intense love affair, and she is likely to register this defeat as her inadequacy on a bodily level: she is rejected for her genitals. This, I think, is a powerful combination. Due consideration has not been given to the possibility of a girl's sense of genital inferiority as derived from her encounter with her mother's heterosexuality. Upon this template a girl's sexuality is then expected to develop in a healthy fashion in relation to the father.

A mother's heterosexuality, if it does not incorporate a healthy integration of homoerotic desire (psychic bisexuality) that can be comfortably acknowledged and expressed in relating to a daughter, can lead to a primal rejection of the girl, of her genitals, and of her sexual power to attract the one she desires (De Lauretis, 1994; Elise, 1998a). Often, a mother has not only in concrete reality chosen a male partner, but has internalized heterosexual assumption and presumes erotic desire to be "naturally" a nonissue with a daughter. Many analysts share in this assumption that heterosexuality is an innate preference and thus also assume that a girl suffers no loss in regard to her mother on an erotic level. But, as Chodorow (1992) challenges: "How do we reconcile a theory that heterosexual preference is innate with our observations and theory concerning the pansexuality of infants and children and . . . with our knowledge that virtually *everyone's* initial bodily erotic involvement is with their mother?" (p. 273). Halberstadt-Freud (1998) sees the mother's central place in a woman's life as meaning that "she is born and continues to live with the legacy of a homo-erotic bond" (p. 42) that has significant implications for her sexuality (see also Bergmann, 1995).

In the situation where heterosexuality is considered to be all that is sexually possible—logically conceivable (Butler, 1990)—a girl is rejected by the object of her desire due to her genitalia, her sex, and then redirected to her father (who has the "right" genitals): a one-down situation, to be sure. How confident can a girl be that these genitals that lost her her mother can now win her father, who, after all, has the best genitals, even though he may desire the mother's, which are still much better than those the girl possesses. A girl can come to feel that her body is inferior to everyone's (Barnett, 1966). Typically, if a father is present for this romance with his daughter, under patriarchal hierarchy he must be dominant (Benjamin, 1988; Butler, 1990; Elise, 1998b)—the sexually active party—and, thus, a girl's sexuality is shaped as a submitting to him, to his desire. Male dominance shapes her sex into that of a passive recipient. A girl "takes refuge" (Freud, 1931b) in being the passive object of the father's desire: this we call the girl's "positive" oedipal.

Herein lies one potential reason for females not to want: active desire could painfully revive the earliest experience of wanting and not getting the mother—never getting the mother—and of having the wrong body/genital.[5] The father is, in this scenario, the booby prize in spite of bisexuality. It is easier for many females to take refuge in being wanted, being the passive recipient. If a more active wanting were to be revived, females might be in touch with wanting specific experiences first known with the mother, and heterosexual females might experience painful disappointment and frustration in relationship to a man (Chodorow, 1978; Dinnerstein, 1976; Halberstadt-Freud, 1998; Rubin, 1983). Lesbians might also experience the devaluing of their erotic selves, but their object choice does indicate that something has led them to maintain, or to return to, their original object. They do not give up on this desire in spite of the odds stacked against this pursuit. I suggest that a woman, lesbian or heterosexual, wants an erotic experience that does not lack in the qualities of desire that she initially experienced in the sensuous bodily contact with her mother (see Wrye & Wells, 1994).

We continually hear in clinical work that heterosexual women feel that they do not get enough of what they *can* identify they want from men: more tenderness, affection, mutual gazing, kissing, emotional exchange, polymorphous perversity (a label clearly invented by the masculine mind), the right kind of touching (usually labelled as "fore-play", which could be rethought as the sexual play a girl had before the turn to the father), more of the right kind of stimulation, orgasm more reliably, and more orgasms. Women want an experience origin-ally based in a relationship with a woman—their mother—who did, or provided the basis for, all of the above in a very effective and gratify-ing manner. It should be clarified that, generally, the ordinarily "good-enough" mother (Winnicott) would provide the sensual foundation for erotic desire to develop. This foundation is undermined when the desire that is stimulated in a daughter for her mother is then deemed nonsexual or viewed as only having a life in relation to the father. Con-siderable variation would occur in every mother–daughter pair regard-ing the relative balance of stimulation and deflection. These individual factors would have much to do, I believe, with the eventual object choice of the same or opposite sex.

Dinnerstein (1976) wrote that men literally reexperience the original embrace with the mother—with a female body—in sex with a woman. Maybe women also want this reencounter with earliest eroticism, and maybe lesbians are women who feel strongly (as do men) that this is a desire not to be denied. Issues of female self-esteem and esteem of the mother are involved, in addition to those of sexual desire.

The mother—a female—would initially be viewed as sexual, agen-tic, active, in a very small child's eyes and experience.[6] This is the mother a girl originally desires, identifies with, relates to intensely, and then loses as a romantic/erotic object and often as ego ideal. When one considers that a girl may experience both her body and her object choice as wrong, the impact cannot be insignificant. Under male dom-inant, patriarchal heterosexuality, a girl is castrated of the erotic tie to the mother, and the mother is castrated at the same time of her previ-ously perceived power (De Lauretis, 1994). Is it surprising that the mother–daughter relationship then frequently takes on an angry, con-flictual cast, as is often noted in analytic literature? It is only now sig-nificant to a girl (although all along to many mothers) that the girl has no penis. She is not recognized in a mother's heterosexual desire, and the mother, in desiring the penis, often comes to be seen as having no desire, which is entirely relocated in the phallus (Benjamin, 1988; Butler, 1990; Irigaray, 1990). The mother is now likely seen as lacking libido, power, agency, activity—all qualities that Hoffman (1999) sees Freud as unable to attribute to female sexuality. She wants for the penis/phallus which the girl cannot deliver. A girl is forced to forego her desire for her mother and also to recognize that the mother, as well, may be viewed as less desirable in an economy that accords "all" to the phallus. Femaleness is now stripped of agentic erotics and becomes a waiting-game. Lesbians typically reject this scenario on grounds both sexual and to do with female esteem. Psychoanalysis has traditionally viewed this refusal as a "masculinity complex" encompassing intense penis envy. We need to rethink the role of envy of the penis in female homoeroticism.

Under conditions of male dominance and heterosexual assumption, what is missing, lacking, in the girl's genital is that which is missing for the heterosexual desire of a mother: and that is a penis. The girl is, simply, not a boy—a person with a penis whom a mother can cathect in a specifically erotic fashion (Braunschweig & Fain, 1993; Burch, 1997; De Lauretis, 1994; Kernberg, 1991; Olivier, 1989). A girl loses out because of her particular equipment not suiting the heterosexuality of the mother. She must accept and mourn that she cannot offer *this* pleasure to the mother—insult added to injury. Unless she is a daughter of a lesbian couple, a girl realizes that mothers only marry people with penises. Lest this seem insignificant, I mention one example described by Frenkel (1996) of a little girl who, after being reasoned with by her mother that the mother had not shown any preference for boys, responded tearfully that "the mother was lying because if she really loved girls more, she would have married one" (p. 152). Schalin (1989) stated that "the realization that only men can marry women may mean a libidinal catastrophe for the daughter. Gradually, the girl realizes that 'the penis is the key to a woman's heart'" (p. 44).

As mentioned above, I am not considering it to be an impossibility for a heterosexual mother erotically to cathect her daughter. However, this would require that a mother could enthusiastically relate (even if only unconsciously) to the lesbian aspect of her psychic bisexuality. It still would be a delicate task, I believe, to deal with the blow to a daughter's narcissism, and to her desire for her mother, dealt by the mother's ultimate choice of a male partner. However, if this choice is not combined with heterosexual assumption, internalized homophobia, and possibly even misogyny, then the daughter's sexuality would have a much improved chance of developing in a healthy, self-validating manner.

Possibly, girls' focus on clitoral masturbation could be understood, in addition to obvious physical pleasure, as having a fantasy-base in relation to the mother's clitoris/nipple: the mouth sucked the nipple to mutual gratification. In cunnilingus everyone is equally equipped (cunnilingus was also the form of sexual contact that women in one study (Kahn & Davis, 1981) ranked as their number one preference, with intercourse placing fourth), with possibly the female lover having an edge in her same body identification and knowledge. Braunschweig and Fain (1993) refer to an "overestimation of the erotic possibilities of the other sex" where the girl "just like Freud and all who have followed him in this line, believes that her sexual organs are not worth as much as the boy's in terms of their resources for pleasure" (p. 137). Women's difficulties with desire might be due to the overvaluation of the object—man/penis (Irigaray, 1990; Riviere, 1929; Torok, 1970)—that, in combination with misogyny of the culture, leads women to feel devalued, less than, lacking—an oedipal narcissistic injury.

When heterosexual assumption buttresses heterosexual practice, then, right from the beginning, a girl's original experience of desire is unlikely to be recognized. What she wants and *that* she wants are then often rendered invisible by heterosexual family structure. As Schafer (1974) states, we insistently shape each sex's psychosexuality, steering children "from their infancy towards procreative male and female roles" (p. 471) in nuclear families. To a certain extent some of this shaping seems to have a potentially deleterious effect on female sexuality. When the father *is* taken as erotic object by a girl, this experience has potential to be a defensive substitution (see Chodorow, 1992) rather than an additional expression of desire's multiple pathways. When the father is not taken as oedipal object and the mother is chosen instead, a girl is pursuing an erotic path deemed deviant by our culture. This pejorative cast cannot fail to have a significant impact on lesbian development. Issues regarding the stigmatization of one's erotic desire would likely pose quite a challenge to the self-esteem of many lesbians. On the other hand, psychoanalysis comprises an extensive literature on the undermining of female sexual self-esteem when a heterosexual path is taken. It is important in clinical work with lesbian patients to be open to a complex interweaving of developmental experiences, varying with each individual, some of which may have been damaging to, and others strengthening of, female sexuality.

Conclusion

The continuous thread of my work (Elise, 1997, 1998a, 1998b, 2000a, 2000b, 2000c, 2001) regarding female development has involved conceptualizing psychic bisexuality and desire for the mother as a primal experience for *both sexes*. If we take infantile sexuality and the psychosexual stages seriously, the mother is, as Freud said, the child's first "seducer". As the early classical analysts emphasized, it is the *transfer* of the oedipal object from the mother to the father that has profound implications for female sexuality and its inhibition. Much of subsequent theorizing reflects an intense need to deny mother–daughter eroticism, and the negative oedipal is frequently given short shrift. Thus, we skip over the meaning to girls of the restriction of their bisexual psychic potential into monosexuality.[7] For the girl, this typically involves the loss of her first erotic object, which has, I believe, potentially damaging consequences for the unfolding and positive recognition of female sexuality and bold female desire. The *Oxford American Dictionary* defines "bold" as "confident and courageous . . . without feelings of shame . . . strong and vivid".

It is paradoxical that mother–child erotic desire, while often not recognized as existing between mother and daughter, is also kept alive in female experience (in the mother–daughter relationship, female friendships, and sexual love relationships, both heterosexual and lesbian) in disguised and not so disguised ways, that may have become less accessible to many heterosexual males given their development in this culture. Women's many levels of sensitivity, sensuality, and—as Schwartz (1998) puts it—"polymorphous diverse" expressions enrich their own and their (female or male) lovers' sexual and emotional experience. Female homoerotic desire has profoundly deep roots in the earliest mother–infant bond. To ignore or deny this primal reality imperils a bold female sexuality.

Notes

1. The question is not so much why the girl would find her father erotically appealing, but what would have her let go of the mother as erotic object.

2. Unfortunately, Olivier (1989) seems to assume that the mother is a nonoedipal object for the daughter as well. Thus Olivier views the daughter as initially *without any* oedipal object rather than as *losing* the maternal object she does desire.

3. In psychoanalytic theory, the girl's genitalia are often viewed as too diffuse or not focalized enough in sensation—a series of lacks and problems. Think of the different quality that would be conveyed if female sexual sensation were to be described as extensive, rather than as diffuse.

4. Referring to oedipal desire for the father as secondary need not be taken to derogate these desires as insignificant. Furthermore, as individual fathers participate more equally in early nurturing of the infant (though it is a question as to how common this practice will ever be), then the above conceptualization would need to shift to encompass primary maternal and primary paternal oedipal situations.

5. Elsewhere, (Elise, 1998a), I have theorized that female genital anatomy, combined with certain object relational experiences, may lead to the sense of wanting as having a hungry, empty quality that, in being unfulfilled, is repressed.

6. See Chasseguet-Smirgel (1976) and Benjamin (1988, 1995) regarding perceived maternal omnipotence versus true maternal subjectivity.

7. By ignoring the boy's negative oedipal relation to the father, we similarly ignore what psychic monosexuality might negatively impose on male development. I am here referring to qualities of mind, not proposing that in actuality people need to live bisexual lives in terms of fluctuating object choice.

CHAPTER SIX

Mending the Symbolic when a place for male same-sex desire is not found

Giorgio Giaccardi

An overview

It has been said that gay men make up their lives as they go along, as if they are building a path at the same time as they are treading on it. For instance, Neil Bartlett states (1988, p. 30): "I subject the whole story of my life as a gay man to constant scrutiny; we all do. We have to, because we're making it up as we go along."

André Gide, in answer to the question whether "homosexuals" have more imagination than others, wrote: "No, but they are more frequently called upon to exercise it" (Gide, 1967, p. 525). This is a manifestation of the broader psychic situation of symbolic fatherlessness, to which James Hillman refers when he writes: "He who has no father is forced to become his own, to create his own pattern, thus becoming the heroic self-created creator" (Hillman, 1960, p. 15).

This invention may be viewed as the response to the challenges that same-sex desire (SSD) meets on the level of the Symbolic—a notion that I would define in a broad sense as the domain of mental life that shapes and confers meaning to our experience through suitable containers (symbols) for both conscious and unconscious processes. From a Jungian perspective, the function of symbols is to allow psychic experiences to be felt and represented by virtue of their capacity to channel psychic energy, on both an individual and a collective level.

Their activation is affected by the way in which the Symbolic shapes the culture of the time, which is what Burgoyne refers to as the "socio-symbolic"—in other words, "the structures of socially and culturally reinforced meanings" (Burgoyne, 2015). The specific socio-cultural dimensions that pose a problem to the symbolization of SSD are usually referred to as "heteronormativity", defined as

> the institutions, structures of understanding, and practical orientations that make heterosexuality not only coherent—that is, organized as a sexuality—but also privileged. . . . It consists less of norms that could be summarized as a body of doctrine than of a sense of rightness produced in contradictory manifestations—often unconscious, immanent to practice or to institutions. [Berlant & Warner, 1998, p. 548]

For the sake of brevity, from here on I use the term "Symbolic" to designate the heteronormative symbolic order.

This chapter examines both the effects of blind spots in the Symbolic on the capacity of men attracted to men to recognize their desire and to attribute meaning to it, and the resulting struggles and endeavours through which they try to adjust to the Symbolic, whether reactively and defensively or more consciously and creatively. Through this process, inchoate emotional stirrings begin to take shape and gradually become thinkable and plastic.

The difficulties posed to SSD by the Symbolic may produce the kind of effects described by the Japanese writer Mishima, which I reference here because of his perceptive descriptions both of the feeling of being barred from a shared Symbolic and of the particular intertwining of having and being that characterize SSD. Evoking his first homoerotic longing for his schoolmate Omi, he writes:

> I tossed my love for Omi onto the rubbish heap of neglected riddles, never once searching deeply for its meaning, . . . I never even dreamed that such desires as I had felt towards Omi might have a significant connection with the realities of my "life". [Mishima, 1948, p. 81]

The problems of symbolization posed by the lack of suitable representations in the collective are of a different order from the difficulties around symbolization usually considered by psychoanalysis as arising out of pre-oedipal or oedipal dynamics. As an instance of the latter, the process of oedipal negotiation is typically seen as contributing to the capacity of forming "symbols [expressing] the absence of what has been renounced" (Perelberg, 2009, p. 123).

Whereas lost objects of desire can be regained on a symbolic level, SSD may face at the onset a lack of suitable containers through which it might be validated and recognized, take shape, and be inscribed in a symbolic dimension. Butler, writing on the melancholic implications of gender identifications in a heteronormative culture, states that

> the loss of homosexual objects and aims (not simply this person of the same gender, but *any* person of that same gender) will be fore- closed from the start. I use the word "foreclosed" to suggest that this is a preemptive loss, a mourning for unlived possibilities . . . a love that is from the start out of the question. [Butler, 1995, p. 171]

For this reason, "it would appear that the taboo against homosexuality must *precede* the heterosexual incest taboo" (Butler, 1990, p. 87). It has also been argued that in Butler's melancholy gender theory the notion of foreclosure of desired objects is more strictly applicable to men than to women, as for the latter—due to the girl's pre-oedipal bond with same-sex mother—the oedipal exclusion of same-sex attraction should be understood as disavowal of loss rather than preemptive foreclosure (Jay, 2007).

Therefore, the psychological movement in the Symbolic for men desiring men is not so much one from desire to its loss and its re-finding via symbolic exchange as one from the lack of a symbolic space in which desire may be conceived to the creation of such a space.

Granted, it has to be recognized that every human experience, including SSD, always has a given place within the Symbolic. As Dolli- more puts it, "desire is always within, and informed by, the very cul- ture it transgresses" (Dollimore, 1991, p. 11). It is also true that any symbol can only capture aspects of a given psychic experience. Lacan- ian psychoanalysis in particular sees the subject as constituted in the world of language and as such inherently alienated from him/herself, and Jung stated that symbols are the best possible expression "of a relatively unknown thing, which . . . cannot be more clearly or characteristically represented" (Jung, 1921/1971, pars. 814–815).

However, the peculiar inadequacy of the way in which SSD is con- ceptualized and inscribed in the dominant Symbolic leaves the experi- encing subject confronting not just a certain inevitable degree of restriction and conditioning of meaning, but an altogether alienating symbolization that Halperin refers to as "a demand to be inauthentic" (Halperin, 2012, p. 457). SSD finds itself constituted by heterosexual fantasies rather than on the basis of the subjects' experience of their desire and the effect it has on their lives. It could be said that SSD undergoes a double process of alienation: one, universal, inherent to the symbolic dimension per se, and an additional one having to do with the heteronormative bias of our culture. Halperin argues that

> gay men are alienated from "nature". . . . They do not experience their desire as proof of their human agency, as a vindication of the natural-ness of their human nature, as an expression of their spontaneous alignment with the natural, given world. They cannot perceive their instincts, their emotions, their longings and lusts as the default settings of a universal human nature. [Halperin, 2012, p. 453]

Conversely, the moment when entry in the Symbolic is experienced as compatible with a sense of oneself, even just as a faint intimation or a dawning possibility, is felt as a defining turning point in one's life. With reference to such a moment for Forster's character Maurice (Forster, 1914), whose compelling process of coming out at a most danger-ous time was so clearly rendered by Forster in all its nuances, it has been written that "the experience of finding even the slightest hint of validation for his inner nature is numinous, and the validating person is likely to become too important" (Beebe, 1993, p. 168).

The choice of the term "same-sex desire" instead of "homosexual-ity" is meant to invite a fresh reflection on how the subject of this desire experiences himself in a heteronormative context, rather than how he has been defined by the latter. The notion of homosexuality was introduced in the second half of the nineteenth century within a heteronormative and pathologizing context, both medical and legal. Its main enduring limitation is given by the conflation of desire with identity, as it usually evokes not just a kind of desire but a set of assumptions about the subject of this desire, mostly based on residual projections of what is excluded by the rigid construction of maleness in a heteronormative culture. An approach that explores the multifaceted aspects of same-sex desire as opposed to an identitarian notion of homosexuality might also bear some relevance for men who, albeit not predominantly attracted to men, nevertheless question the way in which masculinity has been construed and how it may affect their experience of sameness among men, the codification of their sexual body, and the process of construction of a gendered persona.

After a brief review in the second section of the shortcomings of a classical psychoanalytic understanding of SSD, in the third section I consider how the interaction between SSD and the Symbolic in which it is embedded has consequences on one's early development through family interactions. Finally, in the fourth section, I explore a range of dimensions of gay subjectivity, as it constitutes and consolidates itself against this background. Borrowing Halperin's words, I would say that this kind of exploration aims at considering the "conditions under which gay men accede to the subjective experiences of desire and love" (Halperin, 2012, p. 331) and the variety of responses that SSD may engender in a Symbolic experienced as alien, helping one finding a position within it, albeit a provisional one. Some of these adaptive responses may either consolidate as character traits or, in turn, be questioned and partly outgrown, in search of a more personal relation to one's interiority. As a whole, these operations contribute to reshaping the way culture symbolizes SSD.

I base the following reflections both on a psychoanalytically informed understanding of psychic development and on a variety of contributions provided by cultural studies (literary references, gender studies, critical theory) that have fertilized my understanding of SSD in a way that psychoanalytic theory alone did not help me shape. I browse this broad field of references in search of suggestive ideas to frame relevant aspects of psychological development around SSD. In the same vein, I pick some instances from my own clinical practice in order to exemplify, through transference and countertransference, some possible implications of SSD on the formation of gay men's subjectivity.

Jung's emphasis on self and wholeness has also informed my approach, as well as his regard for the variety of subjective experiences and purposefulness of same-sex desire. In a comprehensive review of Jung's statements on homosexuality, Hopcke (1991) has shown that, although most theories adopted by Jung are steeped in binary thinking—for instance, when he understands it as a manifestation of psychological immaturity, a result of mother fixation, or an identification with a feminine Anima—he fundamentally considers that "an individual's homosexuality has a meaning peculiar to the individual in question, and psychological growth consists of becoming aware of that meaning for the individual" (p. 54). He therefore developed a method—the exploration of subjective meaning in the context of the process of individuation—that has the advantage of promoting a more fluid to approach SSD, as well as of considering at least a range of homosexualities.

Subsequently, post-Jungian approaches broadened classical Jungian theory to include both male and same-sex archetypal perspectives, thus countering the predominance of the mother archetype and restrictive notions of otherness permeating both psychoanalysis and classical analytic psychology.

For the reader not familiar with the Jungian notion of archetypes, I would briefly define these as underlying dispositions of the psyche that manifest as patterns of behaviour and cultural products such as myths and other narratives of human experience. When they take shape in a person's life, they are called complexes: clusters of feelings, beliefs, and images revolving around a given archetypal core, rather like knots in one's personal unconscious that tend to attract and shape psychic life according to archetypal patterns. The Oedipus complex is an instance of this notion and represents the only complex spoken of by Freud: one that has, over many decades, dominated the understanding of sexual and gender development, and restricted the symbolic space of SSD.

Archetypes may be regarded as lenses through which human experience is organized, seen, and reflected upon. They are rooted both in the physiology of the body (instincts) and in reflection and imagination (images), thus being partly innate and partly flexible, being shaped by the environment and by one's reflection on them. Jung concisely expresses the relation between these two dimensions by indicating that archetypal images are "self-portraits of the instincts" (Jung, 1948/1975, par. 277). A variety of lenses is needed for such portraits to reflect the complexity of human experience—a view in line with Hillman, who privileges a "polytheistic" perspective over the "monotheistic" vision of the Oedipus complex.

For instance, Hillman (2005) wrote at length about the Senex–Puer archetype, which points to a union of sames and therefore represents a potential for male wholeness. He argues that both polarities of this archetype show similar and connecting traits, such as egocentricity, absence of the feminine, coldness of feelings, resistance to change. Whereas any archetype is inherently "ambivalent and paradoxical" (p. 38), ego consciousness tends to split it in polarities, causing, in the case of this particular male archetype, "frustration of homosexual Eros" and "longing for union of sames". The reunion of Puer and Senex is a way of understanding the psychological search for a kind of male wholeness as a path leading to the integration of many aspects, often oppositional, that coexist in every man.

Lopez-Pedraza, one of the post-Jungians to have explored more extensively the archetypal experience of male sameness, articulates as follows the relation between a plural archetypal perspective on SSD and clinical work: "Psychotherapy could encourage psychic movement by following the dominant archetype in which erotica among men appears, and it would accept this dominant as the very vehicle for psychotherapeutic movement" (Lopez-Pedraza, 2010, p. 135). In the following sections I refer to some archetypal perspectives that post-Jungian studies have variously associated with SSD, namely Puer–Senex, Anima, Pan, Hermaphrodite/Androgyne, Trickster, and the Double.

Lastly, I would like to clarify that in this chapter I take SSD as a given orientation present in men, in some more than in others, that shapes ways of relating and the sense of oneself since early childhood. The American psychiatrists Friedman and Downey, for instance, conclude their broad review of psychological, biological, and genetic studies on this topic, stating that "there is no general theory explaining the balance between genetic effects and other influences on the origins of homosexuality" (Friedman & Downey, 2002, p. 56). The same authors recommend that "it is helpful for clinicians to conceptualize homosexual orientation as being innate" (p. 83).

Psychoanalysis, the Symbolic, and SSD

Much has been written on the heteronormative bias of psychoanalytic theories. Here I would like to consider two types of preconceptions that I regard as particularly restrictive of the symbolic field in which SSD may be represented. As Leo Bersani has succinctly put it: "to a great extent, analysis creates the human it sets out to explore" (Bersani, 1995, p. 145).

First, according to the oedipal model, one is not supposed to desire the same object with which one identifies. Oedipal identification with father happens via a de-sexualization of the parental image. This injunction introduces a wedge between being (identity) and having (desiring). Fletcher expresses this precept in a succinct formula: "you cannot be what you desire; you cannot desire what you wish to be" (Fletcher, 1989, p. 114). As Domenici and Lesser argue, "by positing identification and desire as binary opposites, the normative structure of heterosexuality was buttressed and essentialised" (Domenici & Lesser, 1995, p. 3).

In order to preserve this distinction, Freud introduced SSD in the oedipal model in terms of the so-called inverted or negative Oedipus, in which desire for the same-sex parent implies an identification with the opposite-sex parent. This assumption, while helping to square the oedipal edifice, represents a flaw vis-à-vis actual experience of SSD, as it conflates gender identity with sexual orientation and obscures the reality of men being attracted to men from a position that does not conform to a feminine stereotype. Corbett, a child analyst, points to the following distortions in the construction of maleness in the psychoanalytic binary theory: "the repudiation of homosexual desires; the forsaking of fantastic cross-gendered identifications; the diminution of dependence and passive desires, and the phallomanic onus of sustaining aim over object, penis over person" (Corbett, 2009b, p. 48). As a result, the boy is "formed through competition with men and his repudiation of his desire for them" (p. 51). The paranoid foundation of this notion of maleness has been explored by Silverman through postwar American movies whose "dominant fiction" forces men to deny knowledge of castration and to expect to be desired on account of their unimpaired masculinity, so that when they are confronted with a lack, what is at issue is psychic disintegration. "Male mastery rests upon an abyss" (Silverman, 1992, p. 65).

The oversimplification of desire in the classic oedipal model relies upon the materialistic error of conflating otherness with anatomy. Even when anatomical differences are brought onto a symbolic plane, as both Jung and Lacan have tried to do, the anchorage to their source is hardly overcome. Symbolic imagery in Jung and signifiers in Lacan ultimately do not fully address the problem of defining otherness outside the male–female dichotomy. For instance, in Jung's major and last work on alchemical symbolism and the problem of opposites, only one instance of same-sex *coniunctio* features and only as a transitory stage (Jung, 1955/1970, Pl. 4–6). The notion of *coniunctio* Jung refers to has to do with the question—key to his psychology—of the split of the psyche into opposites as a result of the evolution of consciousness, which he viewed as the basic psychological problem of modernity. In Jung's model, the self-regulatory nature of the psyche responds to the split by activating unconscious processes in the pursuit of forms of integration [*coniunctio*] of the polarities in the direction of greater wholeness. The archetype orienting the search for wholeness is, according to Jung, the Androgyne, an image that in fact hardly allows space for psychic fantasies about the unification of split aspects in the male psyche. As far as Lacan is concerned, whereas some of his interpreters show instances where he envisaged difference as key to male same-sex desire (Nobus, 1997, p. 120), Tim Dean has critiqued his reading of difference as incompletely emancipated from anatomy:

> there remains within psychoanalysis a countervailing impulse to conceptualise alterity in terms of sexual difference. . . . Although [Lacan's] axiom that "there is no sexual relation" counters the heterosexist assumption of

complementarity between the sexes, Lacan's explanations of this axiom nevertheless are invariably couched in terms of male and female failures to relate to each other, rather than in terms of relationality's failure as such, regardless of gender. . . . Often it seems that homosexuality represents the unconscious—the unthought—of Lacanian psychoanalysis. [Dean, 2001, pp. 136, 141]

As Warner concludes, "[psychoanalysis] has totalised gender as an allegory of difference" (Warner, 1990, p. 201).

One lamentable consequence of this conceptual flaw in the psychoanalytic tradition is the equation of homosexuality and narcissism, as both are seen as lacking the capacity to relate to difference. Hanna Segal, for instance, wrote that "homosexuality is of necessity a narcissistic condition, as the name itself betrays. . . . Heterosexuality can be more or less narcissistic, it can be very disturbed or not so. In homosexuality it is 'inbuilt'" (Rose, 1990, pp. 211, 212). The implicit assumption seems to be that if I desire someone of my own sex, this would be somehow equivalent to assuming myself as the object of my desire, or, as suggested by Freud in his essay on Leonardo, to love someone else like one was loved by his mother (therefore out of a "narcissistic" projection). In fact, as Hillman recalls, "Narcissus does not know that it is his own body he sees in the pool. He believes that he is looking at the beautiful form of *another* being" (1979, p. 221). In other words, the experience of SSD is often, albeit not necessarily, marked by an intensification of perception of alterity. Freud himself, after all, oscillates between explanations of homosexuality in terms of sameness (narcissism) and difference (inverted Oedipus). The largely inadequate symbolization of SSD leaves room for it to be used as an empty container for theoretical scapegoating, which is precisely what makes it necessary for SSD to start articulating its own perspective. One such articulation concerns the conjoint importance of dimensions of sameness and otherness in SSD (see "Adaptive processes and formation of subjectivity around SSD").

My second objection to Freud's exploration of SSD concerns the assumption that desire for a same-sex object should be sublimated, put to use socially and channelled into social bonds. In other words, the value of SSD is recognized only in as much as it is de-sexualized and sublimated, while any social expression in an unsublimated form is strongly resisted. Freud couldn't be more explicit about this when he scolded a patient who questioned why people were not supposed to express their homosexual feelings. In his words, the homosexual component should be sublimated as it is now in society; it is one of the most valuable human assets, and should be put to social uses. One cannot give one's impulses free rein. Your attitude reminds me of a child who just discovered everybody defecates and who then demands that everybody ought to defecate in public; that cannot be. [Wortis, 1954, pp. 99, 100]

From this perspective, then, unlike heterosexual desire, SSD would be granted a right to existence only in a socially functional sublimated fashion, thus leaving a symbolic vacuum for the representation of any other declinations of SSD. But then Freud makes a qualification that seems to undo his own argument around sublimation of SSD, when he writes that "it seems certain that homosexual love is far more compatible with group ties, even when it takes the shape of uninhibited sexual impulsions—a remarkable fact, the explanation of which might carry us far" (Freud, 1921c, p. 141). One way of exploring this indeed remarkable fact, which significantly wasn't thought through by Freud, possibly because he intuited its theoretical dangerous implications, might bring us to consider types of "relationality" based on sameness, communality of desires and horizontality (as detailed in the section on "Adaptive Processes").

If Freud believed that homosexuality implies a deficit of sublimation, Jung made a somewhat similar point, albeit from within a very different model. In his discussion of the Hermaphrodite in relation to homosexuality, Jung maintains that homosexuality "is a matter of incomplete detachment from the hermaphroditic archetype, coupled with a distinct resistance to identify with the role of a one-sided sexual being" (Jung 1936/1959, par. 146). Although Jung also indicates advantages of this position, such as preserving "the archetype of the Original Man, which a one-sided sexual being has, up to a point, lost" (par. 146)—where the "Original Man" expresses the idea of a primary, hermaphroditic wholeness preceding psychic polarization—the criticism he makes recalls Freud's argument about homosexuality and de-sublimation. Both Freud and Jung link homosexuality with the avoidance of the loss that would be implied, respectively, in binding the drives and in restricting the range of gender identifications. Although the purpose of psychic development for Jung is indeed psychic integration of masculine and feminine principles, which for Hillman should engender a Dionysian, ambivalent, bisexual structure of consciousness (Hillman, 1960), Jung seems to regard homosexuality as a shortcut through a process which, according to his model, should instead traverse an initial phase of one-sided gender identifications.

I think that both positions overlook the specific reason why some men attracted to men may show a stronger resistance to accepting the sacrifices prescribed by the Symbolic, whether as transformation of the aim of the drive to a non-sexual one or as unilateral and codified gender identifications. I would disagree that this has to do with some inherent greater subjugation to the power of the drives or to an inability to bear the cost that the acceptance of the Symbolic entails. In fact, one can only sacrifice and accept a symbolic exchange for what had been there in the first place, whereas, as I mentioned earlier, the experience of SSD may resist calls for sublimation inasmuch as its existence has not been sufficiently registered. André Green's definition of sublimation as something that "preserves while surpassing" (Green, 1999, p. 216) can hardly apply to a psychic experience that hasn't found a place in the Symbolic and therefore cannot be preserved, let alone surpassed.

If identification with Father is thwarted, as the cultural order he represents is experienced as alien from one's desire, and if, as Freud maintains, it is the internalization of the symbolic father that allows the de-sexualization of the former bodily tie with mother, it then follows that SSD may be consistent with the enduring strength of the ties to the bodily dimension and to a pre-oedipal position in general, as the sublimation process on offer is not viable and Superego remains hard to love. I expand on some of the implications of this difficult relation with the symbolic order in the next sections from a Jungian perspective, with reference to a split archetype Puer–Senex and to the centrality of sex in the gay men's psyche.

Borrowing an André Green's notion, this difficulty may be seen as representing an instance of "dead father" (Green, 2009)—that is, a father unavailable for the process of separation and entry into the Symbolic. Although the kind of scenario Green refers to concerns the absence of a pre-oedipal father due to various reasons such as physical absence, psychic withdrawal, violence, and so on, his is an idea that may be broadly applied, in my understanding, to situations in which identification with father is not available, including the unborn symbolic father of the experience of SSD. If at the beginning there is a dead father, he cannot be oedipally murdered and identified with. The murdered father of *Totem and Taboo* (Freud, 1912–13) "enables individuals to live as members of a group with a shared language, laws and ideals" (Muller, 2009, p. 145), but this totem doesn't work in the realm of desire for men desiring men. If the dead father "has never been integrated into the internal world [as an agent of symbolisation] . . . he seems to remain outside the self" (Green, 2009, p. 37).

And yet, as Lacan points out, every human community—including "communities of *jouissance*", that is, communities that define themselves on the basis of a shared sexual practice (Laurent, 2009, p. 83)—poses limitations to *jouissance* and therefore is bound to be organized around lines of repression. A father function is nevertheless engendered, which shapes desire and limits its potentially unbounded *jouissance*. For Laurent, "we all have to invent for ourselves the father who recognises us or rejects us, even if we want to be self-engendered because of the uniqueness of our sin" (p. 85). How regulation of desire forms and develops within same-sex desiring communities is visible in the institutions and practices they generate—which is a key aspect of the collective process of mending the symbolic (see section on "Communality of Desire and Horizontality"). For instance, in Delany's analysis of collective practices in urban spaces, "public sex [gay cruising] situations are not Dionysian and uncontrolled but are rather some of the most highly socialised and conventionalised behaviour human beings can take part in" (Delany, 1999, p. 53). In Weinberg and Williams' sociological analysis of gay saunas (in the 70s), idiosyncratic rules and etiquette presiding over social interaction are shown to be equally present. SSD does in fact seem to be highly compatible with the adoption of rules, as long as they preside over spaces where SSD is recognized and accepted as relational currency (Weinberg & Williams, 1979).

If anything, gay various "communities of *jouissance*" may show a tendency to overdo the need for regulation, as they seem at times to be invoking a hyper-normative father who lays down very restrictive and often deadening rules. An authoritarian father seems in this case to be born out of reaction to the dead father, anarchy engendering tyranny. Dating apps represent a typical arena where one can observe, among a variety of uses people make of them, a tendency to define one's desire in what appears to be anything but a fluid approach. Sets of preferences are identified very narrowly and desire is coded in a rigid way, to a degree that the actual meeting, as and when it happens, often results in the performance of a predetermined script. Tim Dean observes such outcome particularly with regard to the organization and running of private bareback parties (Dean, 2009). All these rules share the purpose of channelling, organizing and limiting pleasures and ultimately represent a defence against anxiety, to the expense and detriment of desire's inherent openness.

Developmental vicissitudes of men desiring men

If one takes SSD to be an existing disposition of desire around which for some individuals much psychic life is organized, what I think is relevant to understand is the particular history of repression that this desire carries with it and the conditions in which it is first experienced.

Isay highlights the following developmental specificities associated to SSD:

> the special nature of the early erotic attachment of the male child to his father and the ways in which the repression of this attachment may influence later relationships, the nature and importance of coming out first to oneself and then to others, the effect of social and peer stigmatisation on self-esteem, and the particular nature of gay relationships and how they differ from conventional heterosexual relationships. [Isay, 1997, p. 39]

In this section I reflect particularly on SSD and identificatory process. When considering the effect of parental identifications on the psychosexual development of the child, what the child relates to and internalizes is not only the gender roles that the parents embody, but also their conscious and unconscious sexual orientation and, even more crucially, their relation to desire, as well as their expectations of the child.

Whereas the notion of negative Oedipus focuses on the boy's identification with the feminine when desiring the father, this relationship could in fact be more usefully considered in terms of the impact of the son's desire on his father and the effect of the latter's response on the son (Wirth, 1993).

A frequent finding of clinical literature by gay psychotherapists is that what may harm the development of a son desiring his father is not an oedipal issue of diminished masculinity, but the conscious or unconscious rejection by the father of the son's desire, inflicting a blow on the latter's capacity to desire, feel, and fantasize sexually (for instance Beebe, 1993; Hopcke, 1991; Isay, 1997; Lingiardi, 2002; Lynch, 2015; Wirth, 1993). Expectations of rejection and humiliation may then come to harm the capacity for intimacy with another man. Rechy, in his account of his life as a hustler, has defined the resulting anxiety as one "about being busted at any moment" (Rechy, 1977, p. 247)—notably when confirmation of one's attractiveness and desirability is revoked. Rage and identification with the aggressor may also ensue, as described by Beebe who draws on Isay:

> When such crushing rejection constitutes the child's initial experience
> of genital love, the developing homosexual adolescent and young
> adult will almost take revenge on his first sexual partners, turning
> upon them the narcissistic, frustrated rage engendered by the unem-
> pathic, Oedipal father. [Beebe, 1993, p. 162]

The rift that SSD may introduce in the father–son relationship can be
seen from an archetypal perspective as a split in the polarities of the
Puer–Senex archetype, with some consequences that I explore in the
next section. As I mentioned earlier, Hillman argues that it should be
viewed not only as made of two opposite principles along the imaginal
axis "peaks–valley" (high-flying spirit vs groundedness, creative flights
vs repetition, innovation vs conservation, imagination vs structure), but
also as a union of sames, indicating a potential for male wholeness.
Whereas classical Jungian psychology emphasizes the importance of
the union of opposites along lines of otherness often defined according
to heteronormative assumptions (such as male/female or Anima/
Animus), Hillman maintains that psychological development of an
individual also requires the integration of polarities within the same-
gendered archetype:

> the union of opposites—male with female—is not the only union for
> which we long and is not the only union that redeems. There is also
> the union of sames . . . which would heal the split spirit. Adam must
> re-unite with Eve, but there still remains his reunion with God. [Hill-
> man, 2005, pp. 61, 62]

While this archetype in its wholeness requires a complex balance of
sameness and difference, the effect on the father of the gay son's blos-
soming desire may exacerbate the sense of distance between the two
and, archetypally, lead to an imbalance in the relation Puer–Senex as
constellated both in father and son, as the former clings defensively to
his own fixed place in the heteronormative order while the latter
remains trapped in opposition against the Senex qualities of father.

Still from the perspective of archetypal psychology, the impact of
SSD on the father–son couple has also been framed in terms of transmission of Anima from father to son—perhaps the crucial issue for the
formation of masculinity in Jungian terms, as Jung views Anima as the
psychological function connecting men with their interiority. Anima is
the Latin word that Jung adopts to designate his idea of soul. One of
his definitions of Anima is "the archetype of life itself, . . . the living
thing in man, that which of itself lives and causes life" (Jung, 1954/
1959, pars. 56, 66). Hillman specifies that Anima "serves the instinct of

reflection. . . . A man's reflection, those musings he so often mistakes for consciousness, are grounded in an unconscious, archetypal base" (in Beebe, 1985, p. 100). Beebe describes it as "the man's spontaneous working sense of his life, the way he approaches his life and the way he reflects upon it . . . the part of a man that shapes, registers and experiences his life: to be without Anima would be to be depersonalised" (p. 100). It is the psychological function that seduces men into life, unless it remains trapped in a state of identification with mother. Jung describes these properties of Anima as follows:

> the soul lures into life the inertness of matter that does not want to live. She makes us believe incredible things, that life may be lived. She is full of snares and traps, in order that man should fall, should reach the earth, entangle himself there, and stay caught. [1954/1959, para. 56]

Anima, as Beebe points out (2017, p. 70) "is the place in the psyche where a man can transcend his propensity to play roles. When Anima is reached, rigid roles begin to give way to a deeper connection with oneself that is beyond role." If Anima "remains like a flower that hasn't opened", adaptation to the inner world will be faulty and even the performance of social roles will be affected and impaired by "bad moods, resentments, obsessive longings for attachment, uncontrolled emotional outburst" (p. 71).

Some of these aspects of Anima have been considered close to the Lacanian notion of *object a*, as both point to the source/cause of desire and play a function of bridging different realms (consciousness/unconscious in Jung and Symbolic/Real in Lacan) (Henderson, 2018, pp. 186, 188).

Whereas Jung clouded the understanding of Anima by conflating it with a contra-sexual image that would only make it work as a function promoting psychic interiority for heterosexual men, post-Jungians like James Hillman, John Beebe, David Tacey, Scott Wirth, and Andrew Samuels have emancipated such notion from the binary theory of contrasexuality. For Beebe, "the job of the anima is opening up the man's inner depths to himself, and if these depths are homosexual, the Anima engagement will make him more homosexual, not less" (Beebe, 1993, p. 155). Hopcke has noticed that the majority of his gay patients have fantasies and dreams where Anima is personified by male figures (in Thompson, 1994, pp. 225, 226).

Wirth (1993) specifically considers the vicissitudes of Anima for gay men and explores the implications for the son of a father's damaged connection to his own Anima. A father steeped in unreflected or uncritical heteronormativity is unlikely to be in a fertile connection to Anima, particularly if we consider that in his later writings Jung links Anima with Hermes and its androgynous qualities. As a result, his son may cut off from father in rage and risk losing their relationship, or perhaps embark on attempts at repairing father's Anima (a tendency often acted out in gay relationships), or, conversely, try to identify defensively with father's stereotyped Persona in order to be accepted— a "melancholic identification" with heteronormativity, furthering alienation from oneself and one's Anima and thwarting the possibility of a male-to-male relation in which interiority may be preserved and enhanced.

If the possibility for the gay son to identify with the father (or other significant male figures) is blocked for a number of reasons—different object of desire, paranoid defences against SSD, perceived lack of authenticity in the father's desire, sterile and stereotypical performance of masculinity, father's shame at his son's sexual orientation—then the boy will look for it somewhere else, provided he still has developed a minimum level of trust that somewhere in the world there will be some possibility for his desire to take shape, and that someone will help him with that.

Identification with mother is likely to be easier, because she shares both the same object of desire as her son and also, possibly, aspects of his way of desiring, particularly so at least in the case of parental couples in which gender roles are polarized. Mother potentially represents a source of validation for aspects of the boy's psyche that exceed conventional masculinity. Her appreciation can therefore be key in maintaining a degree of self-acceptance and can help him protect himself from internal and external attacks. As Corbett puts it, the mother–son nexus "offers solace in the face of normative cruelty and holds out the hope these boys need to imagine themselves otherwise" (Corbett, 2009b, p. 114). Cross-gender identifications are as equally important as same-sex ones are. Oscar Wilde had made a similar point: "All women become like their mothers. That is their tragedy. No man does. That is his" (Wilde, 1895, p. 334).

By the same token, if mother's validation is revoked and lost, the son might feel as if his self-confidence is shattered, whereas if it is only available in a narcissistic form that objectifies the child as an "it inside the other's theatre" (Bollas, 1993, p. 154) it might deaden the son's own desire. It has also been suggested that mother may be experienced by a gay son as a rival for father's love, in a triangle that would appear more consonant with the mythological reference of Orestes than that of Oedipus (Goldsmith, 2001). In such a scenario, the gay boy may repress his aggression towards mother fearing her oedipal jealousy as well as her anger at feeling rejected as a woman. Hopcke (in Thompson, 1994, p. 221), for instance, talks about a vengeful quality in the incapacity of his mother to mirror his homosexuality, as she might have not felt mirrored erotically by him. As a result the son's aggression could be split off and dissimulated and lead him to constant attempts at being "the best little boy in the world" (p. 221) so as to preserve mother's love. However, aggression is likely to erupt in the crucial experience of coming out, when the son might all of a sudden become cold and detached towards mother, summoning all aggression needed to betray and separate. This eruption may either prove an important rite of passage in the process of male individuation, if it is contained and lived through, or cause a psychic split between festering resentment and attempts at keeping up a good boy persona even in adult life.

Whether successful or not, identification with mother is not sufficient to open up a symbolic space where SSD can find its ground. As mentioned above, Jung perceptively saw the risk of a conflation between Anima and Mother archetypes, which would trap the former in the maternal realm and thwart its potential to bring about psychic engagement with life. As far as I have seen in my work with gay men, this kind of entanglement represents the psychic situation most likely to result in a type of Puer-like narcissism. SSD, far from being in itself a marker for narcissism, in fact often allows a way out of such trap in the search for same-sex validation, which is needed for this desire to be embodied and to initiate the centrifugal process of erotic involvement with others.

In the next section I illustrate how the experience of SSD shapes the formation of men's character and subjectivity as it is encountered, suffered, defended from, reacted and adapted to, reflected on, and, if the process is endured, eventually made one's own. This is the area where I believe psychoanalysis mostly needs the kind of contribution that cultural and gender studies and humanities in general can offer, as the subjective experience of SSD has long remained unheeded and overridden by theoretical assumptions in the psychoanalytic field.

Adaptive processes and formation of subjectivity around SSD

The dimensions of the subjective experience of SSD that I am considering here represent a variety of responses to the inadequacy of the heteronormative symbolic. What follows is a broad but by no means exhaustive description that draws on various sources and voices, which as a whole represent a choral attempt, by men for whom SSD has been a central psychological experience and by thinkers who have given serious and critical consideration to it, to repair the lack of symbolic containers for unseen or misconstrued desires. The transformations that allow the Symbolic to integrate aspects of SSD are the result of cultural, collective processes, triggered and sustained by the emotional and creative capacity of many individuals to endure states of alienation from the Symbolic and to translate the resulting sensibility into new forms. In his autobiography, the American writer Paul Monette (2000, p. 2) refers to the importance of gay men's memoirs as "manifestos piecing together the tales of the tribe", "leaving behind some map, some key, for the gay and lesbian people to follow."

The various instances of emotional responses, defence mechanisms, embodied experiences, and exploratory identifications examined below work as "patches" on the symbolic void. Although they represent a very heterogeneous mix of psychological processes, they all share the function of providing some initial containers for the stirrings induced by SSD, rescuing them from the blind spots of the Symbolic where they might so easily sink. I am using the metaphor of patches also on account of their sticky quality. They replace missing bits of psychic skin, the lack of which would leave the flesh and blood of SSD uncovered and raw, thus holding together aspects of one's desire and allowing one to retain some sensitivity to them.

In some cases, such patches may end up crystallizing throughout life as fixed identity traits, possibly becoming themselves alienating signifiers. To some people, at some point in their lives, these traits represent crucial defences against the fear of dissolution into a state of symbolic nonexistence, and much psychic work is therefore aimed at presiding over the maintenance of the contours of a space in which connection to desire can be kept alive.

However, the awareness and acceptance of some of these aspects may also initiate a deeper process of recognition of one's own position in the symbolic order and attributing meaning to one's desire. Traversing this experience consciously and enduring its various twists and turns may allow one to eventually feel established enough in the Symbolic to learn and live with its inherent provisionality. If this is the case, previously charged formations may lose their grip, be relinquished and eventually be outgrown in the direction of a more personal elaboration of one's relation to desire. At this logical point, and only now, SSD can enter the dynamics of symbolic exchange, entailing loss and substitution. However, the focus of this section, and of this chapter in general, is not so much on this latter development as on the dimensions through which an initial adaptation to the Symbolic is pursued and incomplete skin is patched up.

Even after SSD has undergone a more complex symbolic elaboration, a transformed consciousness that has gained a footing in the Symbolic is still likely to show traces of the troubled history of one's desire as enduring emotional hues, areas of sensitivity, or psychological inclinations that have been intensely cathected and continue to represent possible directions for regression, particularly when the ego feels weakened. Because the original alternative was alienation from the Symbolic, these hard-won formations will often be held onto particularly dearly, whether anxiously, joyfully, nostalgically, or proudly.

It is also important to point out that the collective production of "patches" gradually sediments as a range of cultural acquisitions fertilizing the Symbolic and becoming available to men as containers for the symbolization of SSD. Further down the line these patches may become superseded on a collective level too, as and when new ways of symbolizing SSD develop. Jung maintains that symbols die (i.e. they become signs) once they have fulfilled their function of connecting unconscious processes to consciousness and have been internalized in a new way of consciousness, always subject to further dialectic evolution.

Melancholy

The exclusion from the dominant symbolic is experienced emotionally as a melancholic state, which lingers, often unthought, as long as it is not internalized and integrated as part of one's history. Even so, a melancholic attitude might continue to represent an important emotional chord throughout a gay man's life—a point of regression readily available, or a state that is sought in the pursuit of that ambivalent psychic intensification which uniquely endows early emotional experiences. Borrowing a typical Jungian notion, this withdrawal, resulting from the impossibility to cathect objects, could be described as a state of introversion in which libido (psychic energy) is turned inwardly, characterized by mournful and dreamy qualities. As Jung's biographer, Homans, argues, introversion neurosis was Jung's term for narcissism, which he contrasted with hysteria and transference (Homans, 1979, p. 60).

Millot (2001) refers to an instance of such a feeling complex in her analysis of the "eroticism of desolation" of Mishima with reference to his "Confessions of a Mask", where he traces the development of his relation to SSD. He is "the solitary child [who] watches the others play through a window", who was overwhelmed with affection but missed

> the love . . . that places one in the human community. . . . The [homo-sexual] subject seeks in himself not so much the lost image of the mother's beloved child as something that never gave this love a human face. [Millot, 2001, pp. 210, 215]

She develops this analysis in terms of a psychology of the outcast, attributing to Mishima "a pariah identity developed around his feelings of being 'barred', to which his slow discovery of homosexuality gave meaning only retroactively" (Millot, 2001, p. 215). In the life of Mishima, one can see the attempt at gaining a place in the Symbolic both by becoming a writer ("a separate place—but still a place—among men") and through the eroticization of exclusion ("voluptuous sorrows")—that is, making room for desire by "eroticising the very condition imposed upon you" (Millot, 2001, p. 212). In what could be seen as a description of a sick Anima, Mishima writes: "Some instinct within me demanded that I seek solitude, that I remain apart as something different. This compulsion was manifested as mysterious and strange malaise" (Mishima, 1948, p. 81).

The implications of these kinds of melancholic feelings are wide-ranging. The body, for instance, may be scapegoated in the attempt to concretize (and possibly control) the feeling of non-belonging with the male race. One's body may come to be perceived not just as less than other men's—as it is often the case among heterosexual men—but as somehow radically different and almost not quite a male body itself. The more disparagingly the body is scapegoated, the more sexual (and promiscuous) the search for a connection to it is likely to become. From this perspective (which is only one of many ways to understand it), promiscuity may be viewed as the repetition and variety of encounters in a community of males one looks for in order to establish and validate an embodied gendered sense of oneself. (I say more on this process under the heading, "Sex and the Body".)

Another implication of this melancholic sense of exclusion, which is mentioned by Millot with regards to Mishima's life, is about procrastination: "The silent conviction of being different, excluded from the common destiny, haunted his youth, always holding him back on the threshold of engagements, war, marriage, and a profession" (Millot, 2001, p. 215). The yearned moment of entry into a shared symbolic order is eroticized and activates strong fantasies but often remains subject to the inconceivability of trespassing such a threshold, caught up between a desire to belong and a haunting sense of fated non-existence.

Time

The experience of time may be affected in a variety of ways that deny, bend, restrict, confuse, or reconfigure past, present, and future.

First, as mentioned above, the child or boy for whom same-sex attraction cannot find a space in the dominant culture will be inclined to procrastinate and project into a fantasized future the fulfilment of desire. Present and future are disjointed, one not being felt as conducive to the other. In this gap, fantasies thrive as internal representations of desire, for which no external possibilities of gratification are envisaged. The increasing resort to drugs and chemsex in some gay communities might also have to do with the compulsion to prolong this ensnarement in the fantasy dimension and to experience its unbounded excitement fused with an intense terror of reality. Again, Mishima's autobiography throws a light on this feeling complex:

> During my childhood I was weighed down by a sense of uneasiness at the thought of becoming an adult, and my feeling of growing up continued to be accompanied by a strange, piercing unrest. . . . My indefinable feeling of unrest increased my capacity for dreams divorced from all reality. [Mishima, 1948, pp. 81, 82]

The experience of coming out, as and when it occurs, introduces a watershed in life that marks a new beginning by inaugurating a late adolescence, with different psychological ages possibly coexisting in different areas of life. Paul Monette describes the emergence from the closet as follows: "When you finally come out, there's a pain that stops, and you know it will never hurt like that again, no matter how much you lose or how bad you die" (2000, p. 4). It is quite common to hear gay men describing their life as fully starting only after coming out. New beginnings in life, in general, come to be anticipated as numinous occurrences. This is also due to the fact, pointed out by Isay, that people who have come out experience a sense of power hitherto unknown, because energy previously used to disguise themselves has been freed up in the process (in Thompson, 1994, p. 41).

In Bartlett's concise rendition of this temporal discrepancy, "We are born late" (Bartlett, 1988, p. 221), various sorts of feelings might ensue, from an empowering sense of newly found youthfulness to anxiety around inadequacy, regrets for unlived life, immaturity, or age-inappropriateness. This could be one of the reasons why age difference seems to matter much less in gay relationships. Specific fantasies aside, such as that of a father–son relationship, these differences may be obliterated by a sense of agelessness and a disavowal of the constraints of time, as I expand on in the section on "Puer and Senex".

The lyrics of Jacques Brel's "Song of Old Lovers" come to mind: "Ultimately, in the end, we had to have a good deal of talent to be this old without being grown-ups" (Brel, 1967). Winnicott attributes temporal warps like this to the operation of primary defences when he observes that "the split-off other-sex part of the personality tends to remain of one age, or to grow but slowly" (Winnicott, 1971, p. 104).

Puer and Senex

Connected with time is also the split in the Puer–Senex archetype, which I understand as being brought about by ambivalence around some Senex attributes: those who make such figure a representative of the dominant order such as normality, superego, adult world, and conservation of the status quo. This territory is often experienced by the Puer as inaccessible and is therefore defended against through hatred or idealization, both despised and secretly yearned for.

Senex is a psychic quality that might appear at any age as the archetypal figure presiding over the established order, defining limits and borders, the sick king, cold and distant like Saturn, representing "the hardness of our own ego certainty" (Hillman, 2005, p. 45). Split off from its relation with the Puer, the Senex becomes the "negative lapis, lapis as petrification" (p. 45), ruling out uncertainty and disorder. Hillman argues that the Senex is the archetypal root of ego-formation, promoting consolidation of the ego within stable boundaries. What is referred to as ego here is an embodied awareness of the contours of one's being and the ensuing relative sense of confidence in occupying a place in the world.

If the Senex is mainly experienced as a negative figure, as it may be the case for gay men who perceive him as the guardian of an alien symbolic planet, then ego development may be thwarted. He won't be able to get across to the Puer and attract him into the established symbolic community, thus remaining a kind of dead father. When met in the transference dimension of clinical work, though, opportunities to transform the relationship with him might arise.

One of my patients, a gay man in his late 20s who started analysis a few years after coming out, was intensely ambivalent about entering the "adult" world, which had a stifling effect on some aspects of his life. He found it very stressful to have to perform ordinary administrative tasks such as going to the bank or ringing up utility companies—bureaucracy being perceived as the quintessentially normative adult world towards which he felt anxious and inadequate. It felt as though he experienced these spaces as indecipherable and their representatives as aliens, or himself as an alien in respect to them. At this time, his most powerful sexual fantasies were either about much older men (in their late forties or fifties), whom he would often describe as ugly, or teenagers, usually characterized by some form of excess in their persona presentation or their drug habits. He would describe both kinds of men as cheap, untrustworthy, and ultimately losers, nevertheless feeling at times intensely attracted to them. This appeared to signal an inner Puer–Senex split, engendering extreme and negative representations of these two excessive and degraded figures. In order for him to be able to enter the Symbolic more fully, they would have to be reunited with each other, mutually transformed, and redeemed from the decay they had undergone in their split state.

The analytic frame lent itself to represent an ambivalent but transformative experience that enabled him to internalize enough ground rules and superegoical functions—in which, in other words, the dead father began to come to life and be reckoned with. Unsurprisingly, this process took place through what seemed to be unconscious attacks on the frame of an avoidant nature (disavowing rather than rebellious) such as putting off payments, misplacing invoices, rescheduling sessions, and so on. Initially, for a while, I found myself willing to play along with this, as long as invoices were settled in reasonable time. Gradually his ambivalence towards the frame lessened and, in parallel, he managed to negotiate many of his fears and take some ownership of his adult life, with a reduction in anxiety. My willingness to allow for some unusual flexibility in the frame, and also to abstain for a long while from interpreting his difficulty in sticking to it, probably reflected an intuitive gauge of the absence of a sense of law he could relate to, so that interpretations of this kind might have made it more difficult to recognize the value of a set of rules and pushed him away and back into anxious isolation.

After some work together, he became aware of his idealization of the adult world (dead father now back to existence but experienced as potent and rejecting), particularly when he begrudgingly realized that he found himself intensely attracted to a man working in the City with whom he went out for a short time. He felt at odds with himself, given that consciously he would usually find this type of man uninteresting and difficult to relate to. These objects of desire were in fact to him representatives of a kind of masculine integration in society: decisive, potent, successful and respected, physically attractive, and able to have sex with other men as men. Some kind of *coniunctio* was now beginning to occur, in which aspects associated to the Senex were getting imbued with Puer–like energy and vitality, and the resulting object of desire, albeit not yet fully humanized, showed the potential to transcend both. This more whole figure became a new object of desire for him.

The dawning awareness that it might be possible to achieve some integration of SSD, masculinity and public recognition, can feel both bewildering and compelling and may strongly activate Eros as a force of individuation for a man, calling him to find his own way to pursue it. Eros' work, though, might be thwarted by excessive idealization of the position of the other, who appears to have effortlessly integrated law and desire, hence looking complete, not castrated, having it all. If this is the case, a man would cling to the desired object as an alienating substitute for his own development, while feeling excluded from the possibility of attaining it.

The mystery of the other's world could engender a voyeuristic and idealizing form of curiosity about the nature of the life of the other and what it must feel like. For instance, a maddening recurring question that appears from this position could involve fantasies about how the desired gay man feels about his own male body: is he himself attracted to it? Does he look for a similarly male body in another man, or does he look for different aspects of a male body? If his own body also represents a desired body, how could he also be attracted to another man's body? Underpinning this kind of thought process is a fantasy of the desired other's own self-sufficiency, evoking in the desiring man something similar to what Freud refers to as envy of a narcissistic condition, in which no lack and no desiring tension are perceived: "It is as if we envied them for maintaining a blissful state of mind—an unassailable libidinal position" (Freud, 1914c, p. 89). From this perspective, narcissism appears, in fact, to be in the eye of the beholder, who both desires and feels excluded by a beheld object of desire envied for being fantasized as having-it-all.

The feeling of exclusion from the qualities of the Senex that grant him a successful integration in the Symbolic may, alternatively, lead to the mimetic solution of adopting a rather rigid Senex mask as a currency to buy acceptance from the world and a sense of belonging.

Instead of idealizing a Senex position fantasized as unattainable, there could be rigid identification with its outer qualities (for instance with one's professional position or status or dominant collective values), that would come to represent a shell providing a semblance of being at home in the Symbolic. Like many other "patches" on the symbolic void that I am considering, and depending on the factors that determine the tenacity with which it is clung to, this type of "void-filler" may either serve as a temporary platform, providing some initial reassurance about social validation that may in time help build confidence to connect to and work on deeper areas of alienation, or become itself an alienating position, proving increasingly difficult to outgrow as it can have an annihilating effect on Anima.

Borrowing a Bollas' concept (1987), this type of defensive response could, at its extreme, be described as one of "normotic illness", in which yearning for conformity and homologation leads to "abnormal normality by eradicating the self of subjective life" (p. 156). Bollas envisages the aetiology of this particular defence in a parental attitude that, instead of mirroring the internal world of the child, fosters a deflection onto external, deadened objects, things, impersonal events, routines. I would also see the normotic personality as a defensive response to the lack of representations in the Symbolic of fundamental areas of subjectivity, of which a parental failure to mirror the boy's SSD may be just one of the agents. The adoption of this defence would lead to a "flight from dream life, subjective states of mind, imaginative living and aggressive differentiated play with the other" (Bollas, 1987, p. 146)—in other words, from Puer-like qualities—towards a dry Senex identified and largely blended with the empty, objective, reassuring order of things.

Interestingly, Bollas does not consider the possible connection between SSD and a normotic solution, but, on the contrary, maintains that "some homosexual disturbances" may lead to the formation of an anti-normotic personality. He states that "the homosexual's adornment in exaggerated representations of the subjective elements can be a defiance of the normotic way of life" (p. 147). I argue in the section on "'Transgressive reinscriptions': camp, drag, queering") that what Bollas refers to as "exaggerated representations" may, in fact, constitute a different and just as important attempt at mending the Symbolic, more complex and multilayered than simple defiance and opposition. In general, I regard both a normotic and an anti-normotic position for gay men as alternative responses to the same issue of lack of adequate mirroring by the Symbolic.

Finally, with regard to time and the Puer–Senex split, two dimensions crucially interwoven, gay men also face the problem of an absence of templates for old age. Although for younger generations this might change at some point, until not long ago gay men have certainly had more difficulty in developing comforting fantasies about their old age; this has also been because of the difficulty of imagining their own parenthood and a socially validated role as older men. It has also been argued by Hopcke that "gays awaken in the unconscious of others an intolerant fear of death because we leave no generation to succeed us" (in Thompson, 1994, p. 219).

Unless ways are found to negotiate this anxiety, gay men are likely to grow up with a (Puer-like) lack of familiarity with the anticipation of their real personal future and a sense that the present is the only dimension they are allowed to enjoy. Bartlett captures this state of mind when, drawing on Oscar Wilde, he provocatively writes that "homosexuals, like flowers, have no reason to exist; they delight only themselves. A flower blossoms for its own joy" (Bartlett, 1988, p. 46). The hyacinth, for instance, named after Apollo's lover who was killed by Zephiros out of jealousy, is the flower symbolizing a short-lived, intense same-sex love. Bartlett adds that for gay men "it is specifically abolished . . . the idea of ageing, of being a particular age" (p. 221). One example in which the compelling intensification of the present over duration and development is also visible is the instantaneous character of some codes and practices typical of gay sexuality, such as "the wink on the street, the split-second decision to get it on, the speed with which homosexual relations are consummated", as described by Foucault (1988, p. 297).

Appropriative identifications

Because heterosexual culture is still the first one most children are exposed to, the building blocks of the fantasies associated to SSD will be adopted from such culture but also adapted in order to represent a different kind of desire. An instance of such operation is the way I have used Brel's lyrics, originally referring to heterosexual lovers, to indicate how the experience of time may be affected by SSD. In other words, mental life around SSD takes shape through appropriative identifications, "by identifying with peculiar aspects of those objects that are either non-heteronormative or that lend themselves to non-heteronormative feelings" (Halperin, 2012, p. 346). This is one of the key attempts at mending the symbolic lack: what is not there is found through appropriation and adaptation, a Hermes-like exercise in translation and trickstery stealing. Misappropriation marks the first attempt at building mental representations for SSD and one's identity as a gay man in general, as Bartlett challenges us to consider:

> There is no "real" us, we can only ever have an unnatural identity, which is why we are all forgers. We create a life, not out of lies, but out of more or less conscious choices; adaptations, imitations and plain theft of styles, names, social and sexual roles, bodies. [Bartlett, 1988, p. 169]

Sedgwick, for instance, describes the appropriability of Catholic symbols—the unclothed male body of Jesus to be gazed at and adored, ecstasy and agony, men in dresses, adults who don't marry—as representations of SSD, as they already appear to exceed or contradict the patriarchal order (Sedgwick, 1990, p. 140). Simon Callow, commenting on the 2017 Tate exhibition *Queer British Art*, describes how as a boy his contemplation of the male physique started with representations of Christ on the cross and Saint Sebastian:

> The male physique, tortured but somehow ecstatic, every muscle, every surface, passionately rendered, as if the artist were making love to his subject, the agony of crucifixion or being pierced by arrows strikingly similar to the throes of orgasm. . . . These fleshly images seemed to confirm that it was not just me: men who found other men desirable existed. [Barlow, 2017, p. 80]

If there is trickster-like stealing, there must also be symbolic restitution, as was Hermes' reparative lyre presented to Apollo after he has stolen the latter's cattle. I can see the potential for restitution in the cultural impact that results from gay men having appropriated and elaborated heteronormative codes, which can make it possible for heterosexual men to enrich their relation to desire and gender identity by re-appropriating the transformations of previously fixed codes into more fluid practices, whether sexual or gender-performative (see, for instance, Lingiardi's observations on "metrosexuality", 2015). This can have important effects on the reduction of paranoid defences and binary fences on which the heteronormative construction of maleness rests, as well as on the accessibility of a symbolic space where reflection on aspects of desire involving elements of sameness may become possible. Hopcke (in Thompson, 1994, pp. 216, 217) has suggested that, if we think of the Androgyne as the archetype of the union of any opposites, this could also represent the union of "two different aspects of masculinity as well as two different aspects of femininity. . . . Truly androgynous people exhibit soft masculinity and aggressive masculinity, as well as soft femininity and aggressive femininity." In this sense, restitution to heterosexual men is education to an androgyne style of consciousness. This process is referred to by Hopcke as a work of the Trickster who "grabs people from inside the circle, pulls them out and helps them to become outsiders" (pp. 216, 217). Lopez-Pedraza highlights the essence of hermaphroditism/androgyny in its boundary-weakening potential:

> When the Hermaphrodite appears in psychotherapy, it is accompanied by feelings of weakness in opposition to the illusion of strength of the male and female polarities, with the ingredient of "machismus" they carry. . . . This condition of weakness is essential for making possible the borderline hermaphroditic condition, which marks the psychotherapeutic movement from the old consciousness to a more psychological consciousness. [2010, p. 46]

On a collective level, appropriation is also an important aspect of the development of a mythological frame of reference for SSD. Mythopoesis for SSD often has recourse to the incorporation and adaptation of existing myths. This was already the case for those Greek poets who gave existing legends a homosexual character, as in the case of Herakles and Iolaos, or Poseidon and Pelops. The latter is regarded by the classical scholar Dover as "the most daring and spectacular 'homosexualization' of myth that we have" as told by Pindar, who changed Pelops' fate from being dismembered, cooked up, and served at Tantalos's banquet for the gods, to being ravished by a Poseidon "overcome in his heart by desire" (Dover, 1979, p. 198).

An appropriative structure of consciousness is also likely to be characterized by a *pastiche*-like style, where various elements that have been borrowed from elsewhere coexist while they are experimented with and adapted to represent one's sensibility. The style of this section, in which I am borrowing and juxtaposing a variety of sources as containers for the development of my understanding of SSD, is a case in point. Where a strong blueprint is not available, coherence and consistency might seem to be missing, as the self unfolds in a dowser-like way, browsing across an extended but largely uncharted land and collecting buried metals simply by following the rod's vibrations. The odd gathered scrap metal may be then turned into a sort of alchemical gold—that is, representative of aspects of the self—through a process of appropriative symbolic elaboration.

"Transgressive reinscriptions": camp, drag, queering

Appropriative processes may also take on the meaning and purpose of de-realizing a symbolic world experienced as inauthentic. They represent a particular form of corrosive attack on Father and arise out of a centuries-long practice—inauthenticity being the currency needed to gain a place in the heteronormative world, which has left a legacy of mistrust around the roles meted out by the Symbolic. Also, a gay man whose desire is not reflected in the Symbolic and whose experience is at odds with what he is supposed to feel is more likely to be aware of the performative nature of gender roles and is in a better position to unmask their conventionality.

This is what Susan Sontag identifies as the essence of the camp attitude, which she qualifies as "seeing everything in quotation marks" (Sontag, 1961, p. 280). She considers herself to be "strongly drawn to and almost as strongly offended by it" (p. 276) and uses the following quotation from Oscar Wilde's *An Ideal Husband* (1893) to summarize the artifice of naturalness from a camp perspective: "to be natural is such a very difficult pose to keep up" (p. 282). Camp is an inherently unnatural, exaggerated, passionate, fantastic, self-deprecating and ironically tragic seriousness—a "seriousness that fails" (p. 282).

In this way, as Halperin puts it, "homosexuality dramatises the working of the cultural, rather than the natural, order" and shows its "hypersensitivity to the artificial nature of semiotic systems" (2012, p. 455). Heteronormative roles are caricatured to the point of dissolution, exemplifying Baudrillard's observation that "a system is abolished by pushing it into hyperlogic" (Baudrillard, 1983, p. 46). Dollimore refers to such practices as instances of "transgressive reinscriptions" (Dollimore, 1991, p. 33)—namely, appropriations of aspects of heteronormativity that are then embedded within a different order of desire and identity. They create a degree of proximity between these two domains that poses a threat to heteronormativity, based as it is on a dichotomic structuring of reality. Grotesque identification with gender stereotypes can also target masculine identities—drag kings exist too as parodic representations of muscled, leather or skinhead men, exaggerating aspects of construed personas to absurd proportions.

A drag queen takes on, like a dress, a conventional feminine persona and "queers" it by stretching it to a degree of grotesqueness and abjection that denounces its arbitrariness and artifice through mimicking, veneration, mocking, and intensification to the point of derealization. For Halperin, "gay male culture sees itself, its own plight, in the distorted mirror of a devalued femininity" (Halperin, 2012, p. 182). He goes on to subtly clarify this point by saying that

> a gay subject who is drawn to those affective or discursive possibilities may be expressing not an identification with women so much as an attraction to the cultural values associated with certain practices that happen to be coded as feminine by generic conventions. [Halperin, 2012, p. 338]

In other words, drag queens and camp attitudes are not meant to represent women per se, but only those aspects of a conventional feminine persona that lend themselves to express some emotional dynamics in the life of gay men, like, for instance, passionate outbursts, seductiveness, ecstasy, pain, fragility, hysteria, defeat, primacy of the body, masochism, anger, and so on. In a way, these representations may be seen as requests made to others for a certain kind of anguish to be accepted. Anger, in particular, is a frequent feature of drag queens' representations or of a camp attitude, and it is understandable as an emotional response to the exclusion from or mis-representations by the Symbolic. It produces a tendency to perform women as raging victims. Pain is exhibited, abject masks are put on, debasement is performed, and the stigma is embraced and dramatized. John Beebe views camp as a defensive way of "adapting oppositionally to a world that seems unsafe" (Beebe, 1993, p. 159).

This is, in fact, a complex defensive strategy based on the mechanism of identification with the aggressor, through which one takes control of the attack, throws it in the spectators' face as an indictment of heteronormativity, and at the same time makes a mockery of pain. The latter—irony and mockery—represents a specific camp defence against the violence of the Symbolic that no other minority, to my knowledge, has resorted to. It proclaims that in order to survive a position of disadvantage and inferiority, one should be able to laugh it off: an attitude that, as Halperin has pointed out, developed particularly at the time of the AIDS epidemic among gay men, as a reaction to the stigma culturally attached to them and to the intensity and scale of the tragedy endured—an act of resistance against the pressure to identify as repentant sinners.

In the process of facing and adapting to the AIDS epidemic, a world-wide gay community cemented bonds of solidarity for the first time in history and acquired a much higher and open awareness of its own existence. In this sense, it has been suggested that various aspects of this collective and momentous experience may represent a response to the problem arising from the limited availability of mythological references for SSD in contemporary Western culture and outside a heteronormative frame, as pointed out by Herrada in his *The Missing Myth* (2013). They provide a containing narrative to a historical manifestation of SSD, combining symbolic elements of martyrdom, fighting spirit, mutual recognition, centrality of the body's pleasures and pain, and irony. This mythology has also produced a strong effect on science and economy, from the substantial investment in sexual education in prevention and in the search for vaccines and new drugs to the mass introduction on the market of PrEP, the antiviral prophylaxis taken by an exponentially growing number of gay men across the world, whose promise is to increase the safety of a lifestyle where sex is central and enjoyable without life-changing consequences: a revolution that parallels the huge impact on the psychological relation to sex of the invention of the contraceptive pill for women.

Concealment

At the opposite end of spectrum to the camp solution is the practice of concealment.

Developmentally, it is a habit with which men experiencing SSD often grow up, leading to anxious monitoring of the exposure of one's desire and hyper-control of one's gaze and touch. This intensified self-control process may engender a habit of observing oneself with a third eye and a tendency to constantly imagine how one may be perceived by others, with restrictive consequences on one's spontaneity.

The closet is the symbol of a psychic structure of desire that can only operate in secrecy, representing an internal chamber where desire is stored and kept alive. In order to understand why the tendency to concealment is so strong with SSD, one should bear in mind the obvious but important fact that, unlike other minority-defining traits such as race, SSD is not necessarily shared with other family members, so one is likely to be alone with it from its onset. Prolonged secrecy around a core aspect of oneself is likely to crystallize as a generalized way of going through life, so that, even as and when the "secret" comes out, as Bartlett puts it, "we still have to learn all over again how to give ourselves away" (Bartlett, 1988, p. 74).

Emotionally, this leads to an intensification of affects like shame, self-control, hyper-vigilance, guilt, and anxiety. Proneness to these affective states may continue well beyond the time of coming out, as the rigidity of the internal structural division remains between what is felt as externally communicable and what is not. Frightening and shameful fantasies of the breakdown of such a wall may be recreated, and anxiety may continue to be displaced onto much more ordinary events involving being exposed to the other's gaze—work meetings, travelling on public transport, and so on. This anxiety centres around the fear of a sudden collapse of one's facade and the ensuing humiliating exposure of one's total inadequacy and abnormality.

For the reasons I have recalled above, for a long time heteronormative culture has displayed a strong investment in keeping SSD locked away in the closet, save when it openly portrayed it in order to convey the ridicule or the tragedy of such a desiring position. At the same time, it has shown all along a compelling tendency to hint at the existence of SSD—and not just in a derogatory or pitiful way—without however openly articulating this intrigue. Gore Vidal, interviewed on this topic in the documentary "Celluloid Closet" (Friedman & Epstein, 1995) argues that homosexuality was often referred to by Hollywood, but only in terms of "subtext"—for instance in *Rebel Without a Cause* or in *Ben-Hur*—which was also expedient to circumvent censorship. The "text" is there and the binary construction of heterosexuality evokes it as its oppositional foundation, but one that is not expected to be openly lived. Coming out of the closet, crucially, required emerging to the surface and entering one's text.

Sentimentality

A prolonged state of concealment also shapes the way one learns to experience and express emotions. A key remark by Halperin is that the emotional world is coloured by sentimentality when sentiments are "allowed no real object" (Halperin, 2012, p. 100). When no object can be held in sight, desire falls back on itself and assumes the very emotional state associated with desire as its object, around which psychic energy tends to coalesce. Although these emotional states are associated with fantasized objects, the underlying sense that a real relation to such objects cannot exist leads to cultivating emotionality for its own sake.

One's sensibility thus develops under the sign of an intensified sentimentality—as if in a pressure pan of emotional heat, which can manifest as outbursts of euphoric emotions and hyperbolic passions, often appearing as excessive and unrelated to identifiable objects. Halperin talks about "intense, senseless joy" (Halperin, 2012, p. 102); Monette describes this as "flagrant joy" (in Thompson, 1994, p. 23). All is consigned to the moment, an explosion confined between a melancholic past and unimagined future. As reported by the Jungian analyst Schellenbaum (2005, p. 117), a textual analysis of gay literature reveals how terms like "suddenly", "all at once", "abruptly" are particularly frequent. When kairos presents itself—whether as the moment of coming out, as one's first love, or just as a furtive encounter—at that point in time, in which all emotional life seems to coalesce, the experience may feel infinite, as if hidden aspects of the self are overflowing and bursting out.

Sex and the body

The effects of symbolic void are also visible in the particular importance of sex for men attracted to men. The sense of depersonalization consequent on alienation from the Symbolic often leads a man to find in his sexual body a point of anchoring, of reassurance about the possibility of being seen and desired. Bartlett perceptively says of this process:

> it has been the dynamic of our lives . . . validated our actions and self-esteem . . . organised our relationships, desires, appearances, style and functions of our meeting places . . . most of all, sex has been our Paradise . . . sex is not only a true desire, but an available pleasure . . . sex, and a vague sense that we belong together, will make us stay in even the most uncomfortably crowded room. [Bartlett, 1988, p. 219]

However excessive and absurd this centrality might appear, it often comes with the knowledge that it couldn't be any different. The Greek poet Cavafy, in his poem "Perception" (2007, pp. 79, 81), understands in hindsight the "sensuous" and "wanton life of [his] youth" as the time in which his "poetic will was being shaped" and "the territory of [his] art was being drawn", causing his "useless and futile repentances" and the "resolution to restrain [himself]" to fail, so that his creative self could be preserved and fed.

Archetypally, this is the territory of Pan, closer to the polymorphous perverse: impersonal sexuality, lust for life. The proximity of some manifestations of SSD to the infra-red polarity of the archetype, which for Jung is the bodily–instinctual one (vs. the ultraviolet, spiritual one), is characteristic of experiences that are enacted, rather than symbolized, and are felt as intensely vital. The kind of relationality implied by this perspective leverages sexual energy as an antidote to the deadness caused by the exclusion of one's desire from the Symbolic, without necessarily binding it to a two-person container.

For reasons I mentioned in the section entitled "Developmental Vicissitudes of Men desiring Men", some sexual practices may be viewed as enactments, substitutive for experiences that boys desiring boys may have struggled to access—particularly aggression—in relation both to father and mother. S&M practices, for instance, ritualize aggression and submission in a way that is felt to be accepted by the other, within boundaries expected to be safe. They imply a pact in which the aggressor is entrusted with dispensing a bearable experience of pain. Aggression and pain cause excitement, but the perpetrator, evoked as a potent but involved father figure, is also loved for protecting the victim from its most destructive aspects. Schellenbaum describes this situation as evoking "an archaic felling of immortal virility" (2005, p. 188—translated for this volume).

Other notions and practices developed—or acquired through appropriative identifications—by the gay community, such as the position of power bottom (someone being penetrated but retaining an active role in terms of control of the intercourse and energetic position) or the gang bang situation (being penetrated over a long session by multiple partners), may allow men to experiment with their strength as receivers and their resilience when their usual self is shattered, contaminating potency with passivity in a way that transgresses the heteronormative construction of manhood. Leo Bersani (2010) and Tim Dean (2008, 2009) have both extensively explored contemporary gay men's sexual practices from this perspective. Clearly, these can also have a darker side, particularly when negative power complexes predominate—in other words, when vertical relationships, in which the exercise of power is asymmetric and possibly self-involved and domineering, are not tempered by brotherly, horizontal ones, in which bonding feelings of sameness and communality prevail. Such danger can also manifest when pleasure becomes fused with self-attack, so that the shattering of the usual self, rather than facilitating access to new psychological territory, leaves room for homophobic enactments.

On the broader issue of anal penetration, the sexual practices of men desiring men have contributed to recoding anal sexuality. As cogently argued by Hocquenghem, Freud only considered the excremental and private function of the anus, having construed it as the site of one's hidden away and unsocializable matter and the interface on which one practises and gains control over retention and boundary-keeping and which is, ultimately, the dividing line between individual and society. As Hocquenghem notes, from this perspective the anus expresses only privation and cannot have any social desiring function, whereas the symbolic and socially connecting function of the phallus—that is, penis made into a symbol—is extolled, albeit within oedipal limits (Hocquenghem, 1978, pp. 95, 112). In Freud's own words:

> what is anal remains the symbol of everything that is to be repudiated and excluded from life.   Everything that has to do with these

functions is improper and must be kept secret. [The child] must forego these sources of pleasure, in the name of social respectability. [Freud, 1905d, p. 187]

The anus, unlike the phallus, does not confer gendered identity—in fact, its introduction into the realm of desire risks destroying it. It cannot function as a signifier of difference and hierarchy, given that it is not gender-specific. This explains why, as reported recently with regard to civil war in Libya, warring tribes make recourse to male rape as a way of annihilating the enemy at the core of his identity. The anally penetrated man stops existing as a social being and is often disowned even by his own son, let alone his community.[1] This is an instance that starkly exposes the possibility of exploiting the violence of the (gendered) Symbolic.

Sexual practices between men desiring men in the contemporary gay world challenge the removal of the anus from social exchange as they allow the inscription in the Symbolic of its desiring use in a way that is unprecedented in the Western world. Before the advent of gay men's new sexual paradigm in the second half of last century, the symbolic frame of the sexual use of the anus between men was confined to rigid hierarchies along the dichotomic axis old/young (classic Greece) and masculine/feminine (Mediterranean and Arabic cultures). Both perspectives regard only one partner of the couple as the fully fledged male, whose penis is the only signifier for pleasure and power. The category of power bottom that I mentioned earlier challenges this polarization by queering the anus—that is, recovering his desiring function ("de-sublimating it", in Hocquenghem words) and inscribing it in an exchange in which it becomes an active vehicle for pleasure, no longer representing a signifier of male inferiority. Men also gain an experience of having internal erogenous zones, which is particularly important in crossing binary lines if we think, for instance, of McDougall's differential analysis of women's and men's perversions based on the anatomical distinction between internal and external sexual organs (McDougall, 1990).

Sex can also help to establish an awareness of oneself as a corporeal being: the Freudian body-ego. As Foucault has shown, and as the above considerations on the use of the anus highlight, one's experience of the body, including identification of erogenous zones, is not univocal nor biologically determined, as it depends on the other's gaze and on the inscription in the Symbolic. Heteronormative culture poses a problem to men desiring men as it tends to conflate sexual orientation with gender identity and thus to associate feminine qualities with SSD, which may then restrict the way one connects to the sexual body.

For instance, the patient I mentioned earlier with reference to his struggle with Senex qualities, whose creative and unconventional inclinations also favoured some more feminine gender identifications, showed a lack of connection to his penis, being almost disturbed when a male partner came anywhere near it, as this would reveal to him the existence of something disavowed as a result of the way in which his sexuality had been coded. Analytic work helped him to modify some signifiers through which his body had been mapped, to the effect of including the recognition and enjoyment of his penis, which he gradually allowed his sexual partners to approach as an object of desire.

Although the clinical situation was key to his slowly coming to terms with the anxious experience of exposing his penis to his male analyst by bringing it into the analytic discourse, I also agree with a remark made by Alessandra Lemma where she argues that with individuals suffering from a deficit of bodily mirroring, sexual conflicts may not be worked through exclusively in the transference, and that "only actions that had a physical impact were felt to be able to alter their experience of their body in a sexually aroused state" (Lemma, 2015, p. 201). While transference work opened up possibilities for my patient to develop a more flexible and whole connection to his body, such connection had also to be experienced through a number of sexual encounters in which being desired by a same-sex partner helped him to embody this emerging awareness. This argument is in line with the observation by cultural theorist Teresa De Lauretis that "encouragement given by a partner's physical participation in the sexual activity itself . . . provides a knowledge of the body" and contributes "to the effective reorganisation of the drives" (De Lauretis, 1994, p. 75) and, more recently, with the broader remark by Mary Target that "it is only when [sexual] feelings have been taken in and accepted by another that they can feel authentically part of the self" (Target, 2015, p. 50).

The penis desired by another man, who himself has a penis, can work as an initiation to sameness, a form of reassurance about sharing the same sexed gender, a confirmation of belonging together in a shared symbolic space, a transmission of knowledge on the mysteries of embodied maleness. Particularly for boys whose desire for men has engendered acute physical insecurities, the coming together of two mutually desiring male bodies can be a key experience for a full bodily incarnation.

Communality of desire and horizontality

Another way of pursuing an experience of sameness can be seen in collective situations characterized by communality of desire, which is an extended form of enjoyment of male identification and is key to the formation of institutions where SSD can find a home. In general, same-sex peer groups play an essential part in male development, providing reassurance and confirmation as boys meet a gender discontinuity after initial symbiosis with mother, which had left them exposed to gender anxieties. Friedman and Downey point out that "boys are likely to be faced with the requirement of gaining entry to such groups at a time when their gender-self security systems may be fragile. . . . Boys who are rejected . . . experience a sense of shameful masculine inadequacy" (Friedman & Downey, 2002, p. 133).

However, the communality yearned for by men attracted to men is not only about the coexistence of male bodies (the locker room situation) or shared passions (football fans) but extends to situations of communality of desires—that is, the shared awareness that men can be desirable to each other, which is the ultimate disavowed element of male-to-male connection within the heteronormative order. Bersani describes the peculiarity of men's mutual recognition of desire as simultaneously leading to an awareness of shared identity:

> When a man and a woman pick each other up, there is nothing they have to recognise except the signs of mutual desire; their heterosexuality is assumed; it doesn't make them part of a particular community. When a man recognises another man's desire, he is also learning something about the other's identity, not exactly what kind of person he is, but what kind of groups he belongs to. [Bersani, 1995, p. 147]

A range of practices and behaviours reveal their specific meaning when approached from this premise. A large part of contemporary gay life revolves around the creation of spaces where the inhabiting subject experiences sameness of desire, such as bars, cruising areas, virtual spaces, and so on. It has been suggested that for homosexuals, bars and clubs play the role that family and church play for other groups (Weeks, 1985, p. 192). The moment of entry into this space and its anticipation in fantasy are indeed highly charged, often more than the personal encounter itself as and when it occurs. Halperin (2012, p. 437) defines these kinds of communities as an "unprecedented social experiment". What takes place in them may be viewed as a form of impersonal identification, through which an experience of sameness is pursued through a shared position variously involving bodies, sensorial enjoyment, and mutual desire.

Leo Bersani, for instance, commenting on Jean Genet's *Funeral Rites* (2015), describes the closeness of male bodies "as if they were relay points in a single burst of erotic energy towards the world" (Bersani, 1995, p. 170). Also, with regard to André Gide's *The Immoralist* (2000) and the encounters of its protagonist with Italian and Arab boys, Bersani talks of "intimacies devoided of intimacy . . . moving irresponsibly among other bodies, somewhat indifferent to them, demanding nothing more than that they be [as] available to contact" (Bersani, 1995, p. 128). According to him, this kind of desire is quite different from the traditional way in which desire is conceived as grounded in lack and yearning for the opposite, as it is, in fact, based "on the extensibility of sameness": a kind of enjoyment that can be associated with the expansion of oneself through the experience of communality of being and desiring. It is a notion of relationality distinct from, although possibly coexisting with, imaginary narcissism, intersubjective recognition, empathic identification, and paranoid competitiveness. In Bersani's words, "it defeats narcissism for it erases the individual boundaries within which an ego might frame and contemplate itself" (Bersani, 2010, p. 118).

From a different and complementary perspective, Tim Dean reads gay cruising with a focus on otherness rather than on sameness. He defines it as "a privileged domain in which we encounter otherness" (Dean, 2009, p. 180). It can involve "intimate contact with strangers without necessarily domesticating the other's otherness", as the sexual partner maintains a position of stranger, and this kind of encounter avoids recourse to reassuring practices of establishing familiarity. This understanding counters Christopher Bollas' understanding of gay cruising as "a place of erasure" of the self and an "arena [which] objectifies the child's sense of isolation as an 'it' inside the other's theatre" (Bollas, 1993, p. 154). In the case he reports, this child had been objectified by mother's narcissistic fantasies, obliterating his true self and reducing him to an "it". Where Bollas sees an "it", pleasurably but deadly enacted in the impersonal encounter of gay cruising, Dean envisages the radical other, beyond familiar personhood, through which one can also experience a form of *coniunctio* with the internal other—not dissimilarly, he goes on to suggest, from what happens in the analytic relationship where "one gets involved with an unknown other, a perfect stranger, by means of whom one encounters his or her own otherness" (Dean, 2009, p. 206). Bollas himself allows for the possibility that "for a good many gay men the arena no doubt fulfills important sexual needs and represents significant efforts to be embodied" (Bollas, 1993, p. 151), only to leave this insight unexamined—particularly its implications that the real problem may be one of narcissistic objectification rather than having to do with cruising per se. Another psychoanalytic reductive reading of gay cruising is suggested by André Green, who sees it as a result of a pressing anxiety and the urgent need to make it disappear

> in the realisation of an immediate act, in conditions often harmful to the rest of the personality and to the realization of [the] ego. What is striking, in such moments, is the unexpected eruption of what appears as a disorder of the senses or of sense. [quoted in Lingiardi, 2002, p. 120]

Green's and Bollas' readings have proved important to bring these "arenas" for SSD into the psychoanalytic discourse, but they mostly envisage in them aspects of suffering and self-annihilation. What I think they miss is the fact that pain and a sense of non-existence are often more present and overwhelming in the ordinary life of gay men, inasmuch as they are not able to find a point of entry into an adequate enough, shared Symbolic. Conversely, entry into these (often spontaneous) institutions for SSD offers the possibility of having one's desire seen and recognized—in other words, to feel alive—in a way that might have been previously unthinkable.

The most highly charged psychological movement of men attracted to men, therefore, proceeds horizontally rather than vertically. It centres around the axes of "being left out vs joining in" and "being invisible vs being seen", with a peculiar intensification of energy in the moment of trespassing this boundary. The direction leading from outside to inside is the key one, around which psychic energy coagulates, whereas the various opposites along the vertical axis, such as elevation and degradation, sublimation and de-sublimation, shallowness and depth, sophistication and vulgarity, may coexist with relative ease because, unlike the horizontal inside/outside and same/different dichotomies, they are not experienced as warring opposites. Vulgarity, in particular, in its literal meaning of belonging with the mass, may in itself engender a feeling of commonality, a much cherished and long missed one for gay men, and may coexist in the same person with subtlety and sophistication.

Clearly, there may be a tendency to recreate vertical relationships within the hard-won horizontal ones, also on account of the deep-seated habit to consider oneself as less adequate than the other members of the group. In the kind of spaces I have described earlier, vertical asymmetries, power relations, idealizations, winner and loser outcomes are still likely to occur, just as anywhere else. One instance of such defeat of the search for sameness may be seen in the formation of entrenched spaces called "tribes"—that is, homogeneous groups of people (defined by bodily features, lifestyle, tastes, HIV status, or other signs)—that dating apps often request users to specify, both in terms of self-identification and of preferred category of partners. The fluidity of desire may get trapped and narrowly defined within these precincts, which reintroduce dividing/vertical lines among men desiring men, rather than between gay and straight men. While situations leading to feelings of inadequacy and exclusion cannot therefore be avoided, it still makes a key difference that they are experienced in a context where the existence of SSD, albeit frustrated, can be taken for granted. What can be lost, then, is only the object, not the possibility itself of conceiving desire—just as it happens to the ordinary inhabitants of the heterosexual world.

Sameness and otherness

Finally, most dimensions of subjectivity of men attracted to men that I have explored lead to a redefinition of the notion of sameness and otherness and of the relation between the two. SSD, as I have tried to show, is a multi-faceted experience, which holds together dimensions of sameness and otherness. I am using "otherness" as distinct from "difference", as the latter term usually refers to the axis man–woman, which has long claimed a monopoly on the definition of otherness.

So far I have explored various aspects of the experience of sameness for men attracted to men, particularly focusing on the quest for belonging and on horizontal axes of psychic movement. One way in which this horizontality has been understood, to which I have referred above, is expressed in Bersani's notion of "homo-ness"—that is, the "desire to repeat, to expand, to intensify [have more of] the same" (Bersani, 1995, p. 149).

SSD can also be understood as a particular form of mirroring that takes place through sexual contact with a same-sex partner, which I have examined with regard to the importance of sexual relations for a fuller development of one's embodied sense of oneself. De Beauvoir recognizes and describes same-sex mirroring in relation to women in a way that aptly illustrates this point: "It is only when her fingers trace the body of a woman whose fingers in turn trace her body that the miracle of the mirror is accomplished" (quoted in Warner, 1990, p. 199). Key to this reading of SSD is the emphasis on mutuality, also including the reciprocal connection made possible through a more direct access to the other's pleasure on account of shared physiology.

Furthermore, desires between "sames" creates that particular situation of overlapping between having and being—the oedipal model's ultimate taboo—which led Mishima to write: "My desire to become like Omi had in fact been love for Omi" (Mishima, 1948, p. 120). This awareness is traced back to an armpit fetish that Mishima developed when, as a young boy, he caught sight, for the first time, of hair under his beloved Omi's arm, numinously perceived as opposite to his own completely smooth skin. The interplay between desire and identity operates at times as a consolidating force of one's embodied sense of oneself (as I have argued earlier), while at others it engenders, as in the young Mishima, a defeated sense of gender inadequacy—"Never in this world can you resemble Omi"—a voice told him (Mishima, 1948, p. 83)—in which "not having" may be experienced as bringing with it an excruciating sense of "not being".

The tension between having (or not having) and being (or not being) can never be fully resolved and leaves room for SSD to be also experienced as intense attraction to forms of otherness. Developmentally, SSD is more likely to be experienced at first as a relation to physical otherness, the "other" male body being fantasized as different from one's own, hence intensely desired. The anatomical same may be perceived as an unattainable object, as shown through Mishima's remarks—and, earlier, in the section on "Puer and Senex". When this dimension prevails, SSD has been described as an attempt "to bring into the self what the self recognises as alien . . . the possession of difference is eroticised" (Bersani, 1995, p. 134). The negative side to this complex may consist of destructive envy, excessive competitiveness, and paranoid fears.

Attraction to otherness may also intensify around other dimensions, such as race, culture, age, or status. Dollimore writes about search for fulfilment in the realm of the foreign and of differences of race and class [being] strongly cathected (Dollimore, 1991, p. 250). This might be understood as a consequence of experiencing one's circumstances as incompatible with one's desire, leading to idealization of difference (such as the "exotic", or class difference) as the container into which its fulfilment may be projected. Lacan describes how, in Plato's *Symposium*, the attraction of Socrates to Agathon— a second-rate playwright—can only be understood in terms of difference:

> Agathon . . . has a particular place in society, is not hostile towards philosophers as was the case with other playwrights, and has even managed to gain recognition by producing an inferior kind of poetry. It is this difference which allows Socrates to be attracted to Agathon. [Nobus, 1997, p. 120]

Although any kind of relationship presents a degree of *coniunctio* between sameness and otherness, when SSD constellates, then the same– other axis becomes key to how one experiences relationships. The inherent coexistence of these two aspects and the central space it occupies in one's awareness and psychic life is what poses the most radical challenge to the binary symbolic, particularly as far as paranoid constructions of men's identity are concerned. One archetypal reference to such interplay of sameness and otherness in the same relationship is given by the "Double", which is defined by the coexistence of a sense of both me and not-me. This has been declined in various narratives, from Freud's exploration of the "uncanny" (1919h) to Beebe's notion of "opposing personality (2017)", but it was specifically explored with regard to homoerotic involvement and its individuating function by Mitch Walker (1976). Walker argues that this archetype represents the source of intense bonds between men, albeit not necessarily of an erotic nature, just as is Anima (in the classical archetypal theory) between a man and a woman. The interplay between feelings of sameness and otherness in this archetypal scenario explains the possible oscillations in the experience of the same-sex other between a soulmate and a rival, an ally and a saboteur, love and hatred, fondness and paranoid anxieties.

Botella and Botella (2004) use the notion of the double to indicate a type of analytic interaction that may offer "psychic figurability" to otherwise unrepresented psychic states. Tellingly, they exemplify this notion through a clinical case, loaded with homosexual imagery, involving a male patient–analyst couple. For instance, the patient had this brief dream: "We are together. . . . We are going to have a shower. . . . I don't follow you" (p. 72). This was complemented by some clinical material evoking in both men deep anxiety around loss of identity, which was allowed to emerge through a particular countertransference response that Botella and Botella call "working as a double".

In their reading of this process,

> It is as though [the patient] were caught between the need to invest the analyst as a narcissistic, homosexual double and his terror of losing his boundaries in doing so, of passing over on to the other side of the union. [p. 75]

SSD is not the main focus of Botella and Botella's discussion of this case, and, in fact, they seem to view this patient's homosexual transference as a defence against feelings of destructiveness and fear of depersonalization; nor is it specified whether the patient is gay or not. But my point is that the archetypal dimension of the Double in SSD engenders precisely this charged tension between a compelling desire to become like the other and the fear of losing oneself in the process, which may defensively lead to aggression and destructiveness. In this patient's words: "Either I take an interest in you and forget myself entirely, or I negate you" (p. 75). This resonates with Jung's personal and concise statement to Freud in 1910, expressing the antagonistic quality of SSD in men: "Homosexuality is one of the richest sources of resistance in men" (in McGuire, 1974a, p. 297).

SSD, when embraced in its complexity and embedded in the crucible of relationships, can become an important and, possibly, lifelong task of careful cultivation of the dynamic interplay between sameness and otherness, between "being" the other and "having" him. It requires and promotes the development of a refined capacity to withstand the kind of anxieties, envy, and aggression that this type of human encounter is likely to evoke, particularly at the beginning of its unfolding.

Conclusion: mending the symbolic

I have attempted an exercise in line with the following indication from Edelman: "[We could never be] outside the Symbolic ourselves; but we can, nonetheless, make the choice to accede to our cultural production as figures—within the dominant logic of narrative, within Symbolic reality" (Edelman, 2004, p. 22). Ultimately, I am interested in making a contribution that will allow SSD to think and speak on its own behalf. As Bartlett concisely puts it, after the time of "coming out" it is now more a case of "going in" and developing a knowledge of SSD from within its own psychological language (Bartlett, 1988, p. 206). Foucault (1981) said: "We have to work at becoming homosexuals."

I have described this attempt as a process of mending the Symbolic, in which individual gay men's lives and reflections on their experience cumulatively produce modifications in the way SSD is symbolized, while these new spaces for symbolization facilitate, in turn, the psychological elaboration of one's desire. Mending, as I have explored in some detail, begins with an awareness of specific emotional implications and sensibilities and leads to the development of containing narratives as well as patches (appropriative identifications, defensive formations, same-sex spaces) one needs in order to be able to occupy a place in the Symbolic. The ways in which initial adjustments to an alien Symbolic are sought and variously found leave traces on individual characters and, collectively, are productive of new possibilities—whether as forms of relationality, spaces for belonging, or recodification of the sexed body—through which a more authentic experience of SSD may be gained.

A breakthrough in a gay man's individuation is usually achieved when he is able to accept the effects that SSD has produced on his life, to recognize how the history of his desire has sedimented in his character, and to find in this awareness new possibilities—new working symbols—for channelling psychic resources, given that desire is ultimately a bridge towards one's inexhaustible interiority. As Bartlett points out: "an individual admission that a man is a homosexual . . . does not conclude his history, but begins it" (Bartlett, 1988, p. 161). This I also find to be an important caution against reductive approaches to SSD. I endorse the following words by Camus, resonating with my Jungian formation as it recalls the notion of a soulful life: "living an experience, a particular fate, is accepting it fully. . . . It is not a matter of explaining and solving, but of experiencing and describing" (Camus, 1942, p. 53).

The hard-won "patches" on the Symbolic, which configure a path along which representation of SSD is made possible, may eventually be overcome as the inherent instability of the Symbolic is learnt to be lived with. This psychological movement is in line with the alchemical motto—often taken by Jung (1955/1970) to epitomize the circular nature of psychological work—of making volatile what is fixed following the fixation of the volatile. In other words, to return to the metaphor of the path from where I started, once a road is created by treading on it, and once a new map has been drawn, what may ensue is the discovery of the evanescence of the path. Borrowing Machado's imagery (2003), the path made by walking ("as you walk/you make your own road") fades into a fainter trail, and all that is left is "a ship's wake on the sea"—the sea of interiority where desire has been symbolized and new possibilities for psychological life are set in motion.

Note

1. www.theguardian.com/world/2017/nov/03/revealed-male-used-systematically-in-libya-as-instrument-of-war

PART **III**

PERSPECTIVES ON GENDER

CHAPTER SEVEN

From bisexuality to intersexuality: rethinking gender categories

Jack Drescher

In medical school, during a clinical rotation in the gynaecology clinic, I was asked to obtain a history from a 16-year-old girl. Before meeting with her, I read her chart, and learned that unknown to her, the patient had a genetic condition called androgen insensitivity syndrome (AIS). In possession of a male's XY chromosomes, the developing cells of the foetus with AIS are unresponsive to the masculinizing effects of the androgens secreted by its own testes. Consequently, the newborn's outer appearance is that of a girl. In the case of this patient, her testes were undescended and removed[1] shortly after birth.

The chart said the patient had been raised as a girl; to facilitate the success of that process, and as was the medically recommended custom in these cases (Colapinto, 2000; Money & Ehrhardt, 1996), she had never been told any of the true facts surrounding her birth. Her medical chart contained numerous warnings to whoever might read it, both inside and on the cover, that under no circumstances was the patient to be told about her true nature. Yet I, a complete stranger who would never meet with her again, had been given the above personal information about the patient.[2]

This being one of my first clinical interviews with a "live" patient, I anxiously asked a basic gynaecological history question: "When was your last menstrual period?" She icily responded, "I don't have any." I thought to myself, "Of course she didn't have periods. She had no uterus. How could I be so stupid to ask her *that* question?" I felt guilty and embarrassed. I later came to understand that as an "interesting case", I was not the first curious medical student to bumblingly ask about her gynaecological history.

The patient understood she had been born without a uterus, but she said she could nevertheless be a mother if she chose to marry and adopt children. In fact, she thought of herself as a young woman—as did I. However, the medical profession calls her a male pseudoher-maphrodite—male because she was born with testes, and pseudo-, as opposed to a "true" hermaphrodite, because she was born with testicu-lar but no ovarian tissue. What does all that mean in the clinical set-ting? At the time, the gynaecology chief resident to whom I had to report after speaking with the patient, joked, "Great looking guy, huh?" Still feeling guilty about my own faux pas, I did not find the remark very funny. Yet our reactions may be typical of the kinds of responses evoked when meeting individuals who do not conform to our conventional expectations of "male" and "female".

The study of human sexual identities is changing, and these changes are forcing analysts to think about sexualities in ways never envisioned by our psychoanalytic forbears. These changes also require us to be aware of some of the limitations imposed upon us by our own theoretical traditions. Towards that end, this chapter begins with a definition of terms. This is followed by a review of historical assump-tions underlying the theory of bisexuality. The next section introduces the reader to the role of categories and hierarchies in general, and to the clinical meaning of sexual hierarchies in particular. This is followed by a discussion of the meanings and uses of the concept of "the nat-ural". The final section concludes with a commentary on intersexuality as an example of both the social and surgical construction of gender.

Definition of term

In recent years, the work of lesbian, gay, bisexual, and transgender (LGBT)—and some heterosexual—scholars has increasingly come to be grouped under the umbrella term *queer theory*.[3] Drawing upon the earl-ier work of feminists (Chodorow, 1978; de Beauvoir, 1952; Dinnerstein, 1976; Friedan, 1963) and gay and lesbian studies (Abelove, Barale, & Halperin, 1993), queer theory challenges implicit assumptions that underlie conventional binary categories like "masculinity/femininity", or "homosexuality/heterosexuality". These writers usually seek to challenge cultural norms, seen as oppressive, by "deconstructing" the implicit assumptions upon which such norms are based (Butler, 1990; Foucault, 1978; Rubin, 1984; Sedgwick, 1990). Queer theorists' writings draw attention to the ways in which identities (including, but not limited to, sexual identities) can be socially constructed through history, language, and custom, usually arguing that these identities do not arise from biological (essentialist) factors.

Defining queer theory is in itself a paradoxical act, given that it is a discipline that seeks to destabilize comforting definitions. Nevertheless, one must first have some understanding of the categories being defined before one can understand how they have been constructed. Towards that end, this section provides a glossary of terms intended to aid the reader's understanding of the social construction of gender and sexuality.

Sexual orientation refers to a person's erotic response tendency or sexual attractions, be they *homosexual, bisexual, or heterosexual* (Kinsey, Pomeroy, & Martin, 1948; Kinsey et al., 1953; for further discussion see also Drescher, Stein, & Byne, 2005). Sexual orientation can be assessed through such parameters as the proportion of dreams and fantasies directed to one or the other sex, the sex of one's sexual partners, and the extent of physiological response to erotic stimuli associated with one or both sexes.

The terms *gay, gay man, lesbian, and bisexual* are *sexual identities* and refer to men and women who openly recognize, to some degree, their homosexual or bisexual attractions. Being gay or lesbian is not the same thing as being a *homosexual*. The latter is a medical term—usually with pejorative connotations—that takes one aspect of a person's identity, his or her sexual attractions, and treats it as if it were the sum of the person's entire identity (Magee & Miller, 1997). A *sexual identity* is not the same as a *sexual orientation*. Furthermore, one's sexual orientation and sexual identity can be further distinguished from one's *sexuality or sexual behaviours*. For example, a self-identified "celibate gay priest" has a homosexual orientation, a gay sexual identity, but refrains from sexual behaviour. There is also a range of sexual identities in populations at risk for HIV and AIDS (Halkitis, Wilton, & Drescher, 2005). Described behaviourally as *men who have sex with men* (MSM), such individuals may be gay or they may not necessarily think of themselves as gay, or even as homosexual. For example, a prison inmate with a heterosexual orientation may engage in homosexual behaviour and never consider that he has anything but a heterosexual identity. These examples illustrate how categories and classification systems may conflict with subjective experiences of the meaning of homosexuality.

While *sex* usually refers to the biological attributes of being male or female, *gender*—with which "sex" is often conflated—usually refers to the psychological and social attributes of the sexes. *Gender identity* refers to a persistent sense of oneself as being male or female (Money & Ehrhardt, 1996; Stoller, 1968). Historically, psychoanalysts presumed the cause of homosexuality to be confusion about one's own gender identity, which was, at the time, thought to cause, subsequently, confusion about the sex to which one was attracted. *Gender role* refers to overtly displayed gender-associated social behaviour, which establishes one's position—both for oneself and for others—as a member of one sex or the other (Kohlberg, 1966). It represents the perception of an individual's ability to act as a man or a woman should conventionally behave in public. While *gender identity* describes an inner, subjective experience of being male or female, *gender role* is an external marker of masculinity, femininity, or androgyny.

Gender stability refers to a child's understanding that one's sex at birth remains the same throughout life; it is an understanding that girls are born as girls and grow up to be women and that boys grow up to be men. *Gender constancy* refers to a child's understanding that external changes in appearance or activity do not change one's gender (Kohlberg, 1966). For example, a boy learns that even if he changes his physical appearance by putting on a dress or growing long hair, he remains a boy.

Gender beliefs (Drescher, 1998) are cultural ideas about the essential qualities of men and women. These beliefs are expressed in everyday language regarding the gendered meanings of what people do.

Transsexualism consists of a strong and persistent cross-gender identification, discomfort with one's biological sex (*gender dysphoria*), and a wish to acquire the characteristics of the other sex, which may lead one to seek *sex-reassignment surgery*. An individual born a man who *transitions* to being a woman is called a *male-to-female (MTF) transsexual*. Someone born a woman who transitions to being a man is a *female-to-male (FTM) transsexual*.[4] Complicating matters further, cross-gender identifications give little indication of a transsexual person's eventual sexual orientation. For example, depending upon the individual, a fully transitioned, post-operative MTF transsexual may have sexual feelings for a man (heterosexual MTF) or for a woman (homosexual MTF) (Bornstein, 1994; Lawrence, 2004; Leli & Drescher, 2004).

Not all individuals with cross-gendered identifications desire, seek, or obtain transsexual surgery. Some may undergo a *partial transition*, either by wearing the clothing or accessories of the *non-natal gender* or by taking hormone supplements to acquire secondary sexual characteristics of the other gender (Blanchard, 1993a, 1993b). *Transgender* is an umbrella term and includes both transsexuals and individuals with gender dysphoria who do not fully transition. The term also includes *transvestites*.[5] Cross-dressing is strongly linked in the popular imagination with homosexuality, although fetishistic cross-dressers are frequently married, heterosexual men. While most gay men and women do not cross-dress, there are social venues within gay and lesbian communities that allow for public cross-dressing. These may include community events (Gay Pride, Halloween, or Mardi Gras parades) or paid entertainment (drag shows).

Intersex was once referred to as *hermaphroditism*. In the words of one intersex activist group, the Intersex Initiative, it is

> Technically . . . a "congenital anomaly of the reproductive and sexual system." Intersex people are born with external genitalia, internal reproductive organs, and/or endocrine system that are different from most other people. There is no single 'intersex body'; it encompasses a wide variety of conditions that do not have anything in common except that they are deemed "abnormal" by the society. What makes intersex people similar is their experiences of medicalization, not biology. Intersex is not an identity. While some intersex people do reclaim it as part of their identity, it is not a freely chosen category of gender. . . . Most intersex people identify as men or women . . .[6]

There is a growing movement to redefine intersex conditions as *disorders of sex development (DSD)*.[7]

Bisexuality: tea for two?

Molecular biologist Anne Fausto-Sterling provocatively subtitles her paper, "The Five Sexes" (Fausto-Sterling, 1993), as "Why Male and Female are not Enough". In her system for categorizing the intersexed, Fausto-Sterling places anatomic males and females at opposite poles of a continuum. Males shade into what she called merms, or male pseudohermaphrodites; true hermaphrodites are in the middle; then come ferms, or female pseudohermaphrodites, and then women.[8]

During most of the twentieth century, hermaphrodites were relegated to the shadows. However, by the late 1990s, intersex individuals began appearing publicly. They formed support groups like the Intersex Society of North America (ISNA)[9] and provocatively documented their experiences as "Hermaphrodites with Attitude".[10] Intersex activists and their advocates began a process—one that continues to this day—of questioning both the necessity of genital surgeries and the secrecy that traditionally surrounds the medical treatment of intersex conditions (Diamond & Sigmundson, 1997; Dreger, 1998, 1999; Fausto-Sterling, 2000; Kessler, 1998; Rosario, 2006). Like the sexual minority groups that preceded them—gays, lesbians, bisexuals, transsexuals, transgenders—some intersex activists have raised the question of what an intersex identity is.

Amidst this growing profusion of sexual and gender identities, many analysts are left perplexed. All too often, our training does not include discussions about what it might mean to identify as gay, lesbian, bisexual, transsexual, transgender, or intersex. In part, our difficulties may stem from theoretical traditions, going back to Freud, that skew towards questions about aetiology (i.e. why is the person gay?) rather than focusing on meanings (i.e. what does it mean for this person to call herself gay?) (For more detailed discussions of these questions see Drescher, 1998, 2002b, 2002c).

Based upon ideas developed in his early years of collaboration with Wilhelm Fliess (Freud, 1950 [1892–1899]; Jones, 1961), Freud took a nineteenth-century concept, *bisexuality,* and made it a linchpin of twentieth-century psychoanalysis. In the nineteenth century, physical bisexuality was a popularly held scientific belief. It first referred to the hypothetical ability of an organism to develop as either a male or female of its species. Scientists had observed the capacity in some species to develop and reproduce as either male or female. When it was discovered that human embryos did not develop into either males or females until the 12th week of gestation, it was believed that human beings carried a bisexual potential in them as well. For in that era, scientists still believed that ontogeny, the development of an individual *in utero,* reproduced phylogeny, the evolution of that individual's species. Freud, among others, would take this paradigm one step further and hypothesize that human beings are psychologically bisexual.[11]

Bisexuality, whether biological or psychological, presumes that there are only two sexes: male and female. Girls are made of sugar, spice, and everything nice, and boys of snails and puppy dog tails. In what queer theorists refer to as the *gender binary,* male and female are the only two essential categories: they define all human sexualities, insofar as the wide diversity of sexual identities and practices are envisioned as reflecting some hybrid of these two basic ingredients. The nursery rhyme equivalents would be spiced snails, perhaps, or sugared puppy dog tails. In psychoanalysis, a long-standing formula has been that gay men identify with their mothers (Freud, 1910c) and lesbians are women who act like men (Freud, 1920a).

Formulations based on gender binaries are not limited to psychoanalysis and routinely appear in patient narratives:

> A recounted a dream in which he was kissing a woman. He remembered having the feeling, when he awoke, of being in a therapy relationship with her. In his associations, A wondered if there was some connection between the woman in the dream and his male therapist. The feeling in the dream made him worry whether A might really be "gay", even though he was only aroused by—and his sexual activities were exclusively with—women.

The therapist suggested that perhaps getting help from a man stirred anxiety in the patient because he did not know how to define his *gendered self* in their relationship. They both acknowledged that "A" desired nurturance from the male therapist, just as he had desired it in the past from his unavailable father. However, "A" worried that this desire might mean that he was "gay", by which he meant a man who had the feelings of a woman. In other words, "gay" was the *gendered meaning* that he applied to his desire for nurturance; his awareness of this feeling left him wondering whether having it defined him as masculine or feminine.

"A"'s gender belief about the masculine or feminine meanings of his feelings is one of many examples of gender binaries. In many aspects of their clinical work, analysts find bisexuality to be a useful heuristic. They will routinely offer narratives of bisexuality to widen the two gender categories (male and female) in ways that increase patients' acceptable modes of expression; for example, by affirming a man's wish to cry or a woman's desire to assert herself.

Bisexual narratives may also be reassuring to the preoperative male-to-female (MTF) transsexual, whose subjectivity is captured in the following statement: "I feel myself to be a woman trapped in the body of a man. I want to have surgery so my physical gender matches my psychological gender." Analysts like Robert Stoller (1968, 1985a) theorized that such an individual has a woman's core gender identity in a man's body. In fact, some transsexuals do define their identities using such masculine/feminine binary distinctions. However, not all transgender individuals share that subjectivity. As stated above, not everyone with gender dysphoria wants sex-reassignment surgery (SRS). Nor does every anatomic man who wants SRS feel like a woman inside.[12] In fact, in the transgender community, emerging preoperative and postoperative identities are bending the conventional categories of gender and sexual identity into strange new shapes (Bornstein, 1994; Denny, 2002; Leli & Drescher, 2004; Wilchins, 1997). To paraphrase the subjectivity of another patient, "I feel myself to have a woman's feelings in the body of man. However, I am only attracted to women and not to men at all. So when I make love to my girlfriend, I think of myself as something like a lesbian in the body of a man." It should be further noted that the awkward phrasing reflects the difficulties in capturing this subjectivity in conventional language.

Since the 1950s, the transsexual phenomenon and transgender politics have raised questions about traditional gender beliefs (Garber, 1989). More recently, however, additional challenges to gender categories have been raised as a result of increased attention to the experiences of the intersexed (Dreger, 1998, 1999; Kessler, 1998; Rosario, 2006). One historical account from Fausto-Sterling's *Sexing the Body* (Fausto-Sterling, 2000) reads as a gender-bending tragicomedy:

> In Piedra, Italy, in 1601, a young soldier named Daniel Burghammer shocked his regiment when he gave birth to a healthy baby girl. After his alarmed wife called in his army captain, he confessed to being half male and half female. Christened as a male, he had served as a soldier for seven years while also a practicing blacksmith. The baby's father, Burghammer said, was a Spanish soldier. Uncertain of what to do, the captain called in Church authorities, who decided to go ahead and christen the baby, whom they named Elizabeth. After she was weaned—Burghammer nursed the child with his female breast—several towns competed for the right to adopt her. The Church declared the child's birth a miracle, but granted Burghammer's wife a divorce, suggesting that it found Burghammer's ability to give birth incompatible with the role of husband. [Fausto-Sterling, 2000, p. 35]

Fausto-Sterling notes that prior to the nineteenth century, "biologists and physicians . . . did not have the social prestige and authority of today's professionals and were not the only ones in a position to define and regulate the hermaphrodite" (p. 34). Prior to the ascent of the medical and scientific professions it was the Church, as in the case of Daniel Burghammer, that served as the official regulatory agency of gender. Its reference manual was the Bible, which officially acknowledges the existence of only two sexes. In their decision to assign Burghammer to a female gender, church officials acted upon the belief that *she* having given birth to a child trumped not only *he* being a soldier and a blacksmith, but also a lifetime raised as a man.

In time, many official powers of the church were ceded to what Szasz (1974) calls the "Therapeutic State". In the process, the study of nature moved from the province of religion to that of science. By the nineteenth century, the assignment of hermaphrodites to either one sex or the other increasingly became a scientific and medical concern. However, scientific authorities, much like religious authorities before them, also believed that there were only two sexes. They still divided the gender baby in half, although they did so somewhat differently.

Science's binary categorization of male and female led to a classification system that distinguished between *true* and *pseudo* hermaphrodites. Where individuals with Burghammer's history were once simply "hermaphrodites", scientists decreed the true hermaphroditic condition to be extremely rare. To be true hermaphrodites, individuals had to have some combination of both male and female gonads. Thus, by shared scientific agreement, the organs of sexual reproduction arbitrarily became the defining factor in determining an individual's "true" biological sex. Consequently,

> a body with two ovaries, no matter how many masculine features it might have was [a] female [pseudohermaphrodite]. No matter if a pair of testes were nonfunctional and the person possessing them had a vagina and a breast, testes make the body [a] male [pseudohermaphrodite]. [Fausto-Sterling, 2000, p. 38]

One result of employing this classification system was that the categories of male and female expanded, while the third category—the hermaphrodite—shrank significantly in size. As Fausto-Sterling puts it, "People of mixed sex all but disappeared, not because they had become rarer, but because scientific methods classified them out of existence" (p. 39).

In the nineteenth century, this tendency to reinforce male/female binaries informed Freud's theories as well. His belief in two genders would eventually pit psychoanalysis against *third-sex theories*, the earliest proponent of which was Karl Heinrich Ulrichs (1864). Ulrichs, the historical equivalent of what today might be called a gay political activist, argued, in 1864, that some men were born with a woman's spirit trapped in their bodies. He believed that this explained their attraction to men. Because the terms *homosexuality* and *homosexual* would not be coined until 1869 (Bullough, 1979), Ulrichs designated the condition *Uranism*, and individuals who practised *Uranian* love were called *Urnings*.[13] He believed Urnings constituted a third sex that was neither male nor female.[14]

Almost half a century after Ulrichs, the most prominent spokesperson for third-sex views was Magnus Hirschfeld. As an openly homosexual psychiatrist, he led the German homophile movement in Freud's time (Lauritsen & Thorstad, 1974). Hirschfeld was an early member of the psychoanalytic movement, but he was also an early dropout. After he left, in 1911 Freud wrote to Jung:

> Magnus Hirschfeld has left our ranks in Berlin. No great loss, he is a flabby, unappetizing fellow, absolutely incapable of learning anything. Of course he takes your remark at the Congress as a pretext; homosexual touchiness. Not worth a tear. [in McGuire, 1974b, pp. 453–454]

Hirschfeld's departure, however, eventually led Freud to criticize third-sex theories, although he did so without explicitly mentioning either Ulrichs or Hirschfeld by name. He wrote in a 1915 footnote added to the *Three Essays* (Freud, 1905d):

> Psychoanalytic research is most decidedly opposed to any attempt at separating off homosexuals from the rest of mankind as a group of special character . . . it has found that all human beings are capable of making a homosexual object-choice and have in fact made one in their unconscious . . . psycho-analysis considers that a choice of an object independently of its sex–freedom to range equally over male and female objects–as it is found in childhood, in primitive states of society and early periods of history, is the original basis from which, as a result of restriction in one direction or the other, both the normal and the inverted types develop. [pp. 145–146]

Ironically, in today's climate of rapprochement between the psychoanalytic and gay communities, many cite this footnote to illustrate Freud's pro-gay sympathies. However, in the original, historical context, what sounds like principled opposition to "any attempt at separating off homosexuals from the rest of mankind as a group of special character" was actually Freud's theoretical rebuff to Hirschfeld and the German homophile movement he led: the belief that homosexuals constitute a biological, third sex. If, as Freud argued, all individuals were intrinsically bisexual, there could be no such thing as a third sex. Instead, there could only be two sexes, with everyone having some capacity to express, either consciously or unconsciously, both masculine and feminine instincts.[15]

Hierarchies: who's on first? What's on second?

The concept of bisexuality is not limited to psychoanalytic theory. One scientist who did groundbreaking theorizing about bisexuality was Alfred

Kinsey (Kinsey, Pomeroy, & Martin, 1948, 1953). Like Freud, Kinsey's ideas have had an enormous impact on many contemporary cultural beliefs about human sexuality. Although now embedded in our cultural consciousness as a sex researcher, Kinsey first trained as a taxonomist. He made his first scientific mark by observing gradations of genetic variation among gall wasps. In transferring this scientific approach of insects to studying human sexuality, he placed exclusive heterosexuality, now called a Kinsey 0, at one end of a continuum he created. Exclusive homosexuality, or Kinsey 6, was at the other end. Five types of bisexuality lay in-between, with pure bisexuality, Kinsey 3, in the middle. In defence of his continuum, Kinsey spoke against the dichotomous thinking that characterized much sexual research of his time:

> The world is not to be divided into sheep and goats. Not all things are black nor all things white. It is a fundamental of taxonomy that nature rarely deals with discrete categories. Only the human mind invents categories and tries to force facts into separated pigeon-holes. The living world is a continuum in each and every one of its aspects. The sooner we learn this concerning human sexual behavior the sooner we shall reach a sound understanding of the realities of sex. [Kinsey, Pomeroy, & Martin, 1948, p. 639]

It should be noted that although Kinsey opposed dichotomous thinking, he nevertheless succumbed to it by creating a homosexuality/heterosexuality continuum. Similar to the male/female binary preceding it, this was a polarization of human sexual experience that arbitrarily designated the two ends as essential categories. While this polarization may be a reasonable way to scientifically organize research data for further testing, one might reasonably argue that classification systems are not essentialist truths. To his credit, Kinsey did the best he could: his bisexuality scale was wider in scope than previous classification systems. Furthermore, eliminating categories and continua from thought or speech would be akin to expunging metaphor; it would make normal communication almost impossible. However, although categories cannot be eliminated, queer theorists have demonstrated how they can be deconstructed.

> If these findings are taken into account, then, clearly, the supposition that nature in a freakish mood created a "third sex" falls to the ground. [Freud 1920a, pp. 170–171]

Gender theorists and queer theorists offer alternative ways to think about the cultural underpinnings of "natural" categories like "man" and "woman" (Foucault, 1978). How might one go about reframing a traditional gender narrative? Consider the biblical story of Genesis in which God created man. *Man*, in the Judeo-Christian tradition, is the first gender category. The subsequent creation of *woman* from man's rib produced a second gender category. Perhaps because of humanity's competitive nature—and the subject of nature is addressed below—the existence of two categories has frequently led to discussions of which is the "better" category, man or of woman? There are those who believe that being made first means man is, by birthright, superior. This is, of course, a fundamental tenet of patriarchy. Only recently in the course of human history have feminists countered with the reasonably plausible argument that the later model improved upon the first (de Beauvoir, 1952).[16]

The use of genders as a way to create rankings is a rather common way to organize experience. When categories are compared with each other, they almost inevitably lead to hierarchies. It seems unlikely that any amount of "politically correct" policing of the language will change that. Yet attention to these hierarchies can serve purposes other than political ones. For deconstructing categories and hierarchies offers clinicians a potential way to understand patients' value systems.[17]

Consider the example of *sexual hierarchies*, the ordering of sexual behaviours as either better or worse in terms of implicit or explicit values (Drescher, 1998). Anthropologist Gayle Rubin (1984) refers to such hierarchies in her description of sexual behaviours that lie inside and outside the "charmed circle":

> . . . sexuality in the charmed circle is "good", "normal", and "natural" and should ideally be heterosexual, marital, monogamous, reproductive, and noncommercial. It should be coupled, relational, within the same generation, and occur at home. It should not involve pornography, fetish objects, sex toys of any sort, or roles other than male or female. Any sex that violates these rules is part of the outer limits, meaning it is "bad", "abnormal", or "unnatural". Bad sex may be homosexual, unmarried, promiscuous, non-procreative, or commercial. It may be masturbatory or take place at orgies, may be casual, may cross generational lines, and may take place in "public", or at least in the bushes or in the baths. It may involve the use of pornography, fetish objects, sex toys, or unusual roles. [pp. 14–15]

In clinical practice, patients often discuss their sexual hierarchies—and an individual patient may have more than one. For example, "B" is a thirty-something gay man unsuccessfully struggling to meet someone for a long-term relationship. He is shy and thinks of himself as unattractive. He is dating someone but doesn't feel it is going well:

> B: I had a date last night. There was a very powerful attraction to each other. So much so that we went home and made out. Nothing sexual, we wanted to build a relationship, not just jump in the sack the first night. That was the first week in December, now it is March and it's only been three dates. I try to get more dates, he is not forthcoming. But on the date he is very attentive, tells me how wonderful it is to be with me, how nice it is.

Later in the session, "B" goes on to describe having gone alone to a gay bar where there were half-naked dancing boys. He describes, in critical terms, what he sees as the "sorry spectacle" of a 40-year-old man putting dollar bills in a dancer's G-string. The therapist asks if he has ever paid another man for sex:

> B: No, but I think about it. I think it is degrading. It seems an equal amount of negative reasons not to do it as there are positive. It would be a muscle stud that I could never attract myself. As soon as the hour was up, or my hundred dollars or two hundred dollars is gone, he's not going to call me for a date. I've never been approached by a hustler. If I had been, it would ease the process. I definitely don't see myself going to a hustler. I also see it as a quick fix. I don't see it as an alternative to finding a relationship and a husband. I have nothing against prostitution. I don't see it as wrong. It shouldn't be outlawed. People do need those services, same thing with pornography. I get angry when people try to ban pornography. People need that outlet, people use those services but it's somebody I don't want to be. I don't want to be so desperate to do it.

"B"'s sexual hierarchy might look something like this: waiting to have sex after many dates > having sex on the first date > having paid sexual relationships The latter category could be further broken down hierarchically into being approached by a hustler for sex > approaching a hustler for sex. A therapist could agree with this hierarchy at face value or might question how this arrangement of categories had evolved. In choosing to ask, she might hear a story about what "B" values or devalues in himself and in others. When listened to in this way, patient accounts can be heard as moral narratives (Drescher, 1998, 2002b), stories about what patients believe to be good or bad about themselves or others. Usually these narratives are related in terms of what is better or worse, healthier or sicker, more grown-up or less mature. Sometimes patients think about these rankings consciously. In "B"'s case, his difficulties in achieving a long-term relationship made him think of himself as a failure, presumably destined to pay for sex as he got older.[18]

When listening to the ranking orders of patients, it is also extremely helpful for therapists to be consciously aware of their own hierarchy of values. To know what a therapist values and devalues in patients, or in herself, is a vital way to understand countertransference. When listening to patients, analysts will inevitably filter the material through their own values in general and their own sexual hierarchies in particular (Drescher, 1997). What analysts hear through their own filters may inevitably affect the kinds of interventions they do and do not make with patients.

Freud, for example, draws a charmed circle in the *Three Essays* (Freud, 1905d). There, he classifies homosexuality, along with bestiality and paedophilia, as a "deviation in respect to the object" (p. 136). Freud puts genital sexuality, the insertion of a penis into a vagina, in the charmed circle. Surprisingly, given that he was an avowed atheist, he also puts genitality on a higher spiritual plane as well:

> . . . the perverse forms of intercourse between the two sexes, in which other parts of the body take over the role of the genitals, have undoubtedly increased in social importance. These activities cannot, however, be regarded as being as harmless as analogous extensions [of the sexual aim] in love relationships. They are ethically objectionable, for they degrade the relationships of love between two human beings from a serious matter to a convenient game, attended by no risk and no spiritual participation. [Freud, 1908d, p. 200]

In classical psychoanalysis, sexual hierarchies blend imperceptibly into developmental ones. Oral and anal phases, for example, were considered by Freud and also by Abraham (1924) to be immature stops on the road to mature genitality. Consequently, sexual activities other than inserting a penis in a vagina—which in effect encompasses all homosexual behaviours—are considered either fixations or regressions.[19] Classical analysts are, however, not alone in generating hierarchies. Relational analysts often end reports of "successful" cases with the proud announcement of a patient's marriage or having a child (Trop & Stolorow, 1992).

The nature of nature: doing what comes naturally

To better understand how hierarchies evolve, this section takes up the issue of human nature. Throughout Western history, discussions regarding what is natural and what is not are embedded in moral dis-cussions. The moral implications of discussions on nature are epitom-ized by the teachings of Saint Thomas Aquinas, in *Summa Theologiae*:

> In sins according to nature [*peccata secundum naturam*], the sin is deter-mined as being "contrary to right reason": e.g., fornication, rape, incest, adultery, sacrilege. The lack of conformity to right reason is common to all sexual sins.
>
> In sins against nature [*peccata contra naturam*], the sin contains an *additional* aspect; it is not only against reason but it is also inconsistent with the end of the venereal act—that is, the begetting of children: e.g., masturbation, bestiality, homosexual activity, contraception. [Coleman, 1995, p. 76]

In our culture, a belief in the goodness of nature is a very old one that permeates almost all levels of discourse. That which is natural is given greater hierarchical value than that which is "unnatural". For example, in contemporary culture, *the natural* is a highly prized category used to market commodities. To call something "natural" is another way of saying that it is good, or at least to claim that it is better than some-thing that is not natural. This doctrine does not just operate when sell-ing yogurt or cotton, but in science and politics as well. Saying people are "born gay" is another way of saying it is a natural occurrence, rather than a moral failing.

In Western culture's shift from religious to modern scientific thought, the language of science appropriated and perpetuated trad-itional religion's naturalizing arguments (Szasz, 1974). Aquinas' con-cept of "sins against nature", for example, provides a blueprint for the moral disapproval that flourishes, in thinly disguised forms, in scien-tific and medical theories. Consider the work of nineteenth-century degeneracy theorist, Richard von Krafft-Ebing (1886), whose vision of an intentional evolutionary force is not very different from historical religious beliefs in God's wishes for mankind:

> The propagation of the human race is not left to mere accident or the caprices of the individuals, but is guaranteed by the hidden laws of nature which are enforced by a mighty, irresistible impulse. Sensual enjoyment and physical fitness are not the only conditions for the enforcement of these laws, but higher motives and aims, such as the desire to continue the species or the individuality of mental and phys-ical qualities beyond time and space, exert a considerable influence. Man puts himself at once on a level with the beast if he seeks to grat-ify lust alone, but he elevates his superior position when by curbing

the animal desire he combines with the sexual functions ideas of morality, of the sublime, and the beautiful. [Krafft-Ebing, 1886, p. 23]

It is often true in religion, and unfortunately it is sometimes true in science and psychoanalysis as well, that one can be admonished for behaving in ways that nature presumably never intended. Freud, for example, takes such a moral stance when he chastises an analysand who asks why people should not freely express their natural homosexual instincts:

> Normal people have a certain homosexual component and a very strong heterosexual component. The homosexual component should be sublimated as it now is in society; it is one of the most valuable human assets, and should be put to social uses. One cannot give one's impulses free rein. Your attitude reminds me of a child who just discovered everybody defecates and who then demands that everybody ought to defecate in public; that cannot be. [Wortis, 1954, pp. 99–100]

These moralizing preoccupations with the will of nature persist into modern times as well:

> Psychoanalysis reveals that sexual behavior is not an arbitrary set or rules set down by no-one-knows-who for purposes which no one understands. Our sexual patterns are a product of our biological past, a result of man's collective experience in his long biological and social evolutionary march. They make possible the cooperative coexistence of human beings with one another. At the individual level, they create a balance between the demands of sexual instinct and the external realities surrounding each of us. Not all cultures survive–the majority have not–and anthropologists tell us that serious flaws in sexual codes and institutions have undoubtedly played a significant role in many a culture's demise. [Socarides, 1994]

Whoever defines nature, whether in religion, science, or psychoanalysis, has an opportunity to claim some moral high ground. However among Darwin's most revolutionary ideas was the notion that nature is neither good nor bad. Perhaps even more unsettling to thousands of years of Western tradition and philosophy is Darwin's suggestion that nature cannot be anthropomorphized and as such may be completely indifferent to the moral concerns and intentions of mankind. That insight may have been the nineteenth century's most disturbing paradigm shift. But if that was not disturbing enough, in the early study of hermaphrodites, scientists of that time were realizing that the two sexes were not as neatly segregated as traditional beliefs had previously maintained. Just as substituting evolution's will for God's will shows how difficult it is to change a culture's organizing principles, science, medicine and psychoanalysis seemed likewise unable to relinquish the long-standing cultural idea that "male" and "female" are the standards with which all human expression should be compared. Under the guise of Darwinism, and with heterosexual procreativity (reproduction of the species) as the scientific standard, nonprocreative and unconventional sexualities were redefined as aberrations of nature's evolutionary male–female design.

Thus bisexuality became the compromise made by nineteenth-century scientists unable to rethink the male/female binary. Science, instead, sought a unifying concept that would explain the dizzying array of human sexualities they were discovering. Common sense and tradition decreed that there were only two sexes, while science seemed to be pointing to the potential of human beings to become—at least to some degree—members of either sex. After all, if man's primitive ancestral species could be bisexual, so the theory went, then perhaps the bisexual capacity resided within man as well. As previously stated, Freud took this idea to its psychological limit in his claim that all individuals are unconsciously bisexual. However, one significant problem with psychoanalysis' bisexual narratives, and not the only one, stems from the gender stereotypes that inform them. Freud's sexual theories abound with quaint notions of masculinity and femininity, as in the following example from his paper "On Narcissism":

> Women, especially if they grow up with good looks, develop a certain self-contentment which compensates them for the social restrictions that are imposed upon them in their choice of object. . . . Nor does their need lie in the direction of loving, but of being loved; and the man who fulfils this condition is the one who finds favour with them. [Freud, 1914c, pp. 88–89]

Freud defines activity as masculine and passivity as feminine, illustrating how cultural gender categories become commentaries about male and female nature. Freud, of course, could no more avoid stereotypes of his culture than we can avoid those of our own. Yet, in his bisexual nosology, women *qua* women are objects and men are subjects. Therefore, it is only possible for women to experience themselves as subjects through male identifications. In a 1920 case report, Freud said his lesbian patient was a woman who loved like a man. He called her "a feminist" (1920a, p. 169), which in Freud's time was another way of describing a woman who was too much like a man (Bem, 1993). Similarly, given the economic parsimony of Freud's bisexual world, a man's love for men could only be regarded as a feminine trait. In claiming the artist's homosexuality resulted from a feminine identification, Freud (1910c) said that Leonardo da Vinci was a man who loved like a woman, who, in this case, was his mother. Ironically, Freud's rejection of Ulrichs notwithstanding, the two of them told similar kinds of stories. From a narrative perspective, a man's identification with his mother is not altogether unlike a woman's spirit trapped in a man's body. Both stories imply that there are only two genders, and that some quality of one gender has found its way into the other.

Conclusion

To summarize, it is the "essence" of human nature to create categories. Thus, it is natural for cultures to create categories like "bisexuality". However, bisexuality is more of a social construction than an essential given of human nature. Bisexuality, as I have tried to illustrate, is an artefact of cultural assumptions about masculinity and femininity. In other cultures, gender stories can be told in other ways. Thousands of years ago, Plato told a creation myth with three original sexes—"man", "woman", and androgyne—each split in two for defying the gods:

> Each [of the original three sexes] when separated, having one side only . . . is always looking for his [sic] other half. Men who are a section of that double nature which was once called Androgynous are lovers of women . . . the women who are a section of the woman do not care for men, but have female attachments . . . they who are a section of the male, follow the male. [Kaplan, 1950, pp. 189–191]

Plato's narrative starts with three proto-sexes that go on to spawn four new kinds of gendered beings: (1) men who love men (from the proto-male), (2) women who love women (from the proto-female), (3) men who love women, and (4) women who love men (both from the Androgyne) (see Table 7.1).

In the Symposium's nosology, as women who love women have a different origin from women who love men, they have a different "essence". In this system, transsexuality and tetra sexuality are the gender beliefs that naturalize another culture's sexual behaviours, just as bisexuality has been used to naturalize some of our own.

I have previously noted that *gender beliefs* are not confined to the realm of sexuality: they concern themselves with almost every aspect of daily life (Drescher, 1998). These beliefs are expressed in everyday

Table 7.1 Plato's Creation myth

Transsexuality (three proto-gender types)	*Tetra sexuality* (four gender types)
(1) Male→	(1) Men who love Men
(2) Female→	(2) Women who love Women
(3) Androgyne→	(3) Men who love Women
	(4) Women who love Men

language regarding the gendered meanings of what people do. However, when language is insufficient to the task, belief in the gender binary is also maintained by cultural forces, which insist (1) that every individual be assigned to the category of either man or woman at birth and (2) that they conform to the category to which they have been assigned thereafter. This may explain why, in the last half of the twentieth century, surgery was routinely performed on intersex infants for the purposes of assigning them to either male or female genders (Colapinto, 2000; Diamond & Sigmundson, 1997a; Dreger, 1998, 1999; Fausto-Sterling, 2000; Kessler, 1998).

One explanation for performing these procedures, which usually are not medically necessary, is the social necessity of helping the child fit into a culture that recognizes only two genders. It has even been argued in defence of these surgeries that to make them and those around them more comfortable, intersex children must sacrifice the genitals with which they were born. Thus, boys with micropenises must be castrated to become girls. Or girls with congenital adrenal hyperplasia (CAH) must have their clitorises surgically reduced to "look normal". And, like the AIS patient mentioned in the beginning of this chapter, the truth of who they are and what was done to them must also be kept from them. Resorting to surgery, secrecy, and misleading patients, however, serve as dramatic examples of the lengths to which a culture will go to reinforce illusory binary gender beliefs about the "true" nature of men and women.

Yet what of the majority of people, those born with unambiguous anatomical gender? They, too, must cope with binary gender beliefs. So-called real men and women are powerful cultural myths with which everyone must contend. One compelling aspect of this myth is that "man" and "woman" are mutually exclusive categories. This gender binary is based not only on body parts, for all feelings, thoughts, and behaviours must fall into either one category or the other. Starting in early childhood, everyone must learn a psychological construct of gender that is based not solely on anatomy, but on many social clues (Coates, 1997; de Marneffe, 1997; Fast, 1984). For example, the meaning of aggressivity in girls, or a lack of athletic interests in boys, must be internalized along a family or cultural model that codes these attributes as gender-specific. I have already mentioned one common gender belief, that an attraction to men is a female trait. Others include the kind of clothes men should wear, or the kind of career a woman should pursue.

Judith Butler (1990) calls gender a performance, which I take to mean that one's sense of gender is an ongoing activity occurring in a relational matrix. Thus, if one's gender falls into a more conventional mode of expression—"He's a real boy" or "she's a real girl"—it is usually meant as a compliment. However, if you are not quite a man and not really a woman, then the question may be raised, "What exactly are you?" Or sometimes the question is, "What should be done about you?" Or even, "What should be done to you?" These are, of course, not always easy questions to answer. Nevertheless, all of us, men, women, and everyone else, should give these questions serious thought.

Notes

1. In conventional male development, the foetus is "first female" and then male. In the 12th week of pregnancy, male hormones (androgens) secreted by the testes initiate masculinization of the foetus.

2. There was additional personal and family history in the record: this is omitted here to protect confidentiality. However, the chart informed any reader that the patient was unaware of this history as well.

3. There is a play on the double meaning of the term "queer", historically a disparaging term for gay people. "Queer" is deliberately appropriated as a marker of a unique, outsider's take on cultural conventions.

4. There is a great deal of popular confusion between transsexualism and homosexuality. However, it is extremely rare for those who stably identify as gay, lesbian, or bisexual to have the intense cross-gender identifications associated with transsexualism or to seek sex-reassignment surgery (Drescher, Stein, & Byne, 2005).

5. Unlike homosexuality, which was removed from the American Psychiatric Association's *Diagnostic and Statistical Manual* in 1973 (Bayer, 1981), today's manual, the *DSM–5*, includes three transgender diagnoses: gender dysphoria in children, gender dysphoria in adolescents and adults, and transvestitic disorder (APA, 2013). In a parallel of the homosexual protests of the mid-20th century, there is a growing number of cross-gender identified individuals who challenge the characterization of

their feelings as symptoms of a mental disorder (Drescher, 2002a; Wilchins, 1997). Also see Karasic and Drescher (2006), for a discussion of the gender identity diagnoses of the *DSM*.

6. From http://www.intersexinitiative.org/articles/intersex-faq.html.

7. www.dsdguidelines.org/

8. Had she placed her tongue more firmly in her cheek, she might have designated men as Fausto-Sterling "0's" or women to be F-S "5's."

9. www.isna.org/

10. www.isna.org/library/hwa

11. After Freud's death, his theory of bisexuality was repudiated by Sandor Rado (1940). Of historical significance is that Rado's formulations were a major influence on the subsequent psychoanalytic theorists who regarded homosexuality as pathological (see Bayer, 1981).

12. See Lawrence (2004) for a discussion of autogynephilic transsexuals who are described as men who start out fantasizing about being a woman in a paraphilic/fetishistic way and which may eventually lead to gender dysphoria.

13. Ulrichs defined as *urningin* a woman whom we would today call a *lesbian*.

14. Ulrichs, like Freud, turned to Greek mythology for his etymological sources. His terminology derived from a speech in Plato's *Symposium* that told of the elder Aphrodite, a daughter of slain Uranus, who was born out of the remains of her father's dismembered body. Because she had no mother and her birth involved no female participation, the Uranian Aphrodite, according to Plato, inspired the love of men for men, and women for women (Kaplan, 1950). Heterosexuals in this nosology were *dionings*: descendants of Zeus and the mortal woman Dione.

15. Several years later, Freud (1920a, pp. 170–171) would reiterate this view more disdainfully: "The mystery of homosexuality is therefore by no means so simple as it is commonly depicted in popular expositions—'a feminine mind, bound therefore to love a man, but unhappily attached to a masculine body; a masculine mind, irresistibly attracted by women, but, alas! imprisoned in a feminine body.' . . . Tendentious literature has obscured our view of this interrelationship by putting into the foreground, for practical reasons (the kind of object choice), which is the only one that strikes the layman, and in addition by exaggerating the closeness of the association between this and [physical hermaphroditism]. . . . Two fundamental facts have been revealed by psychoanalytic investigation. The first of these is that homosexual men have experienced a specially strong fixation on their mother; the second, that, in addition to their manifest homosexuality, a very considerable measure of latent or unconscious homosexuality can be detected in all normal people.

16. It is no small irony that science has revealed that all foetuses develop first as females.

17. Analysts trained in the Interpersonal tradition will recognize elements of Sullivan's (1954) "detailed inquiry" in the deconstructive methods of queer theorists.

18. One might add that the "lonely homosexual" is a cultural stereotype that further fuels the development of this kind of moral narrative.

19. I call this Freud's *theory of immaturity* (Drescher, 1998, 2002b); it does not pathologize but, instead, juvenilizes diverse sexualities. In a broader context, this is what Mitchell (1988) calls *infantilism*, a countertransferential use of psychoanalytic developmental theory in which the patient is regarded as a metaphorical baby while the therapist's perspective is assumed to be the adult one.

CHAPTER EIGHT

Notes on a crisis of meaning in the care of gender-diverse children

Bernadette Wren

C linicians in a range of settings are becoming accustomed to meeting young people who question their birth assignation as male or female and who may express intense distress, both at their confinement within their sexed body and/or at the role expectations that are associated with those bodies. In the United Kingdom they are a group protected under the 2010 Equality legislation,[1] and their entitlement to live in their perceived or preferred gender role has come to be widely respected by schools, social care, the NHS, and other state agencies. Gender-diverse[2] feelings are not, of course, a novel phenomenon: they can be a familiar part of childhood development. But the experience and expression of gender diversity—as well as the responses to it—necessarily arise within and take form and colour from particular cultural and historical landscapes, and these become part of the internal experience of gender. And right now, the numbers coming forward, the intensity and urgency of the expressed discomfort with the body, the demands made for physical treatment, and the often unconditional certainty and assertive support of parents and advocacy groups for social and physical transition, *are* new and have led us into deep controversy. Gender-diverse children and adolescents now attract a new descriptive vocabulary, the possibility of a diagnosis ("Gender Dysphoria" in *DSM–5*[3]), dedicated clinics, international guidelines, and the attention of a swathe of professionals and pundits who are trying to make sense of their experiences and their demands for help. While some of these children feel clear that they identify as the "other" gender in a conventional binary sense, other young people are coming to view themselves in ways that radically challenge conventional categories of sex, gender, and sexuality, seeming to show that the "realities to which we thought we were confined are not written in stone" (Butler, 2004).

In a culture increasingly open to hearing about gender-diverse lives, we have begun to listen in new ways to young people's perception of this incongruence of body and sense of self, with a determination to grasp its contours and its significance for the young people themselves. Some of us are in search of models of meaning "that tolerate the real possibility of body/psyche discontinuities" (Saketopoulou, 2014a). But the arguments over the cause, meaning, stability, and significance of these ways of feeling in childhood are engaged with in deeply anxious ways, especially given that we are nowadays equipped with the technologies to make significant bodily interventions. The over-heated public debate reveals that much is at stake for a society struggling to understand this upsurge of gender questioning and the desire for bodily change. Pressing questions arise for clinicians about how to find their feet with these young people: how to make sense of their unhappiness, their yearnings, their identifications, their convictions and how to address their struggles imaginatively, compassionately, effectively, and safely. The Gender Identity Development Service (GIDS) is the one NHS highly specialist service in England and Wales for these children and adolescents. In this chapter the quandaries around gender diversity urgently facing children, parents, carers, GIDS clinicians, and NHS commissioners, and engaging commentators across academia and the media, are identified and located in the context of wider cultural debates about knowledge and its authorization.

The current context

To work in a highly specialized gender identity service for children and adolescents where physical interventions are offered is to feel, and to be, attacked from all sides. From a range of viewpoints we are variously accused of being too rash or too cautious; too politically correct or too naive; too tentative or too arrogant; too neglectful of suffering or too responsive to demands for treatment; too conservative or too radical. Whichever way we act clinically with respect to social transitioning[4] and the provision of puberty blockers and cross-sex hormones—taking account of individual need within a developmental frame, adhering to international clinical guidelines,[5] acknowledging best evidence, and highlighting issues of competence and consent—we offend one or other group of clients, activists, parents/carers, journalists, commentators, mental health colleagues, or allied professionals. We are exposed to attack on multiple fronts. Every week in the media, or so it seems, the predicament of gender-diverse children is transmuted into forms of entertainment, whether presented in broadly factual or fictional forms, and responded to in impassioned and vitriolic voices. Despite, or perhaps because of, this furore, we seem to drift as a society ever further from consensus into polarized positions where each "side" is deaf to the other and further from a comprehensive grasp of the interconnected issues at stake.

Few published papers illuminate how a service operates at the centre of this whirlwind of attention and contestation. While the politicization of gender identity in children proceeds unabated and disputations on professional practice and principles are regular news events, we rarely hear directly from the clinicians whose job it is to help young people grapple with the knowns and unknowns at the interface of sex and gender, and to gate-keep pioneering physical interventions in the face of deep distress and powerful yearning, who observe the porous responsiveness of young people to the ideas and identities on offer around them, who factor in the dearth of substantive evidence on which to base decision-making, who daily juggle the prospects of doing good and doing harm. This chapter is not a personal record of this anxious, watchful clinical work, but I outline briefly how these responsibilities are thought about and managed and describe some of the impacts of the disputatious context on the work. With my own immersion in this work serving as a backdrop, I try to elucidate how powerful positions, taken up in a set of interlinked discourses around knowledge and authorization, create a unique contemporary crisis of meaning about childhood gender identity. I illustrate the way that GIDS sits at the heart of a set of contested and radically unresolved (possibly irresolvable) social and cultural issues of our time.

The child and the clinic

GIDS is the national specialist NHS service for young people up to the age of 18 from England and Wales. Young people are referred to GIDS if they are suffering significant distress associated with a sense of their gender[6] being at odds with the sex assigned to them at birth. Referrals to the service have increased from 27 in 2009/10 to 2,017 in 2017 (Butler, de Graaf, Wren, & Carmichael, 2018). The treatment approach at GIDS is staged and initially involves an extended psychosocial assessment, preceding any further treatment plan. Initially, we have a series of consultations with the young person and family/carers, taking into account the thinking and talking they may have already done as a family and with other professionals. This assessment comprises an exploration of the evolution of the child's gender identity in the context of their broader developmental trajectories, alongside elements of therapeutic support and psycho-education. At this stage we may see parents and young people alone or, in the case of very young children, parents only. We may consult first with other agencies. With very young children, contact may continue regularly if there are conflicts or major distress, or more sporadically if parents and child seem to be coping and are well supported, formally or informally.

Our young clients and their families are offered an opportunity to think with us about the experience of gender diversity and bodily discomfort (and sexual diversity in older children) and about any problematic impacts of this on their wider sense of self, their emotional well-being, their family and peer relationships, their education, and so on. We work alongside carers and relatives and other members of the child's network to appreciate the often profound and unwilled nature of gender identification. We aim to support them to face up to feelings of frustration, confusion, longing, and fear, and to focus both on active coping and on further exploration of the meaning of their feelings of incongruence and bodily discomfiture. We look at their social supports and their sources of information and influence (often online sources). Many of the young people coming to the service suffer a high degree of mood problems, anxiety, self-harm, and social isolation, and many have the social and communication difficulties associated with autistic spectrum conditions. There may be a history of deprivation or trauma. Some, but by no means all, of their difficulties emerge as a result of continuing social disapprobation in the community or in the family. It can be hard to disentangle the difficulties that are specifically gender-related from those that are associated with other developmental challenges, especially among those young people who present post-pubertally. Many young people have identified, or currently identify, as gay or lesbian, and the ways they understand gender in relation to sexuality (and to homophobia) is an important topic for discussion. While most meet criteria for a diagnosis of "gender dysphoria", we are seeing young people presenting in increasingly diverse ways, contemplating a greater range of gender identity options (Twist & de Graaf, 2019).

Historically, the ethos at GIDS has been broadly "affirmative" in taking seriously the intense subjective feelings around gender and the authenticity of feelings of bodily discomfiture (Di Ceglie, 2018). Like many clinicians worldwide (e.g. Hidalgo et al., 2013), we read gender identity as complex and multiply figured, a developmental achievement rather than a biological given, even though experienced as a bedrock of their being by some young people. Importantly, though we may be curious about how and when the young person came to feel as they do, we do not assume psychopathological causality. Rather, we see that gender identity can become threaded through with multiple meanings and "put to the service of crucial psychic work" (Harris, 2005). Hence, a very open exploration of future identity possibilities is advocated, promoting the need to tolerate uncertainty and live with complexity. Increasingly, children and parents come to GIDS with a determination to promote the child's full social transition and to commence the young person on physical interventions. If young people or their parents seem very sure of what the future holds, we put forward, through gentle questioning, the value of reflecting on alternative pathways and as yet unimagined developmental complexities, and of seeing that there are many distinct choices to be made over time. We share our understanding of what the empirical literature illuminates, while acknowledging the modesty of the science thus far. Concurrent emotional difficulties need to be directly addressed, in collaboration with local mental health services, as experience has taught us to anticipate that severe problems may not be readily resolved just because the gender dysphoria is recognized and treated. We keep an awareness of situations where we sense that the gender distress may be secondary to trauma or emotional conflict, while not losing sight of the possibility of more unconflicted transgender experience. But quite apart from any pre-existing difficulties with which the gender issues may become entwined, each trans child may need help to come to terms with the more or less perturbing experiences they have had of body–mind incongruence. They may need support to give up a reliance on idealized solutions to their predicament, to accommodate for now the reality of the body as it currently is, and eventually to face what lies ahead with respect to the opportunities and limitations of the bodily changes that are possible.

At GIDS we serve effectively as NHS gatekeepers to young people accessing hormonal intervention. Depending on the young person's urgency and distress, their evidence of thoughtfulness and capacity to understand what physical intervention could mean, and their stage of pubertal maturity, there may be discussions about whether to embark on our staged programme of physical intervention. In recent years we have seen the emergence of effective endocrinological interventions to delay puberty.[7] A strong case can be made that puberty suspension provides some relief from the anxious anticipation of pubertal changes (Kreukels & Cohen-Kettenis, 2011; Wren, 2000) and supports further exploration of gender feelings and future possibilities. The treatment is increasingly requested for younger children as a way to prevent the development of those unwanted bodily characteristics that may make "passing" as the preferred sex difficult in later life, should this be their wish. While this treatment was originally designed to hold future gender options open, we also have to consider the extent to which it may also serve, for some young people, to narrow options down.

Sex hormones may be available from the age of 16.[8] Before moving to this part of the treatment programme, which brings about partially irreversible changes and may affect fertility, young people are expected to give serious thought to the meaning and direction of their evolving gender identification in the context of greater independence, new life experiences, and increasing curiosity about the self. For some of the young people we see, a non-binary[9] identity may be a possible resolution of their body/mind incongruence, with such an identity not seen as necessarily a state of prolonged uncertainty (Roen, 2011). For such non-binary young people, physical treatment may still be an option, but we strive to keep open the widest range of trajectories, including gender diversity outside the medical. We also anticipate the possibility of the young person never achieving a settled body/mind relation until crucial emotional wounds and associated defences have been worked on and, to some degree, resolved.

At GIDS we are very attuned to the ethical issues the work raises (Wren, 2019a, 2019b) and the need to share our concerns and uncertainties about early social transition and early physical intervention with families, the network of other professionals involved, and, depending on their age, with the young people themselves. We will discuss whether these interventions respect the complexity of gender identity development over the course of growing up. We are very conscious of the accountability of clinicians and parents and carers to fully consider issues of autonomy, competence, capacity, and valid consent in the face of the known benefits, risks, and the as-yet-unknown outcomes of the treatments provided. We will support the importance of exploring how sexuality and its vicissitudes (including internalized homophobia) may be intertwined with an emerging sense of gender. And we repeatedly flag the weighty issue of the need to consider how physical interventions may affect fertility and the possibility of choosing to take steps to preserve this (Butler et al., 2018).

We aim to build resilience, helping young people and families to tolerate waiting for possible intervention and preparing for what lies ahead. While the long wait for complete social transition and bodily intervention can be understood by some as a lack of understanding and compassion by the service or the result of insufficient resources, and can be experienced as unbearable, we continue to believe that delay may have meaning beyond being a form of refusal (Baraitser, 2017): at GIDS we feel a profound responsibility to consider carefully what timely care looks like for any particular child.

GIDS was established to offer non-judgmental care and genuine therapeutic curiosity rather than expert knowingness about gender-diverse children. In the 30 years of the service we have come, over the course of time, to be ready to provide physical intervention. Our psychological exploratory work is never reparative: we have no wish to insist on young people being forced into a reconciliation with their sex-of-birth assignment. And we never claim that as clinicians we can establish the "authenticity" of a child's gender identity. Our role is both to provide the most open platform for identity exploration and to insert time into the process of deliberation. We do question whether early physical intervention is emancipatory for everyone who requests it, as for some young people it may side-step a later adjustment to the body-as-it-is and disrupt pathways to same-sex sexuality. We are also conscious of the way early medical intervention may re-inscribe binary gender conformity by encouraging steps towards rendering trans experience and trans bodies invisible. Further research endeavours will, hopefully, tell us much more about which children will flourish with such medical help and which children may come to feel that it had been an unwise or premature step. To grasp this, we are pursuing very long-term follow-up of young people as they move through our service into early adulthood. Meantime, we have to find ways to proceed as a service in the light of the many and conflicting meanings ascribed to these children's experience.

The work of meaning-making

Within the epistemic frameworks routinely available to us, trans[10] and diverse gender experiences have historically been hard to put into language and render meaningful, both to those who experience it (Prosser, 1999) and to those who witness it from close up or from afar. The terms and definitions in everyday use do scant justice to the range of ways in which gender is experienced: the feelings of intense gender variance often seem to be "fundamentally non-lexical—more like a colour than a word" (Marcus, Marcus, Yaxte, & Marcus, 2015). As well as outrunning our language, these experiences often appear to outrun standard assumptions of meaningfulness. The questions raised by the care of gender-diverse children tap into very strongly held constituents of people's habitual world view. We might say that gender-questioning lays down a challenge to certain foundational logics.

The male/female binary

For instance, it has long seemed to be a founding condition of human subjectivity that, other than for people deemed intersex, who have physical features that are not definitively either male or female, there are two sexed bodies and therefore two ways of being in the body. Certainly every society seems to have evolved ways of identifying and segregating the sexes according to visible bodily signs. This is the process by which we treat male and female people as distinctive with respect to a host of psychological and behavioural characteristics: the process of "gendering". Indeed, it has been a bedrock psychoanalytic assumption that sanity lies in accepting the male/female binary (Chiland, 2011). But there is little evidence, across many eras and cultural contexts, that a settled and non-conflicted cisgender[11] identity is, for many, anything other than a concession to normativity in a world of rigid sexual differences, a submission to the irresistible pressure to conform. This is to see conventional (patriarchal) gender as, at least in part, a social construction rather than an inevitable outcome of the biological differences between males and females. Now, in our time, more and more young people are challenging this rigid articulation of sex/gender prescribed by culture and voicing an incongruity with their sex as inscribed on their bodies in the form of chromosomes, hormones, and genitals. Some of these young people are gender essentialists and feel their cross-gender identity to be a deeply real expression of a core "true" self. Others are questioning all conventional relations between sex, gender, and sexuality in favour of a recognition of more fluid lives, identities, and practices. And many are contemplating making alterations to the non-anomalous body to achieve what they hope will be a more coherent sense of self.

Altering the well body

This desire to change the body, pursued by many, but not all, transgender young people, points to a second major perturbation to conventional meaning-making. Physical treatment for transgender feelings disrupts the underlying logic of age-old medical science: that before intervening physically, one must first have a plausible model of the processes underlying the condition (usually seen as a pathological state) on which the intervention is designed to work. There is no identified physical pathology here (Mueller, De Cuypere, & T'Sjoen, 2017)— although many hope that one day a biological marker of gender variance will be found. (The neuro-biological science, though promising the involvement of genetic or neurological elements in the development of a conscious awareness of gender (Turban & Ehrensaft, 2017), is still in its infancy.) But, increasingly, modern medical practice provides for interventions (like *in vitro* fertilization) that are widely offered for needs associated with identity and self-fulfilment rather than for biological dysfunction.

Autonomy and life choices

This links us to the third foundational idea under challenge in this debate: that children should not make major life decisions until a certain agreed level of maturity has been reached, with that level shifting according to the perceived gravity of the decision. While the ages written into law for voting and marrying can be seen as arbitrary, they are broadly accepted indices of a child's developmental stage. Now some parents support very early intervention with hormone blockers for their assenting children of 10 and under, and advocacy groups agitate for children 14 years old and younger to be permitted to take cross-sex hormones and even undergo surgery (see Ehrensaft, Giammattei, Storck, Tishelman, & Keo-Meier, 2018). In fact, in the United Kingdom[12] and elsewhere (UNCRC, 1989), there is increasing acceptance of the need to consult the wishes of children about major decisions that affect their lives, considered in the light of their age and understanding. In the United Kingdom this is reflected in the notion of

"Gillick competence",[13] which is defined functionally and not in terms of age or stage of development and for which there is no lower age limit.

With such powerful assumptions under challenge—the relation between sex and gender, the justification for medical interventions, and the wariness around children as decision-makers—it is not surprising that consensus over the meaning of childhood gender dysphoria is hard to establish.

Interestingly, many well-regarded reports and commentaries on transgender identities tend to elide the question of meaning altogether, offering justifications or rationales for treatment rather than causal narratives (e.g. Coleman et al., 2012; de Vries & Cohen-Kettenis, 2012). When causal stories are present in the literature, they can comprise somewhat over-confident interpretations of the available evidence in line with the bias of the authors towards a biological grounding for trans experience (e.g. Reed, 2017). Other accounts display a greater tentativeness in the light of the empirical findings but offer a rather romantic view of the emergence of a "true" or "authentic" gender self and propose easy detection of those who will persist and those who will not (Ehrensaft, et al., 2018; Hidalgo et al., 2013). By contrast, in looking at causality, some theorists have focused on trans identification as a developmental crisis, (e.g. Coates, Friedman, & Wolfe, 1991), narrowly hypothesizing the role of anxiety in the development of cross-gender identification in young birth-assigned males. Many prominent clinician–researchers respect complexity and the limits of our current understanding, but the causal stories found in their writing often remain sketchy—not unreasonably, given the absence of an empirically validated and clinically applicable body of knowledge on gender identity development to draw on. de Vries and Cohen-Kettenis (2012) and Zucker, Wood, Singh, and Bradley (2012) refer to broadly bio-psychosocial causes (which may involve pathological processes as well as non-pathological developmental pathways), while leaving the actual patterns and casual links between body, mind, and culture unmapped.

Partly as an attempt to address this, some recent models of the emergence of gender identity draw on a dynamic embodied systems framework, whereby bodies, feelings, behaviours, and cognitions arise from the interaction of a number of contributing systems (Fausto-Sterling, 2012). Such an understanding of biological and psychosocial integration over time emphasizes the non-linear course of developmental change and places a premium on the self-organizing properties of experience: a person's idiosyncratic gender identity as "softly-assembled" (Harris, 2005).

Reflecting on possible causative factors from the recent "trans-critical" perspective, some authors see no basis at all in science for the idea of "true" gender lying in the brain or in a pre-social identity. They pointedly reference the role of normative adolescent dissatisfaction with womanhood, the disparagement of lesbian identities, and the perils of social contagion (see Brunskill-Evans & Moore, 2017) to explain the current surge in numbers presenting to gender clinics, especially among birth-assigned females. These authors work to counter the complacency, as they see it, of adults who are willing to take too seriously the new trans narratives of childhood.

Within the psychoanalytic tradition there is a small host of authors handling quite deftly the relationship between gender-diverse experience and the possibility of troubled relational histories, emotional difficulties, and past trauma (Goldner, 2011; Harris, 2005; Rose, 2016). While they stop well short of asserting an established causal link, they suggest the value of exploration of early personal history as a way to make sense of troubling experiences of body–mind incongruence.

But, for all their potential richness and suggestiveness, neither biological science nor developmental theory (even when highlighting a complex interaction of systems that are variable, flexible, and non-linear), nor social-cultural accounts (critical, feminist, or otherwise) have to date done more than speculate, more or less responsibly and knowledgeably, on what is going on. And we remain very far from achieving a comprehensive, credible, evidenced account of the doubtless complex causes of gender diversity in all its richness and variety.

Yet meaning-making is not just about developing originating stories. Meaning and forms of understanding can also be created out of imaginative and compassionate accounts of unhappiness or confusion, by research endeavours showing how gender non-conforming children suffer in family and community environments that are hostile to their feelings and wishes, and by following the impact of different courses of treatment. Studies tracking very young children who transition socially (Olson, Durwood, DeMeules, & McLaughlin, 2016) and older teens who receive medical intervention (de Vries et al., 2014) show an encouraging picture of the good psychosocial functioning of these young people, even though it is recognized widely that these studies have recruited youngsters with few or no psychosocial complications, living in supportive social settings—not the typical GIDS intake. A less adaptive outcome seems to be in store for those with notable pre-existing emotional and behavioural difficulties (Kaltiala-Heino, Sumia, Työläjärvi, & Lindberg, 2015).

Making meaning within a critical social theory framework, some authors are concerned at the involvement of medical technologies in the bodies and imaginations of gender-questioning young people, while being well aware of the pull of freedom represented by the opportunity to change the sexed body. For these authors, treatments like puberty-suspending hormones may push young people into binary gender boxes and thus serve as "a normalising device" (Roberts & Cronshaw, 2017) to enable passing well as the preferred sex in later life. These authors wonder whether it is possible to "both inhabit and resist—be made within and refuse—sexist medical cultures" (Roberts & Cronshaw, 2017). Like Sadjadi (2013), they query in whose interests is promoted this desire for clarity and conventional intelligibility with respect to a child's future sex and gender, rather than tolerating the possibility of multiplicity, fluidity, and even evanescence. Sadjadi (2013) has been especially critical of the way that lurid accounts of the tragic deaths of adult transwomen (as in Giordano, 2008) have been mobilized to lever support for early intervention with puberty blockers for trans children, asking "which futures are opened by the treatment, and which ones are foreclosed?"

Despite these ongoing and unresolved complex issues arising out of different understandings of the provision of good care to gender-diverse children, it is notable that in their meaning-making efforts, writers across the theoretical spectrum increasingly recognize the pain and confusion caused by the rigid regulation of gender, when subjective experience is so much more diverse. In much clinical writing there is evidence of work to shift diverse genders away from an assumption of pathology, while also paying respect to the paradoxes and contradictions of gendered experience. We have seen that within the psychoanalytic tradition there are several thoughtful authors re-evaluating traditional ideas about sex and gender. But it is striking that none of these compassionate and even-handed psychoanalytic authors directly addresses the wisdom of physical intervention for children. Nor do the imaginative and politically engaged critical social theorists, writing from highly interrogative positions about medical interventions with gender-diverse young people, explicitly suggest that clinicians should stop offering puberty suspension or sex hormones to children and adolescents. Indeed, they offer few suggestions for how a clinician might manage the fraught and controversial task of clinical decision-making in the face of children's deep distress and the widespread normalization of these medical approaches. Roberts and Cronshaw (2017) conclude their critical essay with the well-meaning sentiment that we must "remain open to, and try to address, expressions of need and suffering while also resisting perceived solutions that may cause additional unwanted harm" (Roberts & Cronshaw, 2017). Indeed. Nevertheless, these authors do speak, however tentatively, to a wish—shared by many GIDS clinicians—for genuinely greater social freedom for gender self-definition but un-coupled from the drive to provide earlier and earlier physical treatments.

A crisis of meaning?

Given the complexity of the conceptual, epistemological, empirical, and ethical issues around gender identity development in children, the range of conflicting stances taken on these issues, and the often intemperate nature of the resulting public arguments about appropriate care, it is no exaggeration to say that in both the public and professional domains we are in the midst of a crisis of meaning. With a paucity of established longitudinal empirical evidence, no agreement on the adequacy of explanatory models, no proper grasp of the predictive factors for the fluidity versus the stability of transgender feelings, and limited clarity on the long-term impact of medical interventions for young people, even gender professionals are at odds with respect to their understandings, practices, and ethical stances (Gerritse, Hartman, Antonides, & Wensing-Kruger, 2018; Vrouenraets, Fredriks, Hannema, Cohen-Kettenis, & de Vries, 2015).

In addition, within specialist and public debates we are increasingly seeing challenges to the very business of claiming knowledge and understanding in this field. In this way, the "crisis of meaning" relates not just to fierce competition between different ways of understanding the meaning of the phenomenon, but to the very *possibility* of making meaning, the *right* to make meaning, and the *appropriate focus* for meaning making. There are powerful oppositional dynamics operating in the field, knotted into bigger issues of knowledge and authorization that we are facing in contemporary society. These are deeply contentious debates in contemporary thinking about what can be known, and the foundation of that knowledge; about the value, import, and relevance of different kinds of knowledge; about the capacity of young people to know themselves and the world; about the knowing of the doctor versus the knowing of the patient, the expert versus the lay person; about whose knowing is authorized, who has and should have voice. For clinicians working in the field of gender dysphoria in children and adolescents, these dynamics of argumentation powerfully shape debate and constrain the ways in which meaning may be built up, challenged, and cast aside, militating powerfully against developing shared under-standings of what is ethical and compassionate practice, what "good" care looks like, and who should have a definitive say in treatment decisions.

This is the theme I develop in the rest of the chapter, and I do so under six headings broadly related to the politics of truth.

Knowing and authorizing

What can be known

I have already indicated that when we consider what can be known about gender diversity in children, we may feel some dismay at the state of things. As in so many complex new bio-psychosocial fields of enquiry, studies are still few and limited in scope; the body of research findings is patchy and at times contradictory or inconclusive on key questions. Scientific and clinical observations are taken up and inter-preted differently by groups with conflicting stakes in the matter. Limited data can be read with great optimism about the benefits of social transition and medical interventions and the deleterious effects of withholding very active confirmation of the child's felt identity. Alternatively, the data can be read, equally selectively, as providing inadequate reassurance about how to proceed without risking possible harm. In time, we will have the data from research studies reporting the long-term experiences, internationally, of the cohorts of young people who have pursued, or pulled back from, social transitions and physical treatments at different stages and ages. Properly followed up for 10, 20, 30 years, these young people will be profoundly important witnesses to and judges of our various intervention approaches to sup-porting them through their identity development into adulthood. But in the meantime we are faced with the need to take compassionate and reasoned decisions about how to proceed with the limited knowledge and understandings we currently have.

Avoiding the regulatory gaze

Part of what gives this debate such intensity is the fact that influential bodies, confidently embracing fixed models of meaning, have historic-ally used their regulatory gaze to oppress and diminish the social status of sex and gender minorities. Indeed, in the field of sex and gender, the search for causes always risks being oppressive, threatening to undermine the autonomy of the person whose life is being explained. It can seem—as in investigations of the causes of same-sex attraction—that to look for explanations of why sex/gender minority experiences occur requires not only that they be understood, but that they be open to prevention or suppression (Corbett, 1996, 2009a).

In particular, from within the "psy"-disciplines we have a history of prominent theories disparaging and disqualifying the assertions of gender and sex minorities and legitimizing shameful treatment practices. From punitive aversion therapy for gay men (Smith, King, & Bartlett, 2004) to the once-standard psychoanalytic model seeing all trans people as only ever enacting their psychic conflicts, these traditions have found ways, as Goldner writes, of "separating, classifying, ranking and evaluating persons in hierarchies of normality and morality that are . . . hopelessly entangled" (Goldner, 2011). It seems that in the arenas of sex and gender, clinicians, when faced with the atypical and statistically unusual, are too ready to impose fixed notions of what counts as "normal" or "natural", "deviant" and "disordered". The psychoanalytic world view has had its own particular problems with seeing trans people as perverse and anatomy as destiny (Pula, 2015). Numerous authors highlight the radical potential in Freud's thinking but also see that radical thinking replaced with a conservative theory that reflected the predominant views of the time when homosexuality was seen, if not as a pathological condition, then as a developmental failure (Distiller, 2008). In the face of this, in the political struggle for transgender rights, people can understandably be wary of psychological meaning-making that draws on traditions that have been applied with negative effect in the past.

All this should make clinical professionals very cautious about feeling we know best when claiming sure knowledge around what causes childhood gender identity and how its many manifestations should be treated. There are always dangers in carelessly mapping existing models of identity onto transgender experience. But it can also be seen as a loss if, in the name of dignity and self-definition, this wariness of psychological meaning-making narrows the range of narratives that trans people will themselves draw on (Rose, 2016). Once we abandon a too-knowing, narrowly "pathologizing" therapeutic stance, then developmental pathways may more safely be explored. As Rose argues, looking forward to a world that celebrates trans lives, "why in an ideal world . . . should the ethical questions of how we live be severed from knowledge of how we have come to be who we are?" (Rose, 2016).

Expert knowing dethroned

If knowledge previously relied on to make sense of sex and gender identities can now be regarded as biased and dogmatic, the mistrusted province of discredited and outdated experts, then what may support meaning making, and who may authorize identity? While the United Kingdom may legislate soon, under a current review of the 2004 Gender Recognition Act,[14] to free adults and over-16s to self-declare their legal gender identification rather than rely on a clinical panel to formally recognize them as such, mental health clinicians will still be the gate-keepers for access to medical treatment in the NHS. Many challenge this arrangement. Professional authority may be seen as legitimate when related to ostensibly "objective" data such as blood results and bone scans. With respect to the more diffuse and arguable "knowledge", around such issues as emotional and cognitive development, symbolic representation and psychological distress, professionals struggle for legitimacy in a contested field. And, in particular, our stance of reflective uncertainty can undermine our authority in a world of certain and committed voices.

It is no surprise that debates over who can authorize young gender-diverse people's narratives have arisen in the current intense and polarized form in the hyper-connected world we now inhabit. The availability of information on demand, such a key feature of the Web, has led to a widespread de-throning of professional expertise. Through the Internet and social media platforms all young people and many parents have extensive knowledge and awareness of transgender lives, treatments, and politics. The Web has achieved, like nothing else could, the normalization of transgender experience, and in very many ways this is highly welcome. But there has been an additional, related impact: the professional values that traditionally held sway in the public sphere at its best—uncertainty, reflection, dispassionate assessment, caution in response to evidence—are now pitted online against anecdote, anxiety, emotion, and personal stories (Hodgkin & Metz, 2015). Mis-information, unchallenged, can be replicated rapidly across the Web—for example, in discussion of suicide rates of trans young people (see Mann, Taylor, Wren, & de Graaf, 2019). The hierarchical authority of the "expert" is further disabled by virtue of our multiple accountabilities in the modern era: accountability to the individual parent and family, to a wider public good, to our professional bodies and their ethical codes, to taxpayers, and so on. Being presumptuous, taking an unequivocal moral position, assuming a monopoly on truth—

these cannot be our professional virtues as we negotiate our responsibilities in a rapidly changing treatment landscape.

Knowledge legitimating action

While clinicians and parents may share a wish to promote the flourishing and self-determination of strongly gender-diverse children, prevent their suffering, and avoid harm, we increasingly see a clash of meaning-making practices between these groups. In the clinic, parents or carers, young people, and clinicians wrestle daily over the kind of knowledge that is relevant, and how to interpret that knowledge in the service of good care.

Professionals typically see value in the exploration of flexible and creative possibilities for identities for children who do not conform to gender norms, in critical thinking about conventional notions of masculinity and femininity, and in the possibility of change and development across childhood. They may have worries about overstepping what the evidence can so far tell us about the safety of our interventions. While parents who are antagonistic towards their child's atypical gender expression are unlikely to seek help from GIDS, for parents and carers who do come to GIDS, sensitive responding to the child's emotional needs is likely to be the priority, in line with the attachment-orientation of much contemporary parenting. Many parents coming to GIDS see their child's distress and take it on themselves to bring it to a resolution, with less attentiveness to practices of extended meaning-making, of deliberation, and the deferral of intervention; parents are more likely to speak of moving forward with treatment. There can be acceptance of the child's experience in the here and now, an identification with their suffering, and a wish to end it—a desire for "closure and decisiveness" (Marcus et al., 2015). And medical intervention can seem to offer *the* way to end suffering. Parents and professionals may also be oriented to different kinds of risk, with clinicians more concerned about the possibility of later misgivings around medical intervention, even for the few, while at GIDS parents may worry about the risks to their child of withholding treatment.

There may be clinicians who, in an exercise of knowledge-as-power, encourage children to desist and who justify their stance through appeal to normative theories of development and fear of future pathological developments (Pyne, 2014). But it is also possible to use clinical explanations to support and constrain the gender possibilities for children, amplifying future fears of pathology (suicide and self-harm) as

an ethical warrant for puberty suspension, catastrophizing the outcomes for gender-diverse children left physically untreated. As ethno-
graphic researcher, Meadow (2011), asks: "are these children the
ultimate challenge to patriarchy and heteronormativity, or are they yet
stronger evidence that the sex/gender system retains its vice-like grip
on our social order?" Certainly, the association made between
untreated childhood gender dysphoria and pathology underpins the
logic of seeing the solution lying in direct medical treatment rather
than in advocacy for opening up further identity options for gender-
atypical children. As Latham (2017) argues,

> transgender medicine continues to be based on a paradigmatic narra-
> tive of "being born in the wrong body". This narrative performatively
> reproduces sex, gender and "gender dysphoria" as static, predeter-
> mined and independent of medical encounters . . . [and] flattens out
> the complexities of trans people's experience of gender and sexuality.

But if there is a worry that some groups may proselytize interventions that
can seem premature, given the state of knowledge, equally it is a legitimate
concern that caution and uncertainty may paralyse the clinician. Continuing
to explore may always be the preferred option, an endless deferral of the
decision to medically treat.

Through understanding to the limits of understanding

But perhaps it is the case that the whole field of knowledge in sex and
gender development is just too complex for a solid causal account,
with the origins of gender identity development too dense and too
multi-layered over the lifespan to be captured in a generalizable
explanatory narrative. Transgender experience is not a unitary phenomenon; rather, it is better seen as "the end point of heterogeneous
developmental pathways and complex compromise formations" (Saketopoulou, 2014b). Therefore a tractable explanation for how our gendered selves came about may always be beyond our reach. As Phillips
writes of the endless task of meaning-making: "through understanding
to the limits of understanding—this is Freud's new version of an old
project. Freud's work is best read as a long elegy on the intelligibility
of our lives" (Phillips, 2013).

What may be needed is not just that we take a long hard look at
conventional linear understandings, but that we question all settled
identities and all claims to grasp their source(s). This broadly postmodern stance calls on us to examine the assumptions that produce (and

reproduce) what are intended to be fixed categories of meaning, not least because we can never stand outside the conceptual frameworks we are trying to explain. Alternatively, from a queer perspective, all understandings are perpetually unstable and restless, and trans genders always hold the potential to be uncertain, porous and malleable. Queer gender theorists and queer gender subjects do not subscribe to a belief in "the two territories of male and female, divided by a flesh border and crossed by surgery and endocrinology" (Halberstam, 1998), refusing to situate transition "in relation to a destination, a final form, a specific shape, or an established configuration of desire and identity" (Halberstam, 2018). If motivational complexity, non-linearity and unpredictability are to be expected and indeed welcomed, we should no more wish a trans child to return to an unproblematic gender settlement as push forward to medical treatment to assist a new normative settled gender. From this perpetually questioning position, we can echo Casteneda (2015) who writes, "whereas getting access to medical treatment was an important political goal in its time, the success of the movement that made transgender a 'normalised transgression' in turn calls for newly transgressive political aims" (Casteneda, 2015, p. 268).

Knowing the self

Autonomy is a powerful cultural and moral ideal. In the United Kingdom, as elsewhere, we have increasingly come to think that enabling young people to experience some forms of self-determining freedom is also a social good. The idea is interlinked with the thesis that authentic self-knowledge can be achieved, even by children and adolescents. This is the world in which we can come to trust a child's assertion of their intense cross-gender identification and to be guided by them to initiate medical treatment. And if we conclude that experts exceed their entitlement to making meaning in this domain, we may instead take the view that the relevant kind of "knowledge" to serve as a basis for confident decision-making is actually *self*-knowledge. Historically, as we have seen, trans people have been and still are dismissed in their capacity as knowers within health care systems. When society as a whole has lacked for so long an adequate interpretative framework to understand their experiences, how much more so may children and adolescents be subject to such "epistemic injustice" (Fricker, 2007)? It can be argued that what gender-diverse children consistently feel, demonstrate and assert about themselves is what matters—the kind of knowledge to which the young people themselves have "privileged access" (Wren, 2014).

Indeed, in what can feel like a vacuum of credible theory and established meaning, a fierce and determined trust in the child's apparently confident knowing can fill the space for many parents, carers, activists, support groups and other commentators—even when a child is developmentally in flux. A child's sense of gender can feel like a "given", often in a powerfully embodied way—whether stable or fluctuating, whether embraced or unwelcome to the child. And such beliefs and commitments promote a permissive culture within which children, in the exercise of their autonomy, must be allowed the freedom to make their own mistakes.

Towards unknown conclusions

An essay arguing that we are at a time of crisis for meaning-making around gender identity in children and adolescents cannot end in easy remedies or forward-looking projections: too much is still unresolved about how best to care for these young people, given our thinly evidenced treatments and our differing notions of who should decide about social and physical interventions, and when these should be permitted.

In spelling out the various conflicts—over what the science tells us and how it is to be interpreted, over the respect owing to different kinds of "expert" knowledge versus other kinds of knowing; over the biases operating within certain knowledge frameworks; over the way that different groups of knowers have more clout in different contexts; and over the risks of acting prematurely vs being paralysed by uncertainty—I acknowledge that we are at a point of radical public questioning and professional uncertainty about how best to proceed.

Looking forward, a number of scenarios are imaginable. In one, ethical concerns about medical treatment for gender-diverse and trans children become more widespread and acute—not least if physical interventions for young people come more and more to constitute gender as a strictly normative matter, with an apparent insistence that mental health depends on visible identification with one unambiguous binary sex. Ethical concerns may also surface more urgently about the impact on fertility of childhood interventions—often requested precisely to enable such "invisible transitions" (Casteneda, 2015). We may imagine that clinical ethics boards will come to be more and more alive to the issues of children's capacity to consent, as well as to the possibilities of future regret to which the treatment could give rise. Technological developments may, of course, mitigate against some of these ethical concerns if new methods of DNA retention come on-stream, enabling genetic parenting to be preserved earlier in development and more easily. But until there is a clearer ethical mandate for the care and treatment of children and firmer evidence accrues of who benefits over the long-term from which interventions, we may see a slowdown in available treatment options. This could be framed as a setback, or a backlash, against the expansion of gender norms and possibilities for young people, or it could be regarded as an attempt, in part, to negotiate more carefully the range of authentic, progressive, individual identity narratives that are available to them.

A very different future scenario sees us entering a time when radical alteration of the body—the body made malleable through technology—becomes increasingly commonplace, with hormone therapy and sex confirmation surgery seen as "an expression of the originary technicity of the body" (Gill-Peterson, 2014). As Roberts and Cronshaw (2017) write, this approach sees trans bodily modification, even for children, as "an enactment of a normalised developmental transgression". Some argue that, in an era of widespread availability of pharmaceutical products (contraception, Viagra, pain control, etc.), practices of drug use are constitutive of contemporary subjectivities (e.g. Preciado, 2013). Perhaps it can be imagined that gender-diverse people will organize and find ways to insist on de-medicalized free access to GnRH analogues, testosterone, and oestrogen (of certified quality) to allow anyone to shape their bio-psychosocial sex/gender in ways of their choosing. That such unrestricted access could ever apply to children may seem a development that is unlikely, but no longer unthinkable.

In a world of such identity-oriented socio-medical arrangements, attitudes may broaden further around what count as legitimate and liveable gender identities. We can imagine a time when a person's sex and their gender identity will be less apparent, more idiosyncratically honed, and of less interest in everyday social transactions (other than to intimates). The likelihood of people's bodies, gender feelings, and gender expression lining up in the conventional ways we largely expect today will dissolve. Under these social conditions we may see non-binary, gender queer, a-gender, non-gender, and transgender people opting to undergo individually tailored hormonal or surgical interventions, or no interventions at all.

GIDS, at the sharp end of these social changes, with a remit to care for children safely, justly, and ethically at a time of uncertainty, is not in charge of, and barely able to influence, these changes, although some responsibility must be taken for playing a significant part in the fashioning of the "transgender child" in the public mind (Wren, 2015). GIDS will continue to sit at the epicentre of the continued contestation around these scientifically, ethically, and politically complex issues, carefully negotiating relationships with key ideas and key organizations, naming differences but trying not to replay familiar but unhelpful polarizing dynamics.

To make connections when serious differences are present, considerable relational competence is needed. As the Marcus family say: "The knowledge gap creates a vacuum that permits, even invites, the dynamic play of the irrational, when strong emotion can replace critical thinking in intrapsychic, relational and superordinate social realms" (Marcus et al., 2015). But it can be precisely our isolation from the conflicts, anxieties, and responsibilities borne by others that shields us from understanding where other individuals and groups are speaking from. Polarization is a consequence of strongly held positions, but it also creates a further narrowing of perspective. We have to be answerable for how our social, personal, and professional locations set us up to see certain features of a phenomenon and ignore or downgrade others (Haraway, 1988).

We could call this a clash of cultures between and among children and families, advocates and professionals, reflecting the different emotional and ethical commitments underlying their stances. Here we are talking about "culture" in the widest sense. We need to be readier to see the way that the actions of parents, children, clinicians, and others who partake in the debate only make sense with "some shared and ongoing expectations about the social space in which persons participate" (Krauss, 2012). Creating the relational conditions in which these perspectives can be articulated, explored, and sometimes challenged should be a primary task of GIDS. Agreement cannot be contrived, but an ethos of respect towards the "cultural" understanding of other stakeholders can be. We can surely advance the debate through better ways of conducting dialogue. In what Campbell and Groenbaek (2006) called "dialogical conversations", participants attempt to acknowledge their differences and the "otherness" between them. In such conversations all parties are obliged to be interested in what the other is saying, to allow themselves to be influenced by the conversation, and to speak to one another in such a way that they can disagree and add their own contribution.

The role of process is elevated in such encounters, with time taken to elucidate and clarify deeply held values and biases. The presence of power is not denied; on the contrary, there is a sense of power being constantly negotiated and authority shifting between family, young person, clinician, and advocate, somehow enabling the talking and thinking to continue and, in clinical work, to enable good-enough shared decisions to be made.

Sometimes we hear, usually in scornful terms, about the "politicization of gender". But we cannot take the politics out of the public conversation about trans children, nor should we try. Indeed, "multiple forms of politics" are required (Casteneda, 2015). There are matters of substance to argue over: issues of childhood autonomy, treatment outcomes, the safety of interventions, the psychological cost of rigid patriarchal gender categorization, and norms on developing subjectivity vs the benefits of erasing or blurring all such categorizations—all will be argued over in our changing society. We also need to engage with the broader epistemological questions, highlighted in this chapter, that at times threaten to derail our debates—that is, questions about what kinds of knowledge should be respected, by whom, and in what contexts, carrying what authority, at the expense of which other forms of understanding. These are issues to do with who has power, voice, and legitimacy: what Foucault (1997) calls the politics of truth. The divisions are real; there will continue to be necessary struggles over the power to make meaning, as part of the ongoing fight for the recognition, dignity, protection, and just care and treatment of gender-questioning children and young people.

Notes

1. www.legislation.gov.uk/ukpga/2010/15/contents

2. *Gender diversity* and *gender variance* are umbrella terms used to describe a wide range of gender identifications outside conventional gender categories.

3. *Gender dysphoria* is a general descriptive term referring to an individual's discontent and/or distress with their assigned gender. The term is more specifically defined in the *Diagnostic and Statistical Manual of Mental Disorders–5* (*DSM–5*) (APA, 2013).

4. *Social transition*: a person's change from living socially as the gender that matches the sex assigned at birth to living socially as another gender across several domains of social life.

5. GIDS is commissioned by NHS England, and care is provided according to an agreed service protocol, which takes into account international guidance from the *World Professional Association for Transgender Health* (Coleman et al., 2012) and the recently revised guidelines from the *Endocrine Society* (Hembree et al., 2017).

6. *Gender identity* refers very broadly to the individual's deeply held sense of themselves as male or female, neither or both.

7. The GnRH analogue, known colloquially as "the blocker", prevents the natural pubertal signals from the brain being produced, suspending further pubertal development.

8. Treatment with sex hormones involves physiological doses of testosterone for birth-assigned females and oestradiol for birth-assigned males to induce secondary sex changes associated with the gender of identification.

9. *Non-binary:* a term used to describe someone who does not identify as exclusively male or female.

10. *Trans* or *transgender* refers to the broad spectrum of individuals whose gender identity is not congruent with their sex assigned at birth.

11. A *cisgender* individual identifies with their phenotypical sex.

12. UK Children Act 1989: https://www.legislation.gov.uk/ukpga/1989/41/contents

13. The "Gillick" legal ruling (*Gillick v West Norfolk & Wisbech AHA & DHSS* [1983]. 3 WLR [QBD]) defined a competent child as one who "achieves a sufficient understanding and intelligence to enable him or her to understand fully what is proposed and has sufficient discretion to enable him or her to make a wise choice in his or her own best interests" (http://www.hrcr.org/safrica/childrens_rights/Gillick_WestNorfolk.htm).

14. www.edf.org.uk/government-equalities-office-announcement-gender-recognition-act-consultation/

CHAPTER NINE

Crossing over

Melanie Suchet

I

I look across the room to cold eyes and a body steeled. There is no glimmer of a smile. My few attempts at engagement with Rebecca, a young lesbian lawyer, are rebuffed. I push back in my chair and brace myself for a difficult first session. She has been in one form of therapy or another since the age of 6, after intimidating other kids in the playground. She informs me that she is quite adept at playing mind games, one of the benefits she has gained from therapy. Near the end of the session she manages to tell me that this is the longest time she has felt depressed. Although conflicted about starting therapy again, she has only come out in the last few years, and she wants to try working with a lesbian therapist. When the session ends, I am convinced I will never see her again.

I am surprised, and intrigued, when a few days later she phones. "I was really an asshole", she says to the answering machine. "Will you give me another chance?" Wolverine, her favourite superhero, is named after wolves for his heightened animal senses and his mutant healing powers, which enable his body to regenerate and his mind to heal by driving trauma from his memory. I will, over time, come to appreciate this very complex identification. She tells me very early on that she doesn't like her body, especially her breasts. She feels particularly vulnerable when people stare at them; it makes her feel as if she could be raped. Simultaneously she finds herself riding subway cars alone late at night.

In Rebecca's first dream, three months into our work, she is visiting a prior professor's apartment, where they come close to kissing. The female professor takes her to the bed, pulls her down, and is feeling her breasts, wanting more from her, but Rebecca pulls away. The professor gets angry, calling her a tease.

In the room Rebecca can be engaging and flirtatious but just as easily icy and withdrawn. There is a harsh, attacking quality to her interactions. Sessions begin with long periods of silence. Her facial expression is completely devoid of emotion, as if she has carefully wiped away any evidence of her inner world. When she speaks, it is slowly. Every word is sifted through for any nuggets that might reveal more than she is prepared to give. I am not to know anything she does not already know. Her penultimate need for control and her wariness of me is present at every moment. It can take 40 minutes to begin to talk about what is really bothering her, and then she crams the most painful material in the last 5 minutes, when I can do so little with it in the room. I am left sitting with many thoughts and feelings that cannot be spoken. There are words she will not let me utter. Vulnerable is one of them. I have to remember to say "the V word" instead. She cringes and retreats if I forget.

She cannot speak of her childhood, especially of her mother. Now and then I catch glimpses of whatever trauma I imagine she carries, and there is no doubt in my mind that I am sitting with a hurt bird, hiding her bloody injuries, puffing out her chest to appear that which she is not. I feel enormous pressure in sessions to not fail or disappoint her. It is as if she is watching my every move for any misstep, pouncing on me when I do. I cannot simply be quiet in the room, either; she becomes increasingly anxious, pleading with me to help her start sessions, but then remarks sarcastically, "Is that the best you can do?" Later she calls or writes me long letters, which include descriptions of her despair and thoughts of self-destruction. She is 26 years old and has never been touched.

While I tread so carefully to gain entry into her world, I constantly feel pressured by her to break into mine: can she walk around the room, read my books, sit on my chair, study my keys, go outside with me? And what am I drinking, what do I like to eat, what shoe size do I take? Why did I walk more slowly that day, or greet her differently, or choose to wear that shirt? She also badgers me with questions, feeling dejected and frustrated with my wish to understand rather than answer. "You patrol the borders too vigilantly", she says to me. I feel as if she is the professor of her first dream, seducing and simultaneously pushing me further than I am comfortable going. One of her fantasies is of pacing up and down the room intimidating me, asking if I am afraid. Behind the image of an invader I can feel her fragility. I sense that, all too easily, our work could shatter.

Rebecca is the only child of parents who had married late; her mother was 42 when she was born. Her parents felt more hatred for each other than love and divorced right after her birth. Her father was uneducated, and her mother used her Ph.D. to put him down. He had weekend visitation rights but would be inconsistent, with Rebecca seeing him infrequently. Her mother was convinced he had sexually abused her before the age of 5, bathing her each time she returned home in an attempt to cleanse her, but she could not legally prevent him from seeing Rebecca. When Rebecca reached adolescence, she refused to continue to see him. She describes him as angry, manipulative, and at times verbally abusive. She learned to hide any hurt feelings from her father. She "would not give him the satisfaction of seeing her squirm or show pain". I now recognize the blank expression she gives me. Her life with her mother was "just the two of them", a fused relationship of two outsiders. Initially she refuses to talk about her mother. Over time, a picture emerges of a woman who is narcissistic, harsh, controlling, and intrusive. They appeared to have a close relationship infused with deprivations (of touch, food, and friends). There would be constant fights about issues of control. I start to wonder if my feeling of being invaded by Rebecca is how she experienced her mother. In one of her early childhood dreams her mother is following her through the house and she cannot get away, eventually locking herself in the bathroom.

In the fifth month of a still once-a-week treatment she mentions her conflicted feelings around gender. She does not feel like a woman, but she doesn't feel like a man either, although she feels more like a man than a woman. As an adolescent she hated her breasts, feeling sadness that she could no longer be like a boy, but now she is unsure. She recalls doing push-ups with the image of an ideal muscular male body as early as 7 or 8 years old.

Then she brings in a dream: she is in my office, and 15 minutes before the end of the session I tell her that I know what happened a few nights ago, that a tranny (transgendered person) had been killed and that I am concerned for her. I give her a testosterone pill and a few handwritten pages about taking care of herself and how to pass well as transgendered. I put my arm around her and then give her a hug. She is aroused and pulls away. I won't stand for that and pull her back.

The dream shakes me up. What are the dangers she fears? What is it she wants from me? Testosterone. To be seduced. Sexual abuse is always in the back of my mind. I keep wondering about her relationship with her mother and what of her mother's unconscious she is carrying. When exploring the dream, she can talk only about her anxiety about being aroused by me. She lets me know that sometimes when she pulls back from me, it is because she is actually physically aroused. Her association to the testosterone is of me trying to take care of her. I interpret that she seems to have a very specific fantasy of how I will take care of her, by transforming her into a man. She cannot respond.

An intense erotic transference is beginning that in different forms always permeates our work. She wants to open up with me but is terrified and feels frustrated with herself. Then she walks into a session with a dress on. It is the last time she ever wears one. It is difficult for me to look at her and even harder for me to describe it. She does not even look like a "dyke in a dress", as she refers to herself; it is stranger and more alien. I think to myself: she does not belong in a dress. There is something I do not want to see; her being so out of place, the shame that suffuses her performance.

In her next gender dream I ask her what her bra size is. Then I take off my bra and give it to her to try on. It is too big. She takes it off and gives it back but forgets to pull her shirt down. A friend comes by and tells her to pull her shirt down.

She is reluctant to discuss the dream. She is not only internally conflicted but struggling to figure out what gender I want her to be. I wonder how she reads my femininity and what she thinks I am trying to give her. We explore the dream as a way of her letting me "see" her femininity (as she had tried with the dress), and since the bra is a "measuring tool of femininity", I am trying to give her more. My bigger breasts are a reflection of her seeing me as more comfortable with my femininity. Her dream is quite apt. Then, quite surprisingly, with an openness and vulnerability that can feel so out of place, she writes to me, "I want to give my sensitive, vulnerable, feminine parts to you as a gift." I find myself being moved and touched by her in ways I had not anticipated.[1]

I do have the fantasy that the work would involve her coming to accept and value the feminine parts within her, so she can feel, psychologically, both boy and girl, a similar trajectory to the one I had taken. At this time, in the late 1990s, I had never worked with anyone who is transgendered. I feel anxious as to what transitioning to the other sex would mean. I have vague theoretical ideas circulating in the back of my mind. Would the psychoanalytic world be considering issues of severe pathology, condemning any form of surgery?[2] Would the feminist world be thinking of essentialist notions of gender, returning to rigid stereotypes?[3] I make a conscious decision to resist my urge to read everything I can on the subject, with the fantasy that I will understand it all. I know that for now I must stay close to my experience in the room with Rebecca. I have to let myself feel the anxiety of not knowing, of exploring unfamiliar territory, just as she is.

II

Rebecca decides to come twice a week. Her depressive symptoms have started to lift. She asks me if she can bring in her new stuffed animal, a frog called Ambrosias. I refer to Ambrosias in the feminine, and she tells me immediately that it is a he. It is a male frog with a female name. Ambrosias begins to arrive at sessions, pop out of Rebecca's backpack, and sit on her leg or the edge of the couch, looking up at me with his soft eyes. Sometimes she asks me questions or tells me things through Ambrosias that she otherwise could not. I feel a little wary and restrained at first. I am not sure what the correct psychoanalytic stance is towards stuffed animals.

Rebecca buys a new male frog, Melodius, named after me; he is described as open and kind. Rebecca gently coaxes me to let go a little, nudging me on to play with the boys. Over the months we find new ways to interact. Rebecca likes to keep Ambrosias and give me Melodious, who sits on the arm of my chair. I start to carefully arrange him in different ways, talk to him, and try to make sure he is comfortable. Sometimes I mess up, and Rebecca gently teaches me how to best care for both of them. On occasion we discuss "how the boys are doing", especially if I am away or they have to leave town. At other times the discussion centres on how I hold them, stroke them, and how tender or clumsy I can be with them. Sometimes the frogs leap across the room, and on special occasions they stay overnight, awaiting Rebecca's return.

Through the frogs Rebecca discovers that we can approach more topics than she could on her own. She tests my ability to accept her "boys" and the boy in her. She also uses the frogs as a way of holding me close without cajoling or pressuring me. I "mark" the frogs by touching them so she can embrace them at night, thinking of me. I, too, come to imbue them with emotions, to enjoy them, and find myself eagerly awaiting their arrival. I marvel at the creative solution she has found to help us get close and explore gender. I also feel relief, a sense of being able to breathe again. I am less boxed in, less intruded upon, and less constrained, as is she. It is as if we have created a little respite, a safe sanctuary in a space that otherwise feels so fraught with tension and longing.

In my first dream of Rebecca,[4] *she persuades me to take her with me on vacation. I agree and then regret it.* I think to myself that I must be crazy. What have I done? Have I crossed a boundary?

I fear crossing too many boundaries. Is it a slippery slope, I wonder? Clearly a part of me wants to take her on vacation, adopt her and the boys. She so wants to belong, to find a home. How much has changed from the beginning of our work.

Slowly she allows herself to have fantasies of me touching her breasts and then the rest of her body as a response to feeling deadened. She struggles with dissociation in every session and on her own. "When I can't feel, you bring me back", she says. Having me seduce her, in fantasy, is a way of surrendering her body to me and trusting me to gently bring her back to feeling. She yearns to find a home for herself and speaks poignantly of the desire to be "seduced out of silence".

I explore her wish to surrender and her fear that surrender is a submission, a misuse of power, leaving her open to be abused and exploited.[5] Her wish to surrender is often followed by an attack. She verbally lashes out at me. To be female is linked with vulnerability and the danger of sexual abuse. In addition, it is as if girl is a container, a receptacle for unwanted and hostile projections, whereas male offers protection from that which is thrust into her, including maternal projections. She acknowledges that with her mother it feels as if something noxious is being forced into her.

I learn that her mother's childhood was like a "holocaust". Her mother was one of twins; the other twin, a male foetus, had died in utero. Her mother has no contact with her own mother. Their relationship is "irreparable". Her mother's professional life is centred on sexual abuse. Her mother was sexually abused by her stepfather until she was 11 years old, although at the time she was led to believe that her stepfather was her father. Her mother spent years looking for her biological father, whom she never found.

I begin to wonder if Rebecca is the lost twin or father in her mother's fantasy. What are her mother's dynamics, and what are Rebecca's, and how were they intertwined? Is being boy a fantasy of protecting herself from her mother and/or is it her mother's fantasy Rebecca is enacting? Whose story is she living? Was it her mother who was giving her testosterone, needing her to be a testosterone boy? My thinking is strongly influenced by Laplanche's (1997) ideas on the enigmatic sexual messages transmitted unconsciously from mother to child. The origin of the child's desire is related to the sexual message of the other, to the seduction of the other.

III

With the delicacy of timing in mind, in our third year of twice-a-week work, it feels possible to begin to analyse a central sexual fantasy Rebecca had related to me the year before. The fantasy is, "A woman is sucking my cock, my strapped-on cock. The woman wants to please me but it goes against her politics. It starts with her kneeling down, something she doesn't want to do, but that is okay. I try to explain to the woman that it is about succumbing to my desire, letting someone take me over as I fall back on the bed and they are on top of me. Then I take off the dildo and we have great sex until she tells me she loves my body, my hips, breasts and genitals. I feel very hurt and mocked."

The fantasy comes to be understood as the conditions that will allow Rebecca to surrender. "I have to be boy to be girl", she says. I am puzzled. "You have to be that which you are not to allow for that which you are?" I ask. (My thinking at this time was still limited by biological reductionism.) "YES", is the angry reply. She has to feel more like a boy to let herself express her girl parts. She has to wear the dildo to surrender to her femininity. To be vulnerable from the position of girl is too dangerous; it invites exploitation. Only from a position of power, of strength, of having a penis, can she succumb and "fall back on the bed". She has to protect herself from the humiliation of femininity, of being in the "done to" position. This is a pivotal moment in our work. Girl is such a degraded position. I think to myself that if our work can help her find a different way to be girl, find something strong and powerful in the girl position, she will find a different way to live in herself. I am focusing on gender and the gender identifications she has internalized, particularly her mother's shame and disgust towards her own body.[6]

In addition, the desire to get close, in her mind, is associated with surrender and the girl position, so that as she allows more intimacy with me, which she yearns for; she feels in danger, becoming more hostile. She is terrified of being sexually attacked or harmed by me. In an instant I become the abuser who is penetrating, pushing her too far. Her eager anticipation of our sessions turns to dread. We work on the possible sexual abuse, of which she has no memories. She recalls that the neighbours hated her, as she would scream at night when it was time for bed, imagining someone climbing the stairs to her room to rape and murder her. She would also wake up screaming every night with nightmares until she went to college. She retreats in our work, feeling quite depressed.

Rebecca is also struggling more with her body. Every summer brings an intensification of hatred towards her breasts, which she can no longer hide. She spends hours before the mirror, repulsed by her body. She describes her feelings as intolerable, wanting to "crawl out of her skin". She yearns for all visible traces of femininity to disappear. She wants to be more stone (the impenetrable butch partner who does not want to be touched sexually). She detests her "fat, feminine" shape, particularly her chest. She speaks of how much she wants to "rip her breasts off", followed quickly by fantasies of chest surgery. During this period she has a number of transgender dreams. She finally decides to join a transgender support group.

I show her the path of her associations, from hatred and shame about her body to surgery, as if surgery could be a way of getting rid of her feelings. She is angry with me. I point out that she can't imagine changing her feelings about her chest, only changing her chest. She feels surgery is about changing her feelings. She questions my motivations. She wishes to take a break from me and the work. She is nostalgic for the times when she couldn't wait for a session or fell asleep imagining me holding her.

I have very ambivalent feelings about her going through surgery. Changing one's body doesn't fit with the psychoanalytic model of working through intrapsychic conflict. I am influenced by Kubie's (1973) belief that surgery is an attempt to gain an untenable fantasy of psychic redemption through physical transformation. I have also, at this point, read very closely Ruth Stein's (1995) "Analysis of a Case of Transsexualism", one of the only in-depth clinical papers written from a psychoanalytic perspective. She writes of transsexualism's conceptual challenge to psychoanalysis and tries to explore its relationship to perversion, psychosis, and sexual deviation. She believes it is partially a perversion, in the dynamics of hate, envy, and vengeance, but it is different in that the symptoms of raw terror and anxiety are more open, conscious, and less circumscribed. There is no mention of bodily hate. In her work with this male-to-female transsexual, Stein helps him "become a woman" in the psychological sense; working on his gender identifications, he becomes comfortable with the receptive aspects of his gender and has no desire to physically transition.

I find myself working hard, trying to find a way to explore with Rebecca the possibility of holding the masculine and feminine together, not having to give up either, but finding a way to live with both, a dialectic, a girlboy or boygirl. She believes that her opposite sides, her boy and girl, just cannot be reconciled. She tells me it's "too fucking hard". She starts wishing that I was more butch, that I had more muscular arms, and that I didn't wear eyeliner. She wishes I was like her. She had chosen me at first because I seemed to be more like her in gender terms, but now as she is becoming more trans she wants me to be more of the same. She detests the female aspects of her body, thinks of chest surgery constantly and possibly testosterone. She has no desire for genital surgery. She divides her body into zones: the top half of her body is male—it is the part that the outside world can see—and the bottom half is female, what she can give to her lover. It also becomes clear that with all the increased work on her wish to surrender, her desire to transition is escalating. She explains, carefully and thoughtfully, that masculinity is fragile, more fragile than femininity, so you need something biological, concrete, to affirm it. "You can't just act boy, you have to look boy. Masculinity separate from a male body is even more fragile, more in need of constant assertion", she tells me. This makes holding on to any girl parts, any feminine identifications, threatening to her masculinity; she is not "man enough".

IV

Three years into our work, I am beginning to feel the internal changes in her. Although her gender issues are always central, we also work intensely on her object relations. Our relationship is deepening; she is allowing more intimacy with me and slowly with friends. She starts dating. She is becoming aware of how much she intimidates and shuts people out, how instinctually she wishes to end relationships when feeling hurt or disappointed, and how difficult it is to hold good and bad together, As she is learning to trust me and open up, the sense of a caged animal shifts to more of a wary one, and the amount of dissociation is lessening, allowing us to do more work in the room. She starts to allow her lover to touch her sexually.

However, every time she speaks of sex, her dreams and fantasies are flooded with images of being sexually abused. She can see the links between her desire to surrender and sexual abuse. She goes home and actively imagines severing the ties. She draws pictures of a sledgehammer, an axe, and a sword, trying to imagine how best to symbolize splitting the two experiences apart. She is intent on feeling different. She writes how she imagines surrendering to me. With much work the woman she has started dating turns into a serious relationship of several years. She begins a process of wanting to surrender to her in different ways, very cautiously opening herself up in ways that had been unimaginable. Rebecca cries for the first time in the last session before my summer vacation. She tells her new lover, "the cowards among us spend our lives running away from difficult emotions. Those who are strong feel things deeply."

Over my vacation, I have another dream. Rebecca starts to take off her shirt. I'm surprised because I know how mixed she feels about her chest. We are outside with several people. As she lifts her shirt I notice that she has no breasts. I look at her and it feels okay. I can accept her.

I am surprised by my own dream. Something is shifting in me, too, although I am still conflicted about surgical intervention. In the room Rebecca becomes angry with me. "I'm sceptical and wary of your hypothesis that being vulnerable leads me to wish to transition because of what I think it means to be a woman. It sounds too close to some trans-phobic things out there that transmen are self-loathing women." I answer that it is as if she sees her body as separate from meanings and feelings about her body. I continue by adding that I think it is hard for her to take in what I say about vulnerability and her body because she sees it as threatening the possibility of transitioning. She absolutely agrees with this. I explain that I don't see them as necessarily mutually exclusive. "If my hypothesis is true that you want to get rid of your breasts because you don't want to feel vulnerable as girl, then you are dealing with a psychological conflict by changing your body, the danger being you could be without breasts and still feel the same way." I add that I have changed, though. I am not invested in how she finally defines herself. I would feel differently if the psychological issues are worked through and she still feels the same way about her body. I let her know that, no matter what her decision is, I will go with her to whatever place that takes us. I realize that I am no longer steering her (consciously or unconsciously) to follow my path. I am starting to understand something about the deeply held feelings about her body. Rebecca relaxes. Her body sighs, and I see the tension lifting.

Rebecca tells me about the transgender narratives she is reading. I begin to start to read them, too. My first book is Jay Prosser's (1998) intellectual and erudite *Second Skins*. Prosser, drawing on his own experience, emphasized the "materiality" of trans narratives, exploring how the essence of subjectivity is "bodiliness". To understand transsexuality, one has to grapple with the "materiality of the body itself" (p. 77). He wrote of the transsexual's need to acquire sexed embodiment (a feeling of a coherent, integral, and erogenous body). Prosser based some of his understanding on the work of the analyst Didier Anzieu (1989), who emphasized the skin ego as central to the sense of self. Subjectivity is about feeling one owns one's physical skin; it concerns the "psychic investment of self in skin" (Prosser, 1998, p. 73). One can only feel "at home in one's skin" (p. 73) if one's body image is synonymous with the material body. Moreover, for Prosser, since the problem is located in the material body, intervention needs to be at that level, by surgically altering the flesh rather than psychologically altering body image.

The other most informative book at the time is by the sociologist Holly Devor (1997) on female-to-male transsexuals. It is a comprehensive compilation of trans narratives documenting stages of identity development for female-to-male transsexuals, including experiences pre- and post-surgery. I am struck by the consistent theme that most people are much happier after surgery. In addition, it is clear that breasts are the marker of gender and that surgery for most female-to-male transsexuals is top (breast) surgery. I realize that I need to think about and understand the body differently and contemplate surgery as possibly therapeutic.[7]

Rebecca is having dreams of coming to session wearing only her boxers, which are open, and I can see her genitals. She writes that she never imagined she would feel safe and that when early in the treatment I had said we would never touch, she felt loss, imagining that she would never feel held or comforted by me, but now she can feel all of that. She begins to want her lover to enter her sexually, not just be touched but penetrated. What had been forbidden to even mention, that which had threatened her identity and her masculinity, which opened her up to abuse, is now consciously desired. Rebecca is coming alive. I can feel the changes and hear of them on the outside. I feel excited. We can talk in the room; she can allow herself to feel, and let herself be entered, emotionally. She has her first image of being a young child and fingers coming from above her, opening her genitals, and touching her.

In her next dream she is in a session with me and talking about sexual abuse when she suddenly tells me that she thinks it was her mother that abused her. She is deeply disturbed by the dream. I am not. I have wondered whether her mother actually abused her, given her mother's own history and lack of boundaries. However, we still cannot discuss the possibility and implications of her mother as abuser; she is too frightened and remains dissociated in the room. After a few days her anxiety "gives way to simply feeling supported and held by me, wanting to lean into it more, let more go".

V

We are in the fifth year of our work together. Rebecca comes late to a session. Without a clear precipitant, she starts to jab at me and continues throughout. She doesn't want to be vulnerable. Her relationship is falling apart, and she is angry with me. She wants to end with me, too. I am uncertain as to what is occurring and the cause of her sudden aggressiveness. As the next session unfolds Rebecca refers to herself as "he". Suddenly it becomes clearer. She is struggling to tell me directly that she can no longer refer to herself as "she". It is a turning point. We ponder what it will be like to choose a different name. She has had enormous conflict and ambivalence about how much of a man or woman would best represent her and if she can create something in between. Over the next few sessions, we explore the possibility of making the transition to be named a man.

We speculate on what it will be like for me to shift, too. I realize that I feel anxious and uncertain, despite having known that this moment would come. I understand my anxiety about shifting to see Rebecca as a man is in a very small way what she experiences all the time. It is the struggle Rebecca has lived in, with its ambiguities, contradictions, and unanswerable questions. She lives in the transitional world of in-between, both and neither simultaneously, and crossing the gender divide is a leap fraught with complications, some of them very practical, as in many situations she is now read as a man.

We explore our fears of how things might change. She is concerned that I will relate differently to her as a him; she will no longer identify with me, and perhaps I won't see her as like me, either. There will be something strange and "other" in the room. She is also afraid that she will not be able to flirt with me, that I will not find her attractive as a boy. And if there still is a sexual attraction between us, will it make her a straight man, and will I be a straight woman? I too wonder aloud what we will lose between us. I do not know. What does gender hold? Is it a place setting, a way of announcing how we are to relate to each other? Am I afraid everything will be turned upside down? Would she be the same person or would she become someone quite other? I notice Rebecca has turned away; she is crying. She acknowledges that we have created something that is as close to safe as can be imagined. We both acknowledge some fear of the change, and Rebecca tells me that this fear between us has been one of the greatest barriers to transitioning. I was unaware of how much I was holding her back.

During her vacation Rebecca decides to see her father for the first time in 10 years. She finds he is not who she thought he was and most importantly she is no longer afraid of him. He desperately wants to have a relationship with her. The visit goes so well she decides to see him a second time. This is an enormous step for her. In terms of gender we wonder how much wanting to be male has been a desire for separation and protection from her mother and how much has been a yearning for the father she never had.

On her return, she tells me that she has decided on a name. I am to be the first person that she is trying this new name on. I feel the weight. The name is to be Raphael, healed by G-d. I think, once again of Wolverine, the desire to be healed and the capacity to transform. We explore the biblical meanings and references of the name and what makes it the first choice. I like the name. I am relieved I do not know anyone with that name. I practise the name quietly to myself. I feel the new syllables and sounds swirl around. I want it to flow out of my mouth in an easy, uncomplicated manner. It lodges in my throat. I question myself. What's in a name? So what if Rebecca identifies as a man? What does it mean to me? Is this so different from the regular work of uncovering, discovering, or exploring hidden selves? Why am I getting stuck? I think of analogies—if Rebecca came to me as a heterosexual and then came out as gay, or vice versa, I would make the shift without hesitation. So I ponder, what is it about male and female?

Raphael walks in on Friday wearing a dark pinstriped suit, light blue shirt, and bright yellow tie. His hair is a buzz cut, as short as is possible. His face is soft. He looks like a sharp, tailored young boy. I find myself surprisingly admiring his attire. He uncharacteristically starts talking about gender after 10 minutes into the following session.

He has been thinking about what he is afraid will change in the room. He is concerned that he will have to give up his fantasy of surrender. He is deeply afraid that he will have to give up the girl in him.

For one last time I try to explore if his history of trauma is what needs to be forgotten, excised, an erasure on his body. I return to my thought that his fantasy of being a boy reflects a wish to be closed off, getting away from vulnerability. He refutes this. We explore his wish as a dis-identification with his mother, his mother as intrusive, invasive, as the possible abuser. He becomes angry with me.

"I am frustrated with you", he says to me a few days later. "When you link gender with sexual abuse I feel you are de-legitimating me, invalidating how I feel. It reminds me of when I went to my mother's therapist and he tried to figure out if me being a lesbian was linked to the sexual abuse."

This is one of those moments with him. I have to be absolutely honest. I take a deep breath and start to talk. I tell Raphael that indeed for many years I believed that if we could understand how the sexual abuse was linked to the transgender struggles, then there would be no need to translate those psychodynamic issues into changing the body through surgery, that the issue could be resolved at a psychic not physical level. I believed she could be as much boy or girl as she wanted, she could create and live her own version of gender, without having to construct a body to fit her gender identification. Then when she pushed me two years ago, asking me directly what I would do if she transitioned, either using T (testosterone) or chest surgery, I told her that independent of what I thought was right or not, I would go through the journey with her. Now, in fact, I have come to a different place.

I have watched over the years how he has worked as hard as is possible to understand and explore all the issues before us. And what I have witnessed is a shift in his inner world, in the organization of his object relations, his fantasies and desires. Even his gender identifications have altered as he has allowed himself to express more of the feminine and moved towards a better integration of the feminine with the masculine. Yet what remains untouched is his hatred of his body. I have come to understand that the body feels and means something totally different to him than what my body means to me. He has taught me that his relationship to his body is not easily manipulated and shifted from the inside, and I have always approached change from the inside out. This doesn't seem possible for Raphael. The psychological, inner world does not always take precedence over the physical. He has said it is the container that must shift, and then the contained will be experienced differently. I have slowly, over time, come to understand this. Despite all the insights he has gained from our explorations of the psychodynamics, despite all the awareness and understanding he has attained, and despite his best efforts, he has not come to accept his body as it is.

I now realize that something fundamental cannot shift until he alters his body. I have come to understand the body has its own meanings separate from the psyche. And that these meanings the body carries are not necessarily translatable into words or altered by words. So I now think that changing the body may help to change the psyche. This does not diminish the fact that there are reasons why he feels the way he does regarding his body, but it no longer feels that these reasons have to preclude physical change. An understanding of psychodynamics, work on shifting gender identifications and attachment, does not necessarily alter the embodied experience of being male/female/or differently sexed.

I have slowly come to understand the importance of the body in transgender subjectivity, and that it is a sexed embodiment, a body in which the genitals are experienced as erogenous. For many in the trans world, there is a dis-ownership of their genitals, such that the body remains unsexed and untouchable (Prosser, 1998, p. 77). I have discovered that my psychoanalytic training had not prepared me for the kind of relationship to a body that Raphael has. I am aware of a need to revise our theories, to generate new ideas on the complexity of embodiment. I am tussling with the theoretical challenges as I slowly find myself giving up my allegiance to what I thought I knew. I am increasingly influenced by postmodern gender and queer theory, which has shifted focus to address how the body, especially the trans body, challenges any fixed categories in the sex/gender system. I start to allow more space to think openly, more fluidity in myself. I think about how one comes to inhabit a body and live in it.

I begin to think of this body as the nonverbal imprint of the (m)other, the body as the container of the mother's expelled unconscious phantasies, the body as vessel for memories that cannot be spoken. I find myself drawn to Kristeva's (1995) emphasis on the body, her exploration of the pre-symbolic dimensions of experience, the space in which meaning is below the surface of the speaking being. We are in the realm of the preverbal, the semiotic, the space of rhythms, sounds, colours, and bodily senses. This is where the unconscious makes itself known through the body. There are no words.

Raphael is writing short stories of his longing to find a home. He speaks of nostalgia and melancholia, of loss and yearning. The home he longs for, the search for a bodily container, is not the re-finding of that which has been lost but the home he has never known. When the body does not feel like home, when ownership of the body cannot be attained, when the body has unconsciously been colonized by the other, the deepest unconscious phantasy is of reclaiming the body.[8] And this reclaiming, this attempt to re-inscribe the body, to break free of the confines of the imprisoned self, to decolonize the self from an invasion that has come to inhabit the material flesh, may only be possible through the concreteness of bodily transformation.

I am grasping that how gender comes to be experienced in an emerging body is far more complex than early psychoanalytic models posited. Moreover, embodiment is very different from gender identifications and expressions of gender. And embodiment is not a given (even if never questioned by most of us) but a complex process of acquiring a sense of ownership of one's material flesh, an investment in the bodily self. I can see how it is influenced by physiological, cultural, and unconscious processes and highly sensitive to traumatic disruption. I find Patricia Elliot's (2001) paper on transsexuality very helpful in her exploration of embodiment, integrating psychoanalysis and trans narratives. She wrote of surgery being a necessary means for coming to inhabit a body, and certainly preferable to a "precarious state of disembodiment" (p. 313). According to her, acquiring sexual embodiment is a complex psychosexual process; unlike Prosser, who believes it originates in the body, she emphasized the unconscious dimensions, especially the task of establishing oneself as a separate subject. She articulated that psychoanalysis and surgery should not be regarded as mutually exclusive endeavours.[9] Perhaps, for some, it is necessary to feel the scalpel, to imagine literally excising the trace of the other, cutting the body, the shared common skin of mother and child (Anzieu, 1989), excising the hated other, and demarcating a new body, emerging into a new space of corporeality, into a new sense of self that is habitable.

Raphael and I discuss that I came to the work focusing on the psychological and he on the body. Maybe we can create a space for both. I acknowledge that I have shifted too, that Raphael has taught me much. Now that I have made large conceptual leaps in understanding his need to transition, I find that what is asked of me in the room as he begins his transformation is a different process altogether. If intersubjectivity is an embodied process (Reis, 2009), a way of knowing each other through our bodies, how will his changing body affect my own? Perhaps I am afraid that his transitioning will rock my own gender stability. Will it open options I have never contemplated? Do I fear opening up new realms of possibility? On the other hand, I realize there is also a faint glimmer of envy; does he get to be both sexes?

He tells me that the last time he had sex with his girlfriend, "I wanted her to go inside me. I really did. But I knew if that happened I'd have to end the relationship. . . . You know why, don't look puzzled . . . it would make me . . . a girl!"

I have warned myself to be careful on the last session before my vacation. There is a pattern of intense work that ends the session with Raphael being angry and taking weeks to months to repair the rupture on my return.

"I am confused", I say. "I can't always follow your logic on what allows you to see yourself as boy and what doesn't. You can have a vagina and be a boy but you can't let someone enter you and still be a boy . . . . Sometimes you are so tied to your body as to what a boy is or what a boy does and at other times you are able to transcend that and create your own definition of boy."

Raphael just sits in silence. I have no idea, despite our years of work, what this is going to mean to him. I cannot read his face in these moments. He wipes away any clues, and I wait in a familiar vacuum. Did I go too far, I wonder? I feel conflicted—it is a perfect opportunity, given what we are working on, but simultaneously will he feel that I am being too penetrating. The transference implications are evident. Am I being drawn inside him to be experienced as violating and thereby giving him cause to flee?

Raphael finally responds. "I think of my clit as a dick", he says. "That's how it works for me, but if I am penetrated then I can't see myself as a boy. What you don't understand is that straight boys don't talk about anal penetration. You don't really get it. It's a boy thing to struggle with penetration. It's like a rite of passage."

"And you don't understand because you're not a boy" is the stab at me that is left unsaid. "Surrender is feminized for you", I say, not letting myself be shoved aside. We end the session. I am left with my own thoughts. How much he yearns to have someone enter him, physically and symbolically, and how much shame and fear cover that over. He dresses himself up to mask that longing. And the wish to undress, to surrender, haunts him. I return in my mind to his central sexual fantasy and the only conditions he can imagine that will allow him to attain his longed for surrender.

Raphael is angry with me when I return from my one-week vacation. He is confused by the messages that I am giving him. Four months ago I said that men usually struggle with vulnerability, and that made him feel that I understood him as a man. Now I am saying that he doesn't need to have that struggle, that he should give it up. He tells me, "You can't just alter the meanings of the body. It's not possible to re-read everything, just to change the way you experience your body because you want to." He is so right. I have had to learn over and over with him that the psychological does not always take precedence over the physical, the body. And despite all my own theoretical shifts I have struggled to give up the notion that his sense of embodiment can be shifted as his sense of self shifts.

In the room I agree with him that I can see how I could be confusing and that you cannot simply re-read everything the way I imagine it possible. But I don't think that struggling with vulnerability or surrender is what defines a man. Raphael sits forward and challenges me to define what does make a man. I smile and say, I don't know. I am as confused as he is about what makes him or anyone else a man.

Raphael comes late to the next session. He declares his reluctance to be there at all. I feel the iciness in his blank stare. I say that I think his experience is that I am trying to take something important away from him, how he is boy. I explain that for me this line of thought started with his discussion of wishing to have his girlfriend enter him and how he couldn't do that because it would make him too much of girl. I challenged him in a way to open things up, not take something away. I tell him that I see our work as getting to a space where he could feel comfortable having what he wants without losing who he is.

VI

He is working long hours at his job and being accepted in his masculine identity. In a suit and tie he is always recognized as a man, but summers are difficult; he feels intense shame and layers his body with clothes. He can never go swimming. His friends, a few close people, are accepting of his transitioning. Then, unexpectedly, a few months later, he gets laid off from his job, and his father's health is deteriorating very rapidly. He decides to go across country to take care of his father. This would have been unimaginable previously. He is hoping for the possibility of knowing his father in some deeper way and there being some form of reconciliation. His visit with his father is significant. They discuss many difficult topics, and it becomes very confusing to sort out his mother's version of his father as compared to the man Raphael is interacting with. He discovers that his mother had a serious postpartum depression, and one day, when his father came home, she had taken Rebecca and left a note telling him she wanted a divorce. He finds his father is generous in ways his mother never is and genuinely trying to work things out without holding on to grudges and torturing Raphael the way his mother does. The picture is getting more complicated. He is surprised how much he prefers living with his father. Issues of his purported sexual abuse remain unresolved and in the air. His father goes over the graphic words his mother used when accusing him of abuse and argues that she was reliving her own abuse. His father is adamant he never abused Rebecca. Raphael's father dies while he is taking care of him. Raphael returns to New York six weeks later. He is nostalgic for the father he lost so many years ago and the experiences that were denied him.

He decides to continue with his transitioning. It is difficult in his work to expect everyone to call him Raphael while there are still ways he looks and sounds like a woman. He has thought about what being a man is and decided that it is not defined by what is between his legs but what his body looks like, particularly how muscular it is. It is not genitally based but, rather, based on how one appears to others, the shape of the body and how you move it, what you do with it. Similarly, what defines a woman is mostly what is visible to others, her breasts. I understand more and more that it is not enough to know that you are a man in mind, to act boy, or feel boy, because the body is what holds you back from being recognized and read as boy. "Boy has to be written on the body", he tells me.

Raphael is pushing forward, entering spaces he has never allowed himself to go. He fantasizes about allowing himself to imagine being penetrated by a man. He has dreams of being spread open and of having a man inside him. It is not a rape as it was before in fantasy; he is not terrified, and he tells me that the "focal point is about this pleasurable feeling and my wanting more and more". He starts to draw more images of himself as a girl, sexual images too. For the first time he starts to explore going inside himself, imagining himself as a woman with a woman's body, and he feels sexual pleasure. His sexual fantasy has changed dramatically. He knows he needs to allow himself to be "fucked as a girl, as that traumatized girl". He feels a new compulsion to have someone inside him. I am surprised at the shift and note that this is the first time he does not have to disown or feel shame over his desires. I wonder to myself how much this is a result of the shift in object relations, which are very evident to me, and how much it is a product of the shift in his gender identity. I probably will never be able to separate the two. Could he have done this if identified as female? I think not. He confirms that it is only possible because he is now secure in his masculine identity. If it was in the girl position, it would be submission and rape. If transitioning can allow him the freedom to pursue his desires, without shame and guilt, to feel sufficiently safe within himself to surrender, and this could not be attained as female-identified, then there is no doubt in my mind that this difficult ordeal is worth it.

He trims his pubic hairs, which feels a little transgressive and exciting, and has fantasies of being looked at and seen, not with a penis, but with a clitoris. He is requestioning everything about gender. If his mother didn't want him to be a femme girl but somewhere wanted him to be a boy because of her own history, then was he doing all this for her? If he is trying to not be what she wanted but being boy is unconsciously what she wanted, then the door to the whole gender question is open. Whose gender is it? Could he dress as a girl? Would he be a transman dressing as a girl? He would be a girl who is a boy dressing as a girl. Sometimes this is just all too much to hold for him, the fluidity and uncertainty makes knowing unreachable.

I note how confusing things are with his mother. Recently his mother discovered that there are two birth certificates in her name, from two different hospitals, miles apart. It is all very strange and difficult to sort out. His mother concludes that she was either adopted or a stolen baby. There is an eerie sense of not knowing what is real, of the transmission of intergenerational madness, trauma, and abuse.

Was his unconscious fear of psychosis played out through his gender? I start to believe, more strongly, that gender became the structure he built to protect himself from an overwhelming, emotionally abusive, maybe borderline psychotic mother who invaded him. If he had not had the corporeality of the body, would he have tried to resolve the problem of invasion by a hated object with a flight into delusions and hallucinations? Was the concreteness of the body, in fact, an anchor to reality? I start to think it was perhaps his mother's breasts he wished to cut off, killing off his old self as well as the intruding mother. A sense of certainty, of knowing, eludes us both. We are aware that over the generations what has been transmitted is the feeling that "something cannot be known".

"The gender play is uprooting", he tells me. He writes to me that he actually worries about his sanity. He tries to create a masculinity that doesn't involve a renunciation of the feminine; he calls it a queer masculinity.

Then a strange phenomenon starts to occur; over and over we start to wear the same colour clothes on the same day, from black to pink. Neither of us knows what to make of it. We so feared how his transitioning would alienate us from each other, but it has not at all. I think to myself, is there unconscious communication about gender through the clothing, this being a manifestation of a co-created intersubjective space coming after such intense work with him? Or is this a reenactment of the dynamic with his mother, an unconsciously fused twinship?

VII

He wants to start testosterone. He has been living as a trans man for two years now. He feels he cannot stay in-between; it is difficult internally and even more so in the world. I am also aware that our closeness has scared him. We process it all. But he emphasizes that his voice and breasts startle people. His life feels as if it has "settled into a semi-permanent state of transition". It is difficult to describe the instability of uncertainty, especially living in a space of gender uncertainty in a world that does not tolerate gender ambiguity. In addition, he gets confirmation that his struggle to get a job is linked to being transgendered. He poignantly talks of a desire to be recognized as a guy and to have the kind of freedom to simply walk through the world that other people enjoy. He seizes the moment to begin T (testosterone).

He writes a letter to his friends.

It's taken me a long time to modify my belief in constancy and equally long time to become comfortable with my inconsistencies. I can only tell you about myself . . . if I have permission to be inconstant and inconsistent. Otherwise I am afraid you will be driven insane with illogic. I want you to recognize me as a guy, but I want you to hold on to the fact that I am also female. In a world in which most people are either male or female, man or woman, and they are comfortable there, it may be hard to conceive of someone who is, or would want to be, both . . . . It is hard for me to conceive of myself as a guy, without being female, too. What I like about the label F2M (Female 2 Male) is its multiplicity, being F and M. When I think about my identity, I think about it in terms of layers. On the base layer, I am female. The F is the founding sex, and the known, understood, lived experience of being F in my world. On top of that base I put my lifelong discomfort with being female. I think of M as my discomfort, my desire

to have the body of M, my need to have my small m masculinity seen and recog-
nized and legitimized. I identify with the label F2M because I don't ever think
I could only be M. I wasn't born and raised M. It's also true because in order to only
be M, I would have to give up my experiences as F or pretend that the whole time
that I have been F, I have really been M. I want my body to say, "Here this is Raph-
ael. He's a guy, but he's not only a guy. He's a female guy, who sometimes wants to
be able to be girl."

Despite fears of having to go through puberty in his thirties, in front of
everyone, Raphael starts taking a very low dose of testosterone. It is
the eighth year of our work together. Within a week, his voice begins
to change: it has a gravelly, deeper sound. As the weeks pass, hair
starts to grow on his face and upper lip. He asks me each week if I can
see his moustache. I am aware of my growing maternal feelings
towards Raphael. Raphael plays with the soft fuzz, encouraging it on.
Yet simultaneously hair is now growing on his chest and shoulders, on
the back of his arms, his fingers, and even his butt. This is not all welcome. He is confused and ambivalent.

Very quickly his libido escalates and he starts to have aggressive
sexual fantasies about strangers. "I saw this woman on the platform
the other day", he tells me. "She wasn't particularly attractive, but she
had a good body, a work-out body. In the first second of noticing her
I thought, "I'd like to fuck her in the ass." That was the thought that
came to me. I would never have thought that before. I have chosen to
be part of this straight boys club. That means I am going to be shaped
by them. Do you know what I mean? But what will happen now as
I become a straight guy? I have to fit in. When I said something the
other day to Vince, he looked at me like, What's up with you, man?
Meaning, what kind of a man am I? I can't be confusing. I can't be
a trans guy or something in between. If I want them to treat me like
a guy, I have to be a guy."

He is quiet. We are both quiet. There is a growing sense of unease
in the space between us. I sense my body tensing up. Who am I going
to end up sitting in the room with?

"You really think you have to be in a misogynist to be recognized
as a guy?"

He remains silent. His body has moved along the couch farther
away from me. "I am afraid that I am going to become a complete asshole", he finally says, making sure he is watching me as the words
tumble out. This was the problem he first walked into the room with.
"What if I am this sexist bastard?"

Changing his name was the easy part. Calling him "he" a complicated but relatively simple move. However, losing the sensitive, playful feminist to a misogynist man is not what I had prepared myself for. He has a dream that he is looking for me but can't find me. He finds a man with a beard. He thinks of me as that man. What would I look like as a man? He is missing that we don't wear the same colour clothes anymore. I say that he wants to find himself in me. How different the hormonal changes feel in comparison to the gender identity changes. He is afraid of losing me and the closeness of our relationship. After the session, I think more about the dream and take it as supervision: maybe he is telling me that I am closing off, not giving him access. I think he is right.

We keep exploring, trying to understand, to process, to not be afraid. We know that we are both struggling with the change, but I try to help him separate what will stay the same, what aspects of him and our relationship will not change, despite the bodily shifts. After he has been on testosterone for four months, we both notice that it is harder for him to be intimate, to discuss his feelings. He says he can't access them in the same way; they are harder to define.

The physical changes become more remarkable, dramatic. His voice keeps deepening, moving right into the baritone range. I wish I had recorded his voice before it had changed. It is very odd to watch him metamorphosing right before me. "I am not familiar with who I am", he says. His face looks different, it is longer, more masculine, with less fat. He has far more facial hair, but his hairline is receding, and the texture is changing; it is thicker and coarser. He feels as if he is "sprouting" hair all over. His body shape is shifting, too, which seems to alter the way he walks. It is a bulky, heavy walk. I am surprised that I find him more attractive as a boyish boy than I did as a girl. I can't put my finger on it, but I think it is the increased sense of comfort in his body. What a strange process this all is. I think he can feel I have opened myself up to him again. He now passes regularly as a guy. He feels he is losing access to women's spaces. It is only in bed that he can be read as a girl. He wants to hold on to his queerness, his transness, to look like a gay sailor or a femme boy, not simply a heterosexual male. Perhaps what makes this transgender experience so unknowable, so disorienting, is that it is not simply changing from one gender to another, but the experience of existing outside gender categories, in what Catherine Millot (1990) referred to as "horsexe" or "outsidesex" or it is the experience of exceeding any one category (A. Saketopoulou, personal communication, 11 April 2010). Elliot (2001), too, reading autobiographical, empirical, and clinical readings, spoke of the transgender desire to be beyond sex, to transcend the limits of sexual difference, in the "desire to become the 'Other'" (p. 317).

Raphael feels as if he is losing his footing. He is scared that he will be "slipping away". There is a sense of loss that accompanies us through this process, a strange combination of awe and sadness. I start to forget what he looked like as a woman. I rummage through my memories, but I can't access a clear image. He says he can't, either. I find an old card he sent me with a photograph of him and his girl-friend. I feel relief. I remember Rebecca. I try to carry her with me. It feels important to not lose her completely. We need a hold, an anchor, a stable footing as the familiar material body and all it carried fades out of sight. It is a difficult year of work. His moods fluctuate; he is more irritable, sometimes aggressive, and generally off kilter, though the early misogynist has disappeared.

VIII

"Tectonic plates are shifting", he declares going into his second year of transitioning. His hormones have settled. The epic battle between tes-tosterone and oestrogen has been decided in favour or testosterone. He is happier with himself. He feels so different looking in the mirror at his muscles, his bulk, and his male face. He writes to me about his sexual experiences:

> I used to feel a kind of mind-fuck trying to switch between being male-identified and being female-bodied . . . . Now I feel like not only can I go back and forth, but that I want to. Neither when I am on my back or when I am on top do I feel committed to a certain vision of my body or of my gender.

He talks at length about his sexual fantasies. He tells me how the new fan-tasies that have taken hold are not dominated by rape and violence. We have observed his fantasies over the years, watching if they shift with the changes in his internal world. Initially his repertoire expanded, but the core fantasies remained unchanged. It has taken much longer for the fan-tasies to become less compulsive and less violent. There is no doubt, to both of us, that the different conscious fantasies (reflecting his altered unconscious world) are a direct result of our work.

He is no longer threatened expressing his femininity, or exploring his genitals and female sexuality. He still hates the sight of his breasts, and others' reactions to his breasts, but can feel pleasure when touched. He is set on chest surgery but without the prior urgency. He

begins tossing out everything in his apartment that he feels is not absolutely essential, marvelling at the open floor space that ensures. He
refuses to keep things that are stained or broken. He is trying to teach
himself to act, to change, to try new things and not be afraid of
making mistakes. He is pursuing new kinds of companions, new
friends, new restaurants, new music he has never heard of. He wants
to shift the obsessive ruminations and mind clutter that have dominated his life.

He starts to ask to wear one of my bracelets during sessions, to take
me in, to hold on to me while he feels things are changing so rapidly.
I do not hesitate. We begin wearing the same colours again. He wants
to know if I feel differently about him as he becomes more boy.
I answer "yes and no". There is something that is the same, some con-
tinuity with who he is, and yet so much is different too, but the difference has less impact than I had imagined or feared. He is able to talk
about his relationship to his mother, how she couldn't hold him, literally pushing him off her lap very quickly, and symbolically how she
couldn't make what was unbearable manageable in any way. He wants
to have a different relationship with her, despite her unpredictability
and her need to keep pushing him away. This is his one dissatisfaction
about our work. Despite working hard to be open with his mother, to
understand her, to not get hurt and reject her, their relationship
remains fraught. She has never forgiven him for leaving her. He vows
to continue trying to reach her, to not give up despite her. He has
changed so significantly, it is difficult to recognize the early Wolverine
identification. He is no longer an intimidating, intrusive presence in the
room. He is open, caring, and trusting. His world has expanded; he
has more intimate friendships and is valued and respected in his job.
I no longer feel the sense of being caged in. Our relationship has
changed too, shifting from the erotic to the maternal. He feels I am as
close to a mother he has ever had. He wants me to remain a mother
figure throughout his life. It is clear to us both that he is getting ready
to leave. He gives me permission to write about our work, something
he could not have imagined before. This is a major step. He had never
wanted me to write anything about him, feeling that it was his story to
tell. He could not trust me sufficiently and would have needed to control and edit every line. Now he wants me to tell my story, knowing
that he will tell his own. He wants to share the work, if it will be helpful to anyone else, despite how exposing it will feel. Moreover, it is
a gift to me, and it is a way that we can still hold on to each other. It is
also a way our work will be concretized, something that will have

a material form.[10] "What are you going to do without me?" he asks. "I don't know", I say, only half kidding. I try to imagine a week without him. I choke up, even without him present. I will miss so much of him: his intelligence, his depth, his charm and playfulness, and the way in which he let me into his most private worlds. I think about how much he has given me. Besides the many gifts and exotic fruits and cupcakes over the years, he opened something up in me that I don't want to lose. If I helped him to be more girl, he helped me, too. Not in the same way, but I found a way to be an analyst and be more vulnerable, more human, more open—to expose more of myself.

In the months of saying good-bye, he is ready. He reflects on his ability to hold opposites in mind, to negotiate, compromise, and be open and caring most of the time. He has finally made the decision to change careers, moving to a different city to pursue a graduate degree in the social services, where he can use his emotional resources more. He finds a surgeon and sets a date for top surgery. He finds a long-term partner who already has a child, and his life, which moved so slowly before as he deliberated everything obsessively, is propelled forward.[11]

Notes

1. With hindsight I have wondered, given the sequence of the last two dreams, whether she perceived my surprise at her wish to have me make her a man and was unconsciously trying to be more feminine to gain my approval, or unconsciously to identify with me.

2. See Gershman (1970), Kubie (1973), and Socarides (1970).

3. See Hausman (1995) and Raymond (1979).

4. I did not share any of my dreams with Rebecca during the work.

5. I am indebted to Mannie Ghent's work, especially his 1990 paper on distinguishing surrender from submission and masochism.

6. We also explored the other part of the fantasy: wanting her partner to submit, on her knees, and do something she was not comfortable with, and the transference implications of the fantasy.

7. Other trans narratives I began reading were Bornstein (1995), Califa (1997), Feinberg (1996), and Halberstam (1998).

8. See Lemma (2010) for a similar concept with body modifiers. She discussed three central phantasies (reclaiming, ideal self, and self made).

9. For other early references of analysts who do not see the two as mutually exclusive, see Chiland (2000), Eigen (1996), Person and Ovesey (1974), and Quinodoz (1998).

10. It is only on writing this chapter that Raphael learned of my dreams, and the verbalization of my feelings. He told me there was not much that surprised him, even if there was much that had not been spoken.

11. One and a half years later he continues to excel. He has had top surgery, a decision that he was ready for and that he feels was right. In his new career he has been recognized and is growing emotionally and spiritually. He has become a loving, consistent father to his son, and despite a turbulent relationship with his partner, he has not run away, or withdrawn when injured, but persisted in being kind and caring.

CHAPTER TEN

Gender now

Ken Corbett

ithin this chapter, I set forward a perspective: "Gender Now". I examine the social transformation of gendered life and the ways in which modern theory signifies these transformations as it seeks to undo the normative regulation of gender.[1] Key here is the recognition that norms serve not only as an empirical record (forecasting global regularities) but also as ideals that direct social order. They compel compliance and conformity; they configure that which lies outside the customary as socially unintelligible and psychically incoherent.

Norms morph into that which is considered essential and essentially coherent, ignoring the tempering work of variance and the possibilities of cultural expansion. While norms capture what is most conspicuous about human development (how we are all similar), they do not capture what is perhaps most interesting about human development: norms do not exist without variance; the repetition of patterns or averages is never exact. There is always distinction between humans, and multiplicity within any given human. Static norms impede our capacities to appreciate variance, to reflect justly, and to respond with empathy, even pleasure.

New sustaining ideals are being articulated. New possibilities for recognition are in play. The rigid necessity of the symbolic order has been called into question; consider the widening frame of marriage law, the lessening import of traditional gender codes, the dismantling of binary gender polarities, the widening net of language and modes of communicative exchange, and the redefinition of family, to name a few.

The force field of the symbolic is open to moments of discontinuity, rupture, and mobility. Indeed, the symbolic requires rethinking—a move perhaps towards the consideration of multiple circulating symbolic-s. Psyches need not be fenced in the same old cage. Genders need not follow on the same old identification with the same-sex parent. Paradoxical bodies may stand as such. Genders now come to matter within a less constricting corporeal spectrum. Embodiment and gendered identifications are open to a range of possibilities and differences—perhaps the kinds of differences that make life worth living.

The gendered body is built in a complex psyche–soma–cultural field, open to multiple points of reference, normative expectation, and idiomatic relational meanings. Gender is embodied and constituted via fantasy, organic excitability, desire, neuron, muscle, relationality, injury, and practice. Gender is that which is replicated via normative regulation. But it is also open to transformation and made distinctive through the unique iteration of personhood and the unfolding malleability of social life.

Gender is now conceived as a complex field (imagine a cube filled with floating dots), in contrast to the traditional claim that gender follows in accord with a masculine/feminine gender binary (imagine two dots connected by a taut line) founded on anatomical and developmental determination. Criticism of this gender binary and developmental determinism is not new (not "now"). One can note challenges to the binary before gender was even called "gender", as early as Freud's (1905d) cautionary footnote that seeks to deconstruct the certainty of the masculine/feminine divide: "It is important to understand clearly that the concepts of 'masculine' and 'feminine', whose meaning seems so unambiguous to ordinary people, are amongst the most confused in science" (p. 219). We have, however, come some distance from Freud's scare quotes and marginalia.

Gender and kinship

Despite overwhelming evidence to the contrary, we persist with an idea of family, along with ideas about how that family shapes a child's gender that rarely reflects the lives of our patients. It is intriguing to consider how little we have moved from the guiding symbolic family Freud set forth in his earliest work. His ideas about masculinity and femininity were often at the heart of his early clinical reasoning. In his account, gender is predestined and dispositional, following as it does on biological enunciation, and presumed to bloom through the unfolding of symbolic kin relations. This unfolding pierces the world(s) of family, society, and child, and to that extent it is social and developmental. For Freud, though, these enactments of desire and rivalry are only manifestly social, and as such, they are of limited interest. Instead, it was towards the symbolic oedipally structured account of these relations to which he turned.

Freud's construction has become a powerful part of the daily vernacular that narrates gender; Oedipus tells us, as we tell it. In keeping with Oedipus's reach, the narration of gender most often occurs within a kinship story, just as Freud narrated his report of "Little Hans" (Freud, 1909b): a boy becomes a boy by way of body-based psychic states, conflicts, and pleasures that unfold and fold into a variety of solutions within a set of normative kin relations. Presumed within this model is the work of kin and family as it contributes to gender's making, up to and including the presumption that well-being follows on assimilation to these symbolic norms.

For Freud, the symbolic back-story is set (an inevitable ahistoric unconscious structure), and the psychic action occurs as subjectivities take shape within this pre-determined order. Good-enough parenting within Freud's model affords the emergence and resolution (or "dissolution", as he refers to it) of this ahistoric unconscious complex. He does not pay great heed to the social and psychological work of parenting. At the same time, he does not deny it, and in fact at times illustrates it, or offers advice within this realm.

This model splits the privileged symbolic from what is considered the less determining social and psychological practices of kinship—a split that has set in play the nearly century-long redress of Freud's limited attention to the social-psychological dimensions of parenting, maternity in particular (see, e.g., Benjamin, 1988; Chodorow, 1978; Fonagy, 2001; Fromm & Narvàez, 1968; Sprengnether, 1990). In practice, Freud's proposition flags as the symbolic figures of mother and father conflate and compress the active parenting parent. The focus is on parents as symbolic figures, with too little regard for how parents function to promote growth or to hinder it, and how families come together to transfer and combine the psychic, the symbolic, the cultural, the political, and the material—forces that flow through, assemble, and trump that which we call "family".

Another way this proposition of an inevitable unconscious order falters is that the symbolic back-story is grainy at best: we are copies of copies of copies of copies of Oedipus's children. Copies repeat. Copies degrade. Copies transform. Copies spill out onto gender's complex field. (Imagine an American football field, with most everyone gathered around the 50-yard-line, then imagine others scattered here and there across the field.) A field, yes, with a dense median, and an assiduously controlled mythos, but a field nevertheless that demonstrates how multiple acts of gendered address, affect, and embodiment are equally robust and intelligible, however majoritized or minoritized they may be.

Gender's stories are told within a variety of kinship systems, across a variety of parent–child relations, and on a variety of registers: social, symbolic, political, psychological, biological.[2] Gendered subjects live suspended between these systems, relations, and registers. I write now against an extensive backdrop of feminist and queer response; Freud's abiding assumption of the guiding symbolic has by now been well critiqued (see, e.g., Butler, 2000; Dimen, 1995; Goldner, 1991; Rubin, 1975; Silverman, 1992).

Separating the symbolic from the social results in a set of false and impossible distinctions that perpetuate ill-founded and outmoded presuppositions regarding kinship and gender, setting in play a host of questions: Must one's kinship experience and gendered experience line up with prevailing cultural symbols and ideals? Are these ideals indeed structural and ahistorical? Or are these relations, these structures, culturally contingent, and hence not universal, not ahistoric? Are these ideal oedipal relations primary (as in first) in the formation of gender, or are they re-elaborations of earlier relations (a question analysts such as Klein and Horney began asking as early as the 1930s)? Can we even speak of primary others, when those others are themselves under the contradictory and often enigmatic impress of cultural inscription (Butler, 2004; Dimen, 1991; Fletcher, 1992; Goldner, 1991; Harris, 1991, 2005)? In other words, does a child identify with a mother's femininity as primary, or a mother's complex relationship to femininity as a perplexed social–symbolic category?

Furthermore, one would be led to ask whether symbolic oedipal relations promote or sustain identifications that lead to coherent gendered identities: Does the transfer of gender via gendered correspondence—from primary feminine mother to primary feminine daughter—actually follow in such a linear sociological way, complicated as such transfers are by the personal vagaries of any parent–child relationship and the world within which they reside? What makes for coherent gender? Is it correct to even speak of gender as necessarily coherent?

What makes for a sound body? Who is the coherent qua healthy gendered human?

These are what might be called outsider questions. After all, if one is deemed coherent, if one embodies social ideals and symbols with relative ease, then what would motivate this manner of questioning? Rare is the club member who inquires about those outside the gate. And so it was (and largely continues to be) that the now nearly 75-year-long psychoanalytic debate about gender has followed in response to outsiders knocking on the psychoanalytic door. Beginning with women analysts seeking to join the guild in the 1930s and 40s (Bonaparte, 1935; Deutsch, 1946; Horney, 1926, 1932, 1933; Klein, 1932a, 1932b; Lampl-de Groot, 1927) and leading to today's feminists and queer theorists (Benjamin, 1988, 1995, 1997; Bersani, 1986; Butler, 1990, 1993, 2000, 2004; Chodorow, 1978, 1989; Corbett, 1993, 1996, 2001a, 2001b; Dimen, 1991, 1995; Elise, 1997, 1998b, 2001; Goldner, 1991, 2003; Harris, 1991, 2005; Layton, 1997, 1998; Silverman, 1992), some who have sought a place within the psychoanalytic community, while others have not.[3]

As the outside has seeped in and the guardians at the gate have grown ever more grey, modern theorists, following as much upon Foucault as upon Freud, turn from the structural, symbolic regeneration of gender. We look now at regulatory cultural practices and ask if in fact the cultural regulation of gender may not have pathogenic implications: might gender diminish us, dull us, perhaps even make us ill? In this regard, consider how feminist theory has repeatedly pointed to the ways in which normative gender inscription establishes divisive family dynamics and problematic child-rearing practices (Benjamin, 1988; Butler, 2000; Chodorow, 1978; Dinnerstein, 1976; Goldner, 1991; Rubin, 1975). Or consider how the modern reappraisal of homosexuality points to the ways in which normative conscription leads to a social life of gender that is unliveable for many (Butler, 2004; Corbett, 1997, 2001b; Halberstam, 1998; Isay, 1989, 1997; Sedgwick, 1993b; Silverman, 1992).

In my view, these modern considerations lead to a shift in how we employ oedipal theory as a means to understand the fantastic scenario of family life (a unique and blended scene of unconscious wish and conscious imagination), *not* as a fixed social structure, a universal fundamental language, a determining symbolic order, or primordial law. Shifting in accord with modern cultural practices and evolving symbolic systems, we can no longer continue to presume that gender unfolds within a psychically specific hetero-normative domestic story. We cannot continue to presume that like gender produces like gender—that fathers transfer masculinity to sons, mothers transfer femininity to daughters.

We turn now from our familiar domestic stories to look at how gender is told *from* culture *through* parent to child, or put another way, how masculinity and femininity precedes parents and children. How do governing norms assert and insert? How do they regulate the family and the child? How do they move into the family, into the child? How do they move in a manner that is un-thought, instituted, naturalized? How are they disrupted, challenged, undone by the psychic specificity of any given child, and the unique social world of any given family?

In league with many of my colleagues, I no longer place the Oedipus complex as the major axis for human development or psychopathology, as traditional theorists once did, and some still do. I do, however, keep to the vital nature of the fantastic and intently look for evidence of unconscious infantile wishes, along with the lingering influence of parent–child desire. As Freud (1900a) would have it, there is blood in the water: the unconscious wishes of childhood "are only capable of annihilation in the same sense as the ghosts in the underworld of the *Odyssey—ghosts* which awoke to new life as soon as they tasted blood" (p. 553, fn1).

While I may not grant as much authority to ghosts and the past as did Freud, I do value the psychic ground of early parent–child relations. I do place considerable value on the role of fantasy as it builds the gendered child. I do find clinical merit in the analysis of parent–child desire—how those desires are brought into mind and reflected upon, how they are represented, repressed, negotiated, internalized, reactivated, and rewoven.

In my view, the appeal of oedipal myth is the way in which narratives aid us in coping with the blood and ghosts. My clinical curiosity moves me to try to understand how children and families narrate the stories they collectively tell in order to account for their relations, their overwhelming desires and losses, and how that narration unfurls and refurls in the course of treatment. How is gender desired, how does gender desire within these stories? How is the story positioned in relation to dominant cultural narratives? How is gender signified through fantasy? How is gender fantastically embodied in these stories—in these modes of becoming? Is corporeal embodiment determined by normative order? How is the body made in resisting anxious regulation?

Gender development

Relational theorists have set about to re-theorize development as intersubjectively configured, and this theorizing goes some distance towards capturing the multiple forces at hand in the development of gender and identity. This largely Anglo–American movement has steadily built a theory of gender that rests on the contemplation of a relational–body–mind–social matrix (Benjamin, 1995, 1997; Butler, 1990, 1993, 2000, 2004; Chodorow, 1994, 2002; Coates, 1997; Corbett, 1993, 2001b; Dimen, 1991; Elise, 2001, 2002; Fast, 1984; Goldner, 1991, 2003; Harris, 1991, 2005; Layton, 1997, 1998).

This theoretical move, in my view, represents something of a middle group in the ongoing debate between the developmental forces of attachment versus desire (see Fonagy, 2001; Green, 1995; Laplanche, 1976, 1987a, 1999; Widlocher, 2001). Neither attachment nor desire is privileged in this relational frame; they are interimplicated. Moreover, these Anglo-American theorists have set about to nestle the family in the social order, charting the ways in which gender's becoming is always and already culturally constituted.

Gender is built through the complex accrual of an infinite array of parent–child exchanges, social-child exchanges, symbolic-child exchanges, and body–child exchanges, including the child's experience of his or her body and genitals, the observation of morphological sexual differences, as well as the physiological components of sexual development. This complex matrix (open as it is to enigmatic transfer layered on enigmatic transfer) starts to operate at birth (or even before birth, now that a child's sex is often known to a parent prior to birth) and is crisscrossed by an infinite array of conscious and unconscious meanings for both parent and child.

Distinct from Freud's position, no one aspect of this relational matrix is privileged. There is no originary moment; there is no ordinary pair or triangle, there are instead multiple relations and registrations; there are no dispositional genitalia; gender and genitals, instead, are built through over-determined nonlinear moments. There is no originary desire: desires and gendered states also accumulate through chaotic complexity. The desires that found gender, the desires gender lives to solicit, are manifold. The material body is built, not given and determining. Gender and genital experience are interimplicated; the direction of causality is neither from genital experience to gender nor from gender to genital experience. The direction of causality is neither from the raw materials of physiology to the constructed mind nor from mind to physiology. The network of desires created through the relational excess of human life is too complex for such simplistic causality.

Along with the matrix, another helpful way of imagining how the mind and body come together in the act of gender has been proposed by Elizabeth Grosz (1994), who suggests that we imagine the psyche like a Möbius strip—a topological puzzle, a flat ribbon twisted once and then attached end to end to form a circular twisting surface, whereby inside and outside become continuous. Grosz proposed that we think of the body—the brain, muscles, sex organs, hormones, and more—as composing the inside of the Möbius strip. Culture and experience would constitute the outer surface. One moves from body to culture and back again without ever stepping outside the seamless way in which they are intertwined.

In recognition of this developmental complexity, gender identity—the internal conviction regarding one's gender classification—is no longer positioned as a fixed identity or essence at the core of a person. The structuring and regulating persistence of gender identity is mitigated by our modern recognition of the ways in which all identifications are part of a complex and chaotic open nonlinear system—a system wherein identifications stimulate intricate feedback loops, forming patterns of exchange and transfer. Consider, if you will, how genders are constructed through the transfer of various traits, codes, behaviours, and fantasies. Once transferred, these internalizations come to rest (to the degree that any internalization comes to rest) in exquisitely unique intrapsychic terrains, mapped as they are by idiosyncratic personal histories. These unstable latent terrains, littered with affects and attributes, are the staging ground for significant personal patterns and differences. (Imagine an attic that will not stay organized, no matter one's best efforts.)

It is through the flow, feedback, and repetition of these patterns that structure emerges. As Rappaport (1967) suggested, "Structures are processes of a slow rate of change" (p. 787). Gender identity and gendered embodiments are ongoing events, not discreet endpoints. The structure that emerges is in motion: imagine a building the walls of which are aquiver with atomic movement. Imagine a house that sits well enough on a softly assembled foundation—as Adrienne Harris (2005) might have it.

The gender binary and heterosexual complementarity

The relation between gender and sexuality is also ongoing and open to contradiction. Traditionally it was assumed that sexuality was produced through gender qua anatomy. Furthermore, it was claimed that desire was similarly coded and fixed by gender—female gender traits = the wish for male traits, male gender traits = the wish for female traits—in keeping with the model of heterosexual complementarity.

We now regard this presumption to be a by-product of normative expectation and recognize as well that the chaotic and often contradictory internal world through which any person, homosexual or heterosexual, masculine or feminine, is constructed fractures this normative mirroring of gender traits and sexuality. Once again, the network of identifications and desires created through the relational excess of human life is too complex for such simplistic mapping. In other words, not only are there multiple identifications within any given girl, those identifications do not necessarily correspond to normative patterns of desire. A masculine girl may develop as a masculine girl who desires other masculine girls. A feminine girl may develop as a feminine woman who desires feminine men.

Gender does not dictate desire; it does not even ensure consistency. The masculine boy who develops to desire masculine men may occasionally "flip" between so-called masculine and feminine, or active and passive, desires. Or he may present as masculine, but secretly conceal feminine desires: a state better known as "butch on the streets, femme in the sheets".

And that is to presume that gendered traits on the streets or elsewhere are so easily identified and understood to begin with. Gender is put on with fewer and fewer distinguishing codes, and normative gendered traits become both less compelling and harder and harder to read. One is also left to question the presumption that sexual desires can be so easily separated and distinguished. Indeed, so-called masculine and feminine sexual behaviours, states, and enigmatic conditions collide in acts of desire and often morph in such a way as to be indistinguishable.

In this light, consider a question posed as an organizing gambit for a panel in 2004 presented at the American Psychoanalytic Association on current thinking about gender. The question was posed as, "How is masculinity and femininity expressed in men and women?" In response, I suggest that the only way to answer this question is to *unask* it. To take it off the table and, in so doing, reveal the ways in which a question like this is always haunted by its regulatory function. Listen for the ways in which the word "appropriate" sniffs at, nips at the edges of this question. Even if we were to treat this question more generously, granting the ways in which it invites us to consider how masculinity is expressed in women, or how femininity is expressed in men—granting therein the ways in which this question takes note of gender fluidity, granting therein the permissiveness of the question—the question still invites us to measure. And it is but a short step from measurement to the question of how much is too much. How much femininity can appear in a man before it is too much, before he becomes unintelligible to us as a man and steps out of gender coherence?

Questions such as this serve to create, regulate, and police categories, creating in turn majority and minority categories. You are in, or you are out. And those outside the category serve to help shore up and define those who are exemplars of those who are in, those who are normative. Boys and men, girls and women, who step outside the normative circle and out of cultural intelligibility step into abject and foreclosed identities—identities that are too quickly presumed to be lacking in coherence and well-being.

The exclusionary binary and its splitting action have often created trauma in the name of normative order—trauma that has often been closeted, or presumed as that which inevitably befalls the nonnormative. Consider, for example, how Susan Kessler (1998) and Anne Fausto-Sterling (2000) documented the strong arm of the binary as it has been employed in making decisions concerning surgical options for intersex children. These decisions to alter the manifest gendered surface of a child's body are directed by the overriding belief that a child's body must reflect one aspect of the binary—gender is fixed, not mixed. Underscoring these decisions as well is the belief that the child's physical conformity will aid in the child's adaptation towards a heterosexual system of complementary social relations. Consider what we now know to be the legacy of trauma that such decisions can render, in the face of what we have recently learned about John Money's (Money & Green, 1969) John/Joan case (Butler, 2004; Colapinto, 2000; Diamond & Sigmundson, 1997b). We could not then, and I venture we are still struggling now, to find ways to assist our patients whose bodies and minds do not manifest coherent gender, as dictated by the male/female binary.

As Dimen and Goldner (2005), following on Rubin (1975), argued, "We have often become so fixated on perpetuating, exaggerating, and mythologizing the relatively small physical differences between the sexes, while effacing their obvious commonality and similarity" (p. 96). Our efforts to uphold the binary have as well often left us unprepared to face the dilemmas, and at times trauma, of variance. For example, Money's (Money & Green, 1969) John/Joan solution was to create a girl where there had been a genitally injured boy, to promise (as though this was in fact surgically possible) a coherent gender (qua coherent psyche), in the face of genital injury. Was there, is there, no place for a genitally injured human? Can such a person be acknow-ledged into being? Must such a person endure surgical intervention in order to become intelligible? Must that person's difference be masked in the name of repair, and if so, at what cost? What—who—could this human be in the order of things? And should it not be our task as ana-lysts to question the order of things and refrain from answering ques-tions that regulate and reinforce the order of things?

I do not mean to suggest by these assertions that I believe we can live outside categories. No one lives outside the outside. No one devel-ops outside a system of norms, but at the same time no one develops as a simple mechanical reiteration of such norms (Butler, 1997, 2004; Corbett, 2001b; Layton, 1997). Gendered psyches are formed within and against the "logic" of normative social structure. Gendered bodies come to matter in relation to normative mandates, but importantly they are not fixed by those mandates. Nor is the well-being of gen-dered subjects measured via the simplistic causality of normative order.

Gender and psychic equilibrium

Minds are made in relation, genders are made in relation, and gender is routinely read as a manifest marker of mind; manifest gender attri-butes or performances are routinely linked with psychic equilibrium. In my view, though, we still are not in possession of an adequate model of mind to account for the great variety that marks the relationship between gender, psychological equilibrium, and the indistinguishable work of cultural regulation. Moreover, and perhaps more important, we struggle still to find a way to speak about non-normative genders outside a split that moves between phobia and advocacy.

In a move towards a more complex model of gender and mind, I offer the grounding presupposition that a non-normative gender sur-face can rest on the same degree of psychic equilibrium, or lack thereof, as a normative surface. Gender variance is an expression of subjectiv-ity's wide arc as well as the wide arc that characterizes psychological well-being. Sometimes mixed gender or cross-gendered humans are simply being human, and not to recognize their subjectivities as such is to ignore the tempering work of variance and the possibilities of cul-tural expansion. Genders, both in their central and their marginal expressions, are open to a range of psychic equilibria and structures, however we settle on those terms, which I believe are open to debate—debate that largely centres on the question of how we disentangle the inter-implicated psyche and social. (How do we untangle that which cannot be untangled?)

Is the subject who resists the social, who resists social regulation, who has not automatically internalized our collective norms, lacking in psychic equilibrium? No. In fact, we know (over and over again) many subjects, many of whom are looked upon as the *most* alive, who live at the margins of the social order, live well enough, and live with and through good-enough psychological equilibria.

That is, as a Winnicottian might have it, they live relatively free of psychic disequilibrium wrought by dissociation, chaotic states of regression, splitting, and depersonalization. A Kleinian theorist might speak of their capacity to occupy the depressive position. A relational theorist might note their good-enough capacities to reflect on the complex self-states, self-representations, and object relational networks that compose their intersubjective worlds.

One might argue from any of these psychoanalytic perspectives that the subject's experience of social difference would then be held in reflection (reflection following on the possibilities born of psychic equilibrium). In other words, while it may not be possible to divide the social and the psychological, either in theory or in the act of living, one can nevertheless reflect on a subjective experience of social force and normative expectation. For example, the minority subject may not be able to escape the force of being hated. I suggest, however, that the minority subject who can reflect on that force, who can hold that force in mind, who can redress that force with good-enough psychic equilibrium, is a subject who may fare better as both a social and a psychological being.

In my view, psychoanalysts have not paid sufficient attention to the ways in which cross-gendered states occur, and cross-gendered subjects live at the margin of the symbolic order. Hence, do we look at cross-gendered expressions as incoherent or unintelligible (lacking in well-being) because we have not adequately entertained the ways in which cross-gendered states are a contested realm of human experience? Might we also be overlooking the ways in which marginal cross-gendered subjects employ creative means to reach towards cultural malleability? Is it not through the creative rupture of cultural barriers that new social forms are born? And isn't it the case that such rupture has often been policed as lacking in psychic equilibrium? This raises the question: Is such rupture the consequence of the re-address of pathological gender regulation, or the disquieted consequence of a rupture in psychic well-being?

If it is accepted, following basic psychoanalytic presuppositions, that fantasy is interimplicated with embodiment, and if it is also accepted that genders evolve and become embodied in a relational world, then it follows that embodiment and gendered states are open to a range of fantastic expressions and relational dynamics. It would further follow that gender is always performed with affect, tempered by defence, knit by history, done and undone through the relational excess of human life.

Furthermore, if one accepts that relational dynamics create varying intersubjective spaces, spaces from and through which genders emerge, spaces that are more or less coherent and more or less organizing and loving, spaces that inflect the manner of the transfer of gendered fantasies and attributes, then one also has to be open to considering the ways in which the construction of gender is open to a range of organizations and coherence. These psychoanalytic presuppositions would argue for a way to continue to speak about gender as interimplicated with psychic equilibrium.

Still, we have been too quick to presume gender to be a cohering internalization and identification, as opposed to a complex and enigmatic series of internalizations and identifications that may "cohere" much less than has traditionally been assumed. We have been too quick to categorize, too quick to diagnose, and insufficiently attentive to the complex and perplexed relations established between individuals and cultural mandates. We have been too arrogant in our presumption that we can distinguish, or need not distinguish, the anxious work of cultural regulation and normative force as it intertwines with any person's object-relational history, or as it maps any subject's internal world.

Our theories to date have collapsed gender regulation and gender and offer too little exploration of the ways in which gender regulation constricts gender's wide arc. Authorized mental-health authorities too often fall back on the anxious reinstatement of normative expectations, bypassing a more in-depth analysis of the gendered person before them, overestimating the value of gender coherence, overestimating the value of psychic equilibrium, and overlooking the productive possibilities of gender variance.

Perhaps coherence is not all it is cracked up to be. Too often analysts have looked at variance and called it illness. Too often analysts have failed to note the ways in which the pain of fragmentation is simultaneously the variant construction of a way out. Too often we have looked upon the trauma of difference and sought to cure it through the clumsy application of similarity. Too often have analysts judged gendered behaviours and gendered fantasies as true or false (in accord with the binary), as opposed to examining their discovery, their embodied style, their imagination, the history they may speak, the future they may seek to make.

Listening to gender now

A shift in clinical listening is called for, one that, I venture, is already under way, illustrating something of a developmental lag in our theorizing of gender as opposed to our clinical efforts. Listening to gender now requires a position equidistant from the physiological, the psychological, the cultural, the political, and a reckoning as well with the impossibility of that perplexed position. We used to listen to gender as it was spoken in accord with oedipal–symbolic dictates: the symbolic spoke gender, or spoke through gender. The gendered subject was assessed with an eye towards where and how he or she took their place in the symbolic order. That order was in turn equated with well-being.

We now listen to gender as symbolically regulated and structured. The gendered subject's fit with the normative symbolic order is seen less and less as a matter of well-being per se, and more an indication of the subject's assimilation, an incorporation that comes with advantages and disadvantages. Indeed, an unwavering, unreflective mirroring of the normative symbolic order is now viewed with suspicion, suggesting as it does a subject who is "normotic" (as Bollas, 1989, might have it), a subject who fails to appreciate and make use of gender's wide arc, and the corresponding wide arc of relationship structures and object ties that afford more life.

Listening to gender now also requires a different construction of potential space between analyst and patient, one that is open to the ways in which gender is transferred and forged in over-determined and enigmatic spaces, one that is not so quick to organize normative transferential and countertransferential gendered positions—or, perhaps more precisely, one that questions the rigid organization of gendered positions within the transference/countertransference matrix. Such rigidity would once again be greeted with suspicion and questioned as to the function of these positions as they constrict the patient's personhood and relationship opportunities.

Clinical attention to cultural regulation does not override the necessity at times to also consider how some gendered performances and embodiments may speak to breakdown phenomena relative to both self-state integration and object relations—breakdowns that may reconstitute or unconstitute the gendered materiality of the body. Slipping the symbolic, and stepping out of regulatory norms, can happen through freedom as well as alienation. Moments of malleability open through loving protection, just as they open through malignant seduction. Speaking to power may follow on mental freedom or mental anguish.

Gendered significations, traits, and embodiments may exceed the intentions of the patient or analyst and reveal repressed or dissociated dynamics. The manifest gender performs/speaks and means something in its declaration/expression, and yet something else may also be enacted through the gender performance/address. Some action is taken, some dynamic unfolds, some fantasy comes to life, and in this opening—this potential space—one can seek to understand the desires that inform our gendered subjectivities. Through this opening—this transferential return—one can reflect on gender as it is lived with another, and gender as it reflects one's relational history.

Here, though, one must keep in mind that distressed subjects are always at the mercy of regulatory anxiety, be they normative or nonnormative, be they knowing and relatively free or suffering and aggrieved. Indeed, even those caught in the grip of mental anguish or the enactment of breakdown can often speak to the impact of normative force, sometimes with considerable insight.

Our listening is redirected towards the affects that colour the gendered address and transfer. How is the transfer conveyed, through what manner of psychic action—projection, dissociation, splitting, regression, or identification, to name a few? Is the transfer defensive? Does it open towards recognition? Is the enactment one within which the other is held at bay? Is the transfer an opening for play? Does it open into transitional space, or does it shut down therapeutic action? What might the transfer convey about the subject's personal history and the unique psychic terrain within which her or his gender experience has taken shape? How was the cultural regulation of gender transferred, and with what inflection and impact? To what degree can the patient reflect on that regulatory history? How might the enigmatic transfer of cultural and political mandates be understood, as they commingle and shape the patient's self-representations?

Our task then becomes one of therapeutic action that is shaped by paradox and problem, not one of certainty and solution. Our task is less defined by reparative action and solution as directed by ideal normative mandates, and more one of listening to the unique features of any given subject's gendered experience: the histories, the desires, the personal vagaries, the politics, the style and embodiment of which that experience speaks.

Notes

1. In speaking of modern gender theory, I have in mind a congress of gender theorists, representing different states and constituents. This congress consists of psychoanalysts, psychologists, sociologists, cultural theorists, queer theorists, feminists, philosophers, historians, and literary theorists. I am using the term "modern" to refer to that which is current. I am not using it in the sense of modernism. Much of what I am proposing within this chapter could properly be called postmodern (in particular my emphasis on the role of normative regulation, and my ongoing efforts to deconstruct developmental determinism). But I do not set out here to chart the historical and epistemological evolution of psychoanalytic thought regarding gender—in particular the importance of gender theory as it moves between the modern and postmodern. Others have ably taken up that task (see, e.g., Birksted-Breen, 1993b; Chodorow, 2005; Dimen & Goldner, 2005; Harris, 2005). I am speaking here in a synthesizing current-voice. I do so in order to present a forward-moving position statement. This voice of one should not be mistaken for less than many. Nor should the forward motion be read as unfettered by history.

2. Consider here Butler's (2004) review of analyses of minority kinship systems, including African–American kin (Stack, 1974) and lesbian and gay nonmarital kinship systems (Weston, 1991). Also see Corbett (2001c).

3. There are of course important distinctions one could draw between this vast body of theorists, in respect to both periodization and epistemology (see Chodorow, 2005; Harris, 2005, for an interesting discussion along these lines, or Dimen & Goldner, 2005 for a succinct overview of this history). My interest here is not one of historical accounting per se, rather something more akin to a broad view. I recognize the risk in this move (overgeneralization, intemperance). Still, I believe there is something about the forward motion of such a stance that is vital to, and representative of, our efforts to rethink gender and modern life. Sometimes a sweep and a leap are called for in our efforts to both capture and remake the human.

CHAPTER ELEVEN

A person beyond gender: a first-hand account

D r C and I began our journey seven years ago. I did not come into therapy consciously knowing that I am transgender. I came as a female academic researcher and former competitive bodybuilder, having recently competed in national championships for the second year running. When I began therapy, I was entrenched in my bodybuilding training, eating, and sleeping rituals, to the point that they had completely taken over my life and were threatening to damage my career. I was utterly desperate to escape from myself. I wanted and needed to stop training, I wanted to be able to concentrate on my academic career, but I did not know how to stop or how I would cope with life if I did.

Up to that point, I had managed to juggle the demands of work with the demands of competitive bodybuilding, but this was not sustainable as I progressed professionally, nor was it what I wanted. I wanted a life, friends, a partner one day, a family, to be successful and respected. Instead, outside my research work, my existence had become an isolated ritual of measuring, weighing, and preparing certain bodybuilding foods, training for hours before and after work, and sleeping when not doing any of the above. In my mind, bodybuilding was just as important as academic research—if not more so.

Bodybuilding enabled me to keep going, and all my professional decisions were made to allow me to train.

Early life

Dr C and I have worked hard over the years to understand better my home and family background and the impact they had, and continue to have, on my adult life. I was the daughter of working-class parents who had not had the benefit of a good education themselves and had decided to achieve this for their children, whatever the cost. As a child, I was close to my younger brother: we went to school together and shared friends and everything we had, including a bedroom in our tiny flat until I was 11 years old. We played with everything from dolls to Lego, toy cars and a train set, and spent every summer evening out riding our bikes around our council estate. As young children, we had little concept of "girls' things and boys' things". My Dad would take us both to see ships on the river, the trains going by at the station, and his workshop—in fact, I was the one who most enjoyed this! He would include us both in activities from washing or fixing the car to bike trips along the river path, going to the adventure playground or to museums. Similarly, we did the same things with my Mum like walks in the park or woods and shopping. I wore sensible practical clothes as a child: shorts and T-shirts and nothing white or pale in colour, because I would get it dirty. I didn't like dresses or skirts, and I was never forced to wear them once I was old enough to state my dislike of them. Looking back, those are the happiest years of my life.

When I was 11 years old, I won a scholarship to an Independent Girls' Day School and effectively entered my own private hell. My friends from Junior School were all going elsewhere, and I begged my parents to be able to go with them, but they were overjoyed that I had been accepted at such a good school. From the very first day I felt out of place, awkward, clumsy, stupid, and just so *wrong* in a class of 22 girls. I missed my brother and friends and didn't seem to know how to behave or what was expected of me. I was told off for running in the school yard at break time and climbing over a railing to sit on a grass bank in my first week there because it "wasn't ladylike behaviour". I had never been in trouble at school before. The school uniform was a terrible ordeal. I particularly despised the 6-pleat skirt, which had to come below the knee and prevented me from running properly, but the V-neck striped blouse and V-neck school jumper were not much better. It felt uncomfortable and seemed to drown and suffocate me all at once rather than fit in an attractive way as it did the other girls. On a Sunday night, I would lie awake dreading having to get up the next morning to put on my uniform, and when I got home in the evening, the first thing I would do was rip it off.

I had no interest in the things most of the girls were interested in and couldn't pretend that I did, because I knew nothing about any of it, and they soon figured this out and would delight in quizzing me to prove the point, laughing as I went bright red with shame: makeup, hair- and skin-care products, clothes, current fashion, boys, boy bands, parties. . . . I was shocked and fascinated and frightened in equal measure to learn that the girls in my class already wore makeup, the highest heels they could get away with, and rolled up their skirts (against school rules). They had crushes on boys (particularly each other's older brothers), and they stuck pictures of male popstars and actors in their desks. Some even had boyfriends. I had no pictures in my desk and went home to my tracksuit bottoms and T-shirts, my bike, my brother, and, in later years, our dog, who became my best friend.

I was teased for living in a flat, for the area I came from, for the car we had, for my parents not having professional occupations, for never having been abroad or held a tennis racquet. I quickly learnt to say nothing about myself, my family, or my home. By the end of the first year I had convinced my Mum to hide the car in the car park if she picked me up, and by the third year of school I refused to tell anyone where I was from or where I lived or even which bus I took to get home. I became increasingly withdrawn and isolated.

PE was excruciating. The school uniform was bad enough, but the PE kit was even worse, and I refused to wear the white see-through PE top without my jumper over it (even in summer) or the short wrap-around skirt without shorts underneath it. I was terrified of revealing my body to the other girls and was already becoming very conscious of how fat (I thought) I was, how big my tummy and hips were, how I didn't look like the other girls—but none of this had ever occurred to me until I found myself at secondary school. This was confusing, because I did not want to look like the others and had already assumed that I couldn't and wouldn't. I told myself, I "didn't have the genetics", and from this point, I began to harbour a profound sense of inadequacy. As we grew older, I was fascinated by the girls who already had breasts, tiny waists, and curvy hips, and I wanted to admire them, yet vividly remember puzzling over how uncomfortable and limiting it must be to have breasts. I didn't want them myself, and I tried to ignore the small pointy breast tissue I had begun to develop, already ashamed of what was happening to my body. By the time I was 12 years old, I felt alien among my peers. I wrote about it in my "Secret Notebook" (it had a hard cover, and I made a hole through it so I could put a padlock on it):

I feel like everything about me is wrong. I feel so little and they [the other girls in my class] all seem so much older than me. I feel intensely ashamed about myself and it's so bad it makes me feel quite sick and very frightened all the time. It's like I'm totally empty inside, like a sense of wanting something and never ever finding it or getting it. It feels like something stuck in my throat, a gaping wound or a hole inside me and it hurts so badly . . .

My social background and upbringing were different, so it was easy to attribute my unhappiness to this. I was bullied, teased about everything from my fringe to my flat, sensible school shoes, and the favourite clothes I wore on mufti day. Everything about my home and my family was wrong. I felt utterly worthless and unworthy of being among the other girls.

This evolved into a conviction that I was different and could never look or be like the other girls, because there was something very wrong with me, although I couldn't describe what it was. The only explanation I could find was that I was too fat, and I realized that I could do something about this. When I was 14 or 15, I forced myself to try to be more like the others for a while. I experimented with rolling up my school skirt, but it looked and felt even worse. Although I hated them, I chose shoes that were more like the other girls'. I grew out my fringe, and went on a diet, which meant I stopped eating breakfast at home and threw my lunch in the bin at school. But I felt increasingly uncomfortable and awkward. I eventually stopped talking to anyone unless a teacher forced me to speak in class by asking me a question.

As the girls around me embraced the physical changes of puberty and spoke openly in the classroom about it, I became all the more revolted by my own body and would not even discuss it with my Mum. I resisted wearing a bra for as long as I possibly could and then chose the plainest sports bra I could find. My first period was traumatic. I was momentarily paralysed by the shock, fear, and disgust I felt, and couldn't say a word about it to anyone. I was devastated by the way my body was changing beyond my control. Periods felt like a trauma. I could not use tampons, because I could not bring myself to look, touch, or acknowledge the existence of my female anatomy, and

I could not bear the thought of putting something inside me—and this went on for many years.

In my early years at Secondary School, I "fell in love" with a beautiful girl in sixth form and began to worry that this meant I was gay. It was very clear to me that being gay would not be acceptable to my parents and wider family, and I was terrified of how they might react. But as I grew older and my attraction to this particular girl and subsequently other women continued, I could not *feel* that I was gay—it was just another aspect of what wasn't right about me. I knew how I felt about these women, and I instinctively knew that this was sexual attraction. I experienced this as an intense longing or yearning for something I desperately wanted and needed but could never have. Although I didn't want to be gay, I had grown up next-door to an aunt who was gay and her female partner, and I concluded that if I was gay, there was nothing I could do about it. It did not enter my fantasies that I could have a girlfriend or have a physical sexual relationship with another girl or woman—I did not even imagine kissing the beautiful sixth-former. It was beyond explanation, just another aspect of all that was wrong with me. I knew I was too fat, ugly, thick, stupid, and not "posh enough" for the sixth-former to notice my existence. There was no way that I would ever reveal my body to anyone, because I could not expect anyone else to want to see or touch what I did not want to see or touch.

By the time I was 16, I wanted to leave school. My parents would not listen and constantly reminded me how lucky I was and of the financial sacrifice they were making, telling me I had "nothing to complain about". They didn't seem to notice that I was unhappy and were only interested in my academic results, so I learnt to pretend that I was fine and concentrate on achievement. If I did well at school, I could make my parents happy, and I studied as if my life depended on it. Both of them had been seriously ill, and this intensified my wish to please them. My Dad was beginning to become severely depressed, which affected the whole family. He didn't talk to anyone and would later blame me for his ill health, because he had had to work so hard to support the family financially and send me to school. My Mum turned to me for emotional support and help in dealing with my Dad. I blamed myself for everything and felt it was up to me to make things ok by doing better at school and becoming a better person. Eventually I did do well in my exams, and my parents seemed satisfied. I clung to this positive reinforcement. It was the encouragement I needed to continue.

Body issues

But alongside my ferocious studying, I was starving myself. As with schoolwork, the more I practised starving myself, the better I became at doing it. *As long as I studied and didn't eat, everything would be ok. . . .* Although I could see that I looked unwell, I preferred this to being fat and somehow believed that if I just kept going, it would all work out in the end. I was delighted when I could see the bony prominences of my hips. My body looked straighter again, and my jaw looked squarer. I could see individual muscles, and I liked my body being harder to the touch. But, above all, I rejoiced in not having periods: this was a relief like no other. However hard my "diet" was, however desperately hungry I became, I constantly reminded myself that if I ate too much, I would get fat, and my periods would come back.

I liked the comfort and the security of the eating disorder, with its strict, punishing rules: this was what I deserved, and I welcomed it. If I followed my rules perfectly, the sense of triumph and superiority I felt was worth the pain and difficulty and made me feel better about being me. Anorexia was a distraction. I created my own world, governed by my rules of starvation. Any bad feelings I was suffering became transformed into the need to eat less. I also liked the way that it numbed feelings. I was not so aware of my intense loneliness and longing for human relationships. I did not feel so left out of the normal things in the world around me, and sexual feelings towards other women disappeared altogether.

Bodybuilding

There have been three episodes of severe anorexia nervosa in my life, and the only way I have eventually allowed myself to resume eating is through changing tack completely and constructing my own weight training and nutrition programme to replace the starvation of anorexia with an equally militant level of physical exercise, designed to build muscle. If I could no longer alter my body through starvation, I would spend hours lifting weights to justify every single thing I allowed myself to eat. The rules about what I could eat and in what quantity remained as strict as the rules of starvation had been.

There was never a clear goal in terms of how I wanted to look, but I just kept following the rules to get from one day to the next. Bodybuilding occupied my thoughts and replaced anorexia as my constant companion and comfort. I studied male fitness/bodybuilding magazines to learn as much as possible about how to eat and how to train. In my naivety in those early days, I did not understand the role bodybuilding drugs played in it all. I believed that with dedication, discipline, and hard work I could achieve a muscular physique like the ones in the pictures. When I came across a picture of a competitive female bodybuilder displaying a level of musculature that would be considered extreme by normal standards for men, let alone women, I was transfixed: *this was how I needed my body to be*. I set about transforming my body into what I saw in the magazines.

My approach to training was always in stark contrast to the women around me in the gym. I began lifting weights on my own (surrounded by men) before forming a training partnership with a more experienced male bodybuilder. At that time, there were no other females training in the gym in this way. I lifted the heaviest weights I possibly could, without any modification because I was "a girl". I felt intensely frustrated that I couldn't immediately do the things men could do. I had to train so hard for every little gain and continue to train to maintain this, whereas the men around me would improve in strength and musculature almost daily. I became very strong for my size but had no muscular definition at all and began to believe that I was "too fat" again. I didn't want the physique of a "World's Strongest Woman" competitor: I wanted to look lean and muscular. So I decided to move to another gym, where competitive amateur bodybuilders trained.

By this time, I had started at university, but the move to the bodybuilding gym only intensified my utter determination to transform my body at the expense of everything else in my life. I felt euphoria if something went right—if for example, the muscles in my legs started to grow quite impressively—and utter desolation and mortification if I didn't eat correctly or looked less muscular than I had the previous week. Far from being captivated by my academic work, I was obsessed with training. Although I felt guilty that I wasn't concentrating on my studies, I rationalized that I had to train in order to remain well and keep the anorexia at bay.

I was in my third year when I went to see my first bodybuilding show and saw female bodybuilders, whose appearance enthralled me. By this time I was aware that they had taken drugs to achieve the levels of muscularity they displayed. The physical signs of virilization were apparent, as were their attempts to mask them with layers of make-up, large breast implants, and strikingly feminine choices of clothing (very short skirts, very tight tops, very bright pinks . . .). I felt uneasy about the depth of their voices when they spoke—to me, they sounded like men—but I knew with certainty that I was going to do whatever it took to become like them. This was a pivotal moment in my life, and I never looked back (until many years later, in therapy): I was going to be a female bodybuilder, and I didn't care what anyone else thought or what the potential consequences could be for my future professional life. Now I knew people who wanted the same things and would not question me—I felt as though I could finally belong in a world that wasn't just my own.

It is important to clarify that I saw these female bodybuilders as women who had incredible muscles. I did not imagine that they were "trying to turn themselves into men", or that they had crossed any gender boundary. Their masculinity simply wasn't an issue for me. (*Interestingly, as a group, female bodybuilders are typically very vocal and open in their abuse of transgender people: I have witnessed terrible things as a female bodybuilder that I do not want to write about here.*) From then on, training, eating the right foods at the right time, and sleeping enough to grow were the most important things, and I was obsessed with building muscle, to the exclusion of anything else. This continued throughout university, as an undergraduate and post-graduate student. I did not recognize that the rigid rules and physical damage I inflicted on my body through training to the point of injury and beyond were no different from anorexia.

But, as the years went by, I began to realize that I was not the same as my fellow female bodybuilders after all, and I was in fact as lonely and isolated in their midst as I had been among the girls at my secondary school. I was successful in the female bodybuilding world in the United Kingdom, but an alien among female bodybuilders too. I now had a job in research, but no other female bodybuilder I knew earned money through anything other than bodybuilding or gym-related work. No other female bodybuilder had the self-discipline to train and diet the way I did, to the point of physical failure, with no coach to push me. For a typical female bodybuilder, each appearance in the gym is a performance and a chance to show off her physique to the admiration of the predominantly male gym audience. They wore the tightest, skimpiest gym clothes imaginable, left their long hair loose, and put makeup on to train. In contrast, I was simply not interested in how I looked while training and wore baggy, comfortable clothing designed to hide the body I was so unhappy with. I also lacked the string of boyfriends, male admirers, and ex male training partners who follow a typical female bodybuilder.

I also did not react in the same way to the bodybuilding drugs as did the majority of female bodybuilders. Many become angrier, more aggressive, and more impulsive, and they experience significant increases in libido, leading to reckless promiscuous behaviour. My outward character and behaviour, on the other hand, changed little, but inside I became calmer, more confident, and surer of myself. I felt able to cope with things that otherwise threatened to overwhelm me, including my work, and my mood was lighter and happier. I vividly remember midway through a training session that was going unbelievably well on my very first course of anabolic steroids, thinking, "So *this* is what it feels like to be a man . . ." It felt amazing, and I felt I understood how the men in the gym felt all the time. But I knew that this was not a thought I could ever share with another female bodybuilder in that gym.

Accessing therapy

I chose to remain living at home while I studied. I could not contemplate the change and uncertainty of a normal university experience, and the rules and ritual involved in anorexia and bodybuilding would not allow me to participate in student life. I applied the same survival strategies that I had used at secondary school, studying hard but existing in my own private world. I now look back with deep regret at those years and see many opportunities missed in a blur of anorexia, bodybuilding training, and exams. Far from planning my future career, I struggled to plan the next week. I became increasingly despondent and convinced of my inadequacy. Objectively, this was at odds with my academic performance, and despite my relentless physical self-destruction, I did well and won various merits and distinctions along the way.

But the better I did, the stronger my conviction became that I was fooling everyone and that I was not a good student. In my final year, such was my distress and the incongruence with my academic performance that my educational supervisor introduced me to the concept of "imposter syndrome", but this did little to allay my fears: I *knew* I was an alien and unworthy of a career in academia, and it was only a matter of time before I was *found out*. I carried a conviction that I was not committed enough and too selfish to be accepted in my chosen field, being always preoccupied with managing eating and training.

I reached my lowest point when I was 33.5 years old. A combination of family, financial, and professional pressures, alongside my internal battles and my bodybuilding regimen, became too much for me to manage, and I could see no reason for living: I simply did not have time to train, but if I didn't train, I returned sooner or later to starving myself. This had happened two years earlier, when I had been working in a prestigious academic post and suffered a frightening relapse of anorexia, which led to my resignation. At that time, I had begun therapy with Dr C, which had helped in some ways; but when I left that job, I ended therapy. Now, in a new teaching post in a different setting, I was afraid I was repeating the same pattern. I was so preoccupied with training and eating issues that I felt I could no longer manage to work: it was too exhausting and too difficult to cope with. I didn't want to be living like this, but it was the only way of establishing control that I knew. I remembered my therapy with Dr C but talked myself out of returning.

I was very fortunate to have an unusually supportive and insightful senior colleague at the time, who was astonished to realize the personal difficulties I was having. She told me that whatever was going on outside work was so well hidden, there was no evidence of it in my professional presentation. She helped me to understand that without therapeutic support, the problems I was struggling with were not going to go away, and giving up work was not "the answer". We agreed that I would take a break and go back to therapy. This was the first time I was able to accept that I was not going to get better. I could make myself psychologically strong enough to resist training, but then had nowhere to turn but anorexia.

Having convinced myself that I was "better off without therapy" and that it had been "no help anyway", it took a little while to change course. I spent a long time reading through things I had written to Dr C when I had been in treatment earlier (some of which I had allowed her to read, but most of which I had not) before I finally got in touch with her again. It took courage to contact Dr C, so great was my fear that she would turn me away. I remembered that even when I had allowed Dr C to see how underdeveloped and starved I was, both literally and metaphorically, I had never once felt judged. She had firmly believed that, with time, we could work together to overcome some of my difficulties, and, though never convinced, I had been reassured by her certainty and her greater experience of life. I remembered how she had enabled me to do things, and how we had made some real progress. Finally, I was struck by the realization that I had originally gone into therapy with her for exactly the same reason I needed her now: I wanted to salvage my career and to stop making myself so miserable that I no longer wanted to be alive. I could not do this on my own, but I knew I was going to have to work harder to trust Dr C and to trust in therapy to find a way forward. Dr C's willingness to continue on this journey with me is the only reason I am alive today.

We started again with a new insight I had gained during my most recent period of anorexia. From the age of 14, I had alternated between phases of anorexia and bodybuilding, and had been religiously maintaining an extreme "diet" consisting largely of protein powder. There had been no middle ground and nothing resembling "normality". Over the years, Dr C has repeatedly described my attitude towards myself and my body as *cruel, punishing, masochistic*— words I would never have used, and which I immediately denied: *This was just normal for me, this was how it was to be me, this was what I deserved for being me—and nobody had ever really minded much about it before.* . . . But she refused to agree, and as I learnt to trust her, she enabled me to look at and question my beliefs in ways I had never previously been able to do.

The "driving force"

But what was the driving force? Why had no previous treatment for my eating disorder or trying my hardest to "give up the gym" worked, when I usually had the willpower to do anything I put my mind to? Why was it that this apparently rational and intelligent person could behave in such an irrational way? Crucially, what was it about bodybuilding . . .?

In 2009, having recovered from anorexia to become a competitive bodybuilder, two years before I first met Dr C and when I had no concept of what it meant to be transgender, I wrote:

> Physically, I am a completely different person, but on the inside it's always the same me which is of course the nature of the problem. I hate being me so much that I feel I need to escape from me and the only way I can bear to live as me is to try and change me. . . . I think that is why I restrict what I eat and train the way I do and study the way I do—to try and be better and become something that is more acceptable to me; something I can live with.

In 2011, not long after I first met Dr C, I was beginning to understand this better:

> When I am training like that [at competitive bodybuilding standard] I am me and I love it—I am happy, it makes me feel alive and better about myself for the period of time I am in the gym and trying to improve me, it makes me feel like I am doing something about it . . .

Later, and because of the support of Dr C, I was finally able to start to look deeper:

> There is a feeling I get when I train that I am me and it is ok to be me. I train "like a man" but harder, among men, in my big baggy men's T-shirt, completely oblivious to all that is going on around me and the sensation I am creating by being the only woman among the men, doing whatever exercise it is I am doing. The bodybuilding drugs enhance that feeling and I continue to take them because I want to be able to feel like me in the gym more than I care about the side effects and potential repercussions of what I am doing. Taking drugs for bodybuilding feels like the only thing I have ever done in my life that is truly for me. The only thing that ever stopped me going further [with the drugs in the past] was my concern about what "other people" would think . . . . I was completely ok with what the drugs were doing to me physically—I liked it, and I didn't mind the "unwanted" effects at all [virilisation]. I only minded what other people thought about those unwanted effects . . .

And this was the starting point from which I gradually allowed myself to become conscious of the underlying gender issue. Dr C and I began to understand that the point of bodybuilding was to maximize muscle definition and minimize body fat in a way that no other "sport" or physical pursuit would allow. Bodybuilding was an attempt to *transform my body* into something more acceptable to me—and, ultimately, something not physiologically or physically achievable as an adult female.

There was also my 12-year-history of intermittent use of anabolic-androgenic steroids—perhaps easier to understand in the context of a competitive bodybuilding career, but my last competition had been five years previously. Furthermore, I have never smoked cigarettes or taken recreational drugs, so the use of these illicit substances was out of character. Yet without my bodybuilding drugs, I felt so lost, I hardly knew where to begin. It was not until one day Dr C matter-of-factly referred to these substances as "male hormones" that everything suddenly began to fall into place. Since my last competition, I had stopped taking the drugs only twice: for 6 months and, later, for 18 months. On each occasion, it had been the return of menstruation and the ensuing trauma that had prompted me to resume taking them.

We realized that the times in my life when things had gone really wrong (e.g. resignation of prestigious job, episodes of anorexia nervosa) had been when I had stopped taking these drugs, which had led to my body becoming more "female" again and the return of menstruation.

As the effects of hard training and steroids wore off, it became intolerable for me to be in my own skin, and I felt I needed to "get out of my body" or attack it in some way.

We began to think that the motive underlying the extreme level of control I exerted over my body, from starvation to bodybuilding, was an attempt to eradicate the evidence that it was biologically female. As much as I refused to accept this at first, my behaviour suggested that my sense of self was not female, and that I had been in conflict since the onset of puberty with the person I appeared to be physically. For the first time, with the support of Dr C, I was able to confront the truth I had subconsciously been avoiding or denying for the whole of my adult life: that there was a discrepancy between my mind and the true me (male) and my physical body (female). In a state of internal confusion about what was going on, I had been attacking everything that was female about me, while also trying to conform. In fact, I am a transgender person, a concept that I had never consciously entertained, and the driving force for all these years has been gender dysphoria. The extremes of dieting and training were my desperate attempts to manage this, and they allowed me to bear my existence as well as I did.

So, at 34 years old, and 4 years—albeit with breaks—into therapy, I slowly began to come to terms with the very difficult fact (for me) that my true identity/self is male. It was sobering to realize that I had effectively spent my life trying to prevent the natural biological processes of growing up and developing into an adult woman from happening, without ever acknowledging what I was doing or why. It is very clear to me now that I never wanted breasts, hips, "female curves", or menstrual periods. The few periods that I have experienced were so traumatic there are no words to convey the horror.

With hindsight, my secondary school provided the catastrophic "wrong single-sex" environment for me as a transgender child. Then there was the onset of (the wrong) puberty and the development of (the wrong set of) secondary sexual characteristics, prompting new expectations from others about how I should look, think, behave, and *be* now that I was a "young lady". In my case there were many additional social factors complicating the situation. My deterioration, from the happy child with friends who loved nothing more than playing with her brother to a recluse who did nothing but study and starve herself, was simply ascribed to these external factors, and nobody looked any deeper. By the time I was 15, I had been labelled a "high-flying perfectionist anorexic schoolgirl", and that was that. It was to be another 18 years before I finally began to understand how much more there was to it.

Around the age of 20, I had been treated by an eating disorders team who suggested that I was gay and would not accept it. I tried reluctantly to believe this for many years, tying myself in knots of confusion and despair. I believe now that this was because I always *knew* I wasn't gay, but it was then impossible to explain my sexual attraction to heterosexual women, consistently evident between the periods of starvation or bodybuilding competition preparation, which both effectively suppress those feelings. In the safety of the therapy room with Dr C, it suddenly became obvious to me that my sexual attraction towards heterosexual women is because I am a heterosexual (possibly bisexual—all this has yet to be fully explored) *man*. I see and always have seen women through my male eyes, and my inner male self feels emotional, romantic, and sexual connections with women, which becomes lost in translation through my physical self.

Despite my sexual feelings towards other women, I had never wanted to imagine, and could not have imagined, myself in a physical sexual relationship with another woman. Growing up as female, there was nothing "natural" to me about allowing another human to come close to the body that was so unacceptable to me. I was not in any way averse to others having sexual relationships, but the thought of being female in a straight sexual partnership was abhorrent to me, as was the thought of being a female partner in a gay couple. I simply could not be the female partner in any sexual relationship! As with many other things that divided me from the world around me, sexual relationships just did not apply to me, so I banished this fundamental part of human existence from my life and believed that I was inadequate, unlovable, and unworthy of intimacy.

An unexpected discovery for me post-transition is that, as a man, I can now imagine all these things that had been beyond my comprehension. I can imagine myself as a male partner in a human sexual partnership and feel that is as it should be—I would naturally know what to do (assuming I had a biological male body), and I would want to be there in that situation. However, such is my degree of gender dysphoria and disgust with my trans-male body, that this is not something I feel I could go any further with at this stage: although I have transitioned, this does not mean that my physical body is acceptable to me; I am still nowhere near comfortable enough with it myself to become intimate with anyone else.

I have felt so isolated, that it has taken years to build sufficient trust with Dr C to feel finally safe enough to explore the issues that had remained hidden for so long. I have found it very difficult to believe that Dr C's interest in me as her patient and the continuing relationship we have does not depend on me passing exams or doing really well in my career. It just is. And it is only very recently that I have become able to know and understand without automatically doubting, questioning, and challenging her, that she is just there, regardless.

February 2016:

> Nobody knows me or more about me or what me really is better than you do, and because it doesn't seem to change how you perceive me as a person it makes me feel safe with you and connected with you and free with you in a way I have never felt with another human being. You have given me very, very rare moments of real belief in me—not some act/pretence/highly modified/edited version of me, but the real actual me . . .

Had we not endured the ups and downs, intensities and disappearances of the journey we had been on, and had Dr C not persevered against my greatest efforts at times to make her go away and give up, we would never have reached the point where we were able to face the gender issue together. We ventured into discussions about concepts of biological sex, gender, sexuality, identity, and what constitutes a person, which continue to this day, and which I still can't imagine having with anyone else. I could sit opposite Dr C in therapy, struggling with the fact that I was not sure I was female, not sure I was male, not sure who or what I was or what I was going to do about any of it, but it was ok, because she was there, and she was still going to be there, whatever happened next. She enabled me to begin to realize that I am transgender, and that it is ok to be me. The moment she said to me, as if it were the most ordinary thing in the world, "Well, you are, of course, a person beyond gender . . ." will be ingrained in my memory forever. It was revolutionary—a paradigm shift for me.

In that initial period of realization, the overriding emotions were of relief, elation, and excitement—this was the answer, and suddenly years of confusion, torture, and utter self-loathing began to make sense. . . . I am male but "trapped inside a female body". . . . Only later did I begin to realize that although this was the answer, it was not the answer I wanted. I was finally on the right path, but it was not going to be an easy path to follow.

Pre-transition, when I was exploring this revolutionary idea, Dr C was able to present viewpoints and arguments that I would not otherwise have thought of or considered, and this helped me to achieve balance and maintain perspective. For example she countered my conviction that rather old-fashioned conventional colleagues would be horrified at the prospect of a transgender person in their midst with the suggestion that I might actually be more "acceptable" to them appearing as a "normal male" at first glance than a competitive female bodybuilder.

Dr C's unwavering acceptance of me as "beyond gender" allowed me to remain strong enough to explore, and gradually expose, my transgender identity. I had grown up in a family that did not condone homosexuality, let alone the concept of being transgender or non-binary; that it might be possible to be anything other than male or female and behave other than according to traditional stereotypical male and female roles was simply not spoken of. Furthermore, my time among the female bodybuilders had provided first-hand insight into the discriminatory attitudes and behaviours that exist towards transgender people. I was both ashamed and terrified to be transgender, and it was only with the support of Dr C that I found ways to overcome this. After so many years of never knowing what it meant or understanding how it felt to be accepted and liked simply because I am *me*, Dr C has given me all this and more, and it is quite possibly the greatest gift I will ever receive.

Challenges

The challenge that we have encountered is that no amount of therapy and internal work can change the physical reality of my body, and it is the physical reality (for me) that drives all of the unhelpful behaviours in which I am still entrenched and for which I originally sought help. While therapy has given me a depth of insight that I had no idea was possible—and I know there is potential to go deeper still when the time is right—I still cannot always use this knowledge to react sensibly in a given situation. And because I know that that no amount of therapy can change my physical body to a male one, it can still be all too easy to "blame" it for everything and declare it "useless" and a "waste of time" when I am particularly unhappy or frustrated.

Therapy inevitably stirs things up and brings submerged memories, thoughts, and feelings to the surface. Sometimes I have struggled to return to the present after a therapy session because I am still stuck in whichever moment in the past we were in. Sometimes I have wanted to continue to think and be in that moment for a while longer. There have been times when this has been extremely unhelpful, if I have other things to attend to that require my full concentration, and I become frustrated by the interference of therapy when I am trying to "get on with things" and resentful of the distraction it creates. Dr C has endured several periods over the years where this has become so overwhelming for me that I just disappear until I have been able to admit to myself (once again) that I do need her, and that therapy is extremely helpful.

The contrast between the safety of therapy and the reality of life is another unavoidable challenge. In the world today it is still difficult to be anything other than a "woman" or "man", and I could see that I would find it hard to present myself in my professional environment to colleagues or students as anything outside those categories. Yet in therapy with Dr C, such was the level of trust we had developed that I truly believed I could turn up one week and tell her I was female and then arrive the following week and declare myself male, and it wouldn't make any difference to her at all—in fact, I suspected she might not even notice, if I didn't tell her. This idea frustrated me immensely: it was comforting but also deeply upsetting. I welcomed, craved, and thrived on Dr C's total acceptance of me, beyond gender, and the fascinating idea that gender did not matter at all. But this was not reality and not possible for me as a professional outside the consulting room. And I would become annoyed with therapy for making me believe and feel things I wanted to believe and feel, but that I could not have in the outside world.

Post-transition, when I had returned to work as a man and joined a new gym as male, we had a particularly difficult time, and this triggered my most recent disappearance (to date). At that time, I really thought our journey had ended. Dr C has (of course) always been cautious not to push me one way or the other in terms of gender and transition and so has adopted a neutral position, and I fully understand why this is. However, once I had made the decision to transition and was working hard to cope with it and to keep on top of all it entailed, in terms of health, social, professional, and financial considerations, I found this infuriatingly unhelpful. Such were the difficulties ahead, it often seemed far easier to "go back" and resume my female identity, but I knew without question that this would not be the correct thing for me to do.

In one session alone (just before I disappeared) she talked about me stopping testosterone therapy, not changing my name, and changing my name to something else altogether, as if these things were as inconsequential as choosing which colour shirt to wear. She suggested that the delay my employers had introduced in recognizing my name change could be a positive thing. She even suggested a return to my bodybuilding gym. I was thrown into such a state of uncertainty, bewilderment, and turmoil that I didn't even want to be in the room with her. I became very angry and upset that she could be so seemingly flippant about the issues I was tearing myself apart over, some with potentially irreversible consequences. Therapy had "caused me so much confusion all over again" when the way forward had been clear, albeit not easy: "Whether I like it or not, I am transgender, I am male and I have to transition to my true male role otherwise I will probably end up killing myself, no matter how hard it is. I really need you to help me to be strong and keep moving ahead when I falter . . . ." The difficult nature of the way forward was another stumbling block for us. I would say "This is so hard", and Dr C would say, "I can't make this easy for you." Not once did I think she could make it easy or expect her to be able to make it easy for me. I just wanted and needed her to acknowledge and understand how hard it was, to validate my experience—there was no one else to whom I could talk about it. Similarly, she would suggest the opposite point of view, or a positive way to look at my negative experience, so frequently, that I began to feel as though she was minimizing or dismissing the difficulty of the situation. I began to feel as ashamed and humiliated in front of her as I did outside the therapy room, and eventually I stopped telling her things at all—I felt I was disappointing her by being unable to be more positive.

As an example, I had been trying to explain how horrible the experience of changing in the communal male changing room was when wearing a chest binder—seeking acknowledgement that this was indeed difficult, but that I was doing the best I could. Instead, she responded by suggesting I could change in a toilet. I was so dismayed by her inability to understand what I was trying to convey that I wanted to shout at her "Do you really think I haven't considered every single possible practical way around this countless times, and wouldn't already be doing that if I could?!" Then she asked me what I was so afraid of if someone did see me wearing my chest binder in the changing room, and if it was a fear of being physically attacked. And it was with fear and sadness that I realized that the lack of understanding was growing: I couldn't explain any better, and I knew

I couldn't possibly expect her to understand when I couldn't explain. I wanted to tell her "No, the fear of being physically attacked doesn't occur to me (although yes, it's a possibility) and might be a preferable option. . . . The fear is of rejection. The fear is of not belonging and the reminder of alien status. The fear is of the shame and humiliation I feel because I am not a biological man and wear a chest binder because these feelings are so powerful they make me want to kill myself! The fear is that the men say, "You're not a man—get out of this changing room!" because then what? Then where do I go? Where do I belong? The fear is of how painful it can feel to be transgender in a binary world, and particularly in a part of that world that had always been my sanctuary (the gym). Where do I go when I am not a woman and cannot possibly go into the female changing room? There is nowhere else to go."

We weren't able to overcome this at the time, and I stopped wanting to be in the room with Dr C. At that point I felt just as bad about myself and the difficulties I was having when I was in therapy as I did outside; even worse, I felt I was letting Dr C down. A distance had developed between us, and, much as I wanted to explore the transgender issues I was facing, at that time I could not bring myself to talk to her about any of it. I realized I had reached a point where I wasn't sure there was anything more she could do to help, so I steeled myself to "get on with it" by myself and didn't go back. With hindsight, though, I'm not sure there ever was, or can ever be, a complete break from Dr C, because she is constantly with me in my mind.

My physical experience of transition

> To me gender is not physical at all, but is altogether insubstantial. It is soul, perhaps, it is talent, it is taste, it is environment, it is how one feels, it is light and shade, it is inner music. . . . It is more truly life and love than any combination of genitals, ovaries and hormones. It is the essentialness of oneself, the psyche, the fragment of unity.
>
> [Morris, 1974, p. 20]

I have never *tried* to be male either pre- or post-transition. I have always been me, and "me" is male. So, on the contrary, I have spent the vast majority of my life *trying to be female*, trying to be something I am not, never was, and could not be, trying to fit into and adapt to the uncomfortable limitations of my female body and society's predetermined roles, behaviours, and expectations that are dictated by anatomy. I made my social transition when I was 33.5 years old, and, for me, learning how to "act like a man", "behave like a man", or "sound like a man" were never worries that I had or things that I consciously did: I already did act, behave, and sound like a man sufficiently to "pass" successfully unless I tried very hard not to. So my transition was almost the other way around: it was the moment at which I finally allowed myself to *stop trying to pass as female,* and, as such, it was more of a calm, passive moment of relief than an exciting, active event.

I have never wanted to draw attention to myself, create trouble, or challenge "societal norms". Throughout my time at my all-girls secondary school and university my records remain exemplary. I am not and never will be an activist, and that has nothing to do with my gender identity—that is my personality. The outlet for the distress and frustration and perhaps the expression of my internal conflict has always been through my absolute refusal to accept my physical body and the physical limitations it imposes on me.

Dr C introduced me to Jan Morris' *Conundrum* (1974), and although her transition is male to female, the opposite of mine, this is the closest I have ever come to reading words written by someone else that convey what I feel and experience but find so difficult to explain—and also the true meaning of gender (see above). With regard to identity, she refers to both a description from Kinglake's *Eothen* (1845), "The whole corpus of personality, how others saw him, what he considered himself to be, his status in the world, his background, his taste, his profession, his purposes . . . an entity, the fact of what one is", and the (then) Oxford dictionary definition: "The condition or fact that a person or thing is itself and is not something else" (Morris, 1974, p. 35). She explains "The chief cause of my disquiet was the fact I had none. I was not to others what I was to myself; I did not conform to the dictionary's definition—itself and not something else" (p. 35). This perfectly describes how it feels—and seems to me to be—me. I have never been to others what I am to myself, and have instead spent my life trying to be what I am to others, for others, almost destroying myself in the process. I still do not really have a true sense of there being a "myself", but Dr C says: "Perhaps it's unsurprising that the coherent self feels hard to grasp when one has spent 30 plus years trying to bear the body one is living within, but rebelling against it in various ways, some entirely unconscious." I take comfort in this and remind myself that it is perhaps still early days.

Jan Morris used to sit, alone, and simply watch the daily human goings on around her (as I always have done and still do), feeling unable to be a part of normal human existence. She would marvel that the majority of humans seemed to find the everyday things of life so ordinary that they could be done without a second thought, and I understand this completely. I have complained to Dr C many times over the years that "I can't even do the most basic human things e.g. have a partner, have close friends, go out for lunch." I see, hear, and feel all of this going on around me, but I am not part of it, and it just doesn't apply to me. My exclusion is not a deliberate process, and most of the time I don't feel it emotionally—it is just a fact of my life, as it was for Jan Morris:

> As I watched the world go by, I found myself more than ever outside mankind's commitments. . . . It was not modesty that camouflaged me so, nor even professional technique: it was a detachment so involuntary that I often felt I really wasn't there, but was viewing it all from some silent chamber of my being. [Morris, 1974, pp. 47–48]

Therapy has taught me to look from all angles, ask, and think in ways I was not able to do before. Particularly poignant for me here is that when I read Jan Morris's words, I recognized that as the highly respected and successful male figure that she was, even though she had reached a point at which she felt she could no longer go on, she would have seemed completely "innocuous" to others as that male figure. This has opened my eyes to the possibility that the way others apparently liked me and thought so highly of me as a female professional was genuine. Even though it seemed so heinously wrong to me, maybe to others I really seemed good at my job. It is extraordinary to begin to understand how toxic gender dysphoria can be to everything that constitutes a person.

In the first months post social transition, Dr C would return to the concept of me being a person beyond gender, but I could do nothing with this idea at that time because I still could not get beyond the physical barriers of my female body. I could not see how I could be the person I am *beyond gender* when I was still stuck in the "wrongly gendered" body I so despised, and putting male clothes on it made no difference to me—when I took them off, the same wrong body was still there. It seemed paradoxical that psychological issues such as my feelings about my identity, my alienation and isolation, could have nothing to do with my biological sex and the secondary sexual characteristics and reproductive organs that define it. Indeed, it is the physical things that most transgender people seek to alter in order to find some degree of relief from these crucial psychological issues, and physical interventions do seem to make a difference.

In contrast to the years of internal work and development of the therapeutic relationship with Dr C, the surgeon who performed my top surgery is someone I have spent only minutes with (while conscious). Yet his approach towards me and subsequently his work on my chest have so far been the single most important thing that has reduced my gender dysphoria. Top surgery was the stuff of miracles for me. In my first consultation with the surgeon, I was struck by his total understanding and acceptance of my situation. He did not question me, which was an immense relief, and when he examined me, he prodded my chest muscles and said, "Well that's all you, all that is muscle . . ." and then demonstrated the breast tissue he would remove and said, "And this is what shouldn't be there . . .". I repeated his words over and over again in my mind: "This is what shouldn't be there . . ." Never before had I felt such validation! He saw me as a man who simply should never have had breasts in the first place, and, furthermore, he would remove them for me and create the most masculine chest he possibly could. He understood that top surgery was not about changing my female body into a male body: it was about removing the erroneous female bits from the body I should have had.

The process of surgery itself was not easy. Pain was not an issue, but I bitterly resented the inconvenience, lack of independence, and the actual physical disablement I had to endure after the operation: that I could not drive, could not lift things, and had to take time off work. But, above all, I could not train. I did not go into the gym for five weeks and could not follow my normal upper-body training sessions for the next six months. Today, ten months on, I am still not able to train my upper body in quite the way I used to due to the scar tissue and my fear of irreversible stretching, or worse. I do not regret the surgery for one moment because it has given me a chest that is closer to how my chest should be, but I am still angry about the injustice of having to subject myself to a complex surgical procedure in order to achieve an approximation of the body I should have always had. I am also angry [not with the surgeon—his work is exceptional] that I now have two very long horizontal scars across my chest that extend to under my arms (one 27 cm long, the other 25 cm long) and still at times feel as though I have been "cut in half"—it is not the cosmetic appearance that bothers me most, but that the scar tissue continues to be an area of weakness and vulnerability when I train and still limits what I can do ten months on. It seems ironic to me that I had to become a vulnerable patient, submit myself to the surgeon's scalpel, and now live with two huge scars across myself in order to become more the picture of masculine strength I am on the inside. My top surgery in itself was absolutely brilliant; I was fortunate not to have any complications, and I did not dare hope for the result I got. I will always remember the initial elation and euphoria I felt when I first looked down to see that even with the surgical compression bandages in place, my chest was *completely flat*.

The consistent relief of top surgery is that I can feel more secure in myself about passing as male, because I know I am less likely to be discovered as transgender without a chest binder and clothing designed to hide it. But how I feel about my chest itself is still variable, and there are still times when I become overwhelmed with remorse that it is not and never will be masculine enough. The fact remains that I still have a female chest from which the breasts have been removed and on which male reconstruction was performed. Furthermore, if I look above and below my chest, I still have a female body— perhaps leaner and more muscular than a typical female body, but undoubtedly anatomically female, and this still causes me great sorrow.

I wrote about this to Dr C seven months after my surgery:

Sometimes, if I catch a glimpse of myself in the mirror by mistake instead of when I deliberately want to look, I am shocked by how female my upper body looks, unclothed. I am humiliated and devastated to see my chest—muscular, completely flat, apparently "male"—but it is not the chest I have in my mind's eye. When I am in the gym surrounded by men and looking through my eyes, I am male. But when I suddenly see my physical shell as others see me (e.g. when I catch a glimpse off guard in the mirror) it is a shock and I am mortified. I don't have the physical body of an adult man, or a teenage boy. I am just not what I feel I should be and nothing can take this pain away. Training lessens it, top surgery has made the biggest single difference but nothing ever removes it altogether . . .

Furthermore, I can sometimes look in the mirror and see a female body as if I'd never had top surgery—I see the breasts and female nipples I once had, and it gives me a horrible fright. Looking at the outside world through my own eyes, I feel I am male, and the sense of *wrongness* I imagine others see in my body can still make me want to destroy it—destroy "me". Surely the self I am is physical, just as much as it is psychological? "Me" has consisted of these two components so completely at war with each other, to the point of self-harm and self-destruction, all my teenage and adult life. I simply do not know what it feels like for one's inner self (mind?) to be at peace with one's physical self (body?).

Therapy has helped me to understand that the concept of a person as multifaceted and complex is fundamental to transgender issues. For example, Dr C maintains that I am not *abhorrent as a person*, yet I say I continue to feel *abhorrent to myself*. I am learning that this is an over-simplification and that I have to interrogate such assumptions in order to move forward. Dr C suggests that if I can begin to see myself as a human being who has caring feelings towards others and relationships with them, then I am not abhorrent. The complicated issue of how my feelings about my physical body impact on the definition of myself is something I struggle with as a transgender person.

My body will never have grown and developed like a male body. Surgery alters secondary sexual characteristics: it can remove breasts, it can create a remarkably realistic-looking penis. But this is at the expense of years of medical procedures, significant interruptions to one's life to undergo and recover from these procedures, and enduring scars. I have had brilliant top surgery, but I still do not have a male chest—I have a chest that can now pass as male clothed and unclothed (from a distance). Likewise, metoidioplasty and phalloplasty come at the price of tissue grafting from inner cheek, abdomen, thigh, or forearm with significant and lasting consequences to the donor site. A micropenis or a phallus can be formed with the urethra lengthened to allow urination from the tip of the organ, but that micropenis or phallus cannot necessarily achieve and sustain an erection to allow sexual penetration, and it certainly cannot ejaculate sperm to allow reproduction. Two or three complex surgical procedures are required, multiple complications are possible, and there is no guarantee that any of it will be ok. Bottom surgery better approximates the original female physical body to that of an adult male—but the body is still an altered adult female body. My worry is that even if I have the courage to submit myself to the process of such extensive surgery and cope with all that it entails, it will still never be enough. *Having no breasts and creating a micropenis or a phallus does not make me male!*

I do not disclose that I am transgender to anyone who has not previously known me as female unless there is an explicit reason for doing so. This is a choice I have made for fear of how I will be judged, based on my preconceptions (which could possibly be challenged) and several bad experiences (which cannot be denied). So I am always on the lookout, existing in a constant state of alertness and high awareness, on guard for signs of danger, clues, warnings that others may discover that I am transgender and react badly in some way to this. I am always acutely aware of everyone around me and of myself in relation to others and constantly wonder and worry about what they might be thinking and it can be exhausting.

Physically in the gym, the gap between myself and biological men post-transition is far wider than that between myself (presenting as a female bodybuilder) and biological women, and this was not something I was psychologically prepared for. Such was my excitement at no longer having to deliberately act feminine or cover up the signs of masculinity when I transitioned, I simply hadn't thought about how the goalposts would shift in terms of comparisons made by myself and others. In stature, body shape, and the size and definition of my muscles, little has changed. Although I had been the strongest, most self-disciplined, admired female figure in the gym by many men and women, I had not particularly valued this. Now, suddenly, I was the one of the most pathetic males. Overnight, in the eyes of others, I changed from being an experienced bodybuilder who had clearly spent many hours in the gym, to someone who had possibly never lifted weights or been to a gym before in his life.

Absolutely *nothing* about my physical body or strength could have changed significantly when I presented myself as a man, but the change of my pronoun from female to male meant that *everything* about me effectively changed, as I was perceived in a different context. It has been particularly hard in this setting, not only because of the significance of the body itself, but because the assumed attributes of personality and experience that go with one's physical appearance were also suddenly changed when I was compared with biological men. As a very capable female in the gym, people would approach me for advice, and I would always be ready to help, whether it was showing a novice trainer how to perform an exercise correctly or discussing the intricacies of the final week of contest preparation with a bodybuilder. But this no longer happens. I keep my eyes firmly down, wanting to avoid attention as far as possible.

The male communal area in the changing room is still difficult to this day, because I need to change but keep my transgender body hidden, even after two years of practice. The best option is to avoid having to perform any exchange of clothing in there at all and go straight home, but this is not always possible. Before top surgery, I would be shaking with fear if I was forced to switch T-shirts, in case the door opened and someone came in and caught a glimpse of the chest binder. If I had to take the chest binder off (e.g. it was soaked with sweat), this was magnified a thousand times. Ten months post top surgery, the fear is still there, but less intense. There is no chest binder to immediately give me away, but there are very visible scars from the front, side, and back if I lift my arms. Taking off bottom things remains an art of discretion and speed beneath the cover of long T-shirts and is much easier to accomplish than the top things. It seems most men choose to remain covered on their bottom halves in the changing room, so this sort of routine is not uncommon, but most men are comfortable to be seen topless.

In terms of toilet facilities, as I have not (yet?) had any bottom surgery, I need to use a toilet cubicle. The first problem is that not all male public toilets have one. The second is that when they do, there is often a single cubicle that borders on the un-enterable because it is so disgusting. This is an inevitable worry if I don't know what facilities are available and I am going somewhere for a length of time that will necessitate visiting the toilet (despite my strategic lack of fluid intake). My personal view on the "transgender toilets" issue that generates so much media attention is that any person old enough to enter a public toilet facility unaccompanied (i.e. I do not mean children), whichever gender they identify as, should be able to use a public toilet safely and without causing other users distress in doing so. In my case, I don't mind whether this is a designated men's room, unisex toilet, or disabled toilet and, if faced with the choice of all three, I will pick them in reverse order of preference, prioritizing cleanliness rather than the sign on the door! For reasons I do not yet fully understand, meeting someone I know (and, even worse, someone who knew me as female) in the men's toilet becomes excruciatingly embarrassing for both parties, and I go to great lengths to avoid this. I wonder if it is because this raises uncomfortable questions about masculinity (theirs and mine), because they still see me as a female who should not be in there, or simply because men of my age go into toilet cubicles for one reason only.

Being male

When I meet somebody for the first time now, I am always anxious to know if *they know*, and I follow their gaze as they appraise me, searching for signs that they have figured me out. The first clue is my height, then my ears (small for an adult man and with visible holes from multiple piercings—not a usual sight in a man of my age in my profession, but probably acceptable in a woman), then my flat chest (now not so much of a giveaway post top surgery) but with unusually narrow shoulders for a man who has my hip width. My arms are lean and muscular from years of training and hairy in a typically male way, but unusually small for a man, with tiny wrist joints and hands. When I am working with professional colleagues, I am constantly wondering what they are making of me. On a good day, this can be tedious, but on a bad day, this can be enough to send my mood and self-confidence spiralling downwards and is a constant reminder that *I am not male enough*.

Most people are surprised to discover my age, assuming that I am at least ten years younger than I am because my skin is still unusually smooth for a man of my age, due to lack of testosterone exposure. Facial hair is a clear declaration of masculinity, and one of the first things I wanted to do post-transition was grow a beard. I have always admired light beards and designer stubble and hoped that having my own would help to relieve some of the horror I feel about my "face being too fat", which has been one of my main preoccupations throughout the years. (I now know this is part of the gender dysphoria). But, most upsettingly, my beard still doesn't grow thick or even enough, and after a week of beard growing, I still look more like a 13-year-old boy than an adult man, while my colleagues can grow a thick, full beard in a matter of days!

In addition, the simple and potentially embarrassing things that most people figure out during adolescence, such as trying out a new haircut, all have to be done as an adult man who has apparently always been male. This adds considerably to my anxiety about my transgender status being discovered and now discourages me from trying things out. For instance, I arrived at work one day with my hair much shorter than it had ever been around the back and sides, proudly looking and feeling more masculine (I thought). But the attention it attracted made me feel so conspicuous and afraid that "they suspected something" that my self-belief evaporated, and I felt deflated and wished I had never done it, even though it had made me feel better about myself.

Likewise, I can't walk into a shop and buy the clothes I would choose to wear, because they don't fit me. I am too short for men's high street tailoring, and jackets and shirts big enough to fit my neck and shoulders (due to weight training) come down to my knees; trousers big enough to fit over my hips have handfuls of spare material to gather up around the waist, and I can easily pull them on and off without undoing a button or zip! Men's boxer shorts fit like women's hot pants, and men's briefs fit like women's bikini bottoms, despite extreme stretching procedures, and neither situation does anything to help with gender dysphoria. Men's ankle socks come up to just below my knees, and men's shoes simply don't even come in my size: they begin at size 6 (European 39–39.5), which is far too big, even with thick socks. Consequently, my initial excitement when I first transitioned about being able to dress in men's clothes for work was soon replaced by a heavyhearted lack of interest: looking at all the men's clothes and shoes that I would like to wear but can't because of my size does nothing to help feelings of gender dys-phoria. I get by with the clothes for work that I bought in that initial period of excitement two years ago and one pair of now rather worn-out "proper" men's shoes that were the only design available in men's size 5 and were specially ordered for me by the shoe shop. When not dressed for work, I simply wear the same male sportswear/gym clothes I have worn since I was 12 or 13 and the same unisex-style trainers (technically, women's, due to size).

Overnight, I became a 33.5-year-old man who has had no life experience of growing and developing in a male role but who is sud-denly now recognized and responded to as male by the world around him. I did not experience boy's school, boy's school sports, or male companionship from childhood to adulthood. I was not a Beaver or a Cub but a Brownie and a Guide. I did not play rugby, football, and cricket at school, but hockey, netball, and tennis instead. I can reveal nothing of my competitive achievements as a powerlifter, because it would reveal my transgender status. I feel that there are big gaps that can never be filled, and it is nerve-racking to have no sense of a relatable personal life history, even in the most benign social situ-ations. For instance, a friendly enquiry such as "So which school did you go to in London . . .?" becomes a potential minefield. Meeting new peers at work, having to present my research, and therefore being the centre of attention or having to deal with questions about my name, background, or earlier career by more senior colleagues (some of whom will have encountered me in my previous female role and may or may not remember this) can be so worrying that it can be hard to concentrate on whatever it is I am actually supposed to be doing.

My reputation, achievements, publications, and experience are all inextricably linked to my professional identity, and it is not possible to re-write that history or erase all trace of my previous female name. Key things such as my degree certificate can be changed, but evidence of my achievement cannot be. I can do nothing about presentations and published journal papers. I am known by my name and gender and I work in a small, highly competitive speciality. If I wish to conceal my transgender history to current and new colleagues who know me only as male, I cannot lay claim to any of this history. I feel a great sense of loss and regret about this, and it is bewildering to be faced with a profound sense of discontinuity when I am the same person.

When I first transitioned, I wanted to keep the shortened, gender-neutral version of my original female name. I felt that my name was an integral part of me and should continue post-transition, to reflect that I am the same person—a person, beyond gender. But now I am not so sure. I can see how a new, unequivocally male name that can in no way be linked to my previous female name could be advantageous. I wonder if it would help me to feel more secure in my male role if I could completely deny my former female role. Currently, if I meet someone who wonders whether they know me as female, the similarities between the male and female versions of my name are enough of a clue to suddenly make the connection and understand that I have transitioned, whereas a different name would make this less likely to happen. These sorts of things are particularly difficult in professional situations, such as a conference, where I will encounter people who knew me as female alongside people who know me only as male. It is a constant problem knowing whom to tell and when, what people already know, and where this information has come from.

I have experienced how it feels to have my transgender history deliberately revealed to an entire department of new colleagues without my consent, by someone who recognized me as female. It was such a painful violation of my privacy and my wish to be accepted in a new environment as a man that it has made me even more wary of disclosing anything at all. Similarly, there are inevitable administrative difficulties to overcome when, during the early stages of transition, one's documents are not all aligned in terms of name and gender. Although I began a new post as male, my birth certificate, passport, degree certificates, and so on were still female at that time. I have since discovered that my original female name has a horrible way of popping up in the most unexpected and unhelpful places in the electronic systems we use at work for all and sundry to see—for example, on an electronic training portfolio that a trainer just happened to project onto the screen in front of a classroom of students. Things like this cannot be foreseen; I cannot plan how I will react or manage the situation until it happens, and I am always going to be faced with these issues. I am never going to be truly free of my female history, because I am a transgender person, and I lived for 33.5 years in a female role. But I hope, with time, the worry I have about how I will be perceived and judged and the potential difficulties I will face if people do know I am transgender, will fade. Sometimes I feel fine enough about it all to think it doesn't matter, and I don't mind who knows, because nothing can change what it is. But most of the time I still don't feel sure or safe enough.

Work itself is much easier. I have never been misgendered while presenting myself to people who have not known me as female, and I am far more comfortable in my male clothes than I have ever previously been at work, displaying my apparently masculine mannerisms and behaviours that no longer have to be deliberately suppressed. My height is always a problem wherever I go, but the unhappiness and preoccupation I still have with my physical body is never so much of an issue when I am at work, busy, and absorbed in what I am doing. I am far more confident post-transition—both in myself as a person and myself and my ability. A quote I read on an LGBT website comes to mind: "While confidence comes from within, a major source of that inner strength is whether your outward presentation makes you feel awesome . . .", and I think this is very true. I am more self-assured when meeting people for the first time because I do not have to worry about what they think of my muscular arms or deep voice (as I did when I was still a female). I am also more confident on the phone, having had some painful experiences to be told, after arriving to see someone I had only had telephone contact with: "Oh, there must be some mistake! I wasn't talking to you. The person on the phone was a man!" I would feel mortified, and my thoughts would spiral into negativity: "Everyone thinks I sound like a man, they don't think I'm the same person, what must they think of how I look, do they all know I took bodybuilding drugs, it's all my fault for making them feel confused and uncomfortable, it's so embarrassing, I'm so bad, I don't deserve to do this job, etc."

The turmoil and anxiety that has plagued me since adolescence has lessened since I transitioned. Inside, I am calmer and quieter than I have ever been as an adult, because I understand that the fundamental problem and the inescapable driving force has always been, and always will be, that I am transgender, but I had no conscious awareness of this. Perhaps this was because it was not a concept I knew anything about, but if I had, I would probably have intuitively found it unacceptable. In addition, all trace of it was well disguised by my eating disorder and subsequent total obsession with bodybuilding, gaining muscle, and minimizing fat. It took more than four years of therapy with Dr C for us to be able to find it. I just *knew*, with total conviction, that I was too fat and did not have enough muscle *for me*.

But now I understand that *for me* meant for a boy/teenage boy/man depending on the stage of my life I was at.

While I am calmer knowing that I am transgender, I am not always happier. I am able to recognize and understand when the feelings of gender dysphoria are particularly intense, and how this affects my mood, my ability to see things objectively, and my sense of self-belief and confidence. Some days are far better than others, but generally I am less aggressive, desperate, and impulsive in terms of what I will do to relieve the turmoil. Now that I know what is going on, I am faced with the fact that ultimately anything I "make myself do" to feel momentarily better is pointless, because I cannot make myself biologically male, no matter how hard I try. Being able to recognize the futility of my position can be helpful and unhelpful in equal measure. Now I do not always automatically act on the feelings that used to compel me, and I am better able to stop, reflect, and think. But it can also seem overwhelmingly sad to look back at the years and opportunities I have wasted through my preoccupation with trying to change my body into something that it can never be. So my internal work continues.

Despite all the day-to-day difficulties, I am much more settled presenting myself as male (as I can be). I still feel a little rush of excitement when I am referred to as "Sir" or when I overhear colleagues talking about "he" or "him" and know that they are referring to me—being male and being recognized as male is the way it should be. The terrible sense of awkwardness, clumsiness, and inadequacy I used to feel has evaporated, and I know exactly what is expected of me and how to behave. With biological men, I am wary, in case they think I am not male enough, and I am always reassured by their ready acceptance of me and my masculinity. Men seem to be much friendlier with one another than are women, with a greater sense of camaraderie from the outset. Men (even as strangers) greet each other using terms such as "mate" and "brother", but never in my former female life was I called "sister" by another woman I had just met. Subjectively I *am* male, but I still worry about whether I am objectively male enough for others to assume that I am biologically male and was born male. I think for me, being "male enough" would mean being able to act out my inner maleness and express my inner maleness through my physical body: it would be to experience congruence between my internal psychic and my external physical self. For me, this is not necessarily about having a penis. It would rather be, in a room full of adults, to be among the taller ones, to lift and carry things without a second thought, to have the physical capabilities of men in the gym, to have the physical presence, stature, and natural deepness of voice of a man, and ultimately to be able to use my body to express the love I feel for my sexual partner as a man, and be the father of my own children. Clearly, no amount of any sort of intervention can make this possible for me in my lifetime. But what I can do is work hard to learn to accept and make the best of what I do have, as I continue on this journey.

REFERENCES

Abelove, H., Barale, M. A., & Halperin, D. (Eds.) (1993). *The Lesbian and Gay Studies Reader*. New York: Routledge.

Abraham, K. (1924). A short study of the development of the libido, viewed in the light of mental disorders. In: K. Abraham (Eds.), *Selected Papers on Psychoanalysis* (pp. 418–501). London: Karnac, 1988.

Act Up (1987). *Silence = Death*. New York. Available at: www.actupny.org/reports/silencedeath.html

Akhtar, S. (2014). The mental pain of minorities. *British Journal of Psychotherapy, 30* (2): 136–153.

Allen, D. J., & Oleson, T. (1999). Shame and internalized homophobia in gay men. *Journal of Homosexuality, 37* (3): 33–43.

APA (2013). *Diagnostic and Statistical Manual of Mental Disorders (DSM–5)*. Washington, DC: American Psychiatric Association.

Amsterdam, B. K., & Levitt, M. (1980). Consciousness of self and painful self-consciousness. *Psychoanalytic Study of the Child, 35*: 67–83.

Anonymous (2015). A gay trainee *New Associations (Newsletter of the British Psychoanalytic Council)*, Issue 17 (Spring), pp. 9–10.

Anzieu, D. (1989). *The Skin Ego*. New Haven, CT: Yale University Press.

Balint, E. (1973). Technical problems found in the analysis of women by a woman analyst: A contribution to the question "what does a woman want?". *International Journal of Psychoanalysis, 54*: 195–201.

Balsam, R. H. (2017). Freud, the birthing body, and modern life. *Journal of the American Psychoanalytic Association, 65* (1): 61–90.

Bannister, K., & Pincus, L. (1965). *Shared Fantasy in Marital Problems*. London: Institute of Marital Studies.

Baraitser, L. (2017). *Enduring Time*. London: Bloomsbury.

Barden, N. (2011). Disrupting Oedipus: The legacy of the Sphinx. *Psychoanalytic Psychotherapy, 25* (4): 324–345.

Barlow, C. (2017). Queer British Art 1861–1967. *Tate Etc., Issue 39* (Spring).

Barnett, M. (1966). Vaginal awareness in the infancy and childhood of girls. *Journal of the American Psychoanalytic Association, 14*: 129–141.

Bartlett, N. (1988). *Who Was that Man? A Present for Mr Oscar Wilde*. London: Serpent's Tail.

Baudrillard, J. (1983). *In the Shadow of the Silent Majorities*. New York: Semiotext(e).

Bayer, R. (1981). *Homosexuality and American Psychiatry: The Politics of Diagnosis*. New York: Basic Books.

BBC News (2014). UKIP councillor blames storms and floods on gay marriage. *BBC News,* January 18. Available at: www.bbc.co.uk/news/uk-england-oxfordshire-25793358

Beebe, J. (1985). The father's anima. In: A. Samuels (Ed.), *The Father: Contemporary Jungian Perspectives*. London: Free Association Books.

Beebe, J. (1993). Toward an image of male partnership. In: R. H. Hopcke, K. L. Carrington, & S. Wirth (Eds.), *Same-Sex Love and the Path to Wholeness*. Boston, MA: Shambhala.

Beebe, J. (2017). *Energies and Patterns in Psychological Type*. London: Routledge.

Bem, S. J. (1993). *The Lenses of Gender: Transforming the Debate on Sexual Inequality*. New Haven, CT: Yale University Press.

Benjamin, J. (1988). *The Bonds of Love*. New York: Pantheon Books.

Benjamin, J. (1995). *Like Subjects and Love Objects*. New Haven, CT: Yale University Press.

Benjamin, J. (1997). *The Shadow of the Other*. New York: Routledge.

Bergmann, M. (1995). Observations on the female negative oedipal phase and its significance in the analytic transference. *Journal of Clinical Psychoanalysis, 4*: 283–295.

Berlant, L., & Warner, M. (1998). Sex in public. *Critical Enquiry, 24* (2): 547–566.

Bersani, L. (1986). *The Freudian Body*. New York: Columbia University Press.

Bersani, L. (1995). *Homos*. Cambridge, MA: Harvard University Press.

Bersani, L. (2010). *Is the Rectum a Grave? And Other Essays*. Chicago, IL: University of Chicago Press.

Bersani, L., & Phillips, A. (2008). *Intimacies*. Chicago, IL: University of Chicago Press.

Bion, W. R. (1967). Notes on memory and desire. *Psychoanalytic Forum, 2* (3): 279–281.

Birksted-Breen, D. (1993a). General introduction. In: D. Birksted-Breen (Ed.), *The Gender Conundrum: Contemporary Psychoanalytic Perspectives on Femininity and Masculinity* (pp. 1–40). London: Routledge.

Birksted-Breen, D. (1993b). *The Gender Conundrum: Contemporary Psychoanalytic Perspectives on Femininity and Masculinity*. London: Routledge.

Blanchard, R. (1993a). The she-male phenomenon and the concept of partial autogynephilia. *Journal of Sex & Marital Therapy, 19* (1): 69–76.

Blanchard, R. (1993b). Partial versus complete autogynephilia and gender dysphoria. *Journal of Sex & Marital Therapy, 19* (4): 301–307.

Blechner, M. J. (2009). Psychoanalysis in and out of the closet. In: *Sex Changes: Transformations in Society and Psychoanalysis*. New York: Routledge.

Blum, A., Danson, M., & Schneider, S. (1997). Problems of sexual expression in adult gay men: A psychoanalytic reconsideration. *Psychoanalytic Psychology, 14* (1): 1–11.

Blum, A., & Pfetzing, V. (1997). Assaults to the self: The trauma of growing up gay. *Gender and Psychoanalysis, 2* (4): 427–442.

Bollas, C. (1987). *The Shadow of the Object: Psychoanalysis of the Unthought Known*. London: Free Association Books.

Bollas, C. (1989). *Forces of Destiny*. London: Free Association Books.

Bollas, C. (1993). *Being a Character. Psychoanalysis and Self Experience*. London: Routledge.

Bonaparte, M. (1935). Passivity, masochism and femininity. *International Journal of Psychoanalysis, 16* (3): 325–333.

Bornstein, K. (1994). *Gender Outlaw: On Men, Women and the Rest of Us*. New York: Vintage Books.

Botella, S., & Botella, C. (2004). *The Work of Psychic Figurability: Mental States without Representation*. London: Brunner-Routledge.

Brakel, L. (1986). "Nothing is missing . . . yet": Two disturbances in the sense of reality and a woman's fantasied phallus. *Psychoanalytic Quarterly, 55*: 301–305.

Braunschweig, D., & Fain, M. (1993). The phallic shadow. In: D. Birksted-Breen (Ed.), *The Gender Conundrum: Contemporary Psychoanalytic Perspectives on Femininity and Masculinity* (pp. 132–146). London: Routledge.

Brel, J. (1967). *Song of the Old Lovers* [English translation]. Available at: http://lyricstranslate.com/en/la-chanson-des-vieux-amants-song-old-lovers.html

British Psychoanalytic Council (2011). *Statement on Homosexuality*. Available at: www.bpc.org.uk/sites/psychoanalytic-council.org/files/6.2%20Position%20statement%20on%20homosexuality.pdf

Bronski, M. (2011). *A Queer History of the United States*. Boston, MA: Beacon Press.

Broucek, F. J. (1982). Shame and its relationship to early narcissistic developments. *International Journal of Psychoanalysis, 63*: 369–378.

Brunskill-Evans, H., & Moore, M. (Eds.) (2017). *Transgender, Children and Young People: Born in Your Own Body*. Newcastle upon Tyne: Cambridge Scholars.

Budd, S. (2001). "No sex please, we're British": Sexuality in English and French psychoanalysis. In: C. Harding (Ed.), *Sexuality: Psychoanalytic Perspectives*. Hove: Brunner-Routledge.

Bullough, V. (1979). *Homosexuality: A History*. New York: Meridian.

Burch, B. (1985). Another perspective on merger in lesbian couples. In: L. B. Rosewater & L. Walker (Eds.), *Handbook of Feminist Therapy: Women's Issues in Psychotherapy* (pp. 10–109). New York: Springer.

Burch, B. (1996). Between women: The mother–daughter romance and homoerotic transference in psychotherapy. *Psychoanalytic Psychology, 13*: 475–494.

Burch, B. (1997). *Other Women: Lesbian/Bisexual Experience and Psychoanalytic Views of Women*. New York: Columbia University Press.

Burgoyne, B. (2015). Symbolic functioning. In: J. Borossa, C. Bronstein, & C. Pajaczkowska (Eds.), *The New Klein–Lacan Dialogues* (pp. 255–270). London: Karnac.

Butler, G., de Graaf, N., Wren, B., & Carmichael, P. (2018). The assessment and support of children and adolescents with gender dysphoria. *Archives of Disease in Childhood, 103*: 631–636.

Butler, J. (1990). *Gender Trouble: Feminism and the Subversion of Identity*. New York: Routledge.

Butler, J. (1993). *Bodies That Matter*. New York: Routledge.

Butler, J. (1995). Melancholy gender—Refused identifications. *Psychoanalytic Dialogues, 5*: 165–180.

Butler, J. (1997). Response to Lynne Layton's "The doer behind the deed". *Gender in Psychoanalysis, 2*: 515–520.

Butler, J. (2000). *Antigone's Claim*. New York: Columbia University Press.

Butler, J. (2004). *Undoing Gender*. New York: Routledge.

Califa, P. (1997). *Sex Changes: The Politics of Transgenderism*. San Francisco, CA: Cleis.

Campbell, D., & Groenbaek, M. (2006). *Taking Positions in the Organization*. London: Karnac.

Camus, A. (1942). *The Myth of Sisyphus and Other Essays.* New York: Vintage Books, 1991.

Casteneda, C. (2015). Developing gender: The medical treatment of transgender young people. *Social Science & Medicine, 143*: 262–270.

Cavafy, C. P. (2007). *The Collected Poems.* Oxford: Oxford University Press.

Chasseguet-Smirgel, J. (1976). Freud and female sexuality: The consideration of some blind spots in the exploration of the "dark continent". *International Journal of Psychoanalysis, 57*: 275–286.

Chasseguet-Smirgel, J. (1985a). *Creativity and Perversion.* London: Free Association Books.

Chasseguet-Smirgel, J. (1985b). *The Ego Ideal: A Psychoanalytic Essay on the Malady of the Ideal,* trans. P. Barrows. London: Free Association Books.

Chiland, C. (2000). The psychoanalyst and the transsexual patient. *International Journal of Psychoanalysis, 81*: 21–35.

Chiland, C. (2011). *Changing Sex: Illusion and Reality.* Paris: Odile Jacob.

Chodorow, N. (1978). *The Reproduction of Mothering.* Berkeley, CA: University of California Press.

Chodorow, N. (1989). *Feminism and Psychoanalytic Theory.* New Haven, CT: Yale University Press.

Chodorow, N. (1992). Heterosexuality as a compromise formation: Reflections on the psychoanalytic theory of sexual development. *Psychoanalysis and Contemporary Thought, 15*: 267–304.

Chodorow, N. (1994). *Femininities, Masculinities, Sexualities: Freud and Beyond.* Lexington, KY: University Press of Kentucky.

Chodorow, N. (2002). Gender as a personal and cultural construction. In: M. Dimen & V. Goldner (Eds.), *Gender in Psychoanalytic Space* (pp. 237–261). New York: Other Press.

Chodorow, N. (2005). Gender on the modern–postmodern and classical-relation divide: Untangling history and epistemology. *Journal of the American Psychoanalytic Association, 53*: 1097–1118.

Coates, S. (1997). Is it time to jettison the concept of developmental lines? Commentary on de Marneffe's paper, "Bodies and Words". *Gender & Psychoanalysis, 2* (1): 35–53.

Coates, S. W., Friedman, R. C., & Wolfe, S. (1991). The etiology of boyhood gender identity disorder: A model for integrating temperament, development, and psychodynamics. *Psychoanalytic. Dialogues, 1*: 481–523.

Colapinto, J. (2000). *As Nature Made Him: The Boy Who Was Raised as a Girl.* New York: HarperCollins.

Coleman, E., Bockting, W., Botzer, M., Cohen-Kettenis, P. T., DeCuypere, G., Feldman, J., et al. (2012). Standards of care for the health of transsexual, transgender, and gender-nonconforming people, version 7. *International Journal of Transgenderism, 13* (4): 165–232.

Coleman, G. (1995). *Homosexuality: Catholic Teaching and Pastoral Practice.* Mahwah, NJ: Paulist Press.

Corbett, K. (1993). The mystery of homosexuality. *Psychoanalytic Psychology, 10* (3): 345–357.

Corbett, K. (1996). Homosexual boyhood: Notes on girlyboys. *Gender and Psychoanalysis, 1:* 429–598.

Corbett, K. (1997). Speaking queer: A reply to Richard C. Friedman. *Gender and Psychoanalysis, 2:* 495–514.

Corbett, K. (2001a). Faggot = loser. *Studies in Gender and Sexuality, 2:* 3–28.

Corbett, K. (2001b). More life: Centrality and marginality in human development. *Psychoanalytic Dialogues, 11:* 313–335.

Corbett, K. (2001c). Nontraditional family romance. *Psychoanalytic Quarterly, 70* (3): 599–624.

Corbett, K. (2009a). Boyhood femininity, gender identity disorder, masculine presuppositions and the anxiety of regulation. *Psychoanalytic Dialogues, 19* (4): 353–370.

Corbett, K. (2009b). *Boyhood. Rethinking Masculinities.* New Haven, CT: Yale University Press.

Dean, T. (2001). Homosexuality and the problem of otherness. In: T. Dean & C. Lane (Eds.), *Homosexuality and Psychoanalysis* (pp. 120–147). Chicago, IL: University of Chicago Press.

Dean, T. (2008). Breeding culture: Barebacking, bugchasing, giftgiving. *Massachusetts Review, 49* (1): 80–94.

Dean, T. (2009). *Unlimited Intimacies: Reflections on the Subculture of Barebacking.* Chicago, IL: University of Chicago Press.

de Beauvoir, S. (1952/1978). *The Second Sex.* New York: Vintage Books.

Delany, S. R. (1999). . . . . Three, two, one, contact: Times Square red, 1998. In: J. Copjec & M. Sorkin (Eds.), *Giving Ground: The Politics of Propinquity.* London: Verso.

De Lauretis, T. (1994). *The Practice of Love: Lesbian Sexuality and Perverse Desire.* Indianapolis, IN: Indiana University Press.

de Marneffe, D. (1997). Bodies and words: A study of young children's genital and gender knowledge. *Gender & Psychoanalysis, 2* (1): 3–33.

Denny, D. (2002). A selective bibliography of transsexualism. *Journal of Gay & Lesbian Psychotherapy, 6* (2): 35–66.

Deutsch, H. (1946). *The Psychology of Women: Psychoanalytic Interpretation: Vol. 1, Girlhood; Vol. 2, Motherhood.* London: Research Books.

Devor, H. (1997). *FTM: Female-to-Male Transsexuality in Society.* Bloomingdale, IN: Indiana University Press.

de Vries, A. C., & Cohen-Kettenis, P. T. (2012). Clinical management of gender dysphoria in children and adolescents: The Dutch approach. *Journal of Homosexuality, 59* (3): 301–329.

de Vries, A. L., McGuire, J. K., Steensma, T. D., Wagenaar, E. C., Doreleijers, T. A., & Cohen-Kettenis, P. T. (2014). Young adult psychological outcome after puberty suppression and gender reassignment. *Pediatrics, 134* (4): 696–704.

Diamond, M., & Sigmundson, K. (1997a). Management of intersexuality: Guidelines for dealing with persons of ambiguous genitalia. *Archives Pediatrics & Adolescent Medicine, 151*: 1046–1050.

Diamond, M., & Sigmundson, K. (1997b). Sex reassignment at birth: A long-term review and clinical implications. *Archives of Pediatrics & Adolescent Medicine, 151*: 298–304.

Di Ceglie, D. (2018). The use of metaphors in understanding atypical gender identity development and its psychosocial impact. *Journal of Child Psychotherapy, 44* (1): 5–28.

Dimen, M. (1991). Deconstructing difference: Gender, splitting and transitional space. *Psychoanalytic Dialogues, 1*: 335–352.

Dimen, M. (1995). The third step: Freud, the feminists, and postmodernism. *American Journal of Psychoanalysis, 55*: 303–319.

Dimen, M. (2001). Perversion is us? Eight notes. *Psychoanalytic Dialogues, 11*: 825–860.

Dimen, M., & Goldner, V. (2005). Gender and sexuality. In: E. Person, A. Cooper, & G. Gabbard (Eds.), *The American Psychiatric Association Publishing Textbook of Psychoanalysis* (pp. 93–114). Washington, DC: American Psychiatric Publishing.

Dinnerstein, D. (1976). *The Mermaid and the Minotaur.* New York: Harper & Row.

Distiller, N. (2008). *Fixing Gender: Lesbian Mothers and the Oedipus Complex.* Madison, NJ: Fairleigh Dickinson University Press.

Dollimore, J. (1991). *Sexual Dissidence: Augustine to Wilde. Freud to Foucault.* Oxford: Oxford University Press.

Domenici, T., & Lesser, R. C. (1995). *Disorienting Sexuality.* London: Routledge.

Donne, J. (2005). *The Complete English Poems,* ed. A. J. Smith. Bath: The Folio Society.

Doty, R. C. (1963). Growth of overt homosexuality in city provokes wide concern. *The New York Times,* 17 December, p. 33.

Dover, K. J. (1979). *Greek Homosexuality.* London: Duckworth.

Dreger, A. (1998). *Hermaphrodites and the Medical Invention of Sex.* Cambridge, MA: Harvard University Press.

Dreger, A. (1999). *Intersex in the Age of Ethics*. Hagerstown, MD: University Publishing Group.

Drescher, J. (1997). From preoedipal to postmodern: Changing psychoanalytic attitudes toward homosexuality. *Gender & Psychoanalysis, 2* (2): 203–216.

Drescher, J. (1998). *Psychoanalytic Therapy and the Gay Man*. Hillsdale, NJ: Analytic Press.

Drescher, J. (2002a). An interview with gender PAC's Riki Wilchins. *Journal of Gay & Lesbian Psychotherapy, 6* (2): 67–85.

Drescher, J. (2002b). Causes and becauses: On etiological theories of homosexuality. *Annual of Psychoanalysis (Rethinking Psychoanalysis and the Homosexualities), 30*: 57–68.

Drescher, J. (2002c). In memory of Stephen A. Mitchell, Ph.D. *Studies in Gender and Sexuality, 3* (1): 95–109.

Drescher, J., Stein, T. S., & Byne, W. (2005). Homosexuality, gay and lesbian identities, and homosexual behavior. In: B. Sadock, & V. Sadock (Eds.), *Kaplan and Sadock's Comprehensive Textbook of Psychiatry* (8th edition, pp. 1936–1965). Baltimore, MD: Williams & Wilkins.

Edelman, L. (2004). *No Future: Queer Theory and the Death Drive*. Durham, NC: Duke University Press.

Ehrensaft, D., Giammattei, S. V., Storck, K., Tishelman, A. C., & Keo-Meier, C. (2018). Prepubertal social gender transitions: What we know; what we can learn—A view from a gender affirmative lens. *International Journal of Transgenderism, 19*: 252–268.

Eigen, M. (1996). *Psychic Deadness*. Northvale, NJ: Jason Aronson.

Elise, D. (1997). Primary femininity, bisexuality and the female ego ideal: A re-examination of female developmental theory. *Psychoanalytic Quarterly, 66*: 489–517.

Elise, D. (1998a). The absence of the paternal penis. *Journal of American Psychoanalytic Association, 46*: 413–442.

Elise, D. (1998b). Gender repertoire: Body, mind, and bisexuality. *Psychoanalytic Dialogues, 8*: 353–371.

Elise, D. (2000a). "Bye-bye" to bisexuality? Response to Layton. *Studies in Gender and Sexuality, 1*: 61–68.

Elise, D. (2000b). Generating gender: Response to Harris. *Studies in Gender and Sexuality, 1*: 157–165.

Elise, D. (2000c). Woman and desire: Why women may not want to want. *Studies in Gender and Sexuality, 1*: 125–145.

Elise, D. (2001). Unlawful entry: Male fears of psychic penetration. *Psychoanalytic Dialogues, 11*: 499–531.

Elise, D. (2002). The primary maternal oedipal situation and female homoerotic desire. *Psychoanalytic Inquiry, 22*: 209–228.

Elise, D. (2015). Reclaiming lost loves: Transcending unrequited desires. Discussion of Davies' "oedipal complexity". *Psychoanalytic Dialogues, 25:* 284–294.

Elliot, P. (2001). A psychoanalytic reading of transsexual embodiment. *Studies in Gender and Sexuality, 2:* 295–325.

Fast, I. (1984). *Gender Identity: A Differentiation Model.* Hillsdale, NJ: Analytic Press.

Fausto-Sterling, A. (1993). The five sexes: Why male and female are not enough. *The Sciences,* March/April, pp. 20–24.

Fausto-Sterling, A. (2000). *Sexing the Body: Gender Politics and the Construction of Sexuality.* New York: Basic Books.

Fausto-Sterling, A. (2012). The dynamic development of gender variability. *Journal of Homosexuality, 59* (3): 398–421.

Feinberg, L. (1996). *Transgender Warriors: Making History from Joan of Arc to RuPaul.* Boston, MA: Beacon Press.

Fletcher, J. (1989). Freud and his uses: Psychoanalysis and gay theory. In: S. Shepherd & M. Wallis (Eds.), *Coming on Strong: Gay Politics and Culture.* London: Unwin Hyman.

Fletcher, J. (1992). The letter in the unconscious: The enigmatic signifier in Jean Laplanche. In: J. Fletcher & M. Stanton (Eds.), *Jean Laplanche: Seduction, Translation, and the Drives* (pp. 93–120). London: ICA.

Fonagy, P. (2001). *Attachment Theory and Psychoanalysis.* New York: Other Press.

Fonagy, P. (2008). A genuinely developmental theory of sexual enjoyment and its implications for psychoanalytic technique. *Journal of the American Psychoanalytic Association, 56* (1): 11–36.

Fonagy, P., & Allison, E. (2015). A scientific theory of homosexuality for psychoanalysis. In: A. Lemma & P. E. Lynch (Eds.), *Sexualities: Contemporary Psychoanalytic Perspectives* (pp. 125–137). London: Routledge.

Forster, E. M. (1914/1971). *Maurice.* London: Penguin.

Foucault, M. (1976). *The Will to Knowledge, Vol. I: The History of Sexuality,* trans. R. Hurley. St. Ives: Penguin, 1998.

Foucault, M. (1978). *Histoire de la sexualité 1. La Volonté de savoir.* Paris: Gallimard. *The History of Sexuality, Vol. I: An Introduction.* New York: Vintage Books, 1980.

Foucault, M. (1981). Friendship as a way of life. *Gai Pied,* April. Available at: https://caringlabor.wordpress.com/2010/11/18/michel-foucault-friendship-as-a-way-of-life

Foucault, M. (1988). Sexual choice, sexual act: Foucault and homosexuality. In: L. D. Kritzman (Ed.), *Politics, Philosophy, Culture: Interviews and Other Writings* (pp. 286–303). London: Routledge.

Foucault, M. (1997). *The Politics of Truth*. Cambridge, MA: MIT Press.

Frazer, J. G. (1894). *The Golden Bough*. New York: Macmillan & Co.

Frenkel, R. (1996). A reconsideration of object choice in women: Phallus or fallacy. *Journal of the American Psychoanalytic Association, 44* (Suppl.): 133–156.

Freud, S. (1900a). *The Interpretation of Dreams. Standard Edition*, 4/5.

Freud, S. (1905d). *Three Essays on the Theory of Sexuality. Standard Edition*, 7: 125–243.

Freud, S. (1905e). Fragment of an analysis of a case of hysteria. *Standard Edition*, 7: 3.

Freud, S. (1908a). Hysterical phantasies and their relation to bisexuality. *Standard Edition*, 9: 155–166.

Freud, S. (1908d). "Civilized" sexual morality and modern nervous illness. *Standard Edition*, 9: 177–204.

Freud, S. (1910a). *Five Lectures on Psycho-Analysis. Standard Edition*, 11: 1–56.

Freud, S. (1910c). *Leonardo Da Vinci and a Memory of his Childhood. Standard Edition*, 11: 59–138.

Freud, S. (1912d). On the universal tendency to debasement in the sphere of love. (Contributions to the psychology of love, II). *Standard Edition*, 11: 177–190.

Freud, S. (1912–1913). *Totem and Taboo. Standard Edition*, 13: 1–162.

Freud, S. (1913c). On beginning the treatment (Further recommendations on the technique of psycho-analysis, I). *Standard Edition*, 12: 121–144.

Freud, S. (1914c). On narcissism: An introduction. *Standard Edition*, 14: 73–102.

Freud, S. (1919h). The uncanny. *Standard Edition*, 17: 219–256.

Freud, S. (1920a). The psychogenesis of a case of homosexuality in a woman. *Standard Edition*, 18: 145–172.

Freud, S. (1920g). *Beyond the Pleasure Principle. Standard Edition*, 18: 7–64.

Freud, S. (1921c). *Group Psychology and the Analysis of the Ego. Standard Edition*, 14.

Freud, S. (1923b). *The Ego and the Id. Standard Edition*, 19: 12–66.

Freud, S. (1924d). The dissolution of the Oedipus complex. *Standard Edition*, 19: 173–179.

Freud, S. (1925j). Some psychical consequences of the anatomical distinction between the sexes. *Standard Edition*, 19: 248–258.

Freud, S. (1926d). *Inhibitions, Symptoms and Anxiety. Standard Edition*, 20: 87–175.

Freud, S. (1931b). Female sexuality. *Standard Edition*, 21: 227–243.

Freud, S. (1933a). *New Introductory Lectures on Psychoanalysis* [No. XXIII: Femininity]. *Standard Edition*, 22: 112–135.

Freud, S. (1935/1951). Letter to an American mother. *American Journal of Psychiatry*, *107*: 786.

Freud, S. (1937c). Analysis terminable and interminable. *Standard Edition*, *23*: 211–253.

Freud, S. (1950 [1892–1899]). Extracts from the Fliess Papers. *Standard Edition*, *1*: 175–280.

Fricker, M. (2007). *Epistemic Injustice: Power and the Ethics of Knowing*. Oxford: Oxford University Press.

Friedan, B. (1963). *The Feminine Mystique*. New York: Laurel.

Friedman, J., & Epstein, R. (1995). *Celluloid Closet* [Documentary film]. London: Drakes Avenue Pictures.

Friedman, R. C., & Downey, J. I. (2002). *Sexual Orientation and Psychodynamic Psychotherapy. Sexual Science and Clinical Practice*. New York: Columbia University Press.

Fromm, E., & Narvàez, F. (1968). The Oedipus complex: Comments on "The Case of Little Hans". *Contemporary Psychoanalysis*, *4*: 178–187.

Frommer, M. S. (1995). Countertransference obscurity in the psychoanalytic treatment of homosexual patients. In: T. Domenici & R. C. Lesser (Eds.), *Disorienting Sexuality: Psychoanalytic Reappraisals of Sexual Identities* (pp. 65–82). New York: Routledge.

Frommer, M. S. (2006). On the subjectivity of lustful states of mind. *Psychoanalytic Dialogues*, *16* (6): 639–664.

Garber, M. (1989). Spare parts: The surgical construction of gender. In: H. Abelove, M. A. Barale, & D. Halperin (Eds.), *The Lesbian and Gay Studies Reader* (pp. 321–336). New York: Routledge, 1993.

Genet, A. (2015). *Funeral Rites*. London: Faber & Faber.

Gerritse, K., Hartman, L., Antonides, M. F., & Wensing-Kruger, A. (2018). Moral challenges in transgender care: A thematic analysis based on a focused ethnography. *Archives of Sexual Behaviour*, *47* (8): 2319–2333.

Gershman, H. (1970). The role of core gender identity in the genesis of perversions. *American Journal of Psychoanalysis*, *30*: 58–67.

Ghent, E. (1990). Masochism, submission, surrender: Masochism as a perversion of surrender. *Contemporary Psychoanalysis*, *26*: 108–136.

Gherovici, P. (2010). *Please Select Your Gender: From the Invention of Hysteria to the Democratizing of Transgenderism*. New York: Routledge.

Gide, A. (1967). *Journals: 1889–1949*. Harmondsworth: Penguin.

Gide, A. (2000). *The Immoralist*. London: Penguin.

Gill-Peterson, J. (2014). The technical capacities of the body: Assembling race, technology and transgender. *Transgender Studies Quarterly*, *I* (3): 402–418.

Giordano, S. (2008). Lives in a Chiaroscuro. Should we suspend the puberty of children with gender identity disorder? *Journal of Medical Ethics, 34*: 580–584.

Glazer, D. F. (1998). Homosexuality and the analytic stance: Implications for treatment and supervision. *Gender and Psychoanalysis: An Interdisciplinary Journal, 3*: 397–412.

Goldner, V. (1991). Toward a critical relational theory of gender. *Psychoanalytic Dialogues, 1*: 249–272.

Goldner, V. (2003). Ironic gender/authentic sex. *Studies in Gender and Sexuality, 4*: 113–139.

Goldner, V. (2011). Trans: Gender in free fall. *Psychoanalytic Dialogues, 21*: 159–171.

Goldsmith, S. J. (2001). Oedipus or Orestes? Homosexual men, their mothers, and other women revisited. *Journal of American Psychoanalytic Association, 49* (4): 1269–1287.

Green, A. (1995). Has sexuality anything to do with psychoanalysis? *International Journal of Psychoanalysis, 76*: 871–883.

Green, A. (1999). *The Work of the Negative*. London: Free Association Books.

Green, A. (2009). The construction of the lost father. In: L. J. Kalinich & S. W. Taylor (Eds.), *The Dead Father: A Psychoanalytic Inquiry* (pp. 23–46). London: Routledge.

Grosz, E. (1994). *Volatile Bodies: Toward a Corporeal Feminism*. Bloomington, IN: University of Indiana Press.

Grunberger, B. (1989). *New Essays on Narcissism*, trans. D. Macey. London: Free Association Books.

Halberstadt-Freud, H. (1998). Electra versus Oedipus: Femininity reconsidered. *International Journal of Psychoanalysis, 79*: 41–56.

Halberstam, J. (1998). *Female Masculinity*. Durham, NC: Duke University Press.

Halberstam, J. (2018). Towards a trans feminism. *Boston Review*, 18 January.

Halkitis, P. N., Wilton, L., & Drescher, J. (2005). *Barebacking: Psychosocial & Public Health Approaches*. New York: Haworth Press.

Halperin, D. (2009). *What Do Gay Men Want? An Essay on Sex, Risk and Subjectivity*. Chicago, IL: University of Michigan Press.

Halperin, D. (2012). *How to Be Gay*. Cambridge, MA: Harvard University Press.

Haraway, D. (1988). Situated knowledges: The science question in feminism and the privilege of partial perspective. *Feminist Studies, 14* (3): 575–599.

Harris, A. (1991). Gender as contradiction. *Psychoanalytic Dialogues, 1*: 107–244.

Harris, A. (2000). Gender as a soft assembly. *Studies in Gender Sexuality, 1* (3): 223–250.

Harris, A. (2005). *Gender as Soft Assembly*. Hillsdale, NJ: Analytic Press.

Hausman, B. L. (1995). *Changing Sex: Transsexualism, Technology, and the Idea of Gender*. Durham, NC: Duke University Press.

Heller, Z. (2016). American girls: Social media and the secret lives of teenage girls by Nancy-Jo sales; girls and sex: Navigating the complicated new landscape by Peggy orenstein [book reviews]. *New York Review of Books*, 18 August, *83* (13): 22–23.

Hembree, W. C., Cohen-Kettenis, P. T., Gooren, L., Hannema, S. E., Meyer, W. J., Murad, M. H., et al. (2017). Endocrine treatment of gender dysphoric/gender-incongruent persons: An endocrine society clinical practice guideline. *Journal of Clinical Endocrinological Metabolism*, *102*: 1–35.

Henderson, D. (2018). Staying alive: *Anima* and *object A*. In: *Re-Encountering Jung. Analytical Psychology and Contemporary Psychoanalysis* (pp. 183–1294). London: Routledge.

Herek, G. M., & McLemore, K. A. (2013). Sexual prejudice. *Annual Review of Psychology*, *64*: 309–333.

Herrada, C. (2013). *The Missing Myth: A New Vision of Same-Sex Love*. New York: SelectBooks.

Hertzmann, L. (2011). Lesbian and gay couple relationships: When internalized homophobia gets in the way of couple creativity. *Psychoanalytic Psychotherapy*, *25* (4): 346–360.

Hertzmann, L. (2015). Objecting to the object. Encountering the internal parental couple relationship for lesbian and gay couples. In: A. Lemma & P. E. Lynch (Eds.), *Sexualities: Contemporary Psychoanalytic Perspectives* (pp. 156–174). London: Routledge.

Herzog, D. (2015). What happened to psychoanalysis in the wake of the sexual revolution? A story about the durability of homophobia and the dream of love, 1950s–2010s. In: A. Lemma & P. E. Lynch (Eds.), *Sexualities: Contemporary Psychoanalytic Perspectives* (pp. 19–40). London: Routledge.

Hidalgo, M. A., Ehrensaft, D., Tishelman, A. C., Clark, L. F., Garofalo, R., Rosenthal, S. M., et al. (2013). The gender affirmative model: What we know and what we aim to learn. *Human Development*, *56*: 285–290.

Hillman, J. (1960). *The Myth of Analysis: Three Essays in Archetypal Psychology*. Evanston, IL: Northwestern University Press, 1992.

Hillman, J. (1979). *The Dream and the Underworld*. New York: Harper Perennial.

Hillman, J. (2005). *Senex & Puer*. Thompson, CT: Spring Publications.

Hocquenghem, G. (1978). *Homosexual Desire*. Durham, NC: Duke University Press.

Hodgkin, P., & Metz, B. (2015). *Online Health Communities. Report*. London: Guy's and St Thomas' Charity/The Health Foundation. Available at: http://benmetz.org/project/online-health-communities/

Hoffman, L. (1999). Passions in girls and women: Toward a bridge between critical relational theory of gender and modern conflict theory. *Journal of the American Psychoanalytic Association, 47*: 1145–1168.

Holland, J., Ramazanoglu, C., Sharpe, S., & Thomson, R. (2004). *The Male in the Head: Young People, Heterosexuality and Power*. London: Tufnell Press.

Homans, P. (1979/1995). *Jung in Context*. Chicago, IL: University of Chicago Press.

Hopcke, R. H. (1991). *Jung, Jungians and Homosexuality*. Eugene, OR: Resource Publications.

Horney, K. (1924). On the genesis of the castration complex in women. *International Journal of Psychoanalysis, 5*: 50–65.

Horney, K. (1926). The flight from womanhood: The masculinity complex in women, as viewed by men and by women. *International Journal of Psychoanalysis, 7*: 324–339.

Horney, K. (1932). Observations on a specific difference in the dread felt by men and by women respectively for the opposite sex. *International Journal of Psychoanalysis, 13*: 348–360.

Horney, K. (1933). The denial of the vagina: A contribution to the problem of the genital anxieties specific to women. *International Journal of Psychoanalysis, 14*: 57–70.

Iasenza, S. (2002). Beyond "lesbian bed death": The passion and play in lesbian relationships. In: S. M. Rose (Ed.), *Lesbian Love and Relationships* (pp. 111–120). New York: Harrington Park Press.

Igartua, K. (1998). Therapy with lesbian couples: The issues and the interventions. *Canadian Journal of Psychiatry, 43*: 391–396.

Irigaray, L. (1990). This sex which is not one. In: C. Zanardi (Ed.), *Essential Papers on the Psychology of Women*. New York: New York University Press.

Isay, R. (1986). The development of sexual identity in homosexual men. *Psychoanalytic Study of the Child, 41*: 467–489.

Isay, R. (1989). *Being Homosexual*. New York: Farrar, Straus, & Giroux.

Isay, R. (1997). *Becoming Gay: The Journey to Self-Acceptance*. New York: Holt.

Isay, R. (2010). *Being Homosexual: Gay Men and Their Development*. New York: Vintage Books.

Jalas, K. (2003). Between tomboys and butch lesbians: Gender nonconformity viewed through clinical psychoanalysis and lesbian and gay theory. *Psychoanalytic Review, 90* (5): 655–683.

James, E. L. (2012). *Fifty Shades of Grey*. London: Vintage Books.

Jay, M. (2007). Melancholy femininity and obsessive-compulsive masculinity: Sex differences in melancholy gender. *Studies in Gender and Sexuality, 8* (2): 115–135.

Jones, E. (1927). The early development of female sexuality. In: *Papers on Psychoanalysis* (pp. 459–472). Boston, MA: Beacon Press, 1961.

Jones, E. (1961). *The Life and Work of Sigmund Freud* [Abridged version]. New York: Basic Books.

Jung, C. G. (1921/1971). *Psychological Types. Collected Works, Vol. 6.* Princeton, NJ: Princeton University Press.

Jung, C. G. (1936/1959). Concerning the archetypes, with special reference to the anima concept. In: *The Archetypes and the Collective Unconscious. Collected Works, Vol. 9i.* London: Routledge & Kegan Paul.

Jung, C. G. (1948/1975). Instincts and the unconscious. In: *The Structure and Dynamics of the Psyche. Collected Works, Vol. 8.* Princeton, NJ: Princeton University Press.

Jung, C. G. (1954/1959). Archetypes of the collective unconscious. In: *The Archetypes and the Collective Unconscious. Collected Works, Vol. 9i.* London: Routledge & Kegan Paul.

Jung, C. G. (1955/1970). *Mysterium Coniunctionis. Collected Works, Vol. 14.* Princeton, NJ: Princeton University Press.

Kahn, S., & Davis, J. (1981). *The Kahn Report on Sexual Preferences.* New York: St. Martin's Press.

Kaltiala-Heino, R., Sumia, M., Työläjärvi, M., & Lindberg, N. (2015). Two years of gender identity service for minors: Overrepresentation of natal girls with severe problems in adolescent development. *Child and Adolescent Psychiatry and Mental Health, 9* (1): 9.

Kaplan, J. (Ed.) (1950). *Dialogues of Plato.* New York: Washington Square Press.

Karasic, D., & Drescher, J. (2006). *Sexual and Gender Diagnoses of the Diagnostic and Statistical Manual (DSM): A Reevaluation.* New York: Haworth Press.

Kaufman, G. (1989). *The Psychology of Shame.* New York: Springer.

Keats, J. (1899). *The Complete Poetical Works and Letters of John Keats (Cambridge Edition).* Boston, MA: Houghton, Mifflin and Company.

Kernberg, O. (1991). Sadomasochism, sexual excitement, and perversion. *Journal of American the Psychoanalytic Association, 39*: 333–362.

Kessler, S. (1998). *Lessons from the Intersexed.* New Brunswick, NJ: Rutgers University Press.

Kestenberg, J. (1956). On the development of maternal feelings in early childhood. *Psychoanalytic Study of the Child, 11*: 257–291.

Kestenberg, J. (1982). The inner-genital phase: Prephallic and preoedipal. In: D. Mendell (Ed.), *Early Female Development: Current Psychoanalytic Views* (pp. 81–125). New York: Spectrum.

King, M. (2011). The queer relationship between psychoanalysts and their gay and lesbian patients. *Psychoanalytic Psychotherapy, 25* (4): 308–318.

King, P., & Steiner, R. (1991). *The Freud–Klein Controversies 1941–45.* London: Routledge.

Kingslake, A. W. (1845). *Eothen, or Traces of Travel from the East.* London: John Olliver.

Kinsey, A., Pomeroy, W., & Martin, C. (1948). *Sexual Behavior in the Human Male.* Philadelphia, PA: Saunders.

Kinsey, A., Pomeroy, W., Martin, C., & Gebhard, P. (1953). *Sexual Behavior in the Human Female.* Philadelphia, PA: Saunders.

Kinsey, B. (2011). Gay supervision. *Supervision Review (The Journal of the British Association for Psychoanalytic & Psychodynamic Supervision),* Winter: 8–12.

Kleeman, J. (1976). Freud's views on early female sexuality in the light of direct child observation. *Journal of the American Psychoanalytic Association, 24* (Suppl.): 3–27.

Klein, M. (1928). Early stages of the Oedipus conflict. *International Journal of Psychoanalysis, 9.* Reprinted in: *Love, Guilt and Reparation and Other Works, 1921–1945* (pp. 186–198). London: Hogarth Press, 1975.

Klein, M. (1932a). The effects of early anxiety-situations on the sexual development of the boy. In: *The Psycho-Analysis of Children* (pp. 240–278). London: Hogarth Press, 1975.

Klein, M. (1932b). The effects of early anxiety-situations on the sexual development of the girl. In: *The Psycho-Analysis of Children* (pp. 194–239). London: Hogarth Press, 1975.

Klein, M. (1945). The Oedipus complex in light of early anxieties. *International Journal of Psychoanalysis, 26.* Reprinted in: *Love, Guilt and Reparation and Other Works, 1921–1945* (pp. 370–419). London: Hogarth Press, 1975.

Kohlberg, L. (1966). A cognitive-developmental analysis of children's sex role concepts and attitudes. In: E. Maccoby (Ed.), *The Development of Sex Differences* (pp. 82–172). Stanford, CA: Stanford University Press.

Krafft-Ebing, R. (1886). *Psychopathia Sexualis,* trans. H. Wedeck. New York: Putnam, 1965.

Krauss, I.-B. (2012). *Culture and Reflexivity in Systemic Psychotherapy: Mutual Perspectives.* London: Karnac.

Kreukels, B. P., & Cohen-Kettenis, P. T. (2011). Puberty suppression in gender identity disorder: The Amsterdam experience. *Nature Reviews Endocrinology, 7:* 466–472.

Kristeva, J. (1982). *The Powers of Horror: An Essay in Abjection,* trans. L. S. Roudiez. New York: Columbia University Press.

Kristeva, J. (1995). *New Maladies of the Soul*. New York: Colombia University Press.

Kubie, L. S. (1973). The drive to become both sexes. *Psychoanalytic Quarterly*, 43: 349–426.

Lampl-de Groot, J. (1927). The evolution of the Oedipus complex in women. *International Journal of Psychoanalysis, 9*: 332–345. Reprinted in J. Lampl-de Groot (Ed.). (1965). *The Development of the Mind: Psychoanalytic Papers on Clinical and Theoretical Problems* (pp. 3–18). New York: International Universities Press.

Laplanche, J. (1976). *Life and Death in Psychoanalysis*. Baltimore, MD: Johns Hopkins University Press.

Laplanche, J. (1987a). *Problèmatiques*. Paris: Presses Universitaires de France.

Laplanche, J. (1987b). *New Foundations for Psychoanalysis*, trans. D. Macey. Oxford: Blackwell, 1989.

Laplanche, J. (1995). Seduction, persecution, revelation. *International Journal of Psychoanalysis, 76*: 663–682.

Laplanche, J. (1997). The theory of seduction and the problem of the other. *International Journal of Psychoanalysis, 78*: 653–666.

Laplanche, J. (1999). *Essays on Otherness*. New York: Routledge.

Laplanche, J. (2002). Starting from the fundamental anthropological situation. In: *Freud and the Sexual: Essays 2000–2006* (pp. 99–113), trans. J. Fletcher, J. House, & N. Ray. New York: International Psychoanalytic Books, 2011.

Laplanche, J. (2005). The *Three Essays* and the theory of the unconscious. In: *Freud and the Sexual: Essays 2000–2006* (pp. 249–266), trans. J. Fletcher, J. House, & N. Ray. New York: International Psychoanalytic Books, 2011.

Laplanche, J., & Pontalis, J.-B. (1968). Fantasy and the origins of sexuality. *International Journal of Psychoanalysis, 49*: 1–19.

Latham, J. R. (2017). (Re)making sex: A praxiography of the gender clinic. *Feminist Theory, 18* (2): 177–204.

Laufer, M. E. (1986). The female Oedipus complex and the relationship to the body. *Psychoanalytic Study of the Child, 41*: 259–276.

Laurent, E. (2009). A new love for the father. In: L. J. Kalinich & S. W. Taylor (Eds.), *The Dead Father: A Psychoanalytic Inquiry* (pp. 75–90). London: Routledge.

Lauritsen, J., & Thorstad, D. (1974). *The Early Homosexual Rights Movement (1864–1935)*. New York: Times Change Press.

Lawrence, A. A. (2004). Autogynephilia: A paraphilic model of gender identity disorder. *Journal of Gay & Lesbian Psychotherapy, 8* (1/2): 69–87. Reprinted in: U. Leli & J. Drescher (Eds.), *Transgender Subjectivities: A Clinician's Guide* (pp. 69–87). New York: Haworth Press.

Lawrence, M. (2012). Response to Paul Lynch. Paper given at BPC Conference on Psychoanalysis and Homosexuality: Moving On, 21 January.

Lax, R. (1994). Aspects of primary and secondary genital feelings and anxieties in girls during the preoedipal and early oedipal phases. *Psychoanalytic Quarterly*, 63: 271–296.

Lax, R. (1997). *Becoming and Being a Woman*. Northvale, NJ: Jason Aronson.

Layton, L. (1997). The doer behind the deed. *Gender in Psychoanalysis*, 2: 515–520.

Layton, L. (1998). *Who's That Girl? Who's That Boy?* Hillsdale, NJ: Analytic Press.

Leli, U., & Drescher, J. (Eds.) (2004). *Transgender Subjectivities: A Clinician's Guide*. New York: Haworth Press.

Lemma, A. (2010). *Under the Skin: A Psychoanalytic Study of Body Modification*. London: Routledge.

Lemma, A. (2015a). *Minding the Body: The Body in Psychoanalysis and Beyond*. London: Routledge.

Lemma, A. (2015b). The prostitute as mirror: Distinguishing perverse and nonperverse use of prostitutes. In: A. Lemma, & P. Lynch (Eds.), *Sexualities: Contemporary Psychoanalytic Perspectives* (pp. 189–204). London: Routledge.

Lemma, A., & Lynch, P. E. (Eds.) (2015). *Sexualities: Contemporary Psychoanalytic Perspectives*. London: Routledge.

Levin, S. (1967). Some metapsychological considerations on the differentiation between shame and guilt. *International Journal of Psychoanalysis*, 48: 267–276.

Lewes, K. (1995). *Psychoanalysis and Male Homosexuality*. Northvale, NJ: Jason Aronson.

Lewes, K. (2009). *Psychoanalysis and Male Homosexuality: 20th Anniversary Edition*. Plymouth, MA: Jason Aronson.

Lingiardi, V. (2002). *Men in Love: Male Homosexualities from Ganymede to Batman*. Chicago, IL: Open Court.

Lingiardi, V. (2015). Gender expression and sexual orientation. In: A. Lemma & P. Lynch (Eds.), *Sexualities: Contemporary Psychoanalytic Perspectives* (pp. 101–121). London: Routledge.

Lopez-Pedraza, R. (2010). *Hermes and His Children*. Einsiedeln: Daimon.

Lynch, P. E. (2015). Intimacy, desire and shame in gay male sexuality. In: A. Lemma & P. E. Lynch (Eds.), *Sexualities: Contemporary Psychoanalytic Perspectives* (pp. 138–155). London: Routledge.

Machado, A. (2003). *There Is No Road*. Buffalo, NY: White Pine Press. Available at: www.whitepine.org/noroad.pdf

Magee, M., & Miller, D. (1997). *Lesbian Lives: Psychoanalytic Narratives Old and New*. Hillsdale, NJ: Analytic Press.

Mahler, M., Pine, F., & Bergman, A. (1975). *The Psychological Birth of the Human Infant*. New York: Basic Books.

Mann, G., Taylor, A., Wren, B., & de Graaf, N. (2019). Review of the literature on self-injurious thoughts and behaviours in gender-diverse children and young people in the United Kingdom. *Clinical Child Psychology and Psychiatry, 24* (2): 304–321.

Marcus, L., Marcus, K., Yaxte, S. M., & Marcus, K. (2015). Genderqueer: One family's experience with gender variance. *Psychoanalytic Inquiry, 35* (8): 795–808.

Masters, W. H., & Johnson, V. E. (1966). *Human Sexual Response*. Boston, MA: Little, Brown.

Mayer, E. L. (1995). The phallic castration complex and primary femininity: Paired developmental lines toward female gender identity. *Journal of the American Psychoanalytic Association, 43*: 17–38.

McDermott, E., Roen, K., & Scourfield, J. (2008). Avoiding shame: Young LGBT people, homophobia and self-destructive behaviours. *Culture, Health & Sexuality, 10* (8): 815–829.

McDougall, J. (1990). *Plea for a Measure of Abnormality*. London: Free Association Books.

McGuire, W. (Ed.) (1974a). Letter from C. G. Jung to Sigmund Freud, February 28, 1910. In: *The Freud/Jung Letters: The Correspondence between Sigmund Freud and C. G. Jung* (pp. 296–297). Princeton, NJ: Princeton University Press.

McGuire, W. (Ed.) (1974b). Letter from Sigmund Freud to C. G. Jung, November 2, 1911. In: *The Freud/Jung Letters: The Correspondence between Sigmund Freud and C. G. Jung* (pp. 423–424). Princeton, NJ: Princeton University Press.

Meadow, T. (2011). "Deep down where the music plays": Parents' accounts of their child's gender variance. *Sexualities, 14*: 725–747.

Miller, B. (2015). "Dude, where's your face?" Self-presentation, self-description, and partner preferences on a social networking application for men who have sex with men: A content analysis. *Sexuality & Culture, 19* (4): 637–658.

Millot, C. (1990). *Horsexe: Essay on Transsexuality*, trans. K. Hylton. New York: Autonomedia.

Millot, C. (2001). The eroticism of desolation. In: T. Dean & C. Lane (Eds.), *Homosexuality and Psychoanalysis* (pp. 210–231). Chicago, IL: University of Chicago Press.

Milton, J. (2000). Psychoanalysis and the moral high ground. *International Journal of Psychoanalysis, 81* (6): 1101–1116.

Mishima, Y. (1948). *Confessions of a Mask*. London: Peter Owen, 2007.

Mitchell, S. A. (1988). *Relational Concepts in Psychoanalysis: An Integration.* Cambridge, MA: Harvard University Press.

Monette, P. (2000). *Becoming a Man.* New York: Quality Paperback Book Club.

Money, J., & Ehrhardt, A. (1996). *Man & Woman, Boy & Girl.* Northvale, NJ: Jason Aronson.

Money, J., & Green, R. (1969). *Transsexualism and Sex Reassignment.* Baltimore, MD: Johns Hopkins University Press.

Money-Kyrle, R. (1971). The aim of psychoanalysis. In: D. Meltzer & E. O'Shaughnessy (Eds.), *The Collected Papers of Roger Money-Kyrle* (pp. 442–449). Strath Tay: Clunie Press.

Montgrain, N. (1983). On the vicissitudes of female sexuality: The difficult path from "anatomical destiny" to psychic representation. *International Journal of Psychoanalysis, 64*: 169–186.

Morgan, M. (1995). The projective gridlock: A form of projective identification in couple relationships. In: S. Ruszczynski & J. Fisher (Eds.), *Intrusiveness and Intimacy in the Couple* (pp. 3–48). London: Karnac.

Morgan, M. (2010). Unconscious beliefs about being a couple. *Fort Da, 16*: 36–55.

Morris, J. (1974). *Conundrum.* London: Faber & Faber.

Morrison, A. P. (1983). Shame, ideal self, and narcissism. *Contemporary Psychoanalysis, 19*: 295–318.

Moss, D. (2002). Internalized homophobia in men: Wanting in the first person singular, hating in the first person plural. *Psychoanalytic Quarterly, 71* (1): 21–50.

Mueller, S. C., De Cuypere, G., & T'Sjoen, G. (2017). Transgender research in the 21st century: A selective critical review from a neurocognitive perspective. *American Journal of Psychiatry, 174* (12): 1155–116.

Muller, J. P. (2009). Father culture: Introduction. In: L. J. Kalinich & S. W. Taylor (Eds.), *The Dead Father: A Psychoanalytic Inquiry* (pp. 145–151). London: Routledge.

Nagel, T. (1986). *The View from Nowhere.* New York: Oxford University Press.

Nobus, D. (1997). Theorising the comedy of sexes: Lacan on sexuality. In: B. Burgoyne & M. Sullivan (Eds.), *The Klein–Lacan Dialogues* (pp. 105–124). London: Karnac.

O'Connor, N., & Ryan, J. (1993). *Wild Desires and Mistaken Identities: Lesbianism and Psychoanalysis.* New York: Columbia University Press; London: Routledge, 2003.

Ogden, T. (2005). On psychoanalytic supervision. *International Journal of Psychoanalysis, 86*: 1265–1280.

Olivier, C. (1989). *Jocasta's Children: The Imprint of the Mother.* London: Routledge.

Olson, K. R., Durwood, L., DeMeules, M., & McLaughlin, K. A. (2016). Mental health of transgender children who are supported in their identities. *Paediatrics, 137* (3).

Ossana, S. M. (2000). Relationship and couples counseling. In: R. M. Perez, K. A. DeBord, & K. J. Bieschke (Eds.), *Handbook of Counseling and Psychotherapy with Lesbian, Gay, and Bisexual Clients* (pp. 275–302). Washington, DC: American Psychological Association.

Perelberg, R. J. (2009). The dead father and the sacrifice of sexuality. In: L. J. Kalinich & S. W. Taylor (Eds.), *The Dead Father: A Psychoanalytic Inquiry* (pp. 121–131). London: Routledge.

Person, E. S., & Ovesey, L. (1974). The transsexual syndrome in males. *American Journal of Psychotherapy, 28*: 174–193.

Pett, J. (2000). Gay, lesbian and bisexual therapy and its supervision. In: D. Davies & C. Neal (Eds.), *Therapeutic Perspectives on Working with Lesbian, Gay and Bisexual Clients* (pp. 54–72). Buckingham: Open University Press.

Phillips, A. (2013). *Missing Out: In Praise of the Unlived Life*. London: Penguin.

Piers, G., & Singer, M. (1953). *Shame and Guilt*. Springfield, IL: Charles C Thomas.

Pines, M. (1995). The universality of shame: A psychoanalytic approach. *British Journal of Psychotherapy, 11* (3): 346–357.

Plummer, D. (2014). The ebb and flow of homophobia: A gender taboo theory. *Sex Roles, 71* (3–4): 126–136.

Preciado, P. (2013). *Testo Junkie: Sex, Drugs, and Biopolitics in the Pharmacopornographic Era*. New York: The Feminist Press.

Probyn, E. (2000). Sporting bodies: Dynamics of shame and pride. *Body & Society, 6* (1): 13–28.

Prosser, J. (1998). *Second Skins: The Body Narratives of Transsexuality*. New York: Columbia University Press.

Prosser, J. (1999). Exceptional locations. In: K. More & S. Whittle (Eds.), *Reclaiming Genders: Transsexual Grammars at the Fin De Siecle* (pp. 83–114). London: Cassell.

Pula, J. (2015). Understanding gender through the lens of transgender experience. *Psychoanalytic Inquiry, 35* (8): 809–822.

Pyne, J. (2014). The governance of non-conforming children: A dangerous enclosure. *Annual Review of Critical Psychology, 11*: 80–96.

Quinodoz, D. (1998). A female transsexual patient in psychoanalysis. *International Journal of Psychoanalysis, 79*: 95–111.

Rado, S. (1940). A critical examination of the concept of bisexuality. *Psychosomatic Medicine, 2*: 459–467. Reprinted in: J. Marmor (Ed.), *Sexual Inversion: The Multiple Roots of Homosexuality* (pp. 175–189). New York: Basic Books, 1965.

Rappaport, D. (1967). *The Collected Papers of David Rappaport*, Ed. M. Gill. New York: Basic Books.

Raymond, J. (1979). *The Transsexual Empire: The Making of the She-Male.* Boston, MA: Beacon Press.

Rechy, J. (1977). *The Sexual Outlaw*. New York: Random House.

Reed, T. (2017). Complexities and biological correlations in the development of atypical gender identity. In: Talk given at the Royal College of Paediatrics and Child Health: Hot Topics in Child Health—Transgender and Gender Diverse Conference, Cavendish Conference Centre, London, 12 June.

Reis, B. (2009). We: Commentary on papers by Trevarthen, Ammaniti & Trentini, and Gallese. *Psychoanalytic Dialogues, 19*: 565–579.

Riviere, J. (1929). Womanliness as masquerade. *International Journal of Psychoanalysis, 10*: 303–313.

Roberts, C. M., & Cronshaw, C. (2017). New puberty, new trans: Children, pharmaceuticals and politics. In: E. Johnson (Ed.), *Gendering Drugs: Feminist Studies of Pharmaceuticals* (pp. 59–84). London: Palgrave.

Roen, K. (2011). The discursive and clinical production of trans youth: Gender variant youth who seek puberty suppression. *Psychology & Sexuality, 2* (1): 58–68.

Rohleder, P. (2016). Othering, blame and shame when working with people living with HIV. *Psychoanalytic Psychotherapy, 30* (1): 62–78.

Rosario, V. A. (2006). An interview with Cheryl Chase. *Journal of Gay & Lesbian Psychotherapy, 10* (2): 93–104.

Rose, J. (1990). Hanna Segal interviewed by Jacqueline Rose. *Women: A Cultural Review, 1* (2): 211–212.

Rose, J. (2016). Who do you think you are? *London Review of Books, 38* (9): 3–13.

Rose, S. H. (2007a). Complication in gay men's intimacy: Unconscious derivatives. *Psychoanalytic Social Work, 14* (2): 65–88.

Rose, S. H. (2007b). *Oedipal Rejection: Echoes in the Relationships of Gay Men.* Amherst, NY: Cambria Press.

Rubin, G. (1975). The traffic in women: Notes on the "political economy" of sex. In: R. Reiter (Ed.), *Toward an Anthropology of Women* (pp. 157–211). New York: Monthly Review Press.

Rubin, G. (1984). Thinking sex: Notes for a radical theory of the politics of sexuality. In: H. Abelove, M. A. Barale, & D. Halperin (Eds.), *The Lesbian and Gay Studies Reader* (pp. 3–44). New York: Routledge, 1993.

Rubin, L. (1983). *Intimate Strangers*. New York: Harper & Row.

Russell, G. M., & Greenhouse, E. M. (1997). Homophobia in the supervisory relationship: An invisible intruder. *Psychoanalytic Review, 84*: 27–42.

Ruszczynski, S. P. (1993). *Psychotherapy with Couples: Theory and Practice at the Tavistock Institute of Marital Studies*. London: Karnac.

Ryan, J. (1998). Lesbianism and the therapist's subjectivity: A psychoanalytic view. In: C. Shelley (Ed.), *Contemporary Perspectives on Psychotherapy and Homosexualities* (pp. 44–57). London: Free Association Books.

Sadjadi, S. (2013). The endocrinologist's office. Puberty suppression: Saving children from a natural disaster? *Journal of Medical Humanities, 34* (2): 255–260.

Saketopoulou, A. (2014a). Mourning the body as bedrock: Developmental considerations in treating transsexual patients analytically. *Journal of the American Psychoanalytic Association, 62* (5): 773–805.

Saketopoulou, A. (2014b). To suffer pleasure: The shattering of the ego as the psychic labor of perverse sexuality. *Studies in Gender Sexuality, 15* (4): 254–268.

Saketopoulou, A. (2015). On sexual perversions' capacity to act as portal to psychic states that have evaded representation. In: A. Lemma & P. E. Lynch (Eds.), *Sexualities: Contemporary Psychoanalytic Perspectives* (pp. 205–218). London: Routledge.

Sandler, J. (1960). The background of safety. *International Journal of Psychoanalysis, 41*: 352–363.

Schafer, R. (1974). Problems in Freud's psychology of women. *Journal of the American Psychoanalytic Association, 22*: 459–485.

Schafer, R. (1997). Authority, evidence, and knowledge in the psychoanalytic relationship. In: *Tradition and Change in Psychoanalysis* (pp. 179–193). London: Karnac.

Schafer, R. (2002). On male nonnormative sexuality and perversion in psychoanalytic discourse. *Annual of Psychoanalysis, 30*: 23–35.

Schalin, L. (1989). On phallicism: Developmental aspects, neutralization, sublimation and defensive phallicism. *Scandinavian Psychoanalytic Review, 12*: 38–57.

Schaverien, J. (2003). Supervising the erotic transference and countertransference. In: J. Wiener, R. Mizen, & J. Duckham (Eds.), *Supervising and Being Supervised* (pp. 167–184). Basingstoke: Palgrave Macmillan.

Schellenbaum, P. (2005). *Tra uomini. La Dinamica omosessuale nella psiche maschile*. Milan: Red Edizioni.

Schore, A. N. (1991). Early superego development: The emergence of shame and narcissistic affect regulation in the practicing period. *Psychoanalysis and Contemporary Thought, 14* (2): 187–250.

Schwartz, A. (1998). *Sexual Subjects: Lesbians, Gender, and Psychoanalysis*. New York: Routledge.

Sedgwick, E. K. (1990). *Epistemology of the Closet*. Berkeley/Los Angeles, CA: University of California Press, 2008.

Sedgwick, E. K. (1993a). How to bring your kids up gay. In: *Tendencies* (pp. 154–166). London: Routledge, 1998.

Sedgwick, E. K. (1993b). *Tendencies*. Chapel Hill, NC: Duke University Press.

Semlyen, J., King, M., Varney, J., & Hagger-Johnson, G. (2016). Sexual orientation and symptoms of common mental disorder or low wellbeing: Combined meta-analysis of 12 UK population health surveys. *BMC Psychiatry*, *16* (1): 67.

Shelby, R. D. (1994). Homosexuality and the struggle for coherence. *Progress in Self-Psychology*, *10*: 55–78.

Silverman, K. (1992). *Male Subjectivity at the Margins*. New York: Routledge.

Smith, G., King, M., & Bartlett, A. (2004). Treatments of homosexuality in Britain since the 1950s—An oral history: The experience of patients. *British Medical Journal*, *328* (7437): 427.

Socarides, C. (1970). A psychoanalytic study of the desire for sexual transformation ("transsexualism"): The plaster-of-Paris man. *International Journal of Psychoanalysis*, *51*: 341–349.

Socarides, C. (1994). The erosion of heterosexuality. *The Washington Times*, 5 July.

Solomon, A. (2014). *Far from the Tree: Parents, Children and the Search for Identity*. London: Vintage Books.

Sontag, S. (1961). *Against Interpretation and Other Essays*. London: Penguin, 2009.

Sprengnether, M. (1990). *The Spectral Mother: Freud, Feminism, and Psychoanalysis*. Ithaca, NY: Cornell University Press.

Spruiell, V. (1997). Review of the psychoanalytic theory of sexuality: Comments on the assault against it. *International Journal of Psychoanalysis*, *78*: 357–361.

Stack, C. (1974). *All Our Kin: Strategies for Survival in a Black Community*. New York: Harper & Row.

Stein, R. (1995). Analysis of a case of transsexualism. *Psychoanalytic Dialogues*, *5*: 257–289.

Stein, R. (1997). The shame experiences of the analyst. *Progress in Self Psychology*, *13*: 109–123.

Stein, R. (1998a). The enigmatic dimension of sexual experience: The "otherness" of sexuality and primal seduction. *Psychoanalytic Quarterly*, *67*: 594–625.

Stein, R. (1998b). The poignant, the excessive and the enigmatic in sexuality. *International Journal of Psychoanalysis*, *79*: 254–268.

Stein, R. (2006). Unforgetting and excess: The recreation and refinding of suppressed sexuality. *Psychoanalytic Dialogues, 16*: 763–778.

Stein, R. (2008). The otherness of sexuality: Excess. *Journal of the American Psychoanalytic Association, 56*: 43–71.

Steiner, J. (1985). Turning a blind eye: The cover up for Oedipus. *International Review of Psycho-Analysis, 12*: 161–172.

Stern, D. (1985). *The Interpersonal World of the Infant*. London: Karnac.

Stoller, R. (1968). *Sex and Gender*. New York: Science House.

Stoller, R. (1972). The "bedrock" of masculinity and femininity: Bisexuality. *Archives of General Psychiatry, 26*: 207–212.

Stoller, R. (1974). Facts and fancies: An examination of Freud's concept of bisexuality. In: J. Strouse (Ed.), *Women and Analysis* (pp. 391–415). New York: Grossman.

Stoller, R. (1975). *Perversion: The Erotic form of Hatred*. London: Karnac, 1986.

Stoller, R. (1985a). *Presentations of Gender*. New Haven, CT: Yale University Press.

Stoller, R. (1985b). *Observing the Erotic Imagination*. New Haven, CT: Yale University Press.

Stoller, R. (1991). Eros and Polis: What is this thing called love? *Journal of the American Psychoanalytic Association, 39*: 1065–1102.

Sullivan, H. S. (1954). *The Psychiatric Interview*. New York: Norton.

Szasz, T. (1974). *Ceremonial Chemistry*. New York: Anchor Books.

Target, M. (2007). Is our sexuality our own? A developmental model of sexuality based on early affect mirroring. *British Journal of Psychotherapy, 23* (4): 517–530.

Target, M. (2015). A developmental model of sexual excitement, desire and alienation. In: A. Lemma & P. E. Lynch (Eds.), *Sexualities: Contemporary Psychoanalytic Perspectives* (pp. 43–62). London: Routledge.

Taywaditep, K. J. (2002). Marginalization among the marginalized. *Journal of Homosexuality, 42* (1): 1–28.

Thelen, E., & Smith, L. (1991). *A Dynamic Systems Approach to the Development of Cognition and Action*. Cambridge, MA: MIT Press.

Thompson, M. (1994). *Gay Soul*. San Francisco, CA: Harper.

Thorne, A., & Coupland, J. (1998). Articulations of same-sex desire: Lesbian and gay male dating advertisements. *Journal of Sociolinguistics, 2* (2): 233–257.

Todd, M. (2016). *Straight-Jacket: How to Be Gay and Happy*. London: Transworld.

Torok, M. (1970). The significance of penis envy in women. In: J. Chasseguet-Smirgel (Ed.), *Female Sexuality: New Psychoanalytic Views* (pp. 135–170). London: Karnac.

Trop, J., & Stolorow, R. (1992). Defense analysis in self psychology: A developmental view. *Psychoanalytic Dialogues, 2*: 427–442.

Turban, J. L., & Ehrensaft, D. (2017). Research review. Gender identity in youth: Treatment paradigms and controversies. *Journal of Child Psychology and Psychiatry, 59* (12): 1228–1243.

Twist, J., & de Graaf, N. (2019). Gender diversity in youth attending the UK National Gender Identity Development Service. *Clinical Child Psychology and Psychiatry, 24* (2): 277–290.

Tyson, P. (1982). A developmental line of gender identity, gender role, and choice of love object. *Journal of the American Psychoanalytic Association, 30*: 61–86.

Ulrichs, K. (1864). *The Riddle of "Man-Manly" Love*, trans. M. Lombardi-Nash. Buffalo, NY: Prometheus Books, 1994.

UN (1989). *Convention on the Rights of the Child*. New York: United Nations.

Vrouenraets, L. J., Fredriks, A. M., Hannema, S. E., Cohen-Kettenis, P. T., & de Vries, M. C. (2015). Early medical treatment of children and adolescents with gender dysphoria: An empirical ethical study. *The Journal of Adolescent Health: Official Publication of the Society for Adolescent Medicine, 57*: 367–373.

Walker, M. (1976). The double: An archetypal configuration. In: *Spring 1976: An Annual of Archetypal Psychology and Jungian Thought* (pp. 165–175). Washington, DC: Spring Publications.

Warner, M. (1990). Homo-narcissism; or, heterosexuality. In: J. A. Boone, & M. Cadden (Eds.), *Engendering Men. The Question of Male Feminist Criticism* (pp. 190–206). New York: Routledge.

Watson, N. S. (1996). *Understanding Rainer Werner Fassbinder: Film as Private and Public Art*. Columbia, SC: University of South Carolina Press.

Weeks, J. (1985). *Sexuality and Its Discontents: Meanings, Myths and Modern Sexualities*. London: Routledge.

Weille, K. H. (2002). The psychodynamics of consensual sadomasochistic and dominant-submissive games. *Studies in Gender Sexuality, 3*: 131–160.

Weinberg, M. S., & Williams, C. J. (1979). Gay baths and the social organisation of impersonal sex. In: M. P. Levine (Ed.), *Gay Men: The Sociology of Male Homosexuality* (pp. 164–181). New York: Harper & Row.

Weston, K. (1991). *Families We Choose: Lesbians, Gays, Kinship*. New York: Columbia University Press.

Wickberg, D. (2000). Homophobia: On the cultural history of an idea. *Critical Inquiry, 27* (1): 42–57.

Widlocher, D. (Ed.) (2001). *Infantile Sexuality and Attachment*. New York: Other Press.

Wilchins, R. A. (1997). *Read My Lips: Sexual Subversion and the End of Gender*. Ithaca, NY: Firebrand Books.

Wilde, O. (1893). An ideal husband. In: *The Works of Oscar Wilde*. Leicester: Galley Press, 1987.

Wilde, O. (1895). The importance of being Earnest. In: *The Works of Oscar Wilde*. Leicester: Galley Press, 1987.

Winnicott, D. W. (1965). The theory of the parent–infant relationship. In: *The Maturational Processes and the Facilitating Environment* (pp. 37–55). London: Karnac.

Winnicott, D. W. (1967). Mirror-role of the mother and family in child development. In: P. Lomas (Ed.), The Predicament of the Family: A Psycho-Analytical Symposium (pp. 26–33). London: Hogarth Press.

Winnicott, D. W. (1969). The use of an object. *International Journal of Psycho-analysis, 50*: 711–716.

Winnicott, D. W. (1971). *Playing and Reality*. London: Routledge, 2005.

Wirth, S. (1993). Not "a one-sided human being": Clinical work with gay men from a Jungian perspective. In: R. H. Hopcke, K. L. Carrington, & S. Wirth (Eds.), *Same-Sex Love and the Path to Wholeness* (pp. 231–245). Boston, MA: Shambhala.

Wortis, J. (1954). *Fragments of an Analysis with Freud*. New York: Charter Books.

Wren, B. (2000). Early physical intervention for young people with atypical gender identity development. *Clinical Child Psychology and Psychiatry, 5* (2): 220–231.

Wren, B. (2014). "Thinking post-modern and practising in the enlightenment": Managing uncertainty in the treatment of transgendered adolescents. *Feminism and Psychology, 24* (2): 271–291.

Wren, B. (2015). Making up people: Understanding gender non-conformity of childhood as both biologically grounded and socially constructed. In: Talk given at the European Professional Association for Transgender Health (EPATH) Conference: Transgender Health Care in Europe. Ghent, Belgium, Saturday, 14 March.

Wren, B. (2017). Ethics and consent. In: Talk given at the Royal College of Paediatrics and Child Health: Hot Topics in Child Health—Transgender and Gender Diverse Conference, Cavendish Conference Centre, London, 12 June.

Wren, B. (2019a). Ethical issues arising in the provision of medical interventions with gender variant children and adolescents. *Clinical Child Psychology and Psychiatry, 24* (2): 203–222.

Wren, B. (2019b). Reflections on "Thinking an Ethics of Gender Exploration: Against Delaying Transition for Transgender and Gender Variant Youth". *Clinical Child Psychology and Psychiatry, 24* (2): 237–240.

Wrye, H. K., & Wells, J. (1994). *The Narration of Desire: Erotic Transferences and Countertransferences.* Hillsdale, NJ: Analytic Press.

Young-Bruehl, E. (1990). *Freud on Women.* New York: Norton.

Zak de Goldstein, R. (1984). The dark continent and its enigmas. *International Journal of Psychoanalysis, 65*: 179–189.

Zepf, F., Zepf, S., Ullrich, B., & Seel, D. (2016). Oedipus and the Oedipus complex: A revision. *International Journal of Psychoanalysis, 97*: 685–707.

Zucker, K. J., Wood, H., Singh, D., & Bradley, S. J. (2012). A developmental, biopsychosocial model for the treatment of children with gender identity disorder. *Journal of Homosexuality, 59* (3): 369–397.

INDEX

abandonment and loss, enactment of,
        97–99
Abelove, H., 168
abjection, 33, 34, 149
Abraham, K., 180
abuse:
    homophobic, 52
    sexual, 218, 220, 222, 224, 226, 231
Act Up, 65
adaptive processes, and formation of
        subjectivity, around same-sex
        desire, 137–163
adolescent(s):
    gender dysphoria in, 201
    gender identity in, 208
adultery, 181
affect regulation, 22
Agathon, 161, 162
ageing, 13, 83, 146
a-gender identity, 209
aggressor, identification with, 133, 150
AIDS, 33, 34, 65, 150, 169
Akhtar, S., 45, 65
alchemical symbolism, 128
alcohol:
    abuse of, 52

    use of, 72
Allen, D. J., 51
Allison, E., 23
American Psychiatric Association,
        *Diagnostic and Statistical
        Manual*, 63, 186, 187,
        189, 211
American Psychoanalytic
        Association, 248
    Position Statement, 63
American Psychological
        Association, 15
Amsterdam, B. K., 43
anal intercourse, 28
anal penetration, 154, 155, 229
anal sexuality, 154
analyst(s), openly gay, 62
"analyst-as-person", 60
analytic philosophy, 23
androgen insensitivity syndrome
        (AIS), 167, 185
Androgyne archetype, 127, 128, 147,
        148, 184
androgyny, 148, 170
Anima archetype, 48, 125, 127,
        134–137, 140, 145, 162

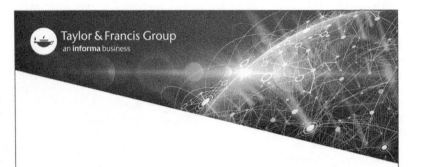